MW00795671

Courteous exchanges

Manchester University Press

THE MANCHESTER SPENSER

The Manchester Spenser is a monograph and text series devoted to historical and textual approaches to Edmund Spenser – to his life, times, places, works and contemporaries.

A growing body of work in Spenser and Renaissance studies, fresh with confidence and curiosity and based on solid historical research, is being written in response to a general sense that our ability to interpret texts is becoming limited without the excavation of further knowledge. So the importance of research in nearby disciplines is quickly being recognised, and interest renewed: history, archaeology, religious or theological history, book history, translation, lexicography, commentary and glossary – these require treatment for and by students of Spenser.

The Manchester Spenser, to feed, foster and build on these refreshed attitudes, aims to publish reference tools, critical, historical, biographical and archaeological monographs on or related to Spenser, from several disciplines, and to publish editions of primary sources and classroom texts of a more wide-ranging scope.

The Manchester Spenser consists of work with stamina, high standards of scholarship and research, adroit handling of evidence, rigour of argument, exposition and documentation.

The series will encourage and assist research into, and develop the readership of, one of the richest and most complex writers of the early modern period.

General Editors Joshua Reid, Kathryn Walls and Tamsin Badcoe

Editorial Board Sukanta Chaudhuri, Helen Cooper, Thomas Herron, J. B. Lethbridge, James Nohrnberg and Brian Vickers

To buy or to find out more about the books currently available in this series, please go to: https://manchesteruniversitypress.co.uk/series/the-manchester-spenser/

Courteous exchanges

Spenser's and Shakespeare's gentle dialogues with readers and audiences

Patricia Wareh

MANCHESTER UNIVERSITY PRESS

The right of Patricia Wareh to be identified as the author
of this work has been asserted in accordance with the
Copyright, Designs and Patents Act 1988.

Published by Manchester University Press
Oxford Road, Manchester, M13 9PL

www.manchesteruniversitypress.co.uk

British Library Cataloguing-in-Publication Data
A catalogue record for this book is available from the British
Library

ISBN 978 1 5261 4985 5 hardback

First published 2024

The publisher has no responsibility for the persistence or
accuracy of URLs for any external or third-party internet
websites referred to in this book, and does not guarantee
that any content on such websites is, or will remain, accurate
or appropriate.

Typeset by Newgen Publishing UK

Contents

Acknowledgments

I have many people to thank for their assistance with this project over its various phases.

My colleagues in the Union College Department of English are, to a person, a remarkable community of encouragement and good sense. I am grateful for the friendship of Claire Bracken, Andrew Burkett, Kara Doyle, Hugh Jenkins, Bernhard Kuhn, Judith Lewin, Katherine Lynes, Harry and Ginit Marten, Shena McAuliffe, Jen Mitchell, Jim and Carol McCord, Jillmarie Murphy, Anastasia Pease, Jordan Smith, Ruth Stevenson, Jenelle Troxell, Bunkong Tuon and Nicole Calandra, and Dan Venning. I note especially Ruth's good humor and mentorship, Judith's extraordinary generosity in helping me polish the final draft of the manuscript, Bunkong's reliable kindness and willingness to trade references to The Smiths, and Jillmarie's friendship, support, and collaboration over the years since we started this journey together. I am thankful to have known Peter Heinegg, April Selley, and Randy Wyatt and return to their memories frequently. I don't know what I'd do without the professionalism and cheerful aid of Debbie Catharine. The clever and patient folks who work at Schaffer Library have also provided frequent help. Union College has assisted this project with sabbatical releases and the Humanities Research Fund.

For their critiques of portions of this work at different stages of its development, I am grateful to Victoria Kahn, Mara Amster, Albert Ascoli, Brian Chalk, Patrick Cheney, Genevieve Guenther, Timothy Hampton, Lorna Hutson, Shannon Kelley, Erzsi Kukorelly, Kristina Lucenko, Robert Reid, John Roe, and Jennifer Vaught.

My local writing group, the Capital District Early Modernists, has offered not only smart and generous comments on multiple drafts of this work, but an incredible camaraderie and excellent culinary taste. I'm so thankful for the work we have done together: Andrew Bozio, David Morrow, Ineke Murakami, Christi Spain-Savage, Eileen Sperry, and Chantelle Thauvette.

Audiences at meetings of the Shakespeare Association of America, the American Shakespeare Center Blackfriars Conference, the Spenser sessions of the International Congress on Medieval Studies at Kalamazoo, the British Shakespeare Association, the South Central Renaissance Conference, the Sixteenth Century Society, and the Centre for Renaissance and Early Modern Studies at the University of York all made this work better. Helen Smith offered a warm welcome as director of the Centre for Renaissance and Early Modern Studies in 2017.

Chapters 3 and 5, and a portion of Chapter 4, include revised versions of previously published articles: "Honorable Action Upstaged by Theatrical Wordplay in *The Faerie Queene* 2.4 and *Much Ado About Nothing*." *Modern Philology* 114.2 (2016): 264–85 (https://doi.org/10.1086/687002) © 2016 by The University of Chicago and reprinted by permission of The University of Chicago Press; "Literary Mirrors of Aristocratic Performance: Readers and Audiences of *The Faerie Queene* and *The Winter's Tale*." *Renaissance Drama* 43.1 (2015): 85–114 (https://doi.org/10.1086/680448) © 2015 by Northwestern University and reprinted by permission of The University of Chicago Press; "Competitions in Courtesy and Nobility: *Nennio* and the Reader's Judgment in Book VI of *The Faerie Queene*." *Spenser Studies* 27 (2012): 163–91 (https://doi.org/10.7756/spst.027.008.163-191) © 2012 by AMS Press, Inc. Reprinted by permission of The University of Chicago Press. In addition to The University of Chicago Press, I thank the editors and anonymous reviewers of *Modern Philology*, *Renaissance Drama*, and *Spenser Studies*.

I am quite sure that this book reflects both explicitly and implicitly the influence of the excellent teachers who mentored me along the way; a very incomplete list includes Paul Alpers, Albert Ascoli, Louise George Clubb, Al Shoaf, and, most especially, Victoria Kahn.

I thank the editors at The Manchester Spenser and Manchester University Press. Julian Lethbridge offered early encouragement for this project, and Joshua Reid provided very helpful guidance over the years of its completion. Two anonymous reviewers offered thorough and perceptive feedback.

I owe the most to my family for their love, support, and well-timed skepticism. Another incomplete list includes Sally Roberts, Jay and Eva Becker, Laura and Faiz Wareh, Meghan Blakeman and John Becker, Lynn and Jay Coles, Marie and Bill Costa, Barb Graber, Susan and Brian McInnis, Rashad Wareh and Erin Ardleigh, and Tarik, Faiz, and Cora Wareh. Tarik read and reread these chapters with good humor, and helped in countless other ways. Faiz provided the necessary distractions as we ventured to cubing competitions around the Northeast. And Cora grew into a writer able to assist me in proofing quotations while taking breaks from her own work.

Introduction

Courteous exchanges: Spenser's and Shakespeare's gentle dialogues with readers and audiences

A contradictory portrait of its author bookends Edmund Spenser's 1590 edition of *The Faerie Queene*. In the proem at the outset of Book 1, Spenser presents himself in a traditional pose of deference, invoking the Muses, Cupid, Venus, and ultimately the Queen, whose divine light he hopes will come to his aid: "Shed thy faire beames into my feeble eyne, / And raise my thoughtes too humble and too vile" (1.Proem.4).[1] Yet appearing at the end of the work is the Letter to Raleigh, a guide that "giueth great light to the Reader," in which Spenser claims, famously, that the purpose of his book "is to fashion a gentleman or noble person in vertuous and gentle discipline." Spenser has moved from being the instrument of the Muses to being himself a source of light. This apparent contradiction between dependence and agency would have been readily legible to readers steeped in a culture of courtesy,[2] however, who would have easily recognized that Spenser's pose of humility in the proem followed both conventions of authorial self-positioning and traditional courtly self-deprecation:

> Lo I the man, whose Muse whylome did maske,
>   As time her taught, in lowly Shephards weeds,
>   Am now enforst a farre vnfitter taske,
>   For trumpets sterne to chaunge mine Oaten reeds:
>   And sing of Knights and Ladies gentle deeds,
>   Whose praises hauing slept in silence long,
>   Me, all too meane, the sacred Muse areeds
>   To blazon broade emongst her learned throng:
> Fierce warres and faithfull loues shall moralize my song.
> (1.Proem.1)

As he modestly places himself among his epic forebears, notably Virgil and Ariosto,[3] Spenser makes a tacit claim to belong to a literary elite. In presenting "the gentle deeds" of his gentle characters, he fashions both his readers and himself, even while raising questions about what it means to be gentle, as Jonathan Goldberg has noted in describing the "puzzle" this Letter offers to readers about the extent to which gentility overlaps with virtue.[4] Despite, or rather through, his courteous self-deprecation, Spenser asserts his own ability to construct a community of gentle readers, one that recognizes itself in his teaching and benefits from its lessons. As suggested by the repetition in his stated aim "to fashion a gentleman ... in ... gentle discipline," these readers are both already gentle and primed to become more so through his literary instruction.

While Spenser's proem clearly attempts to establish *The Faerie Queene*'s place in the epic tradition, at the same time it makes use of a theatrical metaphor for the author in his acknowledgment that his Muse has taken on other guises: "whose Muse whylome did maske." Spenser's gesture toward his own history as a writer of pastoral may well reveal his imitation of Virgil, but it also points toward a theatrical vocabulary and mindset—closely linked to a culture of courtesy—that is absent in the invocations of his models.[5] In taking on a courteous persona as he negotiates his relationships with his readers and addressees, Spenser brings to his epic a discourse of theatricality that will saturate the work as a whole, with its frequent spectacles, its use of stock characters such as the *miles gloriosus*, and most of all, its fostering in readers a heightened sense of how the rhetorical arts of self-presentation figure them as not just readers but spectators of the text.

I argue here that Spenser and Shakespeare share a vocabulary of theatricalized courtesy that shapes how both authors engage with readers and audiences. Strikingly, Spenser's efforts to adjust the mindsets his readers bring to *The Faerie Queene* parallel those of the Prologue that opens William Shakespeare's *Henry V*. Here, too, the Prologue follows up a plea for the aid of a Muse ("O for a Muse of fire") with the language of insistent self-deprecation:

> But pardon, gentles all,
> The flat unraisèd spirits that hath dared
> On this unworthy scaffold to bring forth
> So great an object. Can this cock-pit hold

The vasty fields of France? Or may we cram
Within this wooden O the very casques
That did affright the air at Agincourt?
O pardon: since a crookèd figure may
Attest in little place a million,
And let us, ciphers to this great account,
On your imaginary forces work. (Prologue 8–18)[6]

Repeatedly begging the gentle audience's pardon, just as Spenser does in his proems to Books 2, 3, 5, and 6 of *The Faerie Queene*, Shakespeare's Prologue employs the same topos of modesty, declaring that he and his fellow players are but "ciphers," who will only be able to approximate the "great account" of heroic history with the supplement of the audience's "imaginary forces."[7] Although the Prologue appears to supplicate the audience, he also commands them, deferentially but authoritatively informing them of their imaginative power: "Piece out our imperfections with your thoughts" (23) and "Think, when we talk of horses, that you see them, / Printing their proud hoofs i'th' receiving earth; / For 'tis your thoughts that now must deck our kings" (26–28). Using a metaphorical reference to the world of print,[8] the Prologue calls upon the audience to imagine the impressions made by the pounding of horses' hooves, and simultaneously suggests that the play they will have actively and collaboratively generated will also leave an impression. The audience's *thoughts* are thus both a crucial theme of the Prologue, as well as the means and site of the play's creating making.[9] As the Prologue nears the end of his courteous directions to the spectators, he reminds them of their interdependence with the players: "Admit me Chorus to this history, / Who Prologue-like your humble patience pray / Gently to hear, kindly to judge, our play" (32–34). The humility professed by the Prologue now transfers to an audience asked to judge kindly; their generous, patient response will not only help create the drama, but also establish the audience itself as gentle.[10] As is the case with Spenser's *Faerie Queene*, the active responses of both readers and theatergoers are essential to how the work makes meaning, while they concurrently form a fundamental part of how readers and audiences constitute themselves as courteous actors.

In this book, I demonstrate the significant correspondence in how Spenser's *Faerie Queene* and Shakespeare's plays addressed

rs and audiences; asking for the supplement of their imagin-
is, requiring their active involvement in solving mental puzzles, and prompting them to reflect on how they define themselves
in relation to the text. Focusing on the particularities of Spenser's
and Shakespeare's parallel engagements with the paradoxes of
courtesy (a cultural preoccupation that included the arts of interpreting and creating both literary texts and social performances),
I argue that Shakespeare owes Spenser a more extensive debt than
has generally been acknowledged. At the same time, I suggest a
broader congruity in how readers and audiences engaged with
literary and theatrical works in early modern England. The discourses of courtesy offered the overlapping groups of readers and
playgoers a vocabulary for making sense of the ways in which they
were approached by texts, for recognizing their power to determine a text's meaning, and for understanding the consequences
of those decisions for their own social identities. Making use of
courtesy as a lens for understanding the correspondences between
reading and play-watching, I argue, also helps us see how the discourse of courtesy played a central role in evaluating not only
people, but also texts.

Spenser and Shakespeare—both of middle-class backgrounds,
yet intent on rising—spoke to readers and playgoers who were, like
them, deeply invested in the question of the relationship between
verbal artistry and self-creation. Frank Whigham and Louis
Montrose have argued for the importance of imaginative literature
as cultural capital in the period, with literary mastery serving as a
marker of social belonging.[11] At the same time, the identity crisis
caused by the increasing permeability of the aristocracy, classically
articulated by Lawrence Stone, led to increased attention to debating and defining the nature of aristocratic superiority.[12] The new
possibilities for self-fashioning in the sixteenth century thus helped
to create readers and audiences who were acutely reflective about
the relationship between written word and performance.[13] As Anna
Bryson notes, "historical records of rules of 'courtesy' and 'civility'
can be studied precisely as codifications of codes, which illuminate
the range of social messages available to what Goffman might call
the 'social actors' of the period."[14] I am especially interested here
in exploring how both Spenser and Shakespeare made use of these

codes. The discourses of courtesy, I argue, provided the vocabulary and forms through which authors positioned themselves with reference to readers and playgoers, in dedications, prologues, and epilogues, but also throughout texts, fostering a model of interpretation that was highly attuned to the different layers of social, literary, and theatrical performances. My work establishes courtesy as a generative model that allows for a range of responses to literary and theatrical works, while also attending to the ways it both supports and critiques systems of privilege.

The instruction in courtesy implies an unresolved contradiction, suggesting both that courtesy is a natural expression of aristocratic birthright and that it can be taught. Courtesy literature's dual audience of elites and would-be elites, identified by Whigham as those who sought to "maintain their preeminence," and those who sought to challenge that preeminence through the new possibilities of "social mobility,"[15] reinforces this paradox: refined manners, a marker of separation from the crowd, could, at least in theory, be acquired through the purchase of a book available for sale to a popular audience. While Barbara Correll's point that the readers of courtesy literature cannot be divided so neatly into different camps is well taken, it remains the case that one essential paradox of the genre derives from its attempt to teach that which apparently cannot be taught.[16] A brief illustration from Castiglione's wildly popular 1528 *Book of the Courtier*, the most frequently reprinted courtesy book of the English Renaissance, will illustrate the point.[17] His text offers a vivid depiction of interlocutors gathered together to achieve a consensus about the ideal courtier as well as to shame those who don't meet the standard. Asked by Cesare Gonzaga how grace may be obtained, Count Lodovico demonstrates his reluctance to take on the task of teaching (rather than merely describing) courtesy and grace, and dodges the full import of Gonzaga's question:

> Notwithstanding to fulfill your request in what I am able, althoughe it be (in maner) in a proverbe that Grace is not to be learned, I say unto you, whoso mindeth to be gracious or to have a good grace in the exercises of the body (presupposing first that he be not of nature unapt) ought to begin betimes, and to learne his principles of cunning men.

[Pur, per satisfare ancor quanto è in poter mio alla domanda vostra, benché e' sia quasi in proverbio che la grazia non s'impari, dico che chi ha da esser aggraziato negli esercizi corporali, presuponendo prima che da natura non sia inabile, dee cominciar per tempo ed imparar i princìpi da ottimi maestri.] (1.25)[18]

The Count says, in other words, that grace can't be learned, but this is how one learns it. Just as the meaning of courtly grace is ambiguous, *The Courtier* itself functions on more than one level as it engages both the social and cultural frameworks within which it creates meaning: it neither precisely undercuts the convention of courtly grace as an inborn trait, nor does it fully support it. Even though *The Courtier* describes grace as "the gift of nature and of the heavens" (1.24), readers of the work, in theory at least, may gain from it the necessary skills to *acquire* the gift of grace.

There can be no doubt, however, that a fundamental use of books such as Castiglione's *Courtier* is to help determine, as King Lear puts it, "who's in, who's out," and the social differentiation in which the discourse of courtesy literature participates has a legacy of harm much greater than social shunning. I want to acknowledge this legacy of harm even as I am especially attuned in this project to how these texts undermine systems of discrimination as well as support them. In his work on the "pursuit of civility," Keith Thomas emphasizes how "the ancient and long-enduring opposition between the 'civil' and the 'barbarous'" has been used to justify forced trade, colonization, and slavery.[19] In the case of Spenser specifically, Stephen Greenblatt argues in his influential study of Guyon's destruction of the Bower of Bliss that "civility is won through the exercise of violence over what is deemed barbarous and evil."[20] Moreover, as Melissa Sanchez rightly insists, Spenser's project of fashioning his readers in gentility participates in the harmful project of British colonization and the normalization of ostensible White superiority.[21] Yet, Sanchez's work also points toward the possibility of critique, as she movingly suggests: "The fundamental insight that Spenserians can bring to current scholarly conversations is that seemingly verisimilar representations of race have been allegorical all along."[22] Sanchez underscores that there is no monolithic body of Spenser readers, nor should there be.

In my own work, I aim to do justice to the ways in which both Spenser's and Shakespeare's texts encourage a variety of responses from their readers and audiences, acknowledging that these texts could help uphold harmful systems of discrimination while also being attentive to the ways in which they employ the vocabulary of courtesy to facilitate critique. At the same time that books of courtesy seemed to offer social mobility, they also perpetuated inequality. As Patricia Akhimie argues, courtesy literature could reinforce patterns of subjugation and inequality despite its apparent promise of self-improvement: "The discourse of conduct was as much about the potential for transformation as it was about defining social categories as natural and immovable or immutable."[23] Akhimie responds to what she identifies as a key contradiction in the "culture of conduct": "Systems of social differentiation such as rank and gender, for example, employ opposing ideas about a malleable, performative self, and a natural and immutable self that is essential or biological."[24] A crucial aspect of the ideology of conduct is the critical sensibility it cultivates: "Conduct is not a thing one does, or even a way of doing something. It is a way of evaluating the way other people do things."[25] Conduct literature, in Akhimie's valuable model, provides the idiom through which to evaluate people. In this project, I aim to build on Akhimie's work as I explore how Spenser's and Shakespeare's deployment of the vocabulary of courtesy prods both readers and audiences to develop a sense of judgment about texts as well as people. The explicit attention to judgment that courtesy elicits can help one recognize the artificiality of socially constructed systems of difference even as it supports those harmful systems.

Spenser and Shakespeare addressed audiences attuned to the tensions in courtesy, and their works both evince the symptoms of these tensions and contribute to an ongoing Renaissance discussion about how nature, especially family bloodline, and individual actions, including varying degrees of feigning, determine nobility. While my primary evidence draws on Spenser's *Faerie Queene* and Shakespeare's plays as I claim that their addresses to readers and audiences elicit complicated reactions, my argument attends to readers' and audiences' expectations, especially to their presumed engagement with pressing cultural debates about the constitution of social identity.[26] The connections I make between Spenser and Shakespeare suggest the overlap, not only between Renaissance habits of reading and watching performances, but also between literary and social habits of mind. While a great deal of critical attention has been paid to early modern readers, on the one hand, and early modern theater audiences, on the other, the insights of these two areas of scholarship often remain separate.[27] My exploration of how Spenser and Shakespeare engaged readers and audiences in parallel ways adds to our understanding of both these authors' works on their own terms, and their shared place in the cultural and mental landscapes of the English Renaissance. Renaissance readers and audiences negotiated social identity through active engagement with books and plays, and so I consider here how reading and spectating practices informed and supported each other.

The literary and theatrical uses to which Shakespeare put the works of Spenser, the most important narrative poet of his age, clearly shed light on Shakespeare's engagement with and place in print culture; indeed, Lukas Erne notes that *England's Parnassus*, an anthology of poetry published perhaps as early as 1600, offered sequential extracts from both *The Faerie Queene* and *Romeo and Juliet*, suggesting that Shakespeare's dramatic works could command the same respect as Spenser's literary texts.[28] And yet there is no critical consensus about how much Shakespeare owes to Spenser. Both Jonathan Bate and Stephen Greenblatt doubt Spenser's importance for Shakespeare, with Bate declaring, "it is hard to pin down the extent (if any) of Shakespeare's knowledge of Edmund Spenser's epic romance."[29] Nonetheless, there is increasing attention to the possibility that Spenser played a major role in Shakespeare's formation as an author. In his introduction to *Shakespeare and Spenser: Attractive Opposites*, J. B. Lethbridge claims that "Shakespeare read Spenser with some care," and Judith Anderson suggests, "Shakespeare's familiarity with Spenser's [writing] is also established by specific, recurrent verbal citation," a view I share even as I uncover new examples of it.[30] Patrick Cheney has offered the most extensive and important readings of Shakespeare's engagement with Spenser, arguing that "Shakespeare is an alert reader of Spenser's laureate self-fashioning, and organizes his own art in opposition to it."[31] Cheney's model of Shakespeare's "self-erasure"[32] makes sense: it is the Prologue, however self-consciously presented, who speaks at the opening of *Henry V*, rather than an authorial persona, as in the outset of *The Faerie Queene*. Yet, I contend that an important point of connection between Spenser and Shakespeare is that both revel in *exposing* the tools of their artistic creation;[33] just as Spenser's reference to his previous masking underscores how much his authorship involves assuming a persona, so too does Shakespeare's Prologue make his masking clear, calling himself "Prologue-*like*" (emphasis mine). Both works immediately call on readers and audiences to sort out voices that present dissembling poses; thus, we witness these authors emphatically prodding readers and audiences to consider the relationship between how they define texts and performances, and how they define themselves. This game of mapping personas would particularly attract members of a culture steeped in the social arts of courtesy.

Courteous Exchanges extends current scholarly discussions by confirming the importance of courtesy as a discourse informing the relationships between texts, readers, and audiences. In so doing, my project makes new connections between Spenser and Shakespeare that not only illuminate the relationship between two major authors, but also reveal a significant correspondence between Renaissance reading and theatrical practices. In shedding light on the literary relationship between Shakespeare and Spenser, my argument takes seriously the work that has been done to consider Shakespeare as an author deeply invested in print culture. My new approach, however, points out how the works of both Spenser and Shakespeare encourage explicit reflection on readers' and audiences' power to make sense of texts, and how this complex imaginative labor also facilitates reflection on social performances. The discourse of courtesy informed both rhetorical self-presentation and careful judgment making; as such, I argue first that courtesy constituted an essential component of how the practices of reading and playgoing were understood, and second that reading and playgoing could encourage more critical attention to the process of making social judgments.

In examining the ways in which courtesy is not only a theme in Spenser and Shakespeare but also provides a model for thinking about the relationships among authors, audiences, and readers, my project contributes to scholarly conversations about how social interactions might be mediated through and created by texts. As Louis Montrose aptly states, "Elizabethan poetry is more than an analogue of courtliness: it is a medium of courtliness."[34] Previous studies, such as Daniel Javitch's *Poetry and Courtliness in Renaissance England* and Jennifer Richards' *Rhetoric and Courtliness in Early Modern Literature*, treat the connections between tropes of courtesy and authors' literary self-presentation. Other studies such as Wayne Rebhorn's *Courtly Performances* consider the ties between courtesy and theatricality. In *True Relations*, Frances Dolan discusses "how a textual relation can create, shape, or substitute for social relations," putting forward the notion that in domestic advice texts, the reader is "pulled into relation and invited to construct relations."[35] Christopher Warley's work explores the place of sonnet sequences in the mediation of contested social identities, arguing that "they provided writers with a unique form to describe, and to invent, new social positions."[36] Paul Trolander and Zeynep Tenger parse how manuscript circulation among social groups created a discourse of literary criticism that derived from "the language of sociability and polite behavior," contending that elite writing communities during this time were "using specific critical activities and discourse to gain cultural, political, and social advantage."[37] These studies all shed light on literary and social positioning, a focus this book shares.

While Renaissance courtesy has certainly spurred much important research, my contribution considers its special place in constructing Renaissance readers and playgoers who *recognized* their overlapping roles as judges of texts and people. Spenser and Shakespeare both depict and enact paradoxical courtesy, I argue, educating readers and audiences to reflect explicitly on how poetry and theater mediate pressing social and cultural issues. Although Shakespeare's plays do not advertise the same kind of pedagogical purpose that Spenser claims, they nonetheless enjoin their audiences to be aware of their own processes of making social judgments. Spenser's text encourages a critical attitude toward the reliability of conventional expressions of courtesy (self-deprecation, generosity, polished theatricality) that is instilled in readers by asking them to work through the consequences of their own literary spectatorship. Shakespeare thereby finds in Spenser's *Faerie Queene* an extended example of an author who calls upon his readership to entertain conflicting views about courtesy, texts, and themselves; Shakespeare's own body of work also insists that readers and spectators adopt multiple perspectives when contemplating his contradictory portraits of courtesy and aristocratic identity. The critical categories that have tended to separate scholarship on Spenser and Shakespeare have thus obscured the important similarities in how they address readers and playgoers: seeking their cooperation with courteous dexterity, inciting their critical attention to the fictions of gentility that compose their society, and prompting their thoughtful meditation on the roles of literature and theater in training courteous subjects and interpretive communities.

Courteous Exchanges traces how Spenser's and Shakespeare's explorations of courtesy—a social practice that encouraged a hypersensitivity to artful self-presentation—provided a vocabulary and forum to comment on their own literary practices and for readers and audiences to reflect on the constructed nature of both texts and aristocratic identity. In examining their own reactions to a literary text, Renaissance readers and audiences, I argue, developed habits of thought that encouraged them to evaluate their responses to the cultural fiction of inherited gentility and the social performance of courtesy that supported it. For Renaissance readers and playgoers, reading a poem, creating one's courtly identity, acting a part, and watching a play all shared the potential for habituation to virtue or vice. Fundamentally, then, my project seeks to illuminate how Renaissance writers conceptualized what it meant to be a learning, changing human being, while simultaneously doing justice to the interwoven social history and literary genealogies of early modern England. This book recognizes Shakespeare's close involvement in early modern theatrical practices even as I extend Erne's project of recuperating him as a print author.[38] Also, my contribution to the history of Spenser's engagement of readers underscores the importance of theatricality for his pedagogy of courtesy. Although Spenser spent his working life largely apart from the London theaters,[39] discourses of theatricality nonetheless permeate his work; his *Faerie Queene* speaks to audiences used to thinking with a theatrical mindset both at stage performances and in their own social performances. Spenser's epic, theatrical romance models for Shakespeare an author's complex interactions with his readers.

Reading and playgoing

Renaissance reading and playgoing practices empowered interpreters of both poems and plays to develop their own assessments of texts even as these texts were designed to work changes upon them. The judgment of readers and audiences defined books and plays, then, and also defined the readers and audiences themselves. My argument throughout insists on an important parallel between

Renaissance readers and Renaissance theatergoers: the intellectual responses of both played an active role in determining the significance of the text.[40] As Albert Russell Ascoli aptly notes, "interpretive reading itself is *a*, if not *the*, theme of the Renaissance."[41] Terence Cave suggests that a decisive change occurred in Renaissance reading practices, creating a new emphasis on the reader's interaction with a text that was capable of generating many meanings. For Cave, this new openness to "unfinished and generative readings" leads the reader to become actively involved in the text's process of making meaning, rather than a passive recipient of prepackaged ancient texts and knowledge, thus "inviting the reader to constitute himself as a subject through the act of reading."[42] Commenting on the Renaissance convention of marginalia, Stephen Orgel succinctly observes, "Reading was also writing."[43] And Sasha Roberts, in her study of the reception of Shakespeare's poems, eloquently describes "the agency of (often unidentified) individual readers, wielding power over the texts they manipulated, fashioning meaning from them according to their own interests and agendas."[44] The variation in Renaissance reading practices, which ranged from silent and solitary to audible and communal, inspired readers to engage with texts in different ways.[45]

At the same time, Shakespeare's theater also promoted the active involvement of its audience: spectators were addressed directly and were frequently reminded that they were watching a play.[46] As Tiffany Stern argues, "This drama changes spectators into participants."[47] Matteo A. Pangallo characterizes the early modern "audience–stage relationship" as "intensely dialogic, participatory, and creative," noting that an "assumption of the significant, productive capacity of audience interpretation was a shared theoretical underpinning for both the theater's defenders and its detractors."[48] William N. West aptly states, "Early modern playgoers were reminded continually how the play was soliciting their attentions, and how their attentions made the play."[49] In my examination of how the discourses of courtesy functioned as the medium through which Renaissance authors approached both readers and audiences, I bring into conversation the insights of these two fields of scholarship.

My project pays special attention to Castiglione's *Book of the Courtier* because it not only sets the standard for Renaissance explorations of courtesy, but also intensely explores the interrelatedness of literature and social performance. *The Book of the Courtier* offers multiple competing voices and requires readers' active engagement in considering their relationship to the dialogue, affording them a rich interrogation of the connections among aristocratic identity, literature, theatricality, and spectatorship. In a self-reinforcing cycle, the discourses of courtesy trained subjects to create and seek multiple levels of sophistication. Castiglione's text acknowledges that reading lends itself to ongoing consideration: "writinge keepeth the woordes in store, and referreth them to the judgemente of the reader, and geveth tyme to examyne them depely" (1.29). Yet it also insists on the power of both written words and oral performances to activate the imagination; the ideal courtier uses both to create vivid sensory experiences for his audiences, "and (as it were) draw the matters to the sense of the verye eyes, and (as they saie) make them felte wyth hande, for the delyte of him that heareth, or readeth" (1.34). Throughout *The Book of the Courtier*, the interlocutors both form a model community of courteous performers and challenge readers to reflect on the book's relationship to their own lives. Readers may apply its examples as stylistic models for their social self-presentation, but they are also encouraged to contemplate the relationship between literature and theatricality.[50]

Focusing on how the discourse of courtesy informed Renaissance understandings of reading and playgoing, this book questions the separate consideration of these two experiences, thereby adding to the growing body of criticism that insists on the interrelationship between print literature and theater in the period.[51] In the case of Shakespeare, Erne has argued for the serious readings that Shakespeare's printed playbooks received in his own time.[52] Cheney, in characterizing Shakespeare as a "national poet-playwright," further suggests the need for

> a fuller, more historically accurate classification, one that sees Shakespeare as a collaborative man of the theatre who wrote plays for both page and stage alongside his freestanding poems, and who ended up bridging the divide between the professional exigencies of the bustling commercial theatre and the longer-term goals of literary immortality.[53]

More generally, Tiffany Stern has added to the claims of both Erne and Cheney to emphasize just how much "the practise of reading critically in the theater was melded with the practise of watching critically."[54] Charles Whitney's *Early Responses to Renaissance Drama* also offers a crucial argument that Renaissance audiences engaged with plays outside the theater as well, through allusions and other kinds of creative responses; examining written responses to theatergoing, he suggests, "cuts across the venerable binary of stage *vs.* page, of theatrical presentation *vs.* literary art, perform-ance *vs.* text, play going *vs.* reading."[55] Akihiro Yamada connects Shakespeare's many references to reading, books, and education to England's increases in education and literacy; his book establishes "a historical and cultural interrelation between the reader and the audience of Shakespeare's time."[56] Likewise, Cyndia Susan Clegg, in *Shakespeare's Reading Audiences*, considers the different read-ing experiences that might have affected how audiences interpreted Shakespeare's sonnets and plays: "we can envision Shakespeare's audiences as being composed not only of a 'great variety of playgo-ers,' but also of a great variety of readers—readers who participated in a variety of reading communities."[57] As I build upon this import-ant body of scholarship, I aim to recover how courtesy literature in particular offered models for thinking about both character forma-tion and the related question of the relationships between readers, audiences, and texts. As readers and audiences looked to courtesy literature to reflect on their own self-fashioning, the vocabulary of courtesy also shaped both how texts addressed them and how they responded. I argue that we should take seriously the agency that Spenser and Shakespeare offered readers and playgoers, attending to the ways in which Spenser wrote for a readership attuned to the arts of theatrical and social performance even as Shakespeare's audiences included, but were by no means limited to, those who were well versed in the art of engaged reading.

My project thus offers a fuller picture of how the Renaissance preoccupation with readerly engagement may have informed not only the experience of reading poetry, but also the experience of playgoing—of making sense in a communal theatrical setting of performances that were saturated with intertextuality and influ-enced by a literary tradition of addressing readers implicitly or explicitly. Although mindful of the differences between reading and playgoing, I am also attuned to how the prevailing critical divide obscures important parallels between how the four overlapping groups of Renaissance authors, theatermakers, readers, and play-goers conceived of their activities. By examining the ways Spenser and Shakespeare directly and indirectly connected with readers and audiences, my project underscores how Renaissance expectations about the reception of written poetry and plays coincide.

Defending poetry and theater; fashioning readers and audiences

Renaissance writers often speak of poetry and theater in the same breath. In the October eclogue of Spenser's *Shepheardes Calender*, for example, Cuddie both laments the contemporary neglect of poets and speaks rapturously of the effect that wine could have on his poetic faculties: "Thou kenst not *Percie* howe the ryme should rage. / O if my temples were distain'd with wine, / And girt in gir-londs of wild Yuie twine, / How I could reare the Muse on stately stage" (109–12).[58] Theatrical performance is here treated as a nat-ural extension of the poet's voice. In his *Briefe Apologie of Poetrie* prefacing his translation of *Orlando Furioso*, John Harington also assumes an overlap, speaking of the support given to poetry by rulers, the "honors" they have bestowed on it at "great and mag-nificent cost": "As witnes the huge Theaters, and Amphitheaters, monuments of stupendious charge, made onely for Tragedies and Comedies, the workes of Poets to be represented on" (ii verso).[59]

Indeed, debates about the value of poetry and theater spanning the length of Spenser's and Shakespeare's careers suggest the par-allels in Renaissance understandings of reading and playgoing as well as poetry-making and playwriting. From a negative perspec-tive, the title page to Stephen Gosson's 1579 *Schoole of Abuse*—addressing a readership of "Gentlemen that favour learning" and "all that wyll follow vertue"—lumps together "Poets, Pipers, Plaiers, Jesters, and such like Caterpillers of a Commonwelth." Gosson's rhetoric is typical of antitheatrical writers, yet the responses their work received suggests that his assumption about the common cul-tural work of poets and players is shared by those with a positive view of poetry and theater, including Gosson's poorly chosen dedi-catee, Philip Sidney.

The promise and dangers of both poetry and theater were closely linked to the possibility that they would fashion the characters of readers and audiences. As Jonas Barish observes, "It is the element of spectator complicity which makes the experience perilous."[60] Indeed, the critique of theater's effect on the mind was linked with a critique of poetry at least as early as Plato's *Republic*, in which Socrates describes the effects of theatrical spectatorship:

> That element in yourself which wanted to make jokes, but which you kept in check by means of reason because you were frightened of being thought a buffoon, you now release. You don't realise that giving it its head in this way results in your playing the comedian, over and over again, in your own life. (Book 10, 606c)[61]

Yet this model of character formation through spectatorship also offered the possibility of moral benefit.[62] George Puttenham, for example, includes comedy and tragedy in his *Art of English Poesy*, calling them "poems reprehensive"—that is to say, texts that were created with the aim of correcting humanity's vices (1.13).[63] For Puttenham, comedy "tended altogether to the amendment of man by discipline and example" (1.14).

A comparison of Sidney's 1595 *Defence of Poesy* (also published in 1595 as *An Apologie for Poetrie*) and Thomas Heywood's 1612 *Apology for Actors* suggests the parallels in Renaissance expectations for how readers and audiences responded to texts, including matching their imaginative labor with that of authors and performers as well as making use of texts as spurs for their own self-creation.[64] The active readers and alert playgoers envisioned by Sidney and Heywood would have found their training ground through study of Castiglione's *Courtier*, a text that is obsessed with subject formation through literary and performative models. In an overreaching masculine ideal that nonetheless had real currency in Spenser's and Shakespeare's day, authors such as Sidney and Heywood claimed that poetry and theater could lead Renaissance subjects to create themselves as Cyruses and Alexanders. Poets and theatermakers alike justified their enterprises, at least in part, with the suggestion that readers and audiences could have their dispositions molded by the models of virtue and vice they offered. The fact that Shakespeare himself does not appear to have embraced such an explicitly didactic model does not mean that some of his playgoers did not bring this expectation to the theater—or that his plays had nothing to teach them.

Though Sidney, who died before the heyday of the Elizabethan theater, took a dim view of its practice in his own time, he nonetheless assumes that theater is a subcategory of poetry. This makes sense given the use of verse in both classical and Renaissance drama, not to mention Sidney's own elastic definition of poetry.[65] In speaking of the educational value of the theater, Sidney contrasts poetry (brought alive by performance) to philosophy: "let but Sophocles bring you Ajax on a stage ... and tell me if you have not a more familiar insight into anger than finding in the schoolmen his *genus* and difference" (222). He also emphasizes the role of the poet's art made vivid through theatrical performance in dissuading audiences from vice: "comedy is an imitation of the common errors of our life, which he representeth in the most ridiculous and scornful sort that may be, so as it is impossible that any beholder can be content to be such a one" (229–30). If Sidney seeks to elevate poetry over other competing textual disciplines—if he defends the value of reading one kind of book over others—Heywood's text might initially appear to differ in that the commendatory verses at the outset of his *Apology* defend the value of playgoing over other kinds of recreation. While Sidney claims that poetry is better than philosophy and history, Heywood's praisers suggest that theatergoing is better than drinking and drabbing. Yet to see poetry as involving solely the mind, and theater solely the body, is to create an absurdly reductive dichotomy. What is striking about Heywood's treatise is the degree to which he, like Sidney, sees poetry and theater as imbricated disciplines forming the minds and dispositions of playgoers. Heywood asserts that the "moderne poets" can include those "whose pennes have had the greatest trafficke with the Stage" (B3r), and he cites Harington's *Briefe Apologie of Poetrie* as evidence for his own case: "Tragedies well handled be a most worthy kinde of Poesie" (F4v). Heywood does point to the practical benefits of the theater, in that it keeps the citizenry from worse forms of recreation and occupies them so that they are too busy to foment rebellion (D1r). Yet even this argument has a moral and ideological dimension, as Heywood insists on the role of the theaters as a source of civic pride (an "ornament to the Citty" [F3r]), as well as a crucial aspect of the national identity: "But in no Country they are of that eminence that ours are" (G3r). If poets like Spenser could contribute to the growing sense of national pride, then Heywood sees the theater as a fundamental component of that project.[66]

Both Sidney and Heywood insist on the power of poetry to prompt readers' and audiences' self-reflection on their own faculties of critical judgment. For Sidney, the poet has the power to affect readers in order "to bestow a Cyrus upon the world, to make many Cyruses, if they will learn aright why and how that Maker made him" (217).[67] Sidney thus defends poetry by creating a model of how its formative benefits come from both drawing in readers fully *and* encouraging attention to its own construction. This argument has much in common with Heywood's defense of his own profession through his suggestion that the theater can serve as the training ground for the moral development of the nation, an assessment with which the praisers of his work concur. In his commendatory verse to Heywood's *Apology*, Christopher Beeston suggests that the recreation of the theater can have a lasting effect on those "with a generous minde": "Two houres well spent, and all their pastimes done, / Whats good I follow, and whats bad I shun." John Taylor's commendatory verse similarly argues that the theater may cause audience members to view their vices more clearly as they see them reflected on the stage: "A Play's a true transparant Christall mirror, / To shew good minds their mirth, the bad their terror," a formulation that recalls Hamlet's famous assertion that "the purpose of playing" is "to hold ... the mirror up to Nature" (3.2.20–22).[68] In Taylor's conception, the value of a theatrical event depends on the meaning that the audience gives to it: "For Playes are good or bad, as they are us'd, / And best inventions often are abus'd." (Or, there is nothing either good or bad, but thinking makes it so.)

Though the audience possesses much of the power to determine the meaning and effect of the play, the actors—Heywood's titular subject, after all—are also paramount. Far from diminishing the audience's responsibility, however, this focus on the actors' skill requires playgoers' critique both of the characters *and* of the actors' performances. As Arthur Hopton writes in his commendatory verse, "What profit many may attaine by playes, / To the most critticke eye this book displaies, / Brave men, brave acts, being bravely acted too, / Makes, as men see things done, desire to do." While the "brave men" and "brave acts" are necessary for the audience's mimetic education, the players' performances ("being bravely acted too") are also an essential part of the formula. Indeed, the following line ("as men see things done") suggests that the valor of the character must be matched by the artistry of the actor who presents him; both inform the audience's desire to imitate. Just as Sidney's readers of poetry must consider not only the depiction of a Cyrus, but also "why and how that Maker made him," so too is the playgoers' attention to the craft of the theater itself an important part of their pedagogical process. If readers of poetry and plays created imaginative relationships with characters, playgoers might actually interact with a player on the stage, providing still more material for critically considering their relationship to the process of theatermaking.

Courteous readers

Sidney's defense of poetry and Heywood's defense of theater also share an important assumption: that the pedagogical effects of poems and plays are related to their creation of courteous interpretive communities.[69] The title page of Henry Olney's 1595 publication of Sidney points out the author's social rank ("Written by the right noble, vertuous, and learned, Sir Phillip Sidney, Knight") and includes a tag line from Horace that underscores just how much a proper appreciation of poetry may be bound up with a sense of social distinction: "Odi profanum vulgus, et arceo." As the treatise opens, Sidney speaks with the self-deprecating modesty we expect from the consummate courtier, asking his readers' pardon if he treats his subject "with more good will than good reasons" (212) and, as he nears his conclusion, referring to the entire treatise as an "ink-wasting toy" (249). (Little wonder that Philip Sidney has been proposed, however fancifully, as a possible model for Calidore, Spenser's own knight of courtesy.) Sidney's readers thus have access through purchase of his book to a document that would have circulated in manuscript for a more limited, coterie audience, enabling them to reinforce their status as the non-vulgar elite through their cultural sophistication; as Pierre Bourdieu notes, "Taste classifies, and it classifies the classifier."[70] Here we might compare the disdain expressed in Spenser's *Teares of the Muses* for the vulgar, those who are pleased with the performances of "Blind Error, scornefull Follie, and base Spight": "They to the vulgar sort now pipe and sing, / And make them merrie with their fooleries" (317, 319–20). Further, we might note that a reader of the 1609 edition of *The Faerie Queene* from the library of William Drummond obviously defined himself as one of Spenser's elite readers when he made a notation next to the maxim "So feeble skill of perfect things the vulgar has" (5.3.17).[71]

Heywood similarly poses as a deferential defender of the value of the theater in his dedicatory epistle to Edward, the Earl of Worcester, invoking the conventional modest, courteous touches even as he implicitly argues that the best readers are those who agree with him: "If my industry herein be by the common Adversary harshly received, but by your Honour charitably censured, I have from the injuditious (whom I esteeme not) but what I expect: but from your Lordship (whom I ever reverence) more then I can merit" (A2v). Like Sidney's publisher, Heywood seeks to make clear that good judgment and nobility would be aligned in giving his argument favor. Likewise, in his address to the City-Actors, Heywood wishes them "judiciall Audiences" (A3v), a group of people he no doubt hopes to train as he goes on in the following prefatory letter to address the "judiciall Reader." Heywood approaches the "curteous Reader" with measured decorum, defining the terms of their relationship: "I will neither shew my selfe over-presumptuous, in skorning thy favour, nor too importunate a beggar, by too servilly intreating it." Despite his pose of modesty, Heywood thus claims equal footing with the reader who has the power to judge his treatise, working to establish a community of readers that includes playgoers as well as theater and print professionals. He may refer to his unworthiness ("I thought it better to stammer out my mind, then not to speake at all" [B1v]), but he also employs the traditional markers of literary authority, both in the commendatory verses that preface his work and in his use of ancient citations, such as from the *Aeneid* (B1v) and Ovid's *Ars Amatoria* (B4r–v).

The editors of Shakespeare's First Folio would go even further in pointing to the power of the reader, and be even franker about their desire to see the rewards of their print project:

> It is now publique, & you will stand for your priviledges wee know: to read, and censure. Do so, but buy it first. That doth best commend a Booke, the Stationer saies. Then, how odde soever your braines be, or your wisedomes, make your licence the same, and spare not. Judge

your sixe-pen'orth, your shillings worth, your five shillings worth at a time, or higher, so you rise to the just rates, and welcome. But, what ever you do, Buy.[72]

Yet despite the mercantile terms in which John Heminges and Henry Condell portray the reader's agency here, they too use the conventions of courtesy in the volume's opening address to William Herbert, Earl of Pembroke, and his brother Philip Herbert, Earl of Montgomery, denigrating the work with patently false modesty: "For, when we valew the places your H.H. sustaine, we cannot but know their dignity greater, then to descend to the reading of these trifles." Though the publication of Shakespeare's works may expose Heminges and Condell to the vagaries of common opinion, the artful self-deprecation in the front matter of the First Folio also places them in the same tradition of courteous exchange exemplified by Sidney's and Heywood's texts.

As they lay out the relationships between moral instruction and poetry and theater, both Sidney and Heywood emphasize the importance of social norms for their models. Sidney's Horatian vision of poetry as teaching and delighting involves close attention to social decorum.[73] For a text to "delight" it must be both pleasing and fitting, while laughter is reserved for mocking what goes out of bounds: "for delight we scarcely do but in things that have a conveniency to ourselves or to the general nature; laughter almost ever cometh of things most disproportioned to ourselves and nature" (245). Delight is the response of an in-group that sees an ideal vision of itself and knows how to respond, even as the scorn of laughter defines the outcast. Decorum is also central to Heywood's model, as he envisions the role of the theater in the social instruction of the university, helping the scholar to "keepe a decorum in his countenance" (C3v) and, in another formulation that recalls Hamlet's advice to the players, "to fit his phrases to his action, and his actions to his phrase, and his pronuntiation to them both" (C4r). Theatrical and social performance blur in Heywood's model of the developing scholar. For Heywood, too, an audience's reaction is part of the way in which theater's pedagogy operates, both giving meaning to a performance and helping to determine a social norm. Thus, comedy may offer "mirth ... in the shape of a Clowne, to shew others their slovenly and unhansome behaviour, that they may reforme that simplicity in themselves, which others make their sport, lest they happen to become the like subject of generall scorne to an auditory" (F3v–F4r). The collaboration between the actors' performance and the audience's response establishes a social consensus to guide the future behavior of playgoers; reading communities and audiences establish what is to be scorned while concomitantly teaching others to scorn. Heywood's own opening verse, "The Author to his Booke," suggests that "The world's a Theater, the earth a Stage," one in which each person has his or her role to play: "This plaies an honest man, and that a knave / A gentle person this, and he a clowne ... She a chaste Lady acteth all her life, / A wanton Curtezan another playes." Gentility, chastity, and honesty are all performances, Heywood suggests, and the theater has much to teach its audiences about how to act the part even as, like poetry, it also has the potential to fundamentally affect their character.

Spenser, Shakespeare, and courteous interpretation

Renaissance readers and audiences were thus shaped as courteous interpretive communities and offered flexibility in their responses to poems and plays. Considering these transactions, I argue, yields new insights into the common ground shared by Spenser and Shakespeare despite their differences in genre and approach. My work attends to how readers and audiences both define and are defined by the texts themselves, as they are directly and indirectly addressed by front matter, proems, and prologues. At the same time, I explore how the overlapping categories of books and plays offer readers and audiences the flexibility to use their own judgment in ways that are, paradoxically perhaps, already scripted into these texts.[74] I suggest that paying closer attention to Spenser's and Shakespeare's parallel engagement with and deployment of courtesy sheds new light on how the most important print poet and the most important poet-playwright (to borrow Cheney's useful term) of their time anticipated, figured, and even created their readers and audiences through their writing, while also creating texts that offered tools for flexible, critical responses. If it is axiomatic that stage performances require an audience, it is no less the case that Spenser's winding epic draws in its readers at every turn, challenging them to reflect on how their responses to the text define both it and them.

In a likely reference to Spenser's *Teares of the Muses* in *A Midsummer Night's Dream*, Theseus declines to hear "The thrice-three muses mourning for the death / Of learning, late deceased in beggary" (5.1.52–53).[75] He also argues that the court should offer a courteous reception to the play proposed by the rude mechanicals, considering not only their performance, but their intention:

> The kinder we, to give them thanks for nothing.
> Our sport shall be to take what they mistake,
> And what poor duty cannot do,
> Noble respect takes it in might, not merit.
> Where I have come, great clerks have purposèd
> To greet me with premeditated welcomes,
> Where I have seen them shiver and look pale,
> Make periods in the midst of sentences,
> Throttle their practised accent in their fears,
> And in conclusion dumbly have broke off,
> Not paying me a welcome. Trust me, sweet,
> Out of this silence yet I picked a welcome,
> And in the modesty of fearful duty
> I read as much as from the rattling tongue
> Of saucy and audacious eloquence.
> Love, therefore, and tongue-tied simplicity
> In least speak most, to my capacity. (5.1.89–105)

Theseus here offers a model of attentive, generous reading that I suggest is a fundamental value of Shakespeare's texts; we need only consider how often characters are encouraged to reconsider the first evidence of their senses. "Pause awhile," says *Much Ado About Nothing*'s Friar Francis to a Leonato who is eager to wreak physical revenge on his apparently dishonorable daughter or the men who have wronged her—as soon as he figures out which one. This simple caution, which may also address the audience, is emblematic of a body of work in which characters, readers, and spectators are made more aware of their own faculties of judgment and encouraged to use them with generosity and compassion.

I would be very hesitant to extract a tidy lesson from Shakespeare's corpus; *pace* Heywood, I don't believe that comedies such as *A Midsummer Night's Dream* have much to teach young lovers about how to be less foolish, for example. Nonetheless, I do propose that the model of courteous reading that emerges from

Shakespeare's texts—a model that, like courtesy, is at once generous and cynically aware of the competing interests that texts of all
kinds can embody—finds its fullest Renaissance literary expression
in Spenser's *Faerie Queene*. Here, too, readers are constantly tasked
with re-evaluating their judgments, and encouraged to consider
more thoughtfully how the evidence of their senses may lead them
astray. As the virtue perhaps most connected to outward expression, courtesy forms an ideal lens for considering the complexities
of interpretation faced by Renaissance readers and spectators:

> But in the triall of true curtesie,
>   Its now so farre from that, which then it was,
>   That it indeed is nought but forgerie,
>   Fashion'd to please the eies of them, that pas,
>   Which see not perfect things but in a glas:
>   Yet is that glasse so gay, that it can blynd
>   The wisest sight, to thinke gold that is bras.
>   But vertues seat is deepe within the mynd,
> And not in outward shows, but inward thoughts defynd. (6.Proem.5)

In prompting readers to consider how their own imbrication in the
social discourse of courtesy affects their powers of discernment,
Spenser's text demands their vigilance. In that sense, whether or
not the text can "fashion a gentleman or noble person in vertuous and gentle discipline," it spurs readers to think critically about
the nature of literary discipline and how it relates to courteous
Renaissance subjectivity; they both engage with multiple levels of
signification, and explicitly reflect on why it matters that they do
so. Spenser here both reworks and goes further than Sidney's claim
that "[Nature's] world is brazen, the poets only deliver a golden"
(216): the poet of *The Faerie Queene* requires readers to suspect
his gleaming text even as they learn from it. Indeed, the brass of
the fallen world is not only to be found in nature, as Sidney conceives it. It was also associated with the world of print, as in the
First Folio's address to the Reader, referring to the Graver who
made Shakespeare's image for the opening figure: "O, could he but
have drawne his wit / As well in brasse, as he hath hit / His face; /
the Print would then surpasse / All, that was ever writ in brasse."
Even as Shakespeare's readers were asked to "looke / Not on his

Picture, but his Booke," so too were Spenser's audiences challenged to become cautious spectators as they reflected on the theatrical nature of Renaissance social performances.

Jane Grogan suggests that "the characteristic movement of the reading experience of *The Faerie Queene* ... is involvement and critical distance."[76] Similarly, Jeremy Lopez argues that Renaissance audiences "enjoyed maintaining an ironic distance from the action or words on stage, and also losing that distance, and then being made aware of moments when they had lost it."[77] The argument of this book is that we would do well to integrate such insights into the ways in which Renaissance readers and audiences were fashioned in parallel processes by print texts and theatrical spectacles.

Organization of the book

The book's next chapter is a foundational exploration of how Castiglione's *Courtier* offered new models for considering the relationship between active reading and active spectatorship; I then move to detailed analyses of how Spenser's and Shakespeare's uses of the discourses of courtesy offered them a vocabulary for engaging readers and audiences. Tracing their parallel treatments of the interpretive problems posed by both gender and class, I establish throughout their overlapping development of these themes. In Chapters 3 and 5 especially, I suggest that recognizing Shakespeare's explicit adaptation of Spenser creates new understandings of how his plays offer pointed social critiques.

Chapter 1: Imprinting and performance in Castiglione's Book of the Courtier

This chapter delves into how Castiglione's *Book of the Courtier* spurs reflection about the relationships between reading, performance, and character formation, arguing that the dialogue's recurrent, interwoven vocabulary of print and performance informs readers' experiences of considering critically the relationship between literary and social performances. *The Book of the Courtier*, I propose, encourages its readers not only to observe the debate, but to observe themselves, becoming both actor and specta-tor through their speculative readings of the text. I consider both Castiglione's original text and the editions printed in England in order to demonstrate that the material form of the book as well as its thematic discussions encouraged readers to immerse themselves in the dialogue as they tested out the possibilities of different mental positions. Involving readers in its explorations while also offering them agency to direct their own experiences of it, Castiglione's dia-logue in its various editions facilitates both pleasurable instruction and metacritical reflection and critique. I thus focus on readers' complex experiences rather than on straightforward resolutions to debates within and about the dialogue. One crucial puzzle offered to readers concerns the unity of the book as it moves from a model of courtesy as a performance to a model of courtesy as a discourse capable of changing the natures of both the courtier and those with whom he interacts. This tension in two modes of character forma-tion, I suggest, also emerges in *Hamlet* in Polonius's contradictory advice to Laertes about self-fashioning yet being true to himself. Against the critical tradition, I contend that the book's printed form, with its condensed rules for conduct in the back of English editions, complicates rather than simplifies readers' engagement, giving them an additional puzzle to sort out, prompting them to test the relationship between the straightforward editorial rules and glosses and the text's more complicated discussions. Readers' practice in courtesy as they experience the text involves juggling multiple perspectives, as reflected in both the content and the for-mat of the book; this practice also provides an ideal training for the overlapping tasks of reading Spenser and reading and watching Shakespeare.

Chapter 2: Playing by the rules? Pedagogies of pleasure and inset audiences in Spenser's Faerie Queene and Shakespeare's Love's Labour's Lost

While Chapter 1 focuses on the various methods by which Castiglione instructs his readers in courtesy, Chapter 2 considers how both Spenser and Shakespeare manage the related question of how instruction itself can be courteous, a topic that Roger Ascham also treats in his *Schoolmaster*. I assert that Spenser and Shakespeare both draw from and rework Castiglione's and Ascham's models of courteous pedagogy rooted in pleasure, though in different ways. My reading of selected passages from *The Faerie Queene* and *Love's Labour's Lost* sheds light on how these texts both reflect on and elicit reader and audience awareness of the complexity of courteous instruction. In the case of Spenser, I explore how *The Faerie Queene* explicitly points to the educational process by presenting models of instruction both by potentially coercive precept and by more pleasurable example, thus inviting readers to consider what is at stake in the difference between the two. I am especially attentive to how Spenser's poem represents theatrical moments of education. For example, in Calidore's encounter with the discourteous Briana, simply *watching* Calidore's instruction of another makes Briana "so wondrously now chaung'd, from that she was afore." Briana provides readers with a model of how to read Spenser's text: the poem has the potential to transform them as they critically observe the education of literary characters, and it does so by moving beyond straightforward precepts.

Shakespeare's *Love's Labour's Lost* also involves readers and audiences in thinking about how they are both reflected in and different from its inset audiences. Yet if Castiglione's text asserts that the courtier's pleasing social performances and recreation cohere with his moral role as educator of the prince, Shakespeare's play shows the frequent incompatibility of pedagogy and pleasure. Castiglione's idealistic model is undermined for comic effect in Shakespeare's satire of humanist education; at the same time, the play sends up the epic aspirations of a poem like Spenser's in its presentation of the Nine Worthies. *Love's Labour's Lost* refuses to take seriously the enlistment of courtesy for Christian purposes that Spenser's text offers. Nonetheless, as in both Castiglione and Spenser, the play works by involving readers and audiences in the mental game of thinking about how they are both mirrored in and different from its inset audiences. Taken together, Chapters 1 and 2 show how Castiglione, Spenser, and Shakespeare present interpretive puzzles around problems of courtly social performance for readers and playgoers, challenging them to reflect on the relationship between how they define the text and how they define themselves.

Chapter 3: Honorable action upstaged by theatrical wordplay *in* The Faerie Queene *and* Much Ado About Nothing

In this chapter, I contribute to the ongoing question of Shakespeare's debts to Spenser, arguing that Spenser's Phedon episode in *Faerie Queene* 2.4 is a more important source for Shakespeare's *Much Ado About Nothing* than previously recognized. By setting Shakespeare's comedy alongside a tragic event in Spenser's poem (in which the suspicion of adultery leads to murder rather than an apparently happy ending, as it does in Shakespeare), I show how Shakespeare and Spenser deviate from other versions of the tale, notably Ariosto's *Orlando Furioso*, in their emphasis on courteous theatricality over heroic action. Both texts, I establish, reveal the costs of maintaining the appearance of masculine honor in a culture obsessed with impersonation, especially the danger that substance will be replaced with verbal self-presentation. The movement from action to words contained in Spenser's narrative leaves significant traces in Shakespeare's play as it too registers the loss of authenticity that afflicts its characters.

Chapter 4: Courteous competitions: Blood, gold, *and outward shows in* Nennio, *Spenser's Book of Courtesy, and* The Merchant of Venice

This chapter explores the relationships between Shakespeare's *Merchant of Venice*, Book 6 of *The Faerie Queene*, and the dialogue *Nennio, or A Treatise on Nobility*, published in English translation in 1595 with a commendatory sonnet by Spenser. Despite its important connections to the depiction of courtesy in *The Faerie Queene*, *Nennio* has received little critical attention. In *Nennio*, the characters' debate about whether nobility of blood or nobility of mind is superior concludes with a relatively straightforward victory for nobility of mind, cemented by the generosity of the lower-born Fabricio. But Spenser's poem requires more complicated reactions of its readers, as the Knight of Courtesy's competitions in generosity with the lowly shepherds he encounters have differing outcomes and have encouraged a variety of critical responses to his character. I demonstrate that, in contrast both to *Nennio* and to his own commendatory sonnet, Spenser's concern throughout his treatment of courtesy in *The Faerie Queene* is not to direct his readers toward a particular view of nobility, but to train their judgments in understanding the complexity of courtesy in action. By navigating interrelated examples, Spenser's readers revisit and revise their interpretations and come to understand the shifting relations between nobility and courtesy, and between inner character and outward show. I argue that Spenser's claim that "virtue's seat is deep within the mind" is an acknowledgment of the ultimate unknowability of others' motivations in ambiguous expressions of courtesy rather than a straightforward claim for the importance of inner virtue. Interpreting the characters' competitions in courtesy and the audience's judgment in *The Merchant of Venice*, I show that Bassanio's "impromptu" speech in praise of the lead casket is an example of *sprezzatura* that has significant implications for the play's treatment of the conflict between courteous and mercantile systems of exchange. Self-deprecation becomes self-promotion, as the apparently modest choice of the lead casket is how Bassanio, a young man of noble blood, outshines his competitors. Thus, while with one voice the play suggests the obvious superiority of the Christian aristocrats, it also offers readers the tools to question the nature of inherited nobility and to critique the culturally available, pernicious view that gentility runs in the blood. In their parallel explorations of how self-interested generosity passes as courtesy, Spenser and Shakespeare call upon readers and audiences both to appreciate the complexity of courtesy and to make their own judgments.

Chapter 5: Literary mirrors of aristocratic performance:
Readers and audiences of The Faerie Queene *and*
The Winter's Tale

In this chapter I demonstrate how both Spenser and Shakespeare show the difficulty of establishing noble identity by pointing toward their own authorial roles as fictionmakers, spurring readers and audiences to recognize how their own responses to the text render it meaningful. Taking as my focus two recognition scenes when an apparently rustic young woman (Pastorella in *The Faerie Queene*, Perdita in *The Winter's Tale*) is recognized to be of noble birth, I examine how both authors insist on the obvious fictionality of their work. Spenser's and Shakespeare's texts reject the hidden art of *sprezzatura* and instead make use of metapoetry and metatheater, directly drawing attention to and commenting on the fictional nature of the stories they create. Even as recognition scenes emphasize the fictional nature of the text through their use of highly conventional archetypes that are acknowledged as such, they also denaturalize gentle identity by prompting readers and audiences to connect texts' literary performances and aristocratic role-playing in the wider society. The metapoetic and metatheatrical moments in *The Faerie Queene* and *The Winter's Tale* encourage both explicit reflection on the authors' self-conscious artistry and a critical examination of social fictions.

Conclusion: *Courteous farewells in Spenser and Shakespeare*

This book ends by exploring how the conclusions of *The Book of the Courtier*, the 1596 *Faerie Queene*, and *The Tempest* offer opportunities to both approach and challenge readers and audiences. These are moments, I argue, when readers and audiences are called on to recognize the special power that their own investment—their pleasure, their judgment—in poems and plays has to render these works meaningful, and to decide how they will position themselves with relation to the text. While much of the book focuses on parallels between Spenser and Shakespeare, here I suggest a divergence as Spenserian rupture contrasts with Shakespearean collaboration. At the same time, as both authors offer choices about how to relate to their works, they show their fundamental recognition of readers' and audiences' agency.

Notes

1 All citations of *The Faerie Queene* are from the revised second edition of A. C. Hamilton, Hiroshi Yamashita, and Toshiyuki Suzuki.
2 See Frank Whigham's discussion of "self-deprecation" as a "trope of personal promotion" (*Ambition and Privilege*, 102–12) and Richard Helgerson on the poet's self-promoting self-deprecation (*Self-Crowned Laureates*, 30 and passim).
3 On Spenser's creation of a "Christianized Virgilian career," see Patrick Cheney, *Spenser's Famous Flight*.

4 Jonathan Goldberg, *Seeds of Things*, 63–66.

5 The opening of Ariosto's *Orlando Furioso* does, however, point to
   that poem's interest in courtesy. Patrick Cheney has previously commented on the significance of Spenser's choice of theatrical metaphor
   and its relevance to Shakespeare's career; see *Shakespeare's Literary
   Authorship*, 20.

6 I cite Gary Taylor's edition of *Henry V*.

7 Tiffany Stern offers the suggestion that the apparent "modest humility" of this speech may also mask "an aggressive dimension," if the
   Lord Chamberlain's Men were pointing out that the Curtain Theatre,
   in which the play may have been first performed, was inferior to the
   Globe that they were soon to occupy. This fascinating reading is of
   course not incompatible with seeing the topos of courteous modesty
   as a cover for theatrical pride, as I argue here. See Stern, *Making
   Shakespeare*, 15.

8 Cf. Patrick Cheney's extended argument about the references to
   publication and theater in his discussion of the "printless foot" of
   Prospero's farewell address (*Shakespeare's Literary Authorship*, 1–4).

9 My own approach is not a cognitive one, but I recognize the importance of a number of studies that have explored the way in which
   Shakespeare's language engages the brains of its audiences and readers
   in complicated ways at the same time that it depicts characters undergoing complex thought processes. See Raphael Lyne, *Shakespeare,
   Rhetoric and Cognition*; Bruce McConachie, *Engaging Audiences*,
   65–120; Philip Davis, *Shakespeare Thinking*; and Stephen Booth,
   Precious Nonsense.

10 Robert Hapgood also points to the link between gentleness and the
   audience's imagination in this prologue, emphasizing especially the
   "implied ennoblement" of the audience (*Shakespeare the Theatre-
   Poet*, 20–21). Cyndia Susan Clegg likewise emphasizes the role
   of the audience here, though her focus is different from mine. See
   Shakespeare's Reading Audiences, 17–18 and 68–69.

11 On texts as commodities, see Whigham, *Ambition and Privilege*,
   29. On pastoral literature in particular as a cultural commodity, see
   Louis Montrose, "Of Gentlemen and Shepherds." Robert Matz in
   Defending Literature in Early Modern England pushes against the
   notion (articulated by critics such as Montrose and Whigham) that
   literature at the time is "politically profitable" (11), advocating "a
   more skeptical account of the place of literature in Renaissance culture and society" (128).

12 See Lawrence Stone, *Crisis of the Aristocracy*. David Posner writes
   that in the early modern period, "the nobility found itself, or—more

importantly—perceived itself, to be in a period of difficulty, tension, and transition, in which certain previously secure ideas of what it meant to be 'noble' were being challenged, modified, or replaced" (*Performance of Nobility*, 3). Norbert Elias argues that when the upper class is under threat, there is all the more effort "to observe and polish everything that distinguishes them from people of lower rank" (*Civilizing Process*, 399 and 424). As Anna Bryson discusses in both drawing on and modifying Elias, this attempt to compete through polished behavior took place in large part through customs of manners that paid extreme attention to differentiations of status (*From Courtesy to Civility*, 75–106). For a wide-ranging account of the concept and practice of civility in the period, see also Keith Thomas, *In Pursuit of Civility*. Thomas suggests that both Elias and Bryson have exaggerated the extent to which the sixteenth century offered "a new departure in the history of manners" (15), underscoring that all societies must possess some form of the restraint that Elias considered the hallmark of the early modern period (16).

13 In his foundational treatment of this subject, Stephen Greenblatt asserts that "in the sixteenth century there appears to be an increased self-consciousness about the fashioning of human identity as a manipulable, artful process" (*Renaissance Self-Fashioning*, 2). Harry Berger Jr. notes, "The new representation demands described by Elias have in recent decades been associated with the increasing theatricalization and rhetoricization of culture" (*Absence of Grace*, 44).

14 Bryson, *From Courtesy to Civility*, 13.

15 Whigham, *Ambition and Privilege*, x–xi and passim. Norbert Elias also notes the irony that courtesy manuals "assisted the spreading of their [the nobility's] manners even as they sought to differentiate themselves" (*Civilizing Process*, 387). On the generational tensions between "opportunism" and "conservatism" (4) in the Elizabethan period, see also Anthony Esler, *Aspiring Mind of the Elizabethan Younger Generation*.

16 Barbara Correll, *End of Conduct*, 16–17.

17 On the success of Castiglione, see Whigham, *Ambition and Privilege*, 198–99, and Peter Burke, *Fortunes of the* Courtier, 55–80.

18 Unless otherwise identified, English citations of *The Book of the Courtier* are from Virginia Cox's edition of Hoby's 1561 translation, originally published by William Seres. I have also consulted (and will occasionally cite) the Italian edition of G. Carnazzi and the Charles Singleton translation, edited by Daniel Javitch. Eduardo Saccone provides a useful discussion of the complicated nature of Castiglione's view of grace in "*Grazia, Sprezzatura, Affettazione* in the *Courtier*"; he stresses both its dualistic nature, and its expression through social

transactions. Drawing from Saccone, Berger suggests that "the absence of grace" is what is in fact necessary for the ideal courtier, since it enables him to strive toward the imitation of an elusive ideal (*Absence of Grace*, 17). For a discussion of the importance of the topic of grace in this period, see also Eugenio Garin, *Italian Humanism*, 117–22.

19 See Thomas, *In Pursuit of Civility*, 6 and especially 159–82. Ian Smith tracks the association of "language performance" and "status," arguing that "barbarism demarcated a cultural division of insiders and outsiders that would eventually sharpen into racial awareness" (*Race and Rhetoric in the Renaissance*, 2). Patricia Akhimie's work points to the importance of "identifying processes of inclusion and exclusion by detecting the pain that such operations inflict" (*Shakespeare and the Cultivation of Difference*, 11).

20 Greenblatt, *Renaissance Self-Fashioning*, 186.

21 See Melissa E. Sanchez, " 'To Giue Faire Colour,' " especially 253–54.

22 Sanchez, " 'To Giue Faire Colour,' " 261. Ross Lerner also explores the connection between racialization and allegory in Spenser, suggesting that the poem itself may critique the racialization it produces. See "Allegory and Racialization in *The Faerie Queene*."

23 Akhimie, *Shakespeare and the Cultivation of Difference*, 12. Thus, as Akhimie convincingly argues, literature that offered advice for rising in society could at the same time be a powerful tool of social oppression: "Conduct literature offers the opportunity for social advancement to a broad readership while at the same time suggesting that comportment is the purview and even the natural habit of aristocratic people alone ... the leisure of the landed is created and maintained by working class bodies" (27).

24 Akhimie, *Shakespeare and the Cultivation of Difference*, 13.

25 Akhimie, *Shakespeare and the Cultivation of Difference*, 1.

26 I thus respond in my own way to Jennifer A. Low and Nova Myhill's suggestion that more work should be done on the relationship between "the performance authority of the play" and "the interpretive authority of the playgoer" (*Imagining the Audience*, 2).

27 Two important exceptions to this are the 2017 Globe workshop, "Spenser, Poetry, and Performance," and a pair of seminar sessions on Spenser organized by Joe Moshenska and Leah Whittington at the 2019 Shakespeare Association of America conference. On the overlaps between Shakespeare's and Spenser's circles, see also Willy Maley, "Shakespeare and Spenser: Bards of a Feather?"

28 Lukas Erne, *Shakespeare as Literary Dramatist*, 17–18.

29 Jonathan Bate, *Soul of the Age*, 143. Stephen Greenblatt asserts that "Shakespeare's work" shows "relatively few signs of the influence of Spenser, Donne, Bacon, or Ralegh" (*Will in the World*, 207).

30 See J. B. Lethbridge, Introduction to *Shakespeare and Spenser*, 2, and Judith H. Anderson, *Reading the Allegorical Intertext*, 17. Robert Lanier Reid sees Spenser and Shakespeare as "radically divergent," contrasting "Spenser's *Christianized Platonism*" with "Shakespeare's *sophisticated Aristotelianism*" (*Renaissance Psychologies*, 2).

31 Cheney, *Shakespeare's Literary Authorship*, 22.

32 Cheney, *Shakespeare's Literary Authorship*, 22.

33 For this view of Spenser, see Greenblatt, *Renaissance Self-Fashioning*, 157–92, especially 189–92. For a similar view, see also Paul J. Alpers, *The Poetry of* The Faerie Queene, 36, and Jonathan Goldberg, *Endlesse Worke*, 9–11. See also Harry Berger Jr.'s insights into how Spenser "*represents* storytelling" ("Narrative as Rhetoric in *The Faerie Queene*," 3), which have influenced Judith H. Anderson in her intertextual explorations of how Spenser's narrator is "openly a fiction" (*Reading the Allegorical Intertext*, 28–29 and 32). In her study of allegory, Maureen Quilligan asserts that "allegory is ... the most self-reflexive and critically self-conscious of narrative genres, and ... its purpose is always to make its reader correspondingly self-conscious" (*The Language of Allegory*, 24).

34 Montrose, "Of Gentlemen and Shepherds," 451.

35 Frances Dolan, *True Relations*, 24 and 156.

36 Christopher Warley, *Sonnet Sequences and Social Distinction*, 3.

37 Paul Trolander and Zeynep Tenger, *Sociable Criticism in England*, 18 and 63.

38 See Erne, *Shakespeare as Literary Dramatist* and *Shakespeare and the Book Trade*.

39 The question of Spenser's relationship to the theater has received little critical attention; see Jeff Dolven, "Spenser and the Troubled Theaters" and Charles Whitney, *Early Responses to Renaissance Drama*, 132–47. Dolven suggests that Spenser adopts a complicated perspective on the stage, mindful both of its dangers and the problem of knee-jerk antitheatricalism. Likewise, Whitney suggests that Spenser presents "theatrical experience ... as a dangerous adventure that could have a positive, transformative outcome" (137). See also Charles E. Walton, "*To Maske in Myrthe*."

40 On the general importance of the reader's response to a literary text, Wolfgang Iser offers the foundational assertion that "Central to the reading of every literary work is the interaction between its structure and its recipient" (*Act of Reading*, 20). See also Norman N. Holland, *Dynamics of Literary Response*, and Stanley Fish, *Is There a Text in This Class?* and *Surprised by Sin*.

41 Albert Ascoli, *Ariosto's Bitter Harmony*, 44.

42 Terence Cave, "The Mimesis of Reading," 149–65. Robert Weimann connects the dispersal of textual authority brought on by the Reformation to new power for readers as well as spectators (*Authority and Representation*, 1–22). Victoria Kahn likewise underscores the importance of the reader's active involvement with the text in *Rhetoric, Prudence, and Skepticism*.

43 Stephen Orgel, "The Book of the Play," 30. On early modern marginalia, see also William H. Sherman, *Used Books*, and Erne, *Shakespeare and the Book Trade*, 224–31.

44 Sasha Roberts, *Reading Shakespeare's Poems*, 4.

45 See Heidi Brayman Hackel, "The 'Great Variety' of Readers," 139–57. See also Helen Smith on the variety of ways in which texts engaged early modern women readers (*'Grossly Material Things'*, 174–211). Eugene R. Kintgen emphasizes that in Tudor England, "reading was always preparation for some future action" (*Reading in Tudor England*, 140).

46 On Renaissance metatheatricality and the audience's awareness of fictionality, see Andrew Gurr, *The Shakespearean Stage*, especially 9–10, and *Playgoing in Shakespeare's London*, 124–28. Tiffany Stern also notes that Coleridge's concept of "the willing suspension of disbelief" did not apply to early modern theaters (*Rehearsal from Shakespeare to Sheridan*, 13).

47 Stern, *Making Shakespeare*, 29.

48 Matteo Pangallo, *Playwriting Playgoers*, 3 and 34.

49 William West, *Common Understandings, Poetic Confusion*, 9. On the crucial role of audiences in the early modern theater, see Jeremy Lopez, *Theatrical Convention and Audience Response*; Anthony B. Dawson and Paul Yachnin's *Culture of Playgoing*; Jennifer A. Low and Nova Myhill, *Imagining the Audience*; and Erika T. Lin, *Shakespeare and the Materiality of Performance*.

50 It is certainly the case that conduct literature offers a special example of engaged reading, as Dolan notes in a different context: "domestic advice sought to propel its readers into action" (*True Relations*, 166). She also observes the flexibility that domestic advice texts might offer readers: "domestic conduct books function inefficiently as delivery mechanisms for didacticism. The reader might be as puzzled as to what he has learned from them as from a Shakespeare play. The effect of that puzzlement is to be left to one's own devices to craft a lesson, to determine the relation between what the text offers and what one needs" (*True Relations*, 160).

51 In his introduction to the anthology *Reading and Writing in Shakespeare*, David M. Bergeron notes, "The theater as an institution

especially marks the conjunction of oral and written cultures as actors speak aloud the lines that the playwright has written, before an audience made up of both literate and illiterate spectators. In time some of these spectators will purchase books that contain the words of the play, and they will read the drama in private" (11). For a larger study of the close relationship between print and theater, see Julie Stone Peters, *Theatre of the Book*. See also Barbara A. Mowat, "The Theater and Literary Culture."

52 For an argument about Shakespeare's concern for the print readership of his plays, see Erne, *Shakespeare as Literary Dramatist*; for the complementary argument about his success in acquiring this print readership, see Erne, *Shakespeare and the Book Trade*. David Scott Kastan represents the opposing viewpoint in asserting, "At least in his role as playwright, Shakespeare had no obvious interest in the printed book" (*Shakespeare and the Book*, 5).

53 Cheney, *Shakespeare's Literary Authorship*, xii and 6–11. See also Cheney's *Shakespeare, National Poet-Playwright*. On Shakespeare as an author concerned for metatextuality in addition to metatheatricality, see also Helen Smith, " 'A Man in Print?,' " 59–78.

54 Tiffany Stern, "Watching as Reading," 137.

55 Charles Whitney, *Early Responses to Renaissance Drama*, 4. Whitney recognizes the importance of taking stock of the history of reading in exploring varied audience responses to plays (8).

56 Akihiro Yamada, *Experiencing Drama*, 200.

57 Clegg, *Shakespeare's Reading Audiences*, 11.

58 All citations of Spenser not from *The Faerie Queene* are from *The Yale Edition of the Shorter Poems of Edmund Spenser*, ed. William A. Oram et al.

59 Throughout the book, in cases where I have not made use of modern editions, I have typically silently regularized u/v, i/j, tilde, and long s.

60 Jonas Barish, *Antitheatrical Prejudice*, 80.

61 I cite the edition of *The Republic* translated by Tom Griffith and edited by G. R. F. Ferrari. On Platonic antitheatricalism, see Barish, *Antitheatrical Prejudice*, 5–37.

62 As Tanya Pollard notes, "Defenses of the theater, curiously, tend for the most part to agree with antitheatricalists' primary claim that plays reconstitute us in their own image. For playwrights and other supporters, however, this capacity to mold spectators is the theater's great strength" (*Shakespeare's Theater*, xxi).

63 I cite throughout Frank Whigham and Wayne A. Rebhorn's edition of Puttenham's *The Art of English Poesy*.

64 While I agree with Barish's assessment that Heywood's treatise is "a desultory ramble that repeatedly betrays the cause it is attempting to serve" (*Antitheatrical Prejudice*, 117), I also see an important similarity in how Heywood and Sidney view the relationships between poetry, drama, and character formation.

65 Citations of *The Defence of Poesy* are from *The Major Works* edited by Katherine Duncan-Jones unless otherwise noted. It is hard not to wonder what Sidney would have made of Shakespeare's theater, and whether it might have led him to adjust his arguments. For example, Sidney praises poetry as superior to history in presenting ideal characters, rather than making the reader use his "discretion" in figuring out what and what not to imitate (224). And Sidney also attacks some contemporary versions of the theater that fail to follow Aristotle's unities of time and place, thus requiring the audience to stretch their minds in creating the fiction that two hours spent on one stage have credibly presented actions widely ranging in time and place (243). Sidney's objections fail to give audiences credit for the kind of mental labors in which Shakespeare's plays, with their rich characters and at times wide-ranging plots, engage audiences.

66 On Spenser and nation-building, see especially Richard Helgerson, *Forms of Nationhood*.

67 For a discussion of Sidney's emphasis on the power of both authors and readers, see Margaret W. Ferguson, *Trials of Desire*, 137–62. On the relationship between rhetoric and the reader's judgment, see Victoria Kahn, *Rhetoric, Prudence, and Skepticism*.

68 I cite the edition of *Hamlet* by Ann Thompson and Neil Taylor. Cf. Bruce McConachie's work on the role of "mirror neurons" in allowing audiences to empathize with characters onstage (*Engaging Audiences*, 65–120). On theatergoing as "an intensely corporeal, highly emotive activity," see Allison P. Hobgood, *Passionate Playgoing*, 10.

69 For a fundamental treatment of "the affinities between proper court conduct and the stylistic procedures of poetry," see Daniel Javitch, *Poetry and Courtliness*, 6. On the relationship between "theories of reading" and "notions of gentlemanly conduct" in the period, see also Katherine A. Craik, *Reading Sensations*, especially 3 and 35–51.

70 Pierre Bourdieu, *Distinction*, 6.

71 I am grateful to the Centre for Research Collections library at the University of Edinburgh for permission to consult this book. It includes extensive annotations on sources by Drummond in Book 6, but whether he also made the marginal annotation to which I refer here is not clear.

72 I cite here *The Norton Facsimile*, prepared by Charlton Hinman. Bergeron notes of this letter: "This blatant sales pitch nevertheless also recognizes the right of the reader to respond in whatever manner he or she chooses: that is the privilege and responsibility of the reader" (*Reading and Writing*, 14). There may have been an actual need for such a sales pitch; Gary Taylor claims that, contrary to what we might expect, the First Folio was a losing investment for its publisher Edward Blount; see "Making Meaning Marketing Shakespeare 1623," 61–62.

73 For a discussion of how "Sidney's championing of Horatian profit and pleasure" should "be read with reference to contemporary, politically charged debates over aristocratic leisure," see Matz, *Defending Literature*, 60.

74 In *Shakespeare's Art of Orchestration*, Jean E. Howard emphasizes Shakespeare's "verbal and visual orchestration" of audience response (2).

75 I cite Peter Holland's edition of *A Midsummer Night's Dream*. A. Kent Hieatt considers this to be Shakespeare's "only generally accepted reference to Spenser" ("William Shakespeare," 641), claiming that it is "not mocking," as argued by critics such as James P. Bednarz in "Imitations of Spenser in *A Midsummer Night's Dream*." Bednarz does, however, see Spenser as an important influence on Shakespeare, claiming, "Ridicule of Spenser is an attempt to deny him the paternity of *A Midsummer Night's Dream*" (88).

76 Jane Grogan, *Exemplary Spenser*, 16.

77 Lopez, *Theatrical Convention*, 34.

1

Imprinting and performance in Castiglione's *Book of the Courtier*

Castiglione's *Book of the Courtier* is both a text that Spenser and Shakespeare would have known well and a fundamental exploration of the complex relationship between the self and performance. In this chapter, I suggest that courtesy literature may have appealed to Renaissance readers not simply because of its promise of practical advice, but because it offered them a pleasurable opportunity to explore the same kinds of intellectual problems that are later posed by *The Faerie Queene* and plays such as *Hamlet*. Thinking about *The Book of the Courtier* as combining a series of pleasing mental games will, I suggest, enable us to see just why it served as a useful mine of concepts for Spenser and Shakespeare as they developed their own interpretive problems to engage readers and audiences. As it puzzles out the difficulties that attend the creation and interpretation of human performances, *The Book of the Courtier* offers training in the self-conscious attention to the practices of reading and spectatorship emphasized by Spenser and Shakespeare.

As Polonius's son Laertes prepares to leave for Paris, *Hamlet*'s verbose courtier offers him some fatherly advice that is full of both paradox and measured decorum:

> There, my blessing with thee,
> And these few precepts in thy memory
> Look thou character: give thy thoughts no tongue
> Nor any unproportioned thought his act.
> Be thou familiar but by no means vulgar;
> Those friends thou hast, and their adoption tried,
> Grapple them unto thy soul with hoops of steel,
> But do not dull thy palm with entertainment

Of each new-hatched, unfledged courage. Beware
Of entrance to a quarrel but, being in,
Bear't that th'opposed may beware of thee.
Give every man thy ear but few thy voice;
Take each man's censure but reserve thy judgement.
Costly thy habit as thy purse can buy
But not expressed in fancy—rich, not gaudy;
For the apparel oft proclaims the man
And they in France of the best rank and station
Are of all most select and generous chief in that.
Neither a borrower nor a lender, boy,
For loan oft loses both itself and friend
And borrowing dulleth th'edge of husbandry.
This above all, to thine own self be true
And it must follow as the night the day
Thou canst not then be false to any man. (1.3.56–79)[1]

Polonius's many precepts follow a regular pattern of exhort-
ing Laertes to moderate his behavior by avoiding extremes in his
friendships, appearance, finances, and entertainment: to be "familiar" but to avoid vulgarity, to listen freely but not speak too much,
to dress well but not gaudily. Polonius counsels his son to attend to
every detail of his activities, to engage in constant self-surveillance
in order to control the façade that he presents to others. All of
Polonius's advice emphasizes that social success depends upon
Laertes' ability to control the ways in which his thoughts reach the
public stage, except, of course, for the speech's ironic, culminating
bit of advice: "to thine own self be true / And it must follow as the
night the day / Thou canst not then be false to any man."

On the one hand, Polonius's concluding advice to his son to be
true to himself sounds like the insincere crescendo of a long list
of conventional[2] precepts, rather than a heartfelt recommendation.
On the other hand, Polonius does encourage Laertes to go beyond
merely hearing or learning his advice; he asks his son to make his
words a part of him: "And these few precepts in thy memory / Look
thou character." Signifying in this context "to engrave, imprint,
inscribe, or write on a surface,"[3] the verb to "character" suggests
a permanent inscription of Polonius's precepts through the engrav-
ing of conventional words on the living memory. Polonius implies
that learning his precepts will in some fundamental way alter
Laertes; that is to say, his son's self—his character—will come to be

composed in part by the internal inscription of his fatherly advice.[4] Of course, learning his father's precepts by heart need not imply that Laertes has fully internalized his father's doctrines; in Gregory Doran's 2009 *Hamlet*, for example, Laertes knew his father's precepts well enough to mockingly recite them along with Ophelia as a dismissal of his father. If Polonius's speech suggests the value of playing one's social part, it also suggests that it's not enough simply to learn one's lines. The speech is both a miniature lesson in courteous self-presentation and, with its overwhelming piling on of advice, a lesson in how not to instruct in courtesy. (After all, the fundamental requirement of courtesy is that one adapt the performance to one's audience, and is any audience more resistant to instruction than one's offspring?)

Polonius's speech offers two interpretive possibilities, then, and refuses to choose between them. His fatherly precepts may be seen as purely practical tips for concealing the true nature of the self, precepts to be put into practice at will as various situations demand, or they may be seen as counseling a mode of being, steeped in decorum, that becomes second nature through the inscription of precepts in the memory. Moving from a pragmatic set of rules for curating one's image to a glancing reference to an authentic personal identity that is nonetheless capable of refinement, Polonius's speech reflects the tensions in the genre of courtesy literature itself. Here, clothing is a key locus for the contradictory depiction of the relationship between the inner self and outward appearance: "Costly thy habit as thy purse can buy / But not expressed in fancy—rich, not gaudy; / For the apparel oft proclaims the man." Laertes' wardrobe—his "habit"—will determine how others see him, yet this too is a commodity available for purchase. In using the term "habit," Polonius invokes a discourse about clothing, character, and habitus that would have had currency in Shakespeare's time. Earlier in the play, Hamlet himself proclaims, "'Tis not alone my inky cloak, cold mother, / Nor customary suits of solemn black ... That can denote me truly. These indeed 'seem', / For they are actions that a man might play, / But I have that within which passes show, / These but the trappings and the suits of woe" (1.2.77–78, 83–86). While Hamlet's "customary" clothing (his costume, as he punningly implies) creates meaning for his spectators, he asserts that his real character is hidden inside. Both Polonius and Hamlet suggest that outward self-presentations may

offer clues for observers to decode rather than simply or even necessarily reflecting one's inner state.[5] And, too, Hamlet's metatheatrical
reference to "actions that a man might play" here underscores the
complex irony at work in his pretense of authenticity, raising further questions about the layering of performance and sincerity for
the audience to sort out. The interpretive dilemmas presented by
Hamlet are in many ways the central problems of courtesy literature
itself, and they are thus the kinds of problems that audiences would
have been trained to appreciate through their readings of texts such
as Castiglione's *Book of the Courtier*.

Like Polonius's speech, Castiglione's dialogue admits of a variety
of interpretations of its goals, ranging from radical personal transformation to convincing performance. Does courtesy literature
inscribe its doctrines on the reader's heart, or does it merely supply
a set of tools that courtly readers can take up at will as they seek to
mold the impressions of others? Castiglione's text serves both these
apparently contradictory aims by openly presenting disagreements
about social values. As Jennifer Richards and others have noted, the
dialogue form of Castiglione's *Book of the Courtier* lends itself to
delineating the paradoxical traits of the courtier as well as registering the socially contested nature of courtesy.[6] Virginia Cox suggests
that the Renaissance dialogue is both "a fictional conversation"
and "an actual literary exchange," and that "the dialogue's double
structure ... allows almost endless possibilities for creative manipulation of the relations between reader and text"; for Cox, the effect
on readers of avoiding precepts is to "unfold before them a dialogue between conflicting perspectives, to sharpen their sense of the
issues involved and open a space for the exercise of their moral
judgment."[7] And, too, as Thomas Hoby asserts in the preface to
his translation of the text first published in 1561, different readers
will derive different lessons from the text (4–5).[8] My reading of
Castiglione builds on these insights in order to emphasize how readers of *The Book of the Courtier* garner opportunities to re-form the
character of a text that is itself concerned with the problem of character formation. The dialogue offers a pleasing recreation in two
senses of the term: both in its fictional claim to re-present actual
conversations, and in its suggestion of a literary pastime for readers. Yet, this literary game contains high stakes: even as it affords
readers an entertaining end in itself, it also raises crucial questions

about how they relate to the text and the society it depicts. Likewise, it both embodies and describes a program of disguised instruction through pleasure, encouraging readers both to get lost in the text and to consider it from a critical distance. In offering different versions and views of courtesy, the text implicitly invites its readers to add their own voices to the mix.

The Courtier thus takes seriously learning that occurs through play and resists straightforward messages. The dialogue operates through a productive modulation of pleasure and anxiety, creating entertainment out of questions that may well have had pressing importance in readers' lives. The choice of the first speaker to propose the qualities of the perfect courtier reinforces the pleasure in indeterminacy. Lodovico da Canossa is selected because his propensity to put everything "arsiversy" (1.13) will provoke more conversation and response; there will be more delight in pursuing knowledge than in immediately getting it right: "we shall have somuch the more *pastyme,* and everye one shall be able to answere you" (1.13; emphasis mine). In his influential reading of *The Courtier,* Daniel Javitch emphasizes the close link between courtly codes of conduct and poetry. For Javitch, the dialogue connects learning to ornament and pleasure rather than to deeper concerns.[9] I want to suggest here that the dialogue is bivalent: it offers readers a pleasurable path to meaningful engagement, and gives them the resources to consider critically the nature of their learning. The "pastyme" of the interlocutors is concomitant with the reader's enjoyment of the process of making sense of the text's debates in ways that move beyond simple resolution. Readers may immerse themselves in a work that gently leads them through a program of pleasurable instruction that marks them unawares. At the same time, the dialogue also offers readers the tools to situate themselves at a critical distance from the text and to reflect explicitly on its performances. As Evelyn Tribble points out, *The Book of the Courtier* emphasizes the importance not only of skilled performance, but also of "skilled vision."[10] In drawing attention to its own practices, I argue, Castiglione's text encourages readers to consider critically how they interpret social performances. As the text attempts to dissect the workings of the courtly habitus, it both analyzes and reveals the complexity of judgments at work in an atmosphere of uncertainty.

As they reflect on the judgment revealed by the dialogue's characters, Castiglione's readers are prompted to consider their own social position as well. In finding an entertainment for the evening, the interlocutors judge one another's suggested games even as they propose games concerned with judgment—choosing the ideal fault for one's beloved, determining the folly to which one is most likely to succumb, and so on.[11] Their final selection of the game of describing an ideal courtier emphasizes the reinforcement of the group's own good judgment and social identity, challenging its readers both to understand the origins of social distinctions and to think critically about how they will position themselves:

> Therfore if in any place men may be founde that deserve the name of good Courtyers, and can judge what belongeth to the perfeccion of Courtyership, by reason a man may beleve them to be here. To disgrace therefore many untowardly asseheades, that through malepertnes thinke to purchase them the name of a good Courtyer, I would have suche a *pastime* for this night, that one of the company myght bee picked out who should take in hand to shape in woordes a good Courtyer. (1.12; emphasis mine)

The dialogue's readers are both invited to join the in-group in their scorn of "untowardly asseheades," and prodded to consider if their own "purchase" of the book (Hoby's translation goes even further in suggesting the marketplace than Castiglione's original "acquistar") places them in the outsider category. Thus, while Wayne Rebhorn rightly insists that the text presents an exchange of equals, it also approaches readers in complicated ways, encouraging them to reflect on the interplay between the different relationships that they may have to the text.[12] Readers may at different times and in different ways identify with the text's social circle or feel banished from it, feel absorbed in the dialogue or stand at a distance from it. The vulgarity of easy access against which Polonius cautions ("Be thou familiar, but by no means vulgar"), and to which he contrasts the ideal of polished behavior, could not be completely distinguished from the market in books such as the best-selling *Book of the Courtier*.

The practice of courtesy forces readers to juggle multiple perspectives, then, a demand that is reflected in the content, form, and format of different editions of *The Book of the Courtier*. The dialogue offers its readers the opportunity to test out various mental stances as they decide how they will position themselves in the debates it raises, assuming and creating a nexus of relationships between reading and social performance. By providing examples of readerly character formation, such as Alexander the Great reading Homer, and Scipio Africanus reading Xenophon (1.43), Castiglione's text suggests the key importance of the reader's active engagement. Even as the interlocutors of the dialogue consider how to position themselves with reference to both the models of the past and their own contemporary society, readers explore how both literary and social performances may be imprinted on the mind, creating productive changes in disposition.[13] The work offers readers the chance to analyze the social performances of its characters with the thoughtfulness one can bring to a written text, and even more than that, it asks them to examine its own performative textuality.[14]

While the theatricality of the courtier's self-presentation is, quite rightly, a critical touchstone, Castiglione's dialogue also suggests the interpenetration of textuality and performance. Critics such as Rebhorn and Greenblatt correctly connect courtiership and performance, with Rebhorn asserting, "For Castiglione as well as for many other Renaissance writers, man was always on a stage, performing before an audience which would judge him."[15] Harry Berger Jr. responds to Rebhorn's influential study by emphasizing the "self-surveillance" and anxiety that accompany the cultures of performance.[16] What I want to underscore here is how much the language of textuality saturates the dialogue's discussion of performance, inviting readers to contemplate their concurrent roles as social performers and readers. Even as the meaning of the book itself is socially determined, the book describes social performances themselves in ways that link them to the discourses of print. My reading thus focuses especially on how Castiglione's dialogue enjoins readers to think about the relationship between print and performance, requiring of them a kind of speculative reading in which they engage with both the text's unresolvable puzzles and the question of how the text mirrors their own identities.[17] Reading *The Courtier* requires reflection not only on one's own social performances, then, but also on one's identity as a reader wrestling with the text's literary performances.

Sprezzatura and the art of making a good impression

While it offers advice about managing the impressions of others, then, *The Book of the Courtier* also underscores just how much the meanings of both literary texts and social performances hinge upon an audience's assessment. These assessments, the dialogue suggests, form part of the give and take through which the courtly habitus develops through engagement with literature as well as social interaction.[18] I will argue here that in Castiglione, the frequent use of print metaphors suggests the ultimate durability of both social impressions and literary engagements that accumulate to create social relationships and dispositions.

Castiglione makes clear from the outset the value of readers' own judgments, suggesting in his dedicatory letter to Don Michel de Silva that he will leave the assessment of his book up to "the judgment of the commune opinion" (18). The book format offers readers the power to make their own evaluations through ongoing reflection; as Lodovico da Canossa asserts, "writinge keepeth the woordes in store, and referreth them to the judgemente of the reader, and geveth tyme to examyne them depely" (1.29). Moreover, the text further blurs the distinction between social interactions and writing in suggesting that social performances also leave lasting impressions—"imprintings" in Hoby's translation. So, Count Lodovico emphasizes the importance of the "first imprinting [prima impressione]" (1.16) created by the courtier, going so far as to suggest that noble rank is important not so much for what it implies about the courtier's intrinsic qualities, but for its instrumental role in creating a good social impression:

> the unnoble shall be muche lesse estemed with everye manne, then
> the gentleman, and he must with much travaile and long time imprint
> in mennes heades a good opinion of himselfe [imprima la bona opin
> ion], whiche the other shal geat in a moment, and onely for that he is
> a gentleman: and howe waightye these imprintinges [queste impres
> sioni] are every man may easily judge. (1.16)

In Book 3, Giuliano's task is to try to dispel "the yvell imprintinge in everye mans minde" of a negative view of women (3.17). Even on the battlefield, Federico Fregoso claims in Book 2, the courtier must be mindful of his stage presence; he should take care that his

audience be as noble as possible, making sure to "feede the eyes of
the lookers on wyth all thinges that he shall thinke may geve him a
good grace":

> He shall never be among the last that come furth into the listes to
> shewe themselves, considering the people, and especially women take
> muche more hede to the fyrste then to the last: because the eyes and
> mindes that at the begynning are greedy of that noveltye, note everye
> lyttle matter and *printe* it [notano ogni minuta cosa, e di quello fanno
> impressione], afterward by continuaunce they are not onely full, but
> weery of it. Therefore was there a noble Stageplaier in olde tyme that
> for this respecte would alwaies be the first to come furth to playe his
> parte. (2.8; emphasis added)

Speaking to his own "noble audience" (2.7), Fregoso explicitly compares the courtier and the actor. Meanwhile, the metaphor of social
"imprinting," which Hoby emphasizes even more than Castiglione,
troubles the boundary between speech and written text, between
social and literary performance.

Lodovico da Canossa's discussion of *sprezzatura*, the key term of
Book 1 if not of the whole dialogue, foregrounds the relationship
between theatricality and social competition, paradoxically suggesting that the faux-improvisational performance of *sprezzatura* creates durable social impressions and once again using the metaphor
of print. The Count defines *sprezzatura* in contradictory terms: a
savvy courtier will "use in every thyng a certaine Reckelesnes, to
cover art withall, and seeme whatsoever he doth and sayeth to do it
wythout pain, and (as it were) not myndyng it" (1.26). Lodovico's
claim that courtiers employ *sprezzatura* implies that it is a volitional
skill, rather than an inborn *trait*, yet the text will also go on to dis-
mantle this opposition. At its most sophisticated, *sprezzatura* relies
on an audience simultaneously willing to be impressed by a performance and savvy enough to recognize that manipulation. Berger
accurately notes the different levels of performance that *sprezzatura*
entails, glossing it as "the ability to show that one is not showing
all the effort one obviously put into learning how to show that one
is not showing effort."[19] Or, according to Javitch, "There should
always be an element of mock-disguise in his poses."[20] Yet here,
too, the text's discussions of performance deploy textual metaphors;
the performance of *sprezzatura* is understood to have lasting social

consequences, in that it "imprinteth in the myndes of the lookers on an opinyon [negli animi delli circunstanti imprime opinione] that whoso can so sleyghtly do well, hath a great deale more knowledge then indeede he hath" (1.28). Theatricalized social interactions have indelible consequences, the dialogue underscores, with *sprezzatura* offering opportunities to shape others' minds and be shaped by them. *Sprezzatura* involves both standing out from the crowd and establishing oneself as an insider, competition as well as collaboration with one's audience. Positioning its readers as both fellow interlocutors and audience, Castiglione's dialogue offers them the chance to inhabit multiple critical perspectives on *sprezzatura*.

One way Castiglione approaches readers is with his own performance of *sprezzatura*, suggesting that the text makes meaning through his courteous exchanges with them. As he opens Book 3 of the dialogue, Castiglione makes clear that the reader's imagination will supersede his own efforts:

> For there is no manne that readeth of the wonderfull families of times past, but in his mind he conceyveth a certein greater opinion of them that are written upon, then it appeereth those bookes can express though they have bine written with perfection: even so do we consider that all the readers of this our travayle (if at the least wise it shall deserve so much favour, that it may come to the sight of noble men and vertuous Ladies) will cast in their minde and thinke for a surety, that the Court of Urbin hath bine muche more excellent and better fournished with notable men, then we are able to expresse in writinge. (3.1)

Castiglione and his readers here enact a complex reciprocity. On the one hand, his self-deprecation establishes his own mastery of *sprezzatura*, as Berger has noted.[21] On the other hand, as he directly addresses his readers with consummate courtesy, Castiglione enunciates their paramount importance in the collaborative work of textual meaning-making, revealing the power of their engagement as he anticipates how the required supplement of their imagination might complete his portrait of the excellence of Urbino's court.

In its paradoxical combination of improvisation and preparation, *sprezzatura* also gestures toward the conflicts in Castiglione's own text, and especially its valuing of both the past and present.[22] The text prizes both the authority of time-tested conventions, and improvisational originality; it rejects over-simplifying precepts,[23] and yet the Count's definition of *sprezzatura* connects it both to innovation ("per dir forse una nova parola") and to universal principles ("trovo una regula universalissima" [1.26]). Likewise, in Hoby's prefatory letter to Henry Hastings, he notes the dialogue's nuanced attitude toward the past (valuing it as a source of authority and pleasure while at the same time rejecting the authority of strict rule-making): "Both Cicero and Castilio professe, they folowe not any certayne appointed order of preceptes or rules, as is used in the instruction of youth, but call to rehearsall, matters debated in their times" (5). In Book 3, Giuliano is adjured not to give "to breef rehersall of these vertuous actes done by women" (3.23). The repetition involved in "rehearsal," the reliving and retelling of old stories and disputes, clearly provides pleasure.[24] The dialogue in its entirety rests on the value of going back over the discussions and stories of the past; these form its macrostructure, in the supposed reconstruction of sequential evenings of debate, as well as many of its supporting examples, as characters provide evidence from history and contemporary society to support their claims.

Even as the text values the retelling of shared cultural narratives, it also proposes that the kind of rehearsal associated with preparing for a performance be kept strictly hidden. While the *OED* dates the first usage of "rehearsal" as "a practice performance of all or part of a play or other work, in preparation for later public performance" to 1579,[25] Hoby's use of this term shortly before the dialogue's discussion of *sprezzatura* (which may be defined as the ability to conceal anticipatory rehearsal) shades into the later sense of preparing for performance. Discussing when self-praise is permissible, the Count responds: "But in mine opinion, all doth consist in speaking such thynges after a sort, that it maye appeare that they are not *rehearsed* to that ende: but that they come so to purpose, that he can not refrayne tellyng them, and alwaies seemynge to flee his owne prayse tell the trueth" (1.18; emphasis mine). The account of one's best features must not appear prepared! Lodovico borrows the authority of ancient orators to underscore the importance of feigned spontaneity:

And I remember that I have reade in my dayes, that there were some excellent Oratours, which among other their cares, enforced themselves to make every man beleve that they had no sight in letters, and dissemblinge their *conning*, made semblant their orations to be made very simply, and rather as nature and trueth lead them, then study

and arte, the whiche if it had bene openly knowen, would have putte
a doubte in the peoples minde, for feare least he beguiled them. You
may see then howe to shewe arte and suche bent study taketh away
the grace of every thing. (1.26; emphasis mine)

While the dialogue's discussion of *sprezzatura* reveals its inherent
tensions, it also denotes tensions in the concept of rehearsal: looking back in nostalgia creates the pleasure of a shared community,
whereas standing out from the crowd by zealously preparing an
affected social performance creates embarrassment and isolation.

Discretion and the courtly habitus

Because courtesy cannot be reduced to simple instructions, its
proper expression depends upon the decorum of the courtier who
seeks to display it; he must rely on his own good judgment even as
he calibrates his behavior to the judgment of others.[26] The task of
Book 2, as outlined at the end of Book 1, is for Federico Fregoso
to explain "in what sort, maner and time the Courtier ought to
practise his good condicions" (1.55). The courtier has flexibility of
choice, yet he must also constantly refine his judgment according
to his audience—what Cox aptly refers to as "the *rhetoricization*
of ethics."[27] Federico begins by saying, "I believe a good judgement in the Courtyer is sufficient for al this ... without any other
preceptes, I suppose he may practyse welynough the thynge that
hee knoweth in due time and after a good sorte" (2.6). He resists
specificity ("the whiche to bring more particularly into rule were to
harde a matter" [2.6]), but he clarifies that the courtier must always
use his discretion ("discrezione") in determining the best action;
even when deciding whether to obey wicked requests of the prince,
Federico defers to the courtier: "all is to be referred to your discretion" (2.23). (Indeed, here Federico both counsels and exemplifies
good judgment and taciturnity.) Discretion requires above all the
courtier's attending and adapting to circumstances:

Afterwarde let him consider wel what the thing is he doth or spea-
keth, the place wher it is done, in presence of whom, in what time,
the cause why he doeth it, his age, his profession, the ende whereto
it tendeth, and the meanes that may bring him to it: and so let him

apply himselfe *discreatly* with these advertisementes to whatsoever
he mindeth to doe or speake. (2.7; emphasis mine)[28]

Similarly, in Book 3 Giuliano makes the point that the lady of the
court must also have "discreation to understand the condicion of
him she talketh withall" (3.6) and "beeware of praysing her selfe
undiscreatly" (3.6); in recapping Giuliano's description of the ideal
lady of the court, Federico Fregoso also lists "discretion" first among
her qualities (3.53). Of course, deferring to their audience's role in
shaping their social standing is especially crucial for the women
of the court, since they must assiduously avoid sullied reputations.
Thus, as Giuliano also observes, she must employ both "discretion
and wisdom" in order always to "be counted discreete" (3.54).
The court lady must be especially attentive to combining modesty
with good judgment, but the requirements on her applied to the
courtier, too.[29]

Far from depicting a straightforward set of rules for courtly action,
then, Castiglione's text instead dialogically fashions a courtly habitus that could be compared to an internalized sense of discretion,
a feel for making choices in both the ethical and aesthetic spheres
that will be socially rewarded. Bourdieu defines the habitus as a
learned disposition, which nonetheless "perceives" its judgments
as "natural";[30] he extends this definition to include "classificatory
schemes, principles of classification, principles of vision and division, different tastes. They make distinctions between what is good
and what is bad, between what is right and what is wrong, between
what is distinguished and what is *vulgar*, and so forth, but the distinctions are not identical" (emphasis mine).[31] In Bourdieu's formulations, the differing tastes or dispositions of groups (including, for
example, their manners and their aesthetic sensibilities) are molded
through social processes and serve to distinguish groups from one
another. "Habitus" is a term Bourdieu adapts from a philosophical
usage going back to an Aristotelian idea that Castiglione would
have known and that clearly exerts an influence on *The Book of the
Courtier*; as such, the concept also points to the dialogue's exploration of how recreational pursuits and ethics overlap, a problem
that will be become paramount on the fourth day.[32] Critiques of
Bourdieu's formulation of habitus call for greater attention to the
conscious processes of training and practice; Castiglione's text is

an interesting model for habitus because it offers both implicit and explicit presentations of the courtly habitus at work.[33]

Concern for the Aristotelian concept of the good, on the one hand, and aesthetic appropriateness, on the other, compete and overlap in *The Book of the Courtier*'s evolving model of decorum. Proper action in Castiglione reworks Aristotle's model in the *Nicomachean Ethics* of virtue as requiring persistent attention to changing circumstances, placing greater emphasis on aesthetic display and social approbation while concurrently acknowledging the importance of human efforts toward perfection.[34] Given that the ideal form of the good is elusive, both Castiglione and Aristotle conceive of the practice of virtue as *relational*: that is, performed in a social context composed of complex and changing details. Aristotle writes that "actions are concerned with particulars" (2.7); for him, "moral virtue is concerned with emotions and actions," and, while there are many variations in degree and quality of emotional experiences, the "mark of virtue" is to "experience all this [variety] at the right time, toward the right objects, toward the right people, for the right reason, and in the right manner" (2.6).[35] This concern for circumstances saturates Castiglione's adaptation of Aristotelian ethics for his key concept of courtly decorum; indeed, as Aristotle's language shows, one who seeks to attain the good through the social practice of virtue must be attuned to what is *fitting* rather than what is certain. Castiglione's text therefore draws from Aristotle even as it emphasizes still further how one's audience determines what is appropriate and what is not.

Ottaviano further articulates the nature of the courtly habitus in his discussion of the prince's education in Book 4, focusing especially on the formative role of social performance. His model claims a civilizing force for the courtier's instructional rhetoric, understood broadly as his persuasive inculcation of virtue through an ever-changing self-presentation which, though perhaps flexible, is not free. The costumes that the courtier assumes can neither simply be chosen and abandoned at random nor at will. Rather, through the role of custom (*costume, consuetudine*), the poses that the courtier adopts mold both his own dispositions and those of the people around him. In this early modern elaboration of "fake it 'til you make it," costume becomes custom, and habit becomes habitus; the difference between performance and inner nature is obscure.

Hamlet's admonishment to Gertrude to "assume a virtue if you have it not ... For *use* almost can change the stamp of nature" (3.4.158, 166; emphasis mine) has been anticipated by Castiglione's exploration of the ways in which "use" can alter character. Ottaviano follows Aristotle's *Nicomachean Ethics* in positing that virtue can be acquired; in his view of education, learned actions become characteristic of the person who performs them: "and therfore there groweth a custome in us of bothe the one and the other throughe longe use, so that first we practise vertue or vice, after that, we are vertuous or vitious" ["e però dell'uno e l'altro in noi si fa l'abito (note that this term carries the specific meaning of its Latin cognate *habitus*) con la consuetudine, di modo che prima operiamo le virtù o i vicii, poi siam virtuosi o viciosi"] (4.12).[36] Character changes are effected through practice; rehearsal trains the subject to act in ways that erase the distinction between performance and character. Book 4 thus continues the focus on custom throughout *The Book of the Courtier*; as is asserted early on in the text,

> use maketh us manye times to delite in, and to set litle by the self same thinges: wherby somtime it proceadeth that maners, garmentes, customes, and facions whiche at sometyme have beene in price, becumme not regarded, and contrarywyse the not regarded, becumme of price. Therfore it is manifestlye to be descerned, that use hath greater force than reason. (1.1)[37]

The courtly habitus outlined by the text resists strict definition because its most distinctive feature is the ability to respond to shifting circumstances, deploying a decorum ingrained through repetition, even as it requires explicit consciousness of artful self-presentation.

Aristotle's assertion that moral virtue is concerned with the particularities of time, objects, people, motivations, and manner parallels Horace's definition of aesthetic decorum in his *Ars Poetica*, the early modern *locus classicus* for this subject. Horace repeatedly stresses the need to match art with nature in ways that are appropriate and fitting, considering character, style, the poet's capabilities, and the audience's expectations. Horace's view of decorum intertwines social expectations and manners both in his concept of the artistic object, and in his vision of how that object participates in social exchange. If the writer wishes for the desired response for his effort, for example, he must closely replicate the details of social experience he represents:

> Now hear what I, and with me the public, expect. If you want an approving hearer, one who waits for the curtain, and will stay in his seat till the singer cries "Give your applause," you must note the manners of each age, and give a befitting tone to shifting natures and their years. (153–57)[38]

In pointing out the artist's need to shape his material so as to stir up the emotions of the audience, Horace's work creates an implicit parallel between the tasks of the poet and those of the orator, who also seeks to persuade by affecting the emotions of his listeners.[39] Horace's requirement that theatrical creation combine variety and appropriateness is also good advice for the courtier, who is himself concerned with the audience's approval of his aesthetic self-creation.[40]

The courtier's discretion gives him a measure of personal agency in adjusting his actions to shifting social expectations, finding the balance that will suit his audience of the moment. In his discussion of performing music, for example, Federico asserts,

> But the seasoning of the whole muste bee discreation, because in effect it wer a matter unpossible to imagine all cases that fall. And if the Courtyer be a righteous judge of himselfe, he shall apply himselfe well inough to the tyme, and shall discerne whan the hearers mindes are disposed to geve eare and whan they are not. (2.13)

The focus on the courtier's discretion in his concern for his audience reinforces even further his connection to the actor on the stage, suiting his performances to the evaluations of his spectators, always in pursuit of their pleasure. Here Hamlet's advice to the visiting players is particularly apt:

> Be not too tame neither, but let your own *discretion* be your tutor. Suit the action to the word, the word to the action, with this special observance—that you o'erstep not the modesty of nature. For anything so o'erdone is from the purpose of playing ... Now this overdone, or come tardy off, though it makes the unskilful laugh, cannot but make the judicious grieve, the censure of which one must in your allowance o'erweigh a whole theatre of others. (3.2.16–20, 24–28; emphasis mine)

Hamlet's speech reveals continuity with Castiglione's dialogue in its stress on the ideal mirroring of the courtier/actor's good judgment with that of his audience.[41] The "judicious" audience matters, rather than the "unskilful" crowd; the performance should appeal to one's "noble audience," as Castiglione's Federico terms his interlocutors (2.7). The proper social audiences serve two overlapping functions: they help determine fitting behavior, and they reward that behavior. While how much the rightness of his actions matters to the courtier is subject to debate both within the text and in its long critical reception, it at least offers for readers' consideration a model of behavior that blends aesthetics and ethics in its concern for doing what is proper.

Book 4 and the education of the reader

The first three books of Castiglione's text focus on the durability of social impressions, whereas Book 4 reworks this topic into an account of how social interactions might actually change one's character, as seen in the courtier's education of the prince. Here, Ottaviano Fregoso says that the concealment of the effort and learning that go into *sprezzatura* is what enables the courtier's delightful instruction of the prince through the recreational ornaments of courtesy. In Ottaviano's model, habits of virtue are both inculcated and expressed in the social setting of recreational performance. Likewise, his discourse functions as a complex example of instruction, as it both overtly describes a system of pleasurable instruction that works through indirection, and exemplifies it, by coming once readers' appetites have been whetted with the sweeter discourses of the first three books. Yet readers are no passive receptacles of instruction; the text also challenges them with sorting out how this fourth book relates to what has come before. The question of how the whole dialogue coheres, or does not, has been a recurrent subject of scholarly debate. Valeria Finucci speaks for many in seeing the gap between the fourth book and the remainder of the text as among the dialogue's "badly mended breaks."[42] Others, such as Cesare Vasoli and Dain Trafton, point to a unity in the work's concerns.[43] I propose that we might instead weigh how this question provides an opportunity to ponder the text's complicated

modulation between unity and discord rather than seeing it as a
problem to be solved definitively. By prompting conscious reflection on the nature of education, which combines agency and passivity, the text calls readers to contemplate their relationship to the
dialogue, offering a mechanism to understand Ottaviano's complex mix of direct and indirect instruction as a model for thinking
about the nature of character formation. Understanding how Book
4 relates to the whole is closely connected to the book's productive pedagogical challenge to readers throughout, asking them to
reflect metacognitively on their involvement with the text. Hoby
demonstrates his own understanding of the metacognitive thinking the book encourages in his opening letter to Henry Hastings,
speaking of the book as a personified Courtier, and asserting, "you
may see him confirme with reason the Courtly facions, comely exercises, and noble vertues, that unawares have from time to time crept
in to you, and already with practise and learning taken custome
in you" (4). Hoby points out two methods of learning courtesy—
intentional study and unconscious habituation. In Book 4 most of
all, *The Book of the Courtier* draws attention to these two models,
encouraging readers to reflect *explicitly* on the way in which aesthetic pleasures of all kinds (literary texts, dramatic performances,
recreational pursuits) may *implicitly* shape one's character.

   Ottaviano's claim in Book 4 that recreational pursuits will har-
ness the will of the subject to stay within the bounds of social decorum emphasizes the formative power of the play of appearances
with which the first sections of *The Courtier* are concerned. In this
view, the social games that *The Courtier* describes (including the
dialogue itself) provide a forum not just for "making an impression," but also for impressing a sense of socially determined and
aestheticized ethics on participants. Ottaviano's paradigm thus
anticipates Bourdieu's fundamental assertion that "taste classifies,
and it classifies the classifier."[44] In doing so, *The Courtier* employs
a classical metaphor for how taste as pleasing deception might actually change the prince's character[45]:

> In this wise maye he leade him throughe the roughe way of vertue (as
> it were) deckynge yt about with boowes to shadowe yt and strawinge
> it over wyth sightlye flouers, to ease the greefe of the peinfull journey
> in hym that is but of a weake force. And sometyme with musike,
> somtime with armes, and horses, sometyme with rymes and meeter,

otherwhyle wyth communication of love, and wyth all those wayes
that these Lordes have spoken of, continuallye keepe that mynde
of his occupyed in honest pleasure: imprintynge notwythstandynge
therin always beesyde (as I have said) in companie with these flickeringe provocations some vertuous condicion, and beeguilinge him
with a holsome craft, as the warie phisitiens do, who manye times
whan they minister to yonge and tender children in ther sickenesse,
a medicin of a bitter taste, annoint the cupp about the brimm with
some sweete licour. The Courtier therfore applyinge to such a pour-
pose this veile of pleasure, in everie time, in everie place, and in everie
exercise he shall attaine to his ende.

[In questo modo per la austera strada della virtù potrà condurlo,
quasi adornandola di frondi ombrose e spargendola di vaghi fiori,
per temperar la noia del faticoso camino a chi è di forza debile; ed or
con musica, or con arme e cavalli, or con versi, or con ragionamenti
d'amore e con tutti que' modi che hanno detti questi signori, tener
continuamente quell'animo occupato in piacere onesto, *imprimen-*
dogli però ancora sempre, come ho detto, in compagnia di queste
illecebre, qualche costume virtuoso ed ingannandolo con inganno
salutifero; come i cauti medici, li quali spesso, volendo dar a' fanci-
ulli infermi e troppo delicati medicina di sapore amaro, circondano
l'orificio del vaso di qualche dolce liquore. Adoperando adunque a
tal effetto il cortegiano questo velo di piacere, in ogni tempo, in ogni
loco ed in ogni esercizio conseguirà il suo fine.] (4.10; emphasis mine)

The courtier must be discreet in his courtly actions in the service
of his prince, always choosing at each moment ("in ogni tempo,
in ogni loco") what is best suited to coaxing the prince toward
virtue. In this idealizing model, the courtier's performances imprint
upon the prince's character ("imprintynge notwythstandynge therin
always beesyde (as I have said) in companie with these flickeringe
provocations some vertuous condicion"), using "salutary deception"[46] (the "veile of pleasure") to convert the unknowing prince
to virtue, just as, in Philip Sidney's later model, the pedagogy of the
poet affects readers without their full knowledge, "even as the child
is often brought to take most wholesome things by hiding them in
such other as have a pleasant taste" (227). In laying bare the methods of the courtier, Castiglione's text reveals how readers may mold
their own characters through literary engagement, as well as how
princes might be "imprinted" by the actions of courtiers.[47]

This model of the courtier's instructional performances parallels
the Renaissance claims for the didactic potential of both theater
and poetry, as his acts of self-creation have the potential to transform himself and others. We can recall Sidney's view that poetry can
"take naughtiness away and *plant goodness* even in the secretest
cabinet of our souls" (221; emphasis mine), which is paralleled by
Heywood's view of the theater as refashioning its audiences through
the intertwining of poetry and performance:

> These wise men of Greece ... could by their industry, finde out no
> neerer or directer course to *plant humanity and manners in the hearts
> of the multitude* then to instruct them by moralized mysteries, what
> vices to avoyd, what vertues to embrace ... which borne out as well
> *by the wisedome of the Poet, as supported by the worth of the Actors,
> wrought such impression* in the hearts of the plebe, that in short
> space they excelled in civility and governement, insomuch that from
> them all the neighbour Nations drew their patternes of Humanity,
> as well in the establishing of their lawes, as the reformation of their
> manners. (C3r; emphasis mine)

The subject matter of the play and the power of the acting
must work together, Heywood argues, including the example of
Hercules' character being molded by a play that he saw in his
youth about his father Zeus: "*Which being personated* with
lively and well-spirited action, wrought such *impression* in his
noble thoughts, that in meere emulation of his fathers valor ... he
perform'd his twelve labours" (B3r; emphasis mine). Heywood's
examples suggest that the tug between performance and reality—
between actor and character—is both part of the distinctive value
of theater and part of how it enacts its pedagogy in viewers who
are fundamentally changed by performances, even as they go on to
play their parts in the social world of day-to-day life: "so bewitch-
ing a thing is lively and well spirited action, that it hath power
to *new mold the harts* of the spectators and fashion them to the
shape of any noble and notable attempt" (B4r; emphasis mine).
Castiglione's text strikingly similarly praises music, anticipating
closely Ottaviano's terminology in Book 4: "musicke ... ought
necessarilye to be learned from a mans childhoode, not onely for
the superficial melodie that is hard, but to be sufficient to bring
into us a newe *habite* that is good, and a *custome* enclyning to
vertue, whiche maketh the minde more apt to the conceiving of

felicitie"; music is able to "make swete the mindes of men" (1.47; emphasis mine).

Castiglione's *Courtier* operates on multiple levels, then. On the one hand, it offers readers a structure that resembles the method of instruction proposed by Ottaviano, leading them into a sophisticated discussion of virtue by means of entertainment. On the other hand, it also offers them the tools to recognize and think critically about this process, producing readers who actively engage with a text that also shapes their dispositions, imprinting itself on their self-understanding and generating their sense of decorum. Precisely because of this, they need not buy the text's justification of itself as more than the record of a party game; the tensions in the book's unity mean that readers are at liberty to determine both their own assessment of the role of the courtier and of the text *The Book of the Courtier*.[48]

Paratexts and the reader's agency

In Ottaviano's idealized model, the courtier's instruction of his prince is gentle, and designed to create princes who can likewise rule gently.[49] The prince will have internalized his instruction to such a degree that it forms a part of him:

> it is requisit that he apply all his studie and diligence to get knowleage, afterward to facion within him selfe and observe unchangeablye in everye thinge the lawe of reason, not written in papers, or in mettall, but graven in his owne minde ["sculpita nell'animo suo proprio"], that it maye be to him alwayes not onlie familier, but inwarde, and live with him, as a percell of him: to the intent it may night and day, in everye time and place admonish him and speake to him within his hart, riddinge him of those troublous affections that untemperate mindes feele. (4.23)

In Ottaviano's vision, the prince's self-mastery helps him serve as an example to his subjects, ruling over them "as a good father over his good childe" rather than "as the maister over his bondeman" (4.27). This is not at all to say that the unjust politics of Ottaviano's model should be ignored; he previously refers to those who are "naturallye bondemen" (4.21).[50] Recognizing the ugly reality of Renaissance despotism, what particularly concerns me here is how Ottaviano's *models* of pedagogical and monarchical authority comment on the

authority of Castiglione's text over the reader.[51] Just as the dialogue
offers one model of authoritarian government while allowing readers to imagine other possibilities, so too does it avoid presenting
rules for readers to mindlessly follow. It both embodies and counsels flexible instruction.

The freedom the book granted its readers to choose their stances
was also reflected in the myriad ways that early modern publishers both responded to the text and gave various points of entry to
their readers. And, too, the shifting forms of the published book as
it moved from one country to another similarly afforded readers
different pathways for engaging with it. The disjointed nature of
the book itself, including both its physical format and its shifting
inclusion of paratextual materials, offered readers intellectual puzzles with consequences for how they viewed their own identities. In
her treatment of printer John Wolfe's 1588 trilingual edition of *The
Courtier*, for example, A. E. B. Coldiron has explored how the page
layout, with three columns of text in Italian, French, and English,
may have prompted readers to think more explicitly about the relationship between the text and questions of national identity.[52]

English readers of this Italian text may have especially questioned
not just how they but also how their country measured up against
the ideal society it describes. In his prefatory letter to Lord Henry
Hastings, Hoby suggests a dual purpose for translating *The Book
of the Courtier*: by making the text widely accessible to an English
audience he hoped to raise the stature of England itself. Hoby
admires those nations, especially Italy, who have made advanced
learning readily available in "the vulgar tunge" (6). He also later
remarks that he hopes that other people will follow him in translating from Latin and Greek, so "that we alone of the worlde maye not
bee styll counted barbarous in oure tunge, as in time out of minde
we have bene in our maners" (7).[53] Hoby's impulse to increase the
literature available in "the vulgar tunge" stems from a desire to civ-
ilize the English populace writ large, even as the wide promulgation
of his text—making it available to the "vulgar crowd"—contrasts
with its role in creating social distinctions.[54]

In both Italy and England, publishers packaged the text for readerly engagement, enabling those privileged enough to purchase the
book to write its lessons on their heart as they saw fit. Virtually each
successive edition adjusted or added a new instrument for readers

to employ to approach the text. In Italy, the 1528 folio edition was followed by more user-friendly octavo editions.[55] In a prefatory letter to the 1533 edition, Francesco Asolano specifically counseled female readers that the smaller book size rendered it portable enough always to have it close to their breast: "in forma piu picciola, è manegevole: accio sempre in ogni luogo, è tempo il possiate a vostro bello agro portare in seno, & havere a mano."[56] Readers may make the book's lessons their own, inscribing them on their hearts, consulting the book on any and all occasions. A 1546 edition offered readers a chronological table of contents,[57] while one printed in 1547 included an index and a list of qualities needed by the men and women of the court, both of which it advertised on the title page.[58] Though it may be tempting to see a list that is labeled "Conditioni et Qualità de l'huomo, & della Donna di Corte, brievemente raccolte da tutto'l libro" as a reduction of the text to certain key words ("nobiltà, ingegno, bellezza & gratia di persona & di aspetto," etc.), the fact that they are indeed key words immediately following the index also suggests that they invite further active exploration of the text, perhaps prompting new index searches and a "choose your own adventure"-style movement through the text.

Because Castiglione's text so insists that the flexible skills of discretion cannot be distilled into strict rules, it may seem ironic that early publishers of his text added rules for readers in forms such as tables of contents, marginal glosses, and appended lists. These guidelines could be interpreted as reducing the text to what Peter Burke calls a "recipe-book," a characterization with which other scholars have concurred.[59] On the contrary, I contend, these scholarly readings of the text's reduction run their own risk of oversimplification. The multiplying editions of the book, I suggest, also afforded readers a chance to engage with the text in multiple ways. Even if readers took editor-supplied rules at face value, the movement from practice, to habit, to personal characteristic is far from straightforward. Self-fashioning is far more complex than following a recipe, just as Polonius's counsel to Laertes—"And these few precepts in thy memory / Look thou character"—is revealed by his own speech to be an oversimplification, and indeed one that cries out for a critical response. Likewise, I suggest, editorial additions that could also be accused of simplifying the text might have been prompts for further active exploration, presenting readers with new ways to test their understandings of the text and to ponder the extent of their agreement with its suggestions.

As William W. E. Slights has argued with reference to other early modern books, "an oppositional voice from the margins could encourage a reader in lively debate with the centered text or at least establish an alternative view of the matters it dealt with there."[60] For example, the new marginal editorial glosses in Giolito's 1556 edition can also serve as propositions for the reader to evaluate rather than simple rules for the reader to follow.[61] Glosses might make points that are distinct from the text, such as "La troppa sprezzatura è affettatione [Excessive *sprezzatura* is affectation]" (42), or contradict one another and/or the text, such as two opposing comments on Bembo's Neoplatonic discourse on beauty and love: "La bellezza è sempre buona [Beauty is always good]" (393) and "La bellezza fa le donne superbe [Beauty makes women proud]" (395).[62] While such glosses take on the force of a maxim by removing reference to any particular speaker, they also prompt readers to recognize reductions, contradictions, or distortions. For example, the gloss "Il Cortegiano dee esser nato nobile [The courtier must be born noble]" (22) might result in a reader recalling that the text's discussion of this issue is not so simple. Similarly, tables of contents could convey apparently straightforward rules and also encourage further exploration. A 1587 edition showed that the table of contents could function as both a list of rules and something more complicated; an entry such as "Il Cortegiano deve havere in abhominatione l'affettatione [The courtier should consider affectation an abomination]" (3v) is clear cut, but other listings could leave things more open-ended: "Se la donna è animale imperfetto per colpa di natura [If women are imperfect creatures by the fault of nature]" (5v).[63] Readers of editions of *Il Cortegiano* currently housed at the Folger Shakespeare Library annotated both the text itself and the marginal editorial glosses, for example by underlining them, suggesting that they responded critically to all the printed matter in the book.[64]

Editions of Castiglione printed in England also presented readers with varied possibilities for engagement.[65] The 1561 edition of *The Book of the Courtier* printed by William Seres includes an opening letter to readers soliciting their collaboration with the translator and printer. Seres reminds them of "the diligence of Maister Hoby in penninge, and mine in printing," encouraging them to match this effort in their attention to the book: "so peruse it that for thy profite, first he, and then I, maye thinke our travayle herein wel imployed." While the 1561, 1577, 1588, and 1603 editions of Hoby's translation did not include detailed tables of contents (beyond a listing of the four books) or indexes, they did include printed marginal glosses and appended rules for readers.[66] Here, too, marginal glosses might foster further exploration rather than cut it off; such glosses as "Dolphines delyte in musicke" or "Howe to obtein the good will of women" would seem to pose questions and thus invite more active reading.[67] The concluding recapitulation of the text, entitled "A breef rehersall of the chiefe conditions and qualities in a Courtier" (1561), offers both a reductive repetition of its points and a guide for users to "rehearse" in their own character formation. Subsequent editions of the text (1577, 1588, and 1603) make a small but significant revision to the title of this list, referring to the "conditions and qualities *required* in a Courtier" (emphasis mine), enjoining even further the active efforts of readers toward a goal rather than the innate attributes of the courtier. As was the case in the Italian editions of the text, such appended rules don't need to mean that readers' judgments have been forestalled; readers may evaluate and prioritize these rules as they see fit. One reader of the 1577 edition put exes throughout the text and continued to do so through the end matter, putting exes next to rules that were of particular interest.[68] The editorial paratexts of *The Courtier* may well have expanded readers' opportunities for creatively making the book their own.

Courtesy and/as reading practice

The Book of the Courtier points to the socially constructed nature of both courtly virtue and courtly tastes in its creation of an ideal figure whose dispositions are perfectly suited to a world (albeit imaginary) in which leisurely pursuits are the means to learn virtue. The dialogue suggests that the courtly habitus resists straightforward description or rule following, though it does take its shape in response to the limits imposed by court society. These limits are not simply constraints on the courtier, however; they also shape his habitus in a productive sense, inculcating a practical sense of discretion and of which choices lead to both virtue and success in the courtly milieu.

Making use of a well-known figure for the sweetness of aesthetic pleasure, *The Book of the Courtier* offers its readers a working model of the honey on the cup, or the use of recreational and aesthetic delights as a disguise for the bitter medicine of character formation in virtue. In its presentation of a delightful, engaging dialogue, it entices readers to take part in aesthetic pleasure as a painless means of instructing them. At the same time, in Book 4 it explicitly instructs readers in the pedagogical value of aesthetic pleasure; this embedded meta-commentary on the text itself, I argue, encourages them to regard the dialogue with a critical eye. Readers of *The Book of the Courtier* not only witness the interlocutors of the dialogue explore what it means to receive an education in courtesy, they watch themselves learning about it as well; they are trained to become both performer and audience through their speculative readings of the text. Readers are tasked with considering the varied relationships between reading and character formation as they both indulge in pleasing literary recreation and think explicitly about the puzzles offered by the original dialogue and its varied editions; readers may be wrapped up in and molded by the text unawares, but they are also given the tools to see it from a critical distance. In prodding readers to consider multiple perspectives, courtesy offers an ideal training ground for Spenser's readers and Shakespeare's audiences. In the following chapter, I interpret Spenser's and Shakespeare's own versions of the education through courteous theatricality that *The Book of the Courtier* explores, showing how they critique the link between pedagogy and pleasure that Castiglione's dialogue sought to establish.

Notes

1 On the conventionality of fatherly advice in the period, and the possible link between Henry Sidney's letter to his son and Polonius, see Richard Helgerson, *Elizabethan Prodigals*, 16–20. On Sidney's letter as a pedagogical text that should also be, in the words of its printer, "carried in memorie," see Judith Owens, *Emotional Settings in Early Modern Pedagogical Culture*, 69–77.

2 See R. W. Dent, *Shakespeare's Proverbial Language*, 20, as cited in the Arden *Hamlet*.

3 *OED*. "character" v. 3.

4 The metaphor of the text inscribed on Laertes' memory has resonance with both Foucauldian discipline and Eagleton's ideology of the aesthetic. See, for example, Michel Foucault, *History of Sexuality*, Vol. 1, 133–59, and Terry Eagleton, *Ideology of the Aesthetic*, 31–69.

5 In Castiglione's *Book of the Courtier*, clothing both is and isn't a guide to the courtier's inner nature, with Federico Fregoso suggesting that "outwarde matters manye times are a token of the inwarde" (2.27), and, in response to an objection, "But I saie that the garment is withall no small argument of the fansie of him that weareth it, although otherwhile it appeere not true. And not this alone, but all the behaviours, gestures and maners, beeside wordes and deedes, are a judgement of the inclination of him in whom they are seene" (2.28). Outward self-presentation *may* be a manifestation of the "inclination" of social actors, a clue to their priorities, desires, and aspirations; Hamlet's mournful garb does not preclude authentic grief. Plus, as Castiglione makes clear, some courtiers do look good in black.

6 Jennifer Richards, *Rhetoric and Courtliness*. Peter Burke links the dialogue form of the text to its particularly "open" quality (*Fortunes of the* Courtier, 19).

7 See Virginia Cox, *Renaissance Dialogue*, 5 and 54. For a discussion of how Gabriel Harvey's annotations of Castiglione reveal his desire for both "rules or precepts for jesting which can then be enacted in the realm of social performance" and "pleasure," see Chris Stamatakis, "'With diligent studie,'" 23 and 34. Barbara Correll persuasively argues that the 1554 German conduct manual *Grobianus*, which works by ironically offering disgusting suggestions for comportment, is a site of "instability" and "resistance" (*End of Conduct*, 39); I propose that the instability that Correll describes is also promoted by Castiglione's text and the multiplying variety in its subsequent editions.

8 On Hoby's decision to translate the dialogue and the original obstacles to its publication, see Mary Partridge, "Thomas Hoby's English Translation." See also Carmela Nocera Avila, *Tradurre il* Cortegiano.

9 See, for example, Daniel Javitch, *Poetry and Courtliness*, 29. Cf. as well Louis Montrose's characterization of the courtier himself as an "ornament" ("Of Gentlemen and Shepherds," 440).

10 Evelyn Tribble, *Early Modern Actors*, 18–19. Tribble's argument has important implications for theater audiences more generally; she notes that "Players performed before audiences themselves practised

in observing the minutiae of their social world" (53), and also that the players had the challenge of offering "a credible emulation of aristocratic skill before audiences drawn from the highest orders of society" (16).

11 Thomas M. Greene suggests that their game serves to "define the ideal that underlies their [the courtly group's] own approved conduct, the authorized version that has regulated their day-to-day activity but has heretofore regulated it tacitly" ("*Il Cortegiano* and the Choice of a Game," 4).

12 See Wayne Rebhorn on how as a symposium the dialogue emphasizes the equality of its participants (*Courtly Performances*, 166). For a discussion of the links between social mobility, literacy, and the book trade, see Akihiro Yamada, *Experiencing Drama*, 3–36.

13 See David Bergeron's discussion of Geoffrey Whitney's admonition that readers should "printe in minde, what wee in printe do reade" (*Reading and Writing*, 12).

14 On the ways in which texts may function as performances and vice versa, see Chapter 1 of W. B. Worthen's *Shakespeare and the Authority of Performance*.

15 Rebhorn, *Courtly Performances*, 26. On the ways in which "nobility" may be a "quasi-theatrical performance before a courtly audience" in Castiglione as well as other authors, see also David Posner, *Performance of Nobility*, 2. For an account of social performance in modern life that makes pervasive use of the actor/audience model in recognizing the importance of an audience's judgment, see Erving Goffman, *Presentation of Self*, especially 17–76. Stephen Greenblatt suggests that courtesy books were "essentially handbooks for actors, practical guides for a society whose members were nearly always on stage" (*Renaissance Self-Fashioning*, 162). Cox emphasizes the link between literature and performance (*Renaissance Dialogue*, 40).

16 Harry Berger Jr., *Absence of Grace*, 9–25.

17 With a different focus than mine, Valeria Finucci has explored the key role of women in the text as a mirror of the courtier (*The Lady Vanishes*, 39).

18 As Victoria Kahn argues, "the central assumption of the humanist rhetorical tradition is that reading is a form of prudence or of deliberative rhetoric and that a text is valuable insofar as it engages the reader in an activity of discrimination and thereby educates the faculty of practical reason or prudential judgment which is essential to the active life" (*Rhetoric, Prudence, and Skepticism*, 11). For authors such as Castiglione, Kahn explains, "The point ... is not that the reader should imitate any single example of the text ... but rather that

he should imitate the author's judgment of decorum"; the goal is "to educate the judgment" (*Rhetoric, Prudence, and Skepticism*, 187).

19 Berger, *Absence of Grace*, 9.
20 Javitch, *Poetry and Courtliness*, 57.
21 Berger, *Absence of Grace*, 119–29. Other commentators have also observed that Castiglione exemplifies the *sprezzatura* that his work teaches. See Joseph D. Falvo's discussion of Castiglione's "non-presence" in the dialogue as a strategy of increasing his own authority (*Economy of Human Relations*, 152–53), and Douglas Biow's account of Castiglione's role as a diplomat and his authorial *sprezzatura* (*In Your Face*, 35–59).
22 On *sprezzatura* as a paradox, see also Rosalie L. Colie, *Paradoxia Epidemica*, 34.
23 "We will not in these bookes folow any certaine order or rule of appointed preceptes," he writes at the outset of the dialogue (1.1). Rebhorn sees Castiglione's text as seeking "to make the reader conscious of the general nature of social operations as well as their moral dimension, so that he may then evolve his own, flexible approach to the particular social realities of his own culture" (*Courtly Performances*, 13). On the dialogue's explicit rejection of rules, see also Stephen Kolsky, "Making and Breaking the Rules: Castiglione's *Cortegiano*."
24 On the early modern fascination with rehearsing as a means of testing out new cultural identities, see Steven Mullaney, *Place of the Stage*, 60–87.
25 Definition 2a. The term is used several times with this meaning in *A Midsummer Night's Dream*.
26 Derek Attridge's treatment of the elusive concept of decorum in Puttenham's *Art of English Poesy* provides a particularly useful account of how this text implies that decorum is an innate, aristocratic quality that cannot be taught (see "Puttenham's Perplexity: Nature, Art, and the Supplement in Renaissance Poetic Theory"). Cf. as well Javitch's observation that the decorum described in Puttenham's *Art of English Poesy* lacks fixed rules (*Poetry and Courtliness*, 51–52).
27 Cox, *Renaissance Dialogue*, 57. Kahn notes the close connection between Aristotelian "prudence" and "rhetoric," defining the former as "that faculty of judgment which provides an internal rule of decorum or authoritative standard of interpretation, one that is not logical, but pragmatic, and that enables us to act appropriately within a social and political context" (*Rhetoric, Prudence, and Skepticism*, 9).
28 On the links between discretion, taste, and social distinction, see Ineke Murakami, "'The Fairing of Good Counsel,'" 147.

29 See Joan Kelly's classic treatment of the greater constraints Renaissance noblewomen faced, "Did Women Have a Renaissance?" Kelly suggests that the "merely decorative role" (35) given to women in Castiglione's dialogue parallels "the courtier's posture of dependency" (45). Valeria Finucci similarly emphasizes the erasure of female subjectivity in the dialogue (*The Lady Vanishes*, 3–103).
30 Pierre Bourdieu, *Distinction*, 172.
31 Bourdieu, *Practical Reason*, 8.
32 Latin/Scholastic *habitus* = Greek *hexis* (from Greek "to have"), which in *Nicomachean Ethics* has been translated as "state" (Terence Irwin) or as a "characteristic [condition/attitude]" established by repeated and habitual action (Martin Ostwald). Burke also suggests in a more general way that Bourdieu's habitus is a subject of the book, but not in reference to this specific passage (*Fortunes of the* Courtier, 29). Katharine Breen suggests that Bourdieu did not pay significant attention to the specific medieval usages of habitus, and offers a correction in *Imagining an English Reading Public*, especially 7–8. For a wide-ranging account of the importance of character formation through habit in the Renaissance, see Peter B. Murray, *Shakespeare's Imagined Persons*; Murray's account offers a thorough appendix of classical and Renaissance references to habit, and he points to the centrality of Aristotle.
33 For critiques of Bourdieu, see Greg Noble and Megan Watkins, "So How Did Bourdieu Learn to Play Tennis?," 520–39, as well as Tribble's discussion of this article in *Early Modern Actors*, 6–8.
34 Arthur Kinney traces Castiglione's borrowings from Cicero and Aristotle and others while suggesting that his main topic is "the primary humanist *yearning* for the moral perfectibility of man" (*Continental Humanist Poetics*, 89). Norbert Elias's suggestion that court life involves attention to a more and more complex set of circumstances and relationships is thus reflected in the courtier's ability to make use of decorum in adapting to his shifting relationships (*Civilizing Process*, 406 and passim).
35 I cite the translation of Martin Ostwald.
36 Susan Gaylard also notes the text's exploration of costume and habitus in this passage; her emphasis is on "surface," while I am concerned here to trouble the distinction between inner and outer (*Hollow Men*, 109–10).
37 On custom/costume, note also the subtitle of Giovanni della Casa's 1558 *Galateo*: "Dei costumi e modi che si debbono tenere o schifare nella commune conversatione."
38 Trans. H. Rushton Fairclough.

39 On the importance of "the external demands of the audience" for Horace, see Bernard Weinberg, *History of Literary Criticism*, 71.

40 Cf. Rebhorn's suggestion that the text describes "the self as a work of art" (*Courtly Performances*, 18). Javitch also treats the points of similarity and contrast between the courtier and Cicero's orator, although I find the functions of the courtier more like those of the orator than Javitch allows; see *Poetry and Courtliness*, 18–49. Susan Gaylard argues in "Castiglione vs. Cicero" that Castiglione critiques Cicero in order to emphasize "the advantages of his own, alternative model of political engagement" (83).

41 Leo Salingar places special emphasis on Hamlet's use of "judicious" here, arguing that this speech comes at a time of newly heightened attention to the power of the audience's judgment ("Jacobean Playwrights and 'Judicious' Spectators"). For an argument that this speech is part of the play's overarching questioning of the possibility that theater can act to expose one's inner nature, see Jane Tylus, "'Par Accident,'" 253–72. Javitch emphasizes the prince as the most important audience of the courtier's performances ("*Il Cortegiano* and the Constraints of Despotism"); Eduardo Saccone underscores that the audience's "good judgment" should match that of the courtier ("*Grazia, Sprezzatura, Affettazione*," 64).

42 See Finucci, *The Lady Vanishes*, 7. Wayne Rebhorn emphasizes the "greater seriousness and weightiness of the fourth book" (180) while also suggesting that its form offers it a kind of unity (200); see *Courtly Performances*, 177–204. Stephen Kolsky suggests that Castiglione attempted to unify the dialogue through his description of Plato and Aristotle as courtiers, but was only "partially successful" in obscuring its "discontinuities and gaps" ("Learning Virtue, Teaching Politics," 24). On the fourth book as a later edition to the text, see Ghino Ghinassi, *Fasi dell'elaborazione del Cortegiano*.

43 Cesare Vasoli notes, for example, that the attention to circumstances that characterized contemporary diplomacy is to be found in all books of the text; for him the skills required for *sprezzatura* naturally lead into the education of the prince ("Il cortigiano, il diplomatico, il principe"). On the text's "structural integrity" and its emphasis on the reader's education, see Dain Trafton, "Structure and Meaning in *The Courtier*," especially 284. Others who emphasize the unity of the book include Lawrence V. Ryan ("Book Four of Castiglione's *Courtier*"); Kinney (*Continental Humanist Poetics*, 127); Douglas A. Northrop ("'The Ende Therfore of a Perfect Courtier,'" 295–305); and Eduardo Saccone ("Portrait of the Courtier," 1–18).

44 Bourdieu, *Distinction*, 6. See also Elias's observations on the "prestige value" of "good taste" (*Civilizing Process*, 422).

45 See Lucretius *De Rerum Natura* 1.935–50 for an early use of the metaphor of the honey on the medicinal cup.

46 As translated by Charles Singleton. On the courtier's use of dissimulation in his instruction of the prince, see Javitch, *Poetry and Courtliness*, 40–49, and "*Il Cortegiano* and the Constraints of Despotism."

47 Richard Halpern's discussion of Tudor education differentiates between two models of education, one based on coercion, and one based on the pleasure of mimesis, in which "the subject comes to assimilate or internalize a set of practices and thus enacts his subjection 'automatically,' as if he himself had chosen it" (29); see *Poetics of Primitive Accumulation*, 19–60. In Halpern's model, then, the imitation of the text involves the reader in "ideological domination"; he is fashioned by the text even as he fashions himself. Though Halpern's emphasis is different, his argument is consistent with Greenblatt's account of the relationships between literature, self-fashioning, and social discipline in *Renaissance Self-Fashioning*. As both Halpern and Greenblatt suggest, the formation of the subject is closely bound up with reading and textual practices that participate in a larger social framework of negotiation and exchange.

48 Cf. also Burke: "Despite the editorial interventions which encouraged readers to view the dialogue as a manual, the existence of this ludic tradition may have allowed some of them to treat the *Courtier* more playfully" (*Fortunes of the* Courtier, 46).

49 Ottaviano's courtier will work under an authoritarian model, training a prince who will rule over others, but it is also possible to see a critique of that type of government. Like Machiavelli's over-the-top praise of an iron-willed prince, Castiglione's text also admits of being read against the grain. For a discussion of how Castiglione's text suggests the importance of the courtier's role in dealing with flawed rulers, see W. R. Albury, *Castiglione's Allegory*, especially 129–90.

50 In "The Print of Goodness," Jonathan Goldberg traces this odious concept to the ideologies of race exemplified by Miranda's attack on Caliban in *The Tempest* as someone incapable of receiving instruction or the "print of goodness"; as Goldberg makes clear, the immoral idea of the "natural slave" (243) goes back to Aristotle's *Politics*.

51 On Book 4 as showing how the courtier can make the best of his situation by advising the prince as a form of public service, see Frank Lovett, "The Path of the Courtier."

52 A. E. B. Coldiron, *Printers Without Borders*, 160–98. Coldiron also briefly connects the ways in which this "edition makes a point of

exercising the reader's faculties" to the narrative practices of *The Faerie Queene* and *Paradise Lost* (178).

53 Ian Smith connects Hoby's translation to a national project of developing the vernacular in order to distinguish the English both from their own ostensibly barbarous past and from those who were subject to their incipient imperialism (*Race and Rhetoric*, 98 and 112).

54 On the "status anxiety" that Hoby feels in translating one vernacular language to another, and his related justification of the project by reference to Italy's promotion of classical culture, see Massimiliano Morini, "The Superiority of Classical Translation." In tracing the mythologizing of the origins of English national identity in Roman conquest, Sean Keilen argues for a close connection in how civilizing and conquest were understood (*Vulgar Eloquence*).

55 For the history of *The Courtier*'s publication and reception, see Burke, *Fortunes of the* Courtier, especially 39–80; on the dialogue's editorial history, see Amedeo Quondam's *"Questo povero Cortegiano"*.

56 Aldus Press (Venice, 1533), accessed at the Folger Shakespeare Library (Folger call number 243923).

57 Published by Gabriel Giolito (Venice, 1546), accessed at the Folger Shakespeare Library (Folger call number 216-651q).

58 Aldus Press (Venice, 1547), accessed at the Folger Shakespeare Library (Folger call number BJ1604 .C4 1547).

59 See Burke, *Fortunes of the* Courtier, 75. Douglas Northrop also cites Burke's argument approvingly ("'The Ende Therfore of a Perfect Courtier,'" 296); Finucci suggests that the dialogue was "read fanatically as a homogenous, unified, serene work" (*The Lady Vanishes*, 7). On the prescriptive nature of editors' additions, see also Carlo Ossola, *Dal "Cortegiano" all' "Uomo di mondo"*, 51–59. Javitch describes his recognition that "Castiglione had deliberately refused to write a prescriptive manual" despite the possibility that the book "tended to be mistaken by Tudor readers as a practical handbook of manners" (Preface to *The Book of the Courtier*, vii).

60 William Slights, *Managing Readers*, 8.

61 Edition published by Gabriel Giolito (Venice, 1556), accessed at the Folger Shakespeare Library (Folger call number BJ1604 .C4 1556).

62 I follow here the original pagination of this edition, in which Arabic numerals are given on both sides of the page.

63 Published by Domenico Giglio (Venice, 1587), and accessed at the Folger Shakespeare Library (Folger call number BJ1604 .C4 1587).

64 See, for example, the editions of Aldine Press (Venice, 1533); Gabriel Giolito (Venice, 1546); and Comin da Trino (Venice, 1573; Folger call number BJ1604 .C4 1573).

65 In addition to Hoby's English translation, the Latin translation of Bartholomew Clerke also enjoyed great success, with six editions published between 1561 and 1611 (Burke, *Fortunes of the* Courtier, 65–66); it too contained a wide variety of paratexts, including prefatory letters to Queen Elizabeth, Thomas Sackville, and the reader by Clerke, and commendatory letters to Clerke by Thomas Sackville and Edward de Vere (1571 edition). In his letter to the reader, Clerke defends his translation choices and credits the reader with the good judgment to pardon, understand, and agree with him.

66 All of these editions include appended rules for proper behavior; the only edition that lacks marginal editorial glosses is the three-column edition of 1588.

67 Glosses on 1.47 and 3.62 contained in 1561, 1577, and 1603 editions.

68 See Folger copy 2 of STC 4779.

2

Playing by the rules? Pedagogies of pleasure and inset audiences in Spenser's *Faerie Queene* and Shakespeare's *Love's Labour's Lost*

Castiglione's *Book of the Courtier* invites its readers to participate imaginatively in a scene of recreation even as it offers them a participatory education in courtesy; as I explore in Chapter 1, it asks them to consider carefully both their own roles as courteous readers and the potential ethical dimension of courtesy, seen especially in Book 4's suggestion that the courtier can lead the prince to virtue through the strategic use of pleasure. Both directly and indirectly, Castiglione's text models a vision of courteous pedagogy in which discretion, pleasure, and education work together to construct courteous subjects who can distinguish themselves in front of an audience. In this chapter, I consider further the imbrication of the discourses of pedagogy and courtesy in English texts that respond to Castiglione's ideas, making use of Ascham's *Schoolmaster* as a bridge between *The Book of the Courtier* and the works of Spenser and Shakespeare. In her account of the Renaissance "culture of teaching," Rebecca Bushnell has argued that the "pedagogical texts" of humanism "oscillated between play and work, freedom and control, submission and mastery,"[1] paradoxes that we also see at work in the texts of Spenser and Shakespeare. This chapter focuses on Book 1 of *The Faerie Queene* as it establishes a model of courteous education that Spenser will take up in Book 6, and on Shakespeare's *Love's Labour's Lost* as a forum for testing the compatibility of courtesy and academic pursuits. I show how both texts explore critically the possibilities of pleasure and spectatorship as vehicles of gentle discipline, and specifically how they *depict* audiences even as they reach out to them. *The Book of the Courtier* claims to educate readers and it invites them to make the text their own; as *The Faerie Queene* and *Love's Labour's Lost* engage with the relationship between pedagogy and courtesy, they also explore crucial questions about their relationships to readers and audience members.

Because Spenser is explicit about the didactic purpose for his poem, not least in the Letter to Raleigh, more critical attention has been paid to the education of readers of *The Faerie Queene* than to the possible education of Shakespeare's audiences. As Jane Grogan declares, "It has become a critical commonplace that *The Faerie Queene* teaches the act of reading."[2] In her classic treatment of allegory in the poem, Isabel MacCaffrey likewise asserts, "*The Faerie Queene* is about processes of coming to know."[3] Grogan, rightly insisting on Spenser's "empowering of readers," argues that he encourages "a more active and responsible reader to collaborate in the process of making meaning"; she sees the poem as "demanding increasingly sophisticated forms of readerly self-awareness."[4] That the reader *actively* participates in the poem's learning process is also a critical touchstone.[5]

Meanwhile, scholars have also questioned the efficacy of the pedagogical impulse in Spenser. Jeff Dolven makes clear that early modern poetry is saturated with the habits of the schoolroom, yet also suggests that there can be found in early modern authors such as Sidney and Spenser "a skepticism or even despair about the very possibility of teaching" and "a crisis of confidence in the humanist program."[6] Corey McEleney suggests that Spenser's *Faerie Queene* is typical of Renaissance poetry in taking its justification from the link between pedagogy and pleasure even though it ultimately ends up rupturing that link with a "futilitarian" tendency, especially in Book 6: "In the Legend of Courtesy, Spenser pushes to the extreme an interruptive impulse or drive—the very pleasure of romance—that the previous books try so hard to subdue."[7] The work of both Dolven and McEleney underscores the *indeterminacy* of Spenser's text, and of Book 6 in particular, with Dolven asserting that "*The Faerie Queene* is not finally interested in making final claims about anything, punishment or courtesy or shame. It can only bring itself to dramatize how such claims might work, where they come from, why we make them, and why we lose faith in them."[8] For McEleney, Book 6 is where "Spenser's didactic claims unravel," as the characters are caught up in what he elsewhere refers to as the "perverse wandering" of romance.[9] While acknowledging the ways in which the poem is indeed reasonably characterized as, in Dolven's words, "the sort of idle, profitless toy that the schoolmasters deplored,"[10] I must add that precisely by offering the reader flexible models of judgment, it may provoke the kind of adaptable thinking that is most suited to Renaissance understandings of courtesy, whose practitioners believed that "in everye thynge it is so harde a matter to knowe the true perfeccion, that it is almoste unpossible, and that by reason of the varietie of judgementes" (*The Book of the Courtier*, 1.13). In other words, my argument aims to complement Dolven's valuable attention to the ways in which "humanist habits of mind and ideas of teaching" persist in Renaissance romance by considering how the habits of mind encouraged by courtesy also find their place there; these habits include readers' attention to their own process of making literary and social judgments.[11] As Grogan argues with respect to Dolven, "I can find only a more moderate position, one that ends with a sense of the reader's responsibility rather than with Spenser's scepticism."[12] The schoolmasters may well have found the ideal training for courtesy's critical habits of mind distasteful, though I suggest that the principles of courtesy also found their way into humanist teaching.

Shakespeare's plays are not usually interpreted as didactic, unlike Spenser's poem—though of course they have a major role in the modern classroom.[13] Still, critics such as Judith Owens and Lynn Enterline offer very rich discussions of how his plays were affected by contemporary educational practices. Recently, Owens has explored the emotional aspects of learning in the Renaissance classroom and family as well as in texts by Shakespeare, Sidney, and Spenser.[14] Enterline argues for a connection between the "school disciplinary practices" of Shakespeare's time and his art.[15] In her discussion of the early modern educational preference for imitation rather than rule following, Enterline shows how schoolroom practices might have created in pupils a "habit of alterity," which included both the ability to place themselves in the positions of others and a sense of "self-reflexive division" that encouraged them to see themselves as audiences to their own performances.[16] Taken together, the work of Dolven, Grogan, and Enterline suggests that training in spectatorship developed in the Renaissance classroom

and was refined through engagement with both literature and theater. Building on their insights, I propose that the period's heightened sensitivity to pose taking, which was also fundamental to the
training in courtesy, enabled readers and audiences alike to engage
with the explicitly fictional and theatrical aspects of Spenser's and
Shakespeare's texts.

In both their pedagogical performances and representations of
pedagogy, Castiglione, Spenser, and Shakespeare share a crucial
attention to audience, and they invite readers and audience members to position themselves in a variety of ways. In Castiglione,
readers may function as the audience to the drama of the interlocutors' discussion, but the text also enables them to see themselves as
performers; it both prepares them for performances of courtesy and
allows them to join in the creation of the dialogue by actively making the text their own. Castiglione's dialogue prompts its readers to
engage in both self-aware and speculative reading, as they explore
more fully the roles of social and reading audiences and question
both the open-ended nature of the text and how they are reflected
in it. The focus on audience that is such a fundamental part of courtesy, then, also facilitates self-conscious awareness on the part of
readers and audiences. Readers of Spenser are instructed in courteous performances while serving as the audience to the performances
in the text. Moreover, they are also invited to compare themselves
with fictional audiences within the poem as it presents moments
of theatrical education. Likewise, Shakespeare's audiences would
have been trained by contemporary staging conditions, especially
the absence of a concept of the "fourth wall," to see themselves as
closely involved with the action of the play. Even as Castiglione's
and Spenser's readers actively participated in the meaning-making
of their texts, Renaissance courtly society and theater blurred the
line between performer and audience member.

As readers and spectators of both Spenser and Shakespeare
compare themselves to inset audiences in both works, I argue,
they are challenged to develop their critical sensibilities about the
text, courtesy, and themselves. Both Spenser's and Shakespeare's
texts explore the tension between education by coercion and education through pleasing examples, suggesting both the power and
the limitations of watching the education of others. My argument
thus builds upon the theatrical metaphor latent in titles such as

Owens' *Emotional Settings in Early Modern Pedagogical Culture* and Dolven's *Scenes of Instruction in Renaissance Romance*, considering the importance of education scenes that are observed by other characters and readers.[17] In Spenser, characters who observe the instruction of others, who function as inset audience members, provide clues for readers as they consider how they might respond to the text and be guided by its lessons. The educational mindset that Grogan links to an awareness of fiction in Spenser finds its counterpart in Shakespeare's insistently metatheatrical depiction of the characters' failures to learn.[18]

The Faerie Queene explores both the dangers and the creative possibilities of instruction that is courteous and pleasurable, and, indeed, at times theatrical. I contend that Spenser envisions a poetic education that moves beyond coercive didacticism by modeling characters who actively embrace real change. Spenser's poem proposes a discipline wherein courtesy may play an important part, going so far as to connect courtesy with Christian charity in contrast to the dictates of the law written in stone. This Christian vision is parodied in Shakespeare's *Love's Labour's Lost*, which refuses to take seriously the enlistment of courtesy for the pedagogical or Christian purposes of Spenser's text, suggesting instead that education is more closely tied to a *lack* of courtesy. The play centers on education with its unflattering portrait of Holofernes the pedant and its frequent use of the terms "learn" and "study," both of which appear more often in this Shakespearean work than any other. In its satire of scholarship more generally, *Love's Labour's Lost* explores and critiques many of the defining themes of *The Book of the Courtier*, including Castiglione's notion that courtly recreation can be a site of instruction in virtue. At the same time, its presentation of the obstacles to education, and its ultimately displeasing resolution, may well prompt further audience speculation on what is at stake in their own courteous entanglements in theatrical discipline.

Ascham and pleasure's path

In taking up the problem of the link between education and courtesy, Spenser and Shakespeare had an important predecessor in the English humanist Roger Ascham. His diatribes against the problem of the "Italianate Englishman" in his posthumously published 1570 *Schoolmaster* are well known. As Ascham outlines a program of Latin education for young gentlemen, he simultaneously rails against the excesses of the court, especially its self-indulgence and time-wasting.[19] For Ascham, there is a grave danger that the nobility will be "drowned in vain pleasure" (41).[20] He associates this problem strongly with the vogue for travel to Italy, which is "full of vain pleasures to poison the mind" (62). Ascham repeatedly warns his readers that courtly Italy is a bewitched landscape where the enchantments of Circe will undo them:

> But I am afraid that overmany of our travelers into Italy do not eschew the way to Circe's court but go and ride and run and fly thither; they make great haste to come to her; they make great suit to serve her; yea, I could point out some with my finger that never had gone out of England but only to serve Circe in Italy. Vanity and vice and any license to ill-living in England was counted stale and rude unto them. (66)[21]

For Ascham, the "vanity of licentious pleasure" (65) found in Italy risks corrupting the English court, including through the dissemination of Italian books in England: "And thus you see how will enticed to wantonness doth easily allure the mind to false opinions" (70). The empty pleasures of both court and Italy are similarly able to seduce young men.

Concurrent with cautioning young noblemen about the dangers of Italy and court culture, however, Ascham also establishes himself as a practitioner of courteous pedagogy, making clear the value to his work of Castiglione's *Book of the Courtier*.[22] Ascham's ideal student is directed by a schoolmaster, while he also learns how to take ownership of his education, eagerly participating in it and actively developing his own sense of judgment; Ascham's model both draws from and modifies the educational program proposed in Castiglione, in which the prince is passively deceived by the courtier's program of pleasure. *The Schoolmaster* follows Castiglione in presenting as its pretext an evening of elite conversation and debate, in this case recalling a dinner in 1563 at the home of William Cecil, Lord Burghley, attended by many members of Elizabeth's Privy Council; Ascham describes the gathering as a "company of so many wise and good men together as hardly then could have been picked out again out of all England beside" (5). Like Castiglione, Ascham uses aristocratic dialogue as a springboard to establish consensus about the norms of education for courtly service.[23] In addition to its opening focus on elite conversation, Ascham's treatise also refers to Castiglione's fundamental concept of *sprezzatura* as a criterion of literary value; though he doesn't use Castiglione's term specifically, Ascham clearly draws from his predecessor's concept of concealed art when citing John Cheke's criticism of the work of Sallust as "more art than nature, and more labor than art" (156). He similarly critiques Thucydides as a tryhard, "not so much benefited by nature as holpen by art and carried forth by desire, study, labor, toil, and ouergreat curiosity" (159). While Castiglione's company discusses an ideal courtier, the men of Elizabeth's court follow Burghley's custom of talking "pleasantly ... of some matter of learning, wherein he will courteously hear the mind of the meanest at his table" (6). On the night in question, Burghley expresses his "wish that some more discretion were in many schoolmasters in using correction than commonly there is" (6). Burghley's emphasis on both gentleness and discretion, key terms of *The Courtier*, is in accord with Ascham's opposition to beating students. When "courteously provoked" by Burghley, Ascham asserts that "young children were sooner allured by love than driven by beating to attain good learning" (7). In taking on the subject of "the private bringing-up of youth in gentlemen's and noblemen's houses" in the full title of the work, Ascham addresses a gentle audience in whom he encourages a gentle means of instruction; rather than relying on fear or violence, Ascham's schoolmaster should, in his frequently used term, *allure* them. Castiglione's text models not only the kind of learning that the student should pursue, but also the kind of teaching that Ascham himself enacts in his treatise: prioritizing readers' pleasure and constructing them as wise and courteous.[24]

So, while Ascham is emphatic that young men should beware the ways in which both travel and books can "allure" them from the proper path of virtue, "allure" is also a key term for him in suggesting that the pleasures of learning should entice the will of the student.[25] Hoby's translation of Castiglione's Book 4, in which Ottaviano explains how the courtier must deftly educate the prince, also underscores the need for pedagogical seduction:

> the Courtier by the meane of those honeste qualities that Count Lewis and Sir Friderick have given hym, may soone, and ought to

go about so to purchase him the good will and *allure* unto him the
minde of his Prince, that he maye make him a free and safe passage
to comune with him in every matter without troublinge him. (4.9;
emphasis mine)

As discussed in Chapter 1, because the path of virtue is initially
steep, the Courtier must use both inspiration and recreation to help
the Prince:

maye he leade him throughe the roughe way of vertue (as it were)
deckynge yt about with boowes to shadowe yt and strawinge it over
wyth sightlye flouers, to ease the greefe of the peinfull journey ...
keepe that mynde of his occupied in honest pleasure ... beeguilinge
him with a holsome craft. (4.10)

Castiglione here recognizes the power of pleasure to effect real
change—to imprint upon the prince. Yet the nature of that pleasure is complicated: it is both an "honest pleasure" and a "veile
of pleasure," that is, both true and deceptive, healing while also
"beeguilinge." Until the Prince has developed enough virtue that
his senses become a reliable guide, the courtier must disguise his
lessons as pleasing courtly pastimes. This educational program of
using pleasure on the path to learning is crucial for Ascham, though
he also modifies it in important ways.

Ascham's clearest reference to Castiglione underscores their
shared sense of the value of pleasure. He counsels his readers to
learn from reading *The Book of the Courtier*, which will also help
them avoid the perils of an Italian journey:

To join learning with comely exercises, Conte Baldassare Castiglione
in his book *Cortegiano* doth trimly teach; which book, advisedly read
and diligently followed but one year at home in England, would do
a young gentleman more good, iwis, than three years' travel abroad
spent in Italy. And I marvel this book is no more read in the court
than it is, seeing it is so well translated into English by a worthy
gentleman, Sir Thomas Hoby, who was many ways well furnished
with learning and very expert in knowledge of divers tongues. (55)

Ascham points out Castiglione's key pedagogical link between
learning and pleasure, suggesting the value of active engagement
with the Italian dialogue; it is to be "advisedly read and diligently
followed," reinforcing both the judgment and caution that the text
requires.[26] He even encourages his readers to differentiate themselves

from Castiglione's original readers by seeking out Hoby's English translation, advice that potentially strengthens the virtues of the English court. He also nominates Castiglione himself as a courteous pedagogue, one who in his text "doth trimly teach." While the adverb "trimly" is later used disparagingly by Shakespeare's Hotspur to describe the courtier who demanded his prisoners from him on the battlefield, here Ascham indicates his approval of both Castiglione's theory of courteous pedagogy and his demonstration of it in his text.[27]

Like Castiglione's, Ascham's text, I argue, not only *describes* the teaching of students, but also *teaches* its readers with the variety of models it recommends, attempting to develop their own skills in judgment and alluring them with pleasing examples. Ascham's exemplum of Lady Jane Grey demonstrates well his insistence on the role of pleasure both in his own text and in the school. Ascham prefaces the example by drawing attention to the pleasure it will give to readers: "And one example, whether love or fear doth work more in a child for virtue and learning, I will gladly report; *which may be heard with some pleasure and followed with more profit*" (35; emphasis mine). He then recounts how Jane preferred reading Plato to hunting in the park with the rest of her gentle household, justifying her choice by asserting that "all their *sport in the park is but a shadow to that pleasure* that I find in Plato. Alas, good folk, they never felt what true pleasure meant" (36; emphasis mine). Here, Ascham foresees that his readers' pleasure in hearing of Lady Jane Grey's own pleasure in the reading of Plato will entice them to follow her example. Unlike Castiglione's prince, who must be deceived into following the path of learning, Ascham's readers will, he asserts, recognize the true pleasure in the pursuit of knowledge. For Ascham, indulgence in the wrong kind of pleasure leads to "a mind embracing lightly the worse opinion and barren of *discretion* to make true difference betwixt good and ill, betwixt truth and vanity" (64; emphasis mine). Thus, while Castiglione accentuates the need for discretion in shaping a courtly performance suitable to its audience, Ascham's concept of discretion is less concerned with social decorum and more with what McEleney calls "the judgment to distinguish honest pleasure from dishonest pleasure."[28] McEleney's reading of Ascham holds that his attempt to write a straightforward educational treatise ends up reproducing the same kind of romance wandering that he criticizes, suggesting the ultimate impossibility of distinguishing between different kinds of pleasure.[29] For my part, I contend that for Ascham, pleasure and courtesy are both essential yet perilous components of his peda- gogical project of heightening the reader's self-aware judgment of true virtue.

Ascham seeks to develop a more fully virtuous, English commu- nity of elite learners, drawing on Castiglione while addressing the frivolity of the court. Even as Ascham praises Castiglione's model of incorporating pleasure and learning, one key difference is that he envisions true pleasure as that which the best student takes in learning for its own sake:

> by this way prescribed in this book, being straight, plain, and easy, the scholar is always laboring with pleasure and ever going right on forward with profit. Always laboring, I say, for or he have construed, parsed, twice translated over by good advisement, marked out his six points by skillful judgment, he shall have necessary occasion to read over every lecture a dozen times, at the least. Which, because he shall do always in order, he shall do it always with pleasure. And pleas- ure allureth love; love hath lust to labor; labor always obtaineth his purpose. (79)

Castiglione insists that the courtier should adorn the prince's path to learning with metaphorical flowers of fun; in contrast, Ascham responds that learning will be pleasurable for his students precisely because they are following the "straight, plain, and easy" path to it. Ascham's idealized model of education links pleasure, love, labor, and learning, emphasizing the reader's or student's recogni- tion of their active role in the learning process rather than pleasing deception.

The project of distinguishing oneself as a member of a social elite, central to Castiglione, does not disappear in Ascham, but is uneas- ily mapped onto his joint project of defining a gentle pedagogical program for the gentility and critiquing the self-indulgence of the court. Like Castiglione's readers, Ascham's students are trained in judgment to satisfy the most important audience; in Ascham's case, that audience's wisdom takes precedence over its savoir faire. Ascham's method of instruction "shall work such a right choice of words, so straight a framing of sentences, *such a true judgment,* both to write skillfully and speak wittily, as *wise men* shall both praise and marvel at" (19–20; emphasis mine). As in Castiglione, judgment, discretion, and the best form of social approbation all work together.[30] Like Castiglione as well, Ascham challenges his readers to recognize the merits of his method for themselves and to join in the elite community of the learned formed in part by his own book: "whether a schoolmaster shall work sooner in a child by fearful beating or *courteous* handling, you that be wise judge" (31; emphasis mine). Ascham's text constructs its readers as both wise and courteous, able to form their own consensus about the pedagogical values his book espouses and also to turn that judgment onto the values of the court itself.

Spenser's pedagogy

Given the range of anti-court sentiment in Ascham's *Schoolmaster*, Richard Helgerson clearly distinguishes between its values and those of Spenser's chivalric romance.[31] Yet, I argue that Spenser follows Ascham in insisting on both the dangers and the necessity of courtesy, employing courtesy as an educational model even as he warns of the pitfalls of pleasure. As Robert Matz argues in his account of Guyon's destruction of the Bower of Bliss, Spenser's readers must differentiate between types of pleasure: "Distinguishing between the pleasures of the text and those of courtly material culture, Spenser puts at stake the relative values of different forms of material and symbolic capital." For Matz, the destruction of the Bower, coded as feminine, permits Spenser to carve out a place as the masculine poet who uses pleasure for moral purposes.[32] In my own exploration of the relationship between pleasure and didacticism, I am particularly concerned with exploring how both Spenser's and Shakespeare's texts use models of courtesy for thinking through the effects of their texts on readers and audiences. If Castiglione, with at least one voice in his dialogue, suggests the compatibility of courtly pleasures and moral virtue, and Ascham the need to detach true pleasure from its deceptive double, Spenser's allegorical project further posits the necessity of testing characters and readers in order to sharpen their judgment about the possibilities of courteous education and the related role of pleasure. *The Faerie Queene* draws overt attention to the educational process by contrasting instructional modes such as potentially coercive precept and more pleasurable example, thus inviting readers to consider the stakes in the difference between the two and to reflect explicitly on their relationship to the poem. The shaping of characters within the narrative, then, has important implications for the shaping of the reader's character through the process of reading the book.

Spenser's Letter to Raleigh, included at the end of the 1590 edition of *The Faerie Queene*, offers the author's direct reflections on how readers might engage with the text. In the letter, Spenser offers help for readers' "better light in reading" the book, the "generall end" of which is to "fashion a gentleman or noble person in vertuous and gentle discipline" (714). Yet Spenser's defense of his text's methods reveals suspicion of his book's audience, since he criticizes the kind of techniques that have the best chance of reaching his readers.[33] In explaining his choice of "historicall fiction," for example, Spenser also acknowledges that this genre runs the risk of entertaining, rather than instructing: "Which for that I conceiued shoulde be most plausible and pleasing, being coloured with an historicall fiction, the which the most part of men delight to read, rather for variety of matter, then for profite of the ensample" (714–15). The author has limited power over his readers, the bulk of whom may fail to appreciate his text's pedagogical value as they get lost in its pleasing fictions. These fictions may even tinge on deception, as Spenser's use of "coloured" suggests; in the Proem to the Book of Courtesy in the 1596 *Faerie Queene*, Spenser's narrator will criticize the "fayned shows" of courtesy, "which carry colours faire, that feeble eies misdeeme" (6.Proem.4). Furthermore, Spenser suggests, among the presumably more discriminating members of his readership, some would have preferred a more clear-cut form of literary pedagogy:

> To some I know this Methode will seeme displeasaunt, which had rather haue good discipline *deliuered plainly in way of precepts*, or sermoned at large, as they vse, then thus clowdily enwrapped in Allegoricall deuises. But such, me seeme, should be *satisfide with the vse of these dayes* seeing all things accounted by their showes, and nothing esteemed of, that is not delightfull and pleasing to commune sence. (715–16; emphasis mine)

As Jonathan Goldberg notes of this passage in his aptly titled *Endlesse Worke*, "What gives pleasure gives displeasure."[34]

Strikingly, Spenser allies the techniques of his poem with a pejorative description of the courtly social performances of his time, even going so far as to suggest that his savvier readers might have to be swept along with the crowd in taking pleasure in delightful shows. In characterizing both his literary project and his audience in contradictory ways, Spenser's letter functions as a complicated provocation for readers who must reach their own conclusions about how they define themselves and the poem. Indeed, Spenser closes by noting that he has written these explanations so readers may avoid finding the whole poem "tedious and confused" (718). In addressing how readers should engage with his text, Spenser painstakingly clarifies both the hard intellectual labor involved and the ethical and pleasurable benefits to be derived from that labor. At the same time, he presents readers with further questions of their own to resolve.

"So much more profitable and gratious is doctrine by ensample, then by rule" (716), Spenser asserts, articulating a preference for exemplum that places him in a long pedagogical tradition that includes Castiglione and Ascham as well as English humanist Thomas Elyot, who also owned a copy of *The Courtier*.[35] In *The Book Named The Governor*, Elyot claims that "in every discipline example is the best instructor" (2.9).[36] For Ascham in *The Schoolmaster*, students' connecting rules to examples is fundamental to their ability to make the matter of the lesson their own:

> For when the master shall compare Tully's book with his scholar's translation, let the master at the first lead and teach his scholar to join the rules of his grammar book with the examples of his present lesson, until the scholar by himself be able to fetch out of his grammar every rule for every example. (16)

Spenser similarly requires his readers to sort out the relationships between rules and examples, yet he offers them less straightforward tasks than mastering Latin grammar; as I discuss in greater detail in Chapter 4, his text is not simply composed of narrative examples from which the reader can distill straightforward rules, but rather an oftentimes contradictory blend of precepts and illustrative examples of which the reader is challenged to make sense.[37] Here, I show how Spenser's text offers readers multiple models of instruction, encouraging them to position themselves in a text that provides the possibility of teaching *with* courtesy as well as *learning* the techniques of courtesy. In presenting a variety of "discipline problems"—not only characters who misbehave, but also pedagogical conundrums—Spenser's text requires the mental effort of both empathy and critique, of identification and recognition from a critical distance, as readers are tasked with fashioning themselves both as readers and gentle persons.

Book One: Detouring from pleasure's path

In Book 1 of *The Faerie Queene*, the narrator charts a path for the development of the Redcrosse Knight, the knight of holiness, that emphasizes both the ambiguity of pleasure and the efficacy of instruction that takes place through theatrical spectatorship. As is the case with Ascham, Spenser's engagement of readers in literary pleasure both follows and critiques Castiglione's educational model of having the courtier lead the prince "throughe the roughe way of vertue ... deckynge yt about with boowes to shadowe yt and strawinge it over wyth sightlye flouers" (4.10). The flower-strewn paths of the courtier's pedagogy suggest the landscape of romance, and indeed Hoby's translation reveals both the similarity and contrast between Castiglione and Spenser; even as Castiglione's courtier brings the prince to virtue by "beeguilinge him with a holsome craft" (4.10), Spenser's narrator recounts how at the outset of their journey, the Redcrosse Knight and Una are "with pleasure forward led" (1.1.8) into the Wandering Wood. They continue to be passively drawn into pleasure as "led with delight, they thus beguile the way" (1.1.10).[38] But they are on the path that leads to Errour's Den and to the Redcrosse Knight's being wrapped up in "*Errours* endlesse traine" (1.1.18) and becoming the "beguiled guest" (1.2.11) of the deceptive necromancer Archimago. While Castiglione's account moves rather hastily from an oxymoronic honest deceptive pleasure that leads to true learning, Spenser's poem, over six books, troubles the link between pleasure and learning. Ascham suggests that the schoolmaster should "allure" students even as he cautions them away from the Circe-like enchantments of the court; Spenser's poem likewise highlights the seductive, deceptive nature of pleasure as the Redcrosse Knight becomes a temporary follower of Duessa, "Who with her witchcraft and misseeming sweete, / Inueigled him to follow her desires vnmeete" (1.7.50). Spenser, like Ascham, insists that his readers must ultimately become *aware* of the nature of the learning process, recognizing and distinguishing between the different kinds of sweetness.

The episode in the House of Pride offers both characters and readers an early opportunity to distinguish between good and bad forms of pleasure and courtesy, suggesting a strong link between courtesy and vanity. The atmosphere of the House closely ties courtesy to a superficial attention to fashion: "Some frounce their curled heare in courtly guise, / Some prancke their ruffes, and others trimly dight / Their gay attyre: each others greater pride does spight" (1.4.14). Yet at the same time that Duessa basks in the "faire courtesie" that the company offers her, Redcrosse scorns this competition in coiffure: "Yet the stout Faery mongst the middest crowd / Thought all their glorie vaine in knightly vew" (1.4.15). The punning reference to vainglory raises both the self-importance and the pointlessness of the court atmosphere according to the Redcrosse Knight. The progress of the Seven Deadly Sins in the House of Pride similarly connects empty pleasures with vanity. While the courtly company enjoys the opportunity to view the pageant, "in fresh flowring fields themselues to sport," the Redcrosse Knight declines to participate as either performer (like Duessa) or audience member (like the many gathered people): "But that good knight would not so nigh repaire, / Him selfe estraunging from their ioyaunce vaine" (1.4.37). The "pleasuance" (1.4.38) of the scene only alienates the Redcrosse Knight, and readers may learn from his reaction. By the end of the episode, the courtly atmosphere of Lucifera's court has been decisively joined with empty pleasure, as the Dwarf uncovers the dungeon full of those who wrecked their lives with "ydle pomp, or wanton play" (1.5.51). Most of the characters in Lucifera's court learn nothing from the pleasure they experience there, though Redcrosse makes some progress in the displeasure he takes in this form of courtesy, and readers may emulate him in beginning to think about different forms of pleasure.

In its depiction of the Redcrosse Knight's battle with Sansjoy, the House of Pride episode calls upon readers to weigh the learning that occurs through critical spectatorship. Readers may well have difficulty differentiating the two contestants in the narrator's description of them: "With hideous horror both together smight, /

And souce so sore, that they the heauens affray: / The wise
Southsayer seeing so sad sight, / Th'amazed vulgar telles of warres
and mortall fight" (1.5.8). The audience within the poem responds
with sympathy but not understanding: "Great ruth in all the gazers
harts did grow, / Seeing the gored woundes to gape so wyde, / That
victory they dare not wish to either side" (1.5.9). Here readers of
the poem are prompted to distinguish themselves from "th'amazed
vulgar": their understanding may exceed that of the poem's internal
audience, even as the internal audience may also be on to something in their sense that there is not yet the difference between the
Redcrosse Knight and Sansjoy that develops by the end of Book 1.[39]

Attending to the responses of audiences within the poem thus
provides vivid examples, rather than the direct instruction of precepts, that readers may use for their own education. In Canto 6,
readers observe two possibilities for tutelage through the character
of Satyrane, the son of a satyr who grows up "from lawes of men
exilde" (23) and spends his time indulging in hunting; his form of
"sportes, and cruell pastime" (27) is to make wild creatures fear
him as "tyrans law" (26). As Satyrane progresses in the civilizing process, he first receives instruction through his mother's lectures: "Ah *Satyrane*, my dearling, and my ioy, / For loue of me leaue
off this dreadfull play; / To dally thus with death, is no fit toy, /
Go find some other play-fellowes, mine own sweet boy" (28). This
attempt to steer her son away from the wrong kind of "play" and
toward the right one works about as well as most such lectures;
neither Satyrane nor Spenser's narrator dignify "these womanish
words" (28) with a response, but simply move directly (at the start
of the next stanza) to stating that Satyrane continues to go about
his wild business: "In these and like delightes of bloody game /
He trayned was" (29). Later, however, Satyrane comes upon the
spectacle of Una teaching the satyrs, a pleasing interlude depicted
as a respite from his "long labours" (30). As a secondary audience to Una's impressive education of the satyrs, Satyrane sees her
"teaching the Satyres, which her sat around / Trew sacred lore,
which from her sweet lips did redound" (30). This scene causes
both wonder and pity in Satyrane: "He wondred at her wisedome
heuenly rare, / Whose like in womens witt he neuer knew; / And
when her curteous deeds he did compare, / Gan her admire, and her
sad sorrowes rew" (31). Watching Una's instruction as a bystander

provokes an active mental engagement in Satyrane. This *spectator-ship* of teaching does what his mother's lecture cannot: he joins the audience of satyr students who have already reacted with "pitty and vnwonted ruth" to Una: "Thenceforth he kept her goodly company, / And learnd her discipline of faith and verity" (12, 31). While Una still laments her separation from the Redcrosse Knight, Satyrane nonetheless provides her what cheerful society he can and, in helping her, is "glad to gain such fauour" (32). The real learning that Una affords Satyrane through his observation of her teaching is accompanied by real pleasure. Spectatorship can certainly continue to be self-indulgence in the poem—the canto ends with Archimago delightedly viewing a battle between Sansloy and Satyrane that he has engineered (48). And yet, this too offers readers the opportunity to reflect upon what kind of readerly audience they want to be for the poem, discriminating between the various kinds of courtesy and pleasure it offers.

Courtesy and true pleasure in the House of Holiness

The educational program of Book 1 culminates with the Redcrosse Knight's movement through the House of Holiness in Canto 10; this episode provides a vision of education as Christian discretion that revises Castiglione's discourse by clarifying the proper role of pleasure. The House of Holiness is portrayed as a place of true pleasure and courtesy, even as it shows the hard work of Christian discipline. Passing through an entrance that is "streight and nar-row" (5), Una and the Redcrosse Knight enter "a spatious court ... Both plaine, and pleasaunt to be walked in" (6); they are greeted by a franklin who treats them with "comely courteous glee" (6) and by a squire who also offers "rare courtesee" (7). Readers are chal-lenged to see the difference between this kind of courteous speech and those they have previously encountered in Book 1: "He them with speaches meet / Does faire entreat; no courting nicetee, / But simple trew, and eke vnfained sweet, / As might become a Squyre so great persons to greet" (7). The House of Holiness offers pleas-ure and sweetness without deception, echoing Una's "sweet" teach-ing of Satyrane and opposing the sweet deception of Castiglione's courtier. The education in the House of Holiness also offers a contrast to the pleasurable paths that have led the Redcrosse Knight astray: "So few there bee, / That chose the narrow path, or seeke the right: / All keepe the broad high way, and take delight / With many rather for to goe astray" (10). It is nonetheless depicted as a place of true courtesy; Dame Caelia also provides "all the court'sies, that she could deuyse" (11) and the two sisters Fidelia and Speranza exchange "like courtesee" with Una (15). In the vision of Spenser's poem, true courtesy and virtue are found by the narrow path, in contrast to Belphoebe's later account of the broad road to the empty pleasures of the court: "But easy is the way, and passage plaine, / To pleasures pallace; it may soone be spide, / And day and night her dores to all stand open wide. / In Princes court" (2.3.41–42).

As the Redcrosse Knight progresses through the House of Holiness, pain and pleasure modulate as he continues to learn the true nature of joy through courteous instruction. Fidelia's "schoolehous" (18) gives Redcrosse a place of respite from his "labors long" (17), but it also involves him in a new kind of strenuous education, as he learns to read "her sacred Booke" (19). Fidelia's teaching involves a blending of lecture and the example of spectacle; not only does she "preach" (19) to Redcrosse, she also vividly demonstrates the powers of faith by halting the course of the sun and moving mountains (20). The narrator suggests the almost theatrical nature of her instruction when he asserts "that wonder was to heare her goodly speach" (19). The Redcrosse Knight's training in "celestiall discipline" (18) leads to a variety of reactions on his part; when he is "greeued" (21) and in "distressed doubtfull agony" (22), Speranza offers him "comfort sweet" (22). Watching all of this, Una herself may guide readers' responses; even she finds "her selfe assayld with great perplexity" (22). As the Redcrosse Knight submits to truthful communication with the "Leach" (23), who provides him with the honest "salues and med'cines" (24), and then proceeds to the path of painful purgation, full of "torment" (28), Una continues to feel emotions linked to theatrical response: "His owne deare *Vna* hearing euermore / His ruefull shriekes and gronings, often tore / Her guiltlesse garments, and her golden heare, / For pitty of his payne and anguish sore; / Yet all with patience wisely she did beare" (28). Una's observational response to the drama of Redcrosse's healing instruction yet again provides a possible model for readers in pondering the relationship between pain and learning, until the Redcrosse Knight's encounter with Charissa spurs pleasure and virtue to unite once more, albeit temporarily. Charissa's children are characterized by their "sportes" (31), and she combines courtesy with pleasure: "them requites with court'sies seeming meet, / And entertaynes with friendly chearefull mood" (32). Yet Charissa still involves the knight in learning her "vertuous rules" (32), suggesting the unification of pleasure and the law as she shows him the "ready path" to heaven (33). The Redcrosse Knight is taught to follow the straight and narrow path ("a narrow way") as opposed to the dictates of pleasure, but the matron Mercy also does her best to remove the "bushy thornes, and ragged breares" (35) as the Redcrosse Knight treads a more explicitly Christian version of Castiglione's "roughe way of vertue."

While the Redcrosse Knight's path to holiness certainly includes a relationship to pleasure, more than anything it requires rejecting a passive model of education and moving through active pursuits toward a true joy seen only fleetingly on earth. The trek to the hermitage of Contemplation includes a "painfull way" up a hill (46), with Una herself remarking on the "paine" of their journey (50). Although the path to Contemplation is difficult, it results in Contemplation's ultimate promise to show Redcrosse the way "that neuer leads the traueiler astray, / But after labors long, and sad delay, / Brings them to ioyous rest and endlesse blis" (52). Contemplation offers Redcrosse a mountaintop vision comparable to that of Mount Sinai, the Mount of Olives, or Mount Parnassus, thus bringing together the pain of the law ("The bitter doome of death and balefull mone" [53]) and the pleasure of poetry ("like that pleasaunt Mount, that is for ay / Through famous Poets verse each where renownd" [54]).[40] From there, he is shown the "steepe and long" path to the New Jerusalem (55), where the Angels have "gladsome companee" and "great ioy" (56). Though the Courtier's education uses pleasure as a gateway to learning, the Redcrosse Knight in the House of Holiness moves through pain to joy. Variations of the word "joy" and "joyous" abound in this canto, all connecting the charitable hospitality of the House to the instruction of the Redcrosse Knight; Dame Caelia's "onely ioy was to relieue the needes / Of wretched soules" (3), Una is "ioyous" to see Redcrosse's "cured conscience" (29), and Charissa is "right ioyious" (33) of the opportunity to teach the Redcrosse Knight. To

these moments of true joy—or honest pleasures—the narrator contrasts Redcrosse's disappointment that he must eventually leave the
Mount of Contemplation and return "backe to the world, whose
ioyes so fruitlesse are" (63). Here we might adduce Ascham's suggestion that the study of virtue inoculates against the temptations
of pleasure:

> The true medicine against the enchantmentes of Circe, the vanity of
> licentious pleasure, the enticements of all sin, is, in Homer, the herb
> *moly*, with the black root and white flower, sour at the first but sweet
> in the end, which Hesiodus termeth the study of virtue, hard and
> irksome in the beginning but in the end easy and pleasant. And that
> which is most to be marveled at, the divine poet Homer saith plainly
> that this medicine against sin and vanity is not found out by man but
> given and taught by God. (65)

By the end of his education, the Redcrosse Knight has learned a
Christian model of distinguishing the best forms of pleasure and
the best paths to walk, rejecting the empty pleasures of this world.
At the same time, the poem emphasizes the incomplete nature of
Redcrosse's human journey. Even after his slaying of the dragon in
Canto 12, the insistent description of his wedding to Una as a time
full of "great ioy" and "exceeding merth," in which "his heart did
seeme to melt in pleasures manifold" (40) and he can partake of
her "ioyous presence and sweet company" (41), is soon undercut
by his need to return to fulfilling his oath of service to the Faerie
Queene, leaving Una "to mourne" (41). Spenser's idealized model
of Christian education through courtesy prods readers to recognize
the different paths of pleasure they may choose, but it also makes
clear the impossibility of attaining perfection.

Calidore's courteous instruction?

While the question of the proper role of courtesy threads through
all of *The Faerie Queene*, Book 6 places the problem of courteous instruction at the forefront of the reader's experience. Here
the narrator underscores the pleasure of his own journey, suggesting that pleasure can now be joined more directly with pedagogy;
"the waies" he travels through fairy land "are so exceeding spa-
cious and wyde, / And sprinckled with such sweet variety, / Of all

that pleasant is to eare or eye" (6.Proem.1). He further credits the
Muses, who "keeping haue of learnings threasures," with providing
him with "heauenly pleasures" (6.Proem.2). In Book 6 as a whole,
however, as I will trace both here and in Chapters 4 and 5, the narrator's instruction is far from seamless. Instead, the text continues
to explore different teaching methods, encouraging the reader to
adopt a variety of positions toward the text.

Calidore's first exploit in Canto 1 depicts two models of instruction, highlighting the difference between simple precepts and other
forms of pedagogy. First, in the case of Crudor, readers witness the
coercion connected to teaching by precept, and next, in the case of
Briana, they see how education through spectatorship might truly
alter one's mental disposition. In order to fulfill the irrational condition the disdainful Crudor has set on his love, Briana attempts to
fashion a mantle lined with the hair and beards of the ladies and
knights unlucky enough to pass her way. In response to Briana's
campaign of discourtesy, Calidore chops off the head of Maleffort,
who leads Briana's endeavor (23), and kills the rest of her retinue
as easily as a steer swishing away the gadflies (24). When Briana,
joined perhaps by the reader, objects to this seemingly excessive response, the text somewhat uneasily defends it; Calidore is
"abashed," but also didactically asserts, "Bloud is no blemish; for
it is no blame / To punish those, that doe deserue the same," and
he goes on to counsel Briana to "mild curt'sie showe / To all, that
passe" (26–27).[41] His precepts thus run the gamut from the highly
debatable (his defense of blood justice in dispensing punishments)
to the banal. His little lecture has no effect on Briana, who continues to "disdaine" his "courteous lore" (27). Finally, Calidore
battles Crudor himself, and, instead of killing him, accepts his plea
for mercy on the condition that Crudor will agree to treat other
knights better and come to the aid of ladies in need (42); Calidore's
mercy to Crudor is also accompanied by a lecture about how courteous knights should act (40–42). Without much choice, Crudor
"promist to performe his precept well" (43) and agrees to be bound
to Briana without further compensation.[42] In a sense, this brief episode follows what Northrop Frye has identified as the classic structure of comedy, with the unjust law that is an obstacle between
lovers being removed by the end: "So suffring him to rise, he made
him sweare / By his owne sword, and by the crosse thereon, / To take

Briana for his louing fere, / Withouten dowre or composition; / But to release his former foule condition" (43).[43]

Of course, Calidore's ostensible mercy to Crudor may simply substitute one unreasonable rule for another. The narrator's description of Crudor makes it clear that his willingness to act courteously may be no more than going through the necessary motions: "All which accepting, and with faithfull *oth* / Bynding himselfe most firmely to obay, / He vp arose, *how euer liefe or loth*, / And swore to him true fealtie for aye" (44; emphasis mine). While Crudor mends his ways, he does so under duress, by adopting a simplistic view of courtesy as the golden rule—he may "performe" courtesy, but it is doubtful that he will *become* courteous. Spenser's narrator here recognizes the problems with education by compulsion that Ascham critiques in *The Schoolmaster* when he draws on the views of Socrates via Plato: "No learning ought to be learned with bondage, for bodily labors wrought by compulsion hurt not the body, but any learning learned by compulsion tarrieth not long in the mind" (32).

Even as Calidore's first exploit models a lesson in courtesy that resembles the coercion of precepts, it nonetheless also depicts an example of learning that works at least in part through spectatorship. When Crudor fades into the background after having pledged himself to follow Calidore's precepts of courtesy, the spotlight shifts to Briana, who has witnessed Crudor's reform ("which all this beheld" [44]). Calidore adds a verbal gloss to Briana's visual appreciation of the scene, letting her know that he has forced Crudor to release her from his unreasonable requirement of a hair-lined coat, and to agree to marry her as is. So, while Calidore's original straightforward address to Briana fails, it seems to work pretty well when intermingled with both tangible prospects for adjusting her life *and* her experience as a witness to Calidore's treatment of Crudor. Together, they have a powerful effect on her; Crudor will perform courtesy regardless of his inner disposition, but Briana undergoes a marked internal shift: "Whereof she now more glad, then sory earst, / All ouercome with infinite *affect*, / For his exceeding courtesie, that *pearst* / *Her stubborne hart* with inward deepe effect" (45; emphasis mine). Without any direct prompting from Calidore, she "her selfe acknowledg'd bound for that accord" (45). Briana's education ultimately ties true pleasure with true learning, as the narrator reiterates how "glad" she is (45,

46) alongside her genuine expressions of courtesy: "Most ioyfully she them did entertaine / Where goodly glee and feast to them she made, / To shew her thankefull mind and meaning faine" (46). Her marvelous reversal of character occurs because she watches Calidore teach and, as the narrator relates, "She freely gaue that Castle for his paine, / And her selfe bound to him for euermore; / So wondrously now chaung'd, from that she was afore" (46). Not only does she "acknowledge" a new relationship to Calidore, she also mirrors Crudor's state of being bound—though she also supersedes it by volunteering to become a member of polite society rather than being forced to accept this role. Her encounter with Calidore changes her very heart.

In a short space, then, the Spenserian narrator offers two opposed, yet interrelated models of instruction. While Calidore seems to be a poor teacher in handing down coercive precepts to Crudor, his instruction of Briana operates by both performed example and direct instruction, and effects a profound inner change in her. A clear distinction between precept and example thus proves difficult to maintain in the poem. As it offers different models for instruction in courtesy, *The Faerie Queene* asserts the importance of this virtue both for how readers define themselves as readers, and for how they define their relationship to the poem's lessons. These examples will of course multiply throughout Book 6, as I will continue to explore in Chapters 4 and 5. It takes the whole of Book 1 of *The Faerie Queene* to reconcile true pleasure, courtesy, and learning; Book 6 offers a tidy resolution in its first canto that it will trouble throughout the remainder of the book.

Love's Labour's Lost

Shakespeare's references to the schoolroom tend toward the negative. In *Romeo and Juliet*, Romeo laments his first parting from Juliet by comparing it to the pain of attending school: "Love goes *toward* love as schoolboys from their books, / But love from love *toward school* with *heavy looks*" (2.1.198–99; emphasis mine). In *As You Like It*, Jaques' second age of man is "the whining schoolboy with his satchel / And shining morning face, creeping like snail / Unwillingly to school" (2.7.145–47). These brief allusions to the displeasure school causes echo the dim view of book-learning that is most fully expressed in *Love's Labour's Lost*, a play that takes on questions of pedagogy and courtesy from a variety of angles. With the ridiculing not only of Holofernes the pedant, but more importantly, of the educational aims of the four central courtiers, the play suggests both the absurdity and the tedium of learning.[44] While both Ascham and Spenser, in their different ways, argue for at least the *possibility* of education through pleasure, Shakespeare's *Love's Labour's Lost* questions the plausibility of this connection. In its mockery of court culture, this play severs the link between pleasure and learning, implying that education involves a *lack* of courtesy.

My aim in this chapter is not to establish a direct allusion to *The Faerie Queene* in *Love's Labour's Lost*; the play may well have preceded the 1596 version of Spenser's poem.[45] I do, however, argue that this play's exploration of audience response raises similar questions about the possibility of courteous education and its limits, even as its depictions of the relationships between inset audiences and learning contrast to Spenser's. Readers of *The Faerie Queene* must use their discretion in contemplating the tensions in courteous education between compulsion and freedom, between precept and example, and between oath and agency. These tensions are also at the forefront of *Love's Labour's Lost*, in which, as in Spenser, characters' reactions to the disciplinary experiences of other characters provide important prompts for audience member reflection. In this case, even though much less learning takes place on the part of the play's characters, its frequent presentations of onstage entertainments may prod audience members to consider the dynamic between audience and player and to reflect on their own roles in interpreting a performance. This foregrounding of the role of audience assessment, I argue, is what most connects *Love's Labour's Lost* to the culture of courtesy. Others have previously linked the play to Castiglione's text; Thomas M. Greene sees in it a deep engagement with civility as it demonstrates the courtiers' lack of decorum; Louis Montrose emphasizes its "critique of courtly styles"; and Donatella Baldini points to the play's emphasis on games and "the constructed character of social life" as linking the play to Castiglione.[46] My reading focuses on how *Love's Labour's Lost* points to the power of both characters and audiences to judge performances of courtesy. As we have seen in Chapter 1,

Castiglione's text emphasizes throughout the notion of judgment; the discernment of the courtier is crucial to creating his social performances, and the judgment of his social audience is what gives these performances their meaning. *Love's Labour's Lost* glances at this idea in the Princess's early assertion to Boyet that "beauty is bought by judgement of the eye" (2.1.15), and it later returns in full force as the play suggests that audience interpretation determines a play's meaning.[47] In Shakespeare's play, audiences receive little guidance about what, if any, lessons should be distilled from its scenes of education, though Montrose has aptly suggested that "*Love's Labour's Lost* has an intrinsic didactic and rhetorical dimension because the play is itself a manifestation of Elizabethan cultural form and because its author, actors, and audience are social players engaged in the same kind of strategies as those of the characters."[48] Developing further Montrose's point about the social training the play gives, I argue that in contrast to Spenser's apparent design for his poem, the lessons that Shakespeare's characters learn may differ sharply from the multiplying meanings audiences extract from *Love's Labour's Lost*. Thus, even as the play pokes fun at humanist aspirations more generally, it also offers the possibility of a wider range of learning opportunities, as both characters and audiences confront how their own identities are constructed with relationship to courtesy, pleasure, and theatergoing.

Study and recreation

In Ascham's model, the self-reinforcing connections among love, labor, and pleasure all maximize the student's learning. Ascham argues that "where love is present labor is seldom absent," citing Aristotle's belief that "love refuseth no labor; and labor obtaineth whatsoever it seeketh" (30). In contrast to those students who are "always laboring with pleasure," Ascham claims that those who learn by rote fail to truly learn: "Their whole knowledge, by learning without the book, was tied only to their tongue and lips, and never ascended up to the brain and head, and therefore was soon spit out of the mouth again ... For their whole labor, or rather great toil without order, was even vain idleness without profit" (79). And yet, in the opening scene of *Love's Labour's Lost*, when the

four courtiers vow to devote themselves to study, they make clear
that their view of learning is closely tied to coercion, discourtesy,
and pointless suffering, all things that Ascham and Spenser oppose
to true education in various ways. Just as Spenser's Crudor takes
a merely formulaic oath, the four courtiers swear to follow their
strict regime to the letter, and in so doing aim for the outward trappings of an impressive education rather than actually changing their
minds or hearts.

So, while *The Book of the Courtier* proposes that courtly entertainments can be used to inculcate virtue, the opening scene of
Love's Labour's Lost questions this possibility, underscoring a self-
denial that is closely linked to a project of social distinction. King
Ferdinand attempts through his rhetoric to link the men's scholarly pursuits to the action of the battlefield: "Therefore, brave
conquerors—for so you are, / That war against your own affections /
And the huge army of the world's desires" (1.1.8–10). He suggests
a view of education as temperate self-conquest, but the hyperbolic nature of his metaphors also renders absurd the link between
action and writing he advocates. Matz has described the way in
which, for Spenser, "scholarly labor may figure knightly service";
here, Ferdinand's words underscore the absurdity of that position.[49]
Ferdinand also makes use of a vocabulary associated with both
theatrical and courtly performance, speaking of the "fame" that
will "grace" the four men "in the disgrace of death": "Navarre
shall be the wonder of the world, / Our court shall be a little academe, / Still and contemplative in living art" (1.1.12–14). In their
reference to the "disgrace" that the men will bring to death, Peter
Burke notes an echo of Hoby's use of "disgracing" as a translation for *sprezzatura*.[50] The men follow Castiglione, perhaps, in
their quest for social approbation, but diverge from his model
in their extreme practice of self-deprivation. Longaville blithely
brags: "I am resolved: 'tis but a three years' fast. / The mind shall
banquet though the body pine" (1.1.24–25). His ascetic practice
mirrors Spenser's Contemplation, who also keeps a "long fast" that
feeds his spirit: "His mind was full of spirituall repast, / And pyn'd
his flesh, to keepe his body low and chast" (1.10.48). Yet, while the
allegorical figure of Contemplation is content with his solitude, the
proposed "still and contemplative" academe is designed to bring
social distinction, as Dumaine also brags: "The grosser manner of

these world's delights / He throws upon the gross world's baser slaves" (1.1.29–30). Dumaine here underscores the performative class dimension of their project, regardless of its claims for inwardly focused scholarship; as Akhimie has shown, the Renaissance "cultivation of difference" involved reinforcing ostensibly natural differences between the privileged class and those marked as other.[51]

While Dumaine's noxious elitism echoes Castiglione, the four men's educational program goes against the grain of *The Book of the Courtier* by depending on painful self-deprivation. When Berowne suggests that study might be best used to find workarounds to their oath in seeking out feasts and mistresses, the King responds: "These be the stops that hinder study quite / And train our intellects to *vain delight*" (1.1.70–71; emphasis mine). Ferdinand sees all pleasure as empty pleasure, but Berowne offers a corrective to this: "Why, all delights are vain, but that most vain / Which, with pain purchased, doth inherit pain" (1.1.72–73). Berowne here nods toward the kind of vain delights that Ascham scorns and Spenser typifies in the Bower of Bliss; indeed, as H. R. Woudhuysen points out, his phrasing echoes Spenser's here: "The vyle *Acrasia*, that with vaine delightes, / And ydle pleasures in her *Bowre of Blisse*, / Does charme her louers" (2.5.27).[52] Berowne's mockery of the men's plan of study suggests that it is worse than simply indulging in pleasure for its own sake; their plan is senseless because it is completely detached from both pleasure and the real world, a point that he later echoes when he criticizes the dictate that women must avoid the court: "Therefore this article is made in vain, / Or vainly comes th'admired Princess hither" (1.1.137–38). Even as the four courtiers seek fame from their own pursuits, Berowne's emphasis on the *vanity* of their scheme underscores both its prideful turning inward for scholarly navel-gazing, and its likely fruitlessness.

In its planned divorce from the world of sociability, then, the men's scholarly project goes against the grain of courtesy, both in its inhospitable asceticism and, even more, in its self-imposed laws that prohibit responding to the specific circumstances of social situations with the flexibility that defines courtesy. Even as the men style themselves as living artistic creations, they also subscribe to dead letters with the signing of their names; Berowne eventually assents, saying, "to the strictest decrees I'll write my name" (1.1.117) and "to the laws at large I write my name" (1.1.153). At the same time as he grudgingly signs on to the plan, Berowne refers to the dictate that women are forbidden from the court as "a dangerous law against gentility" (1.1.127).[53] Here, too, as in Spenser's Briana episode, we see the kind of discourteous edict that it will be the work of the comedy to overcome, although in this case it is an especially odd version of it in that the four courtiers are blocked by their own self-sabotage. The men's program has fatal contradictions from the start; it cares too much about empty names, and it cares too little about actually behaving in a way that is fitting. In setting themselves fixed, unreasonable rules, they neglect the decorum that defines courtesy, thus making themselves recognizable buffoons to audiences familiar with its dictates.

It is in keeping with the impracticality of the men's plan that immediately after Berowne signs his oath, their thoughts turn to taking a break; their "quick recreation" is something outside their educational project, not in tune with it, an "interim to our studies" (1.1.159, 169). While Ascham's Jane Grey takes "true pleasure" in her reading of Plato in contrast to those who enjoy "sport in the park" (36), the four courtiers of *Love's Labour's Lost* make it their "sport" *apart* from their study to poke fun at Don Armado, the *miles gloriosus* of the play. Not only is Armado a braggart soldier, he also exemplifies the affectation against which *The Book of the Courtier* warns: "A man in all the world's new fashion planted, / That hath a mint of phrases in his brain, / One who the music of his own *vain* tongue / Doth ravish like enchanting harmony, / A man of compliments" (1.1.162–66; emphasis mine). Despite having little insight into the vanity of their own project, the four courtiers are admirably attuned to Armado's vanity; they mimic the interlocutors of Castiglione's dialogue, who choose as their "pastime" to "disgrace therefore many untowardly asseheades, that through malepertnes thinke to purchase them the name of a good Courtyer" (1.12).[54] Epitomizing the narcissism of small differences, the men delight in scorning Armado's desire for reputation without recognizing their similarly motivated desire for fame.[55] Even as the men attempt to differentiate themselves from "the gross world's baser slaves" (1.1.30) and from Armado, Armado seeks to distinguish himself from "the rude multitude" (5.1.82) (or the "base vulgar," as his knowing companion Moth puts it [1.2.48]), using language to separate himself from the crowd: "We will be singuled from the barbarous" (5.1.74–75). With his constant use of archaism, Armado entertains by recounting fanciful stories in outdated language; it's also tempting to see in Berowne's mocking description of him an echo of Spenser's diction: "Armado is a most illustrious wight, / A man of fire-new words, fashion's own knight" (1.1.175–76). As spectators watch the four courtiers watch Armado, then, they are offered both an inset audience to the braggart soldier's antics and an example of the kind of dismissal that might accompany the reading of Spenser's romance. Unlike the inset audiences in Spenser's poem, the four courtiers seem to learn very little from observing Armado on their study breaks, even about the absurdity of their project of social distinction. But that need not mean that audiences of the play itself cannot be drawn into their own lessons while the courtiers play the truant.

The eavesdropping scene: Revising the curriculum?

In *The Faerie Queene* readers are invited to consider their relationship to inset audience members as a technique of pedagogy; in *Love's Labour's Lost* the educational role of theater is raised more as a question as the four young men move away from their studies. The virtuoso eavesdropping scene at the center of the play—in which the members of the quartet sequentially spy on one another as they offer declarations of love—gives both characters and audiences the opportunity for vain delight as well as learning through observation and comparison. Erika T. Lin suggests in a different context that the play's eavesdropping scene involves a "modulation of audience identification and disidentification," which is typical of the kind of mental processes that Jeremy Lopez has argued are prompted by early modern theater more generally.[56] My own reading here underscores how the scene prompts audiences to consider the relationship between theater and character formation as they process the variety of ways of relating to the interlude. As the scene opens, Berowne notes that he has become a successful disciple of romance: "By heaven, I do love, and it hath taught me to rhyme, and to be melancholy" (4.3.11–12). Shortly thereafter, Dumaine also speaks of replacing suffering for scholarship with suffering for love, referring to "my true love's fasting pain" (4.3.119). While the scene is a potential goldmine of physical comedy, one's appreciation of the silliness of the players' actions increases as one makes sense of the different layers of dissimulation as well as the ways in which the completeness of each character's knowledge of the others differs, with no one knowing the same amount about which members of the group have succumbed to love. In her work on theory of mind, Lisa Zunshine has demonstrated that the enjoyment of fiction is related to our human interest in ascribing motivations to others and sorting out layers of intention. Much of Zunshine's work concerns the cognitive ability to process meta-representation—that is, "our tendency to keep track of sources of our representations," a mental ability that allows us to adopt a skeptical attitude toward information we receive, or "to store certain information/representations 'under advisement.'"[57] Although Zunshine focuses on the novel, I propose that her model also works well as a partial explanation for the pleasure we might take in watching Shakespeare's plays, especially those that deal with the layers of performance required by courtly self-presentation.

So, just as being a savvy reader of courtesy means sorting out levels of performance, so too does watching the eavesdropping scene involve the audience in keeping track of an increasingly complicated chain. We observe four characters, each with a diminishing understanding of the emotions of the others: Berowne sees that the King thinks that Berowne does not know about the King's own love, and so will join him in scorning Longaville and Dumaine for being lovers. It's tricky to sort out, and indeed one reader of the 1598 quarto, William Drummond, put asterisks and the numbers 2 and 3 next to the poems that the King and Longaville speak at their entrances, in addition to marking Berowne's previous misdirected poem with the number 1.[58] It's possible that Drummond was simply drawing attention to these inset poems, but it's also possible that he was trying to keep track of how they are related to the layering of characters' performances in the theatrical situation. In any case, the humor of the scene depends upon the audience's ability to track the progressively outrageous hypocrisy of the four courtiers, deriving enjoyment from appreciating the mismatch between the characters' words and their feelings. In the 2014 Royal Shakespeare Company production of the play directed by Christopher Luscombe, Edward Bennett as a hidden Berowne looked on gleefully as the King sobbed for love; when Berowne later metatheatrically chastises his three friends for the "scene of foolery" (4.3.160) created by their love declarations, he presents himself as a disgusted spectator of what he was actually glad to witness.

The eavesdropping scene, considered as a version of a play within a play, both proposes and rejects the possibility that Berowne will profit from his experience as an audience member. Recalling Sidney's view that "comedy is an imitation of the common errors of our life, which he representeth in the most ridiculous and scornful sort that may be, so as it is impossible that any beholder can be content to be such a one" (229–30), we might wonder if Berowne will be prompted by the ridiculous examples of his fellow courtiers to amend his own lovesick ways. While he does indeed comment on his viewing and learning ("Once more I'll mark how love can vary wit" [4.3.97]), his overarching response to this "scene of foolery" is to take delight in the foibles of his fellow courtiers. The audience may well join Berowne in his mockery of the other three, as well as being positioned to anticipate that Berowne himself will soon be exposed. Even as Berowne delights in his compatriots' break with study, so too does the audience watching Berowne take pleasure in his own failure to learn, and all the more so because he demonstrates that failure of education through a hypocritical speech that parodies righteous indignation, chastising the degradation of his peers: "O me, with what strict patience have I sat, / To see a king transformed to a gnat! / To see great Hercules whipping a gig, / And profound Solomon to tune a jig, / And Nestor play at push-pin with the boys, / And critic Timon laugh at idle toys" (4.3.162–67). Although Berowne describes feeling pain in seeing the downfall of his noble peers, the audience knows he has taken pleasure in his spectatorship of what he calls their "infant play" (4.3.75) and "idle toys" (4.3.167). Characters and audience both may revel in the contrast between the men's epic aspirations and their human weakness.

The subsequent exposure of the four courtiers' hypocrisy is both playful and serious, making light of the young men's foibles while also revealing their participation in a damaging discourse of privilege. When Costard and Jaquenetta disclose Berowne's own letter declaring his love (which he also seeks to dismiss as "a toy" [4.3.197]), the four courtiers decide to revert to Berowne's original proposition for their study: "having sworn too hard-a-keeping

oath, / Study to break it, and not break my troth" (1.1.65–66).
Berowne is tasked by the other three to play fast and loose with
words in order to "prove / Our loving lawful" (4.3.280–81), giving "some flattery for this evil" (4.3.282) and "some salve for per-
jury" (4.3.284). Identified from the outset as a convenient fiction,
Berowne's argument rejects the program of asceticism to which the
men had previously subscribed themselves, now identifying it as
"leaden contemplation" (4.3.295). He postulates that the disciplines of love teach the whole person; though they are "first learned
in a lady's eyes" (4.3.301), they soon give "to every power a double power" (4.3.305). In addition to offering the senses super-
human force, love also acts as a civilizing influence: "Never durst
poet touch a pen to write / Until his ink were tempered with Love's
sighs. / O, then his lines would ravish savage ears / And plant in
tyrants mild humility" (4.3.320–23). While the justification that
Berowne offers the men is copiously prefaced with references to
its self-serving rhetoric, the proposition that love offers a taming,
civilizing force must be examined in the context of the men's racist
and sexist bickering about which of their loves is the most genuinely "dark," "black," or "fair" that precedes Berowne's speech
(4.3.228–77).[59] Thus, while the play reveals that Berowne's argument about the civilizing power of love is dubious from the start,
I would also underscore that he makes this case in the context of
the four men's self-definition through classist and racist othering,
offering still further support to Akhimie's fundamental work on the
link between discourses of courtesy and the unjust reification of
supposedly natural differences between humans.[60]

With the four courtiers having realized that a prescriptive oath is
inadequate for their project of self-development, it's possible to see
this scene as displaying their movement to a more flexible approach
of the kind Spenser espouses, a movement beyond the verbal coercion of precepts or oaths toward an education that fulfills an idealized Christian vision of hard-won, pleasurable virtue. Yet it's also
possible to see the four courtiers as simply having exchanged one
empty promise for another. Earlier in the eavesdropping scene,
Longaville rather justly accuses Dumaine that his "love is far from
charity, / That in love's grief desirest society" (4.3.124–25); as
Berowne continues his rationalizing speech, he elides the difference
between romantic love and charity that is so fundamental to Book 1

of *The Faerie Queene*. While the Redcrosse Knight's encounter with Charissa combines courtesy with education, preparing him to take the "painfull way" (1.10.46) toward Contemplation, Berowne's speech provides the rationalization for the men to abandon their "painful study" (2.2.23): "It is religion to be thus forsworn, / For charity itself fulfills the law, / And who can sever love from charity?" (4.3.337–39). Berowne makes an audacious defense of their love matches on religious grounds, insisting that the men have moved beyond the constraints of the biblical Old Law when in reality they've simply broken their own silly self-imposed precepts in the service of new romances.[61] The audience is asked to engage with Berowne's speech on at least two levels; they are both in it *and* above it, cringing along with the characters and mocking them too, enjoying the literal content of the men's romance woes even as they may be disgusted by their racism, and also enjoying the fact that all of it is, as it were, in double quotation marks, as a speech said on a stage by a character who is also performing authenticity. The central questions that Castiglione and Spenser ask about the difference between really being morally educated or simply playing the part are thus especially pertinent here, and the culmination of this scene allows for the reading of the men's development as either a genuine change of heart or mere verbal game playing. The possibility of two very different answers to the question of whether or not Berowne's argument is just empty rhetoric is affirmed by the fact that the 2009 Globe performance of the play directed by Dominic Dromgoole encouraged the audience to see it as ironic by including physical humor such as slaps when Longaville seemed to take his defense of their masculine heroism too seriously, while in the 2014 RSC performance, the face of Edward Bennett's Berowne streamed with tears as he delivered it.

Inset entertainments and the audience's lessons

Even though the four courtiers decide to revise their program of study into nonexistence, the play still offers audiences the opportunity to consider the relationship between theater and what it means to "fashion a gentleman ... in gentle discipline." The inset entertainments of the visiting Russians (impersonated by the quartet) and the Nine Worthies (impersonated by Armado, Moth, Costard, Holofernes, and Nathaniel) present the possibility that theater is only about pleasure at the same time that they prompt audience members to reflect on their own power to make meaning. In the first scene of the play, the men move readily from calling themselves "brave conquerors" (1.1.8) to casting about for "quick recreation" (1.1.159); in a replay of this, the four men quickly establish that being "soldiers" on "the field" of Love (4.3.340) means providing "entertainment" (4.3.347) for the women—the same word used by Holofernes to describe the presentation of the Nine Worthies: "some entertainment of time" (5.1.110–11). So, while in Spenser's Book 1 the movement toward charity requires a shift to an understanding of the proper role of pleasure, in *Love's Labour's Lost* the parodic version of this movement ("who can sever love from charity?") simply involves the four young men seeking the diversions that they judge best nurture romantic love: "We will with some strange pastime solace them, / Such as the shortness of the time can shape; / For revels, dances, masques and merry hours / Forerun fair Love, strewing her way with flowers" (4.3.351–54). The men's entertainments are designed to construct a pleasurable path toward love, just as Castiglione's courtier makes the path to learning pleasurable for his prince, "strawinge it over wyth sightlye flouers." While Spenser's Charissa "entertaynes" the Redcrosse Knight as part of her hospitable instruction (1.10.32), Shakespeare's four courtiers seek to make pleasure the path to more pleasure.

Although the men's portraying themselves as love-struck Russians for the entertainment of the ladies provides obvious comedic value both for the women and the audience, it also raises questions about interpretation and authenticity that are crucial to how the audience makes sense of the play. To begin, disguising themselves as Muscovites displays the men's failure of courtly savvy despite their professed intention to return to the ways of courtesy. Castiglione's text provides both useful advice for those engaging in role play and important insights into the mental habits of spectators, suggesting that what delights audiences is the *discrepancy* between the costume and the player, and that a disguise that is too close to the truth doesn't have the same value; if a prince should disguise himself as a prince, "the *pleasure* that the lookers on receyve at the noveltye of the matter should want a great deale, for it is no noveltie at all to any man for a prince to bee a prince" (2.11; emphasis mine). If this discrepancy between player and character is crucial for the audience's delight, the heroes of *Love's Labour's Lost* err in presenting themselves as lovesick young men who are ready to use their hyperbolic linguistic skill to make their cases ("Vouchsafe to show the sunshine of your face, / That we like savages may worship it" [5.2.201–02]). Even though the four men are admittedly not Russians, their disguise still comes too close to how the men actually see themselves, and the performance is thus too close to ostensible reality; indeed, Berowne's words as a Russian echo very closely his previous declaration of love in his own person in the eavesdropping scene: "Who sees the heavenly Rosaline / That, like a rude and savage man of Ind, / At the first opening of the gorgeous east, / Bows not his vassal head and, strucken blind, / Kisses the base ground with obedient breast?" (4.3.217–21). Berowne's excessive (and offensive) comparison of the courtly lovers to "savages" is presented both as a genuine private expression of his love and as a performed game of courteous courtship. The danger lies in taking away the ground for authenticity—as Castiglione goes on to say of the prince who poses as a prince, "beside that, doing in *sport* the very same he should do in good earnest whan neede required, it woulde take away his authoritye in deede and would appeere in lyke case to be play also" (2.11; emphasis mine). By pretending in *sport* to be true lovers (a term that Berowne himself will use as he complains that Boyet has "forestall[ed] their sport" [5.2.473]), the wooers make it hard to pass themselves off as true lovers in *fact*.

Throughout the final act of the play, the characters echo one another's references to inset entertainments as games, calling into question both the meaning of these performances within the play and the meaning of the play as a whole. So, for example, the Princess acknowledges that she understands the men's courtship as disguised Russians as insincere and will receive it in the same spirit that it is intended: "The effect of my intent is to cross theirs. / They do it but in mockery merriment, / And mock for mock is only my intent" (5.2.138–40). And Berowne later complains, "Here was a consent, / Knowing aforehand of our merriment, / To dash it like a Christmas comedy" (5.2.460–62), echoing the Princess's use of the term "merriment" as he characterizes his supposedly genuine courtship in theatrical terms. The fact that both the Princess and

Berowne refer to the wooing Russians as a "merriment" implies a shared recognition that they are all playing the same theatrical game, albeit not on the same team. While the four courtiers regard their impersonation of wooing Russians as a *path* to their romantic goals, the Princess sees it differently, as simply entertainment for its own sake. Even before the "Muscovites" make their entrance, she is ready to best them at their own game: "There's no such sport as sport by sport o'erthrown, / To make theirs ours and ours none but our own. / So shall we stay, mocking intended game, / And they, well mocked, depart away with shame" (5.2.153–56). For the Princess, the point of this game is the sport that it offers, not any enduring outcome; she will later refer to it simply as "pastimes ... and pleasant game" (5.2.360).[62]

The play links layers of performance, social distinction, and mockery, then; just as the four courtiers make Armado their "sport," the four ladies make "sport" of the four courtiers. The audience is also bidden to ask how they position themselves in this game of social identification and distinction as the play moves to the final presentation of the Nine Worthies, which Holofernes also refers to as "sport" (5.1.146) and which Berowne suggests will put the quartet in a good light by comparison: "'tis some policy / To have one show worse than the King's and his company" (5.2.510–11). Berowne's comment shows his failure to appreciate the extent to which he and his companions resemble the court outsiders they scorn, a point the play underscores with verbal echoes. In the eavesdropping scene, Berowne hypocritically and disgustedly compares his three friends' declarations of love to "infant play" (4.3.75) and degraded versions of the ancients playing at games, including "great Hercules whipping a gig"; in the Nine Worthies presentation, the young page Moth, who has been compared by Holofernes to an "infant" and told to go "whip" his "gig" (5.1.61–62), is assigned to play "Hercules in minority" (5.1.126). In short, the botched performance of the Nine Worthies is closer to the four lovers than they might willingly admit, and it also provokes a variety of reactions.

Like *Love's Labour's Lost* as a whole, the performance of the Nine Worthies both presents and undermines examples of masculine bravery, mocking the concept of exemplary models of heroism that is so central to Spenser's *Faerie Queene*. While Spenser's Satyrane and Briana learn by virtue of having served as audiences to disciplinary scenes, Shakespeare depicts audiences with more complicated reactions to the inset performances. One possibility is that, rather than imitating good examples, they take pleasure in failed performances. The Princess notes, "That sport best pleases that doth least know how— / Where zeal strives to content and the contents / Dies in the zeal of that which it presents; / Their form confounded makes most form in mirth, / When great things labouring perish in their birth" (5.2.514–18). Berowne calls these words "a right description of our sport" (5.2.519), and, with their suggestion of wasted labor, they also apply well to the play as a whole, gesturing to its title; the failed heroic performances of the Nine Worthies underscore just how much the men's own mock-heroic labors have miscarried.[63] Although Berowne is unable to profit from the ostensibly bad example of his lovesick peers in the eavesdropping scene, perhaps here he moves at least a little toward recognition of his own vain efforts.

The conclusion of the play continues to present the audience with multiple ways to respond even as it takes a contradictory attitude toward the four men's study of love. While Berowne claims that the men have learned something about using "honest plain words" (5.2.747), he also persists in the kind of verbal self-indulgence for which he mocks others. He asserts that the four courtiers have only "played foul play with our oaths" (5.2.750) because of the women's influence, and further claims that falsity to their oath is the men's only path to grace: "And even that falsehood, in itself a sin, / Thus purifies itself and turns to grace" (5.2.769–70). Earlier Berowne casuistically conflates religious charity and romantic love; here he similarly draws on a discourse of religious "grace" when he means something much closer to romantic favors and secular courtesy. Indeed, even as he suggests (twice!) that the women's "heavenly eyes" (5.2.761, 763) have led to the men's genuine love, he also acknowledges the playful, theatrical nature of that love, comparing it to a "child, skipping and vain" (5.2.755) and a jester's costume, a "parti-coated presence of loose love / Put on by us" (5.2.760–61). Berowne's vacillating accounts of the men's feelings for the ladies do not convince the Princess, who insists on her own interpretation of the men's endeavors: "We have received your letters full of love, / … And in our maiden counsel rated them / At courtship, pleasant jest and *courtesy*, / As bombast and as lining to the time. / But more devout than this in our respects / Have we not been; and therefore met your loves / In their own fashion, like a *merriment*" (5.2.771, 773–78; emphasis mine).[64] She thus suggests that although the men's performance of love was not convincing, they *have* succeeded in presenting the jesting entertainment that she equates, dismissively, with courtesy.

While the ladies judge that the men have continued to err in their romantic pursuits, they also contend that the men must learn lessons in courtesy, particularly the need for decorum and attention to their audiences. The King's desire to brush past the fact that it is the wrong time to pursue their love interests ("though the mourning brow of progeny / Forbid the smiling courtesy of love" [5.2.738–39]) is unsuccessful, with the women insisting that the men refocus their attention to the power of the audience to determine meaning. Mere oaths will not be enough to convince them; the men must experience penance over time to teach them that courtesy is not just performance, but a dynamic exchange between performer and audience. As Rosaline puts it in instructing Berowne to spend a year telling jokes in a hospital, he must learn that "a jest's prosperity lies in the ear / Of him that hears it, never in the tongue / Of him that makes it" (5.2.849–51). Her proposed program of true learning means that Berowne must put away his "idle scorns" if they fail to please his audience, which will make her "right joyful of your reformation" (5.2.853, 857). Rosaline may in time come to resemble Spenser's Una in her joy at the hero's progress, but that is outside the scope of the performance, as Berowne metatheatrically observes that his yearlong penance is "too long for a play" (5.2.866). He nonetheless acknowledges Rosaline's instruction about the audience's power in asserting "Our wooing doth not end like an old play: / Jack hath not Jill. These ladies' courtesy / Might well have made our sport a comedy" (5.2.862–64). Though Berowne points to the lessons that he and his mates may be beginning to learn about an audience's power, he underscores, yet again, the "sport" of their whole venture. While Berowne rhetorically claims at multiple points that the men are undergoing a process of self-improvement in which romantic love and divine charity become one, the play ultimately emphasizes that that sort of talk may be nothing more than a courtly and theatrical game. Still, at the same time that he raises conflicting possibilities about the meaning of the play, he points to the audience's role in determining it.

The play is, then, doing something more interesting than merely implying that our four young men should brush up on their Castiglione, Ascham, or Spenser; in representing courtesy on stage, and in enacting it through its transactions with the audience, it also illuminates the paradoxical nature of courtesy by prompting a range of contradictory emotions and thought processes in its audience. The audiences of *Love's Labour's Lost* may find themselves mirrored in the onstage spectators as they are called on to determine the meaning of the play, and are therefore encouraged to turn that same kind of watchful gaze on themselves, recognizing even more clearly their choices as spectators. Thus, after the barrage of insults he receives for his performance of Judas Maccabaeus, the pedant Holofernes berates the onstage audience of the Nine Worthies for being "not generous, not gentle, not humble" (5.2.623), urging a link between being courteous and being an appreciative audience member. The audience is charged throughout to recognize how courtesy is characterized by *both* gentle humility and nasty snobbishness, and thus to decide on its own reactions to the play.

In making their assessments, audiences may also weigh how the play treats *them*. As Berowne underscores, the men's wooing, and by extension *Love's Labour's Lost* itself, do not end as one might expect. Not only do our four young men break their oaths to one another, the play also breaks its implicit contract with the audience when it withholds the resolution expected from a comedy. For most of the play, audiences are rewarded for not taking it seriously— yet at the end, they are also punished for getting too caught up in the action. Like the courted ladies, audiences may think that the play itself is nothing more than a "merriment"—until it stops being one. Both the 2009 Globe Production and the 2013 American Shakespeare Center production directed by Jim Warren delighted audiences with increasingly frenzied performances of fun (including, at the Globe, a food fight that escalated into actors running out into the audience) before catching them up short with the arrival of Marcadé and the announcement of the Princess's father's death. Yet while *Love's Labour's Lost* may be seen as playing a discourteous trick on audiences familiar with the rules of comedy, it also offers pleasing humor, at least to some. The title page of the 1598 quarto version emphasizes the pleasure it affords audiences in calling it "a pleasant conceited comedy," a view that is in accord with audience

member and lovelorn poet Robert Tofte, who wrote in a poem published in 1598, "To every one (save me) twas *Comicall*."[65] Tofte's
assessment of the play as a "Jest" to others, but a "Plague" to himself, offers support for a view of the play as a comic success even as
it underscores Rosaline's point about the power of the audience to
determine meaning.[66]

At the same time, the play also celebrates the pleasures of failure. In the first instance, the audience will certainly enjoy the men's
failure to pursue their education more than its success—it is hard
to imagine an interesting play based on a diligent program of
reading![67] But the play's refusal to live up to the generic expectations of comedy may also cause delight. In that sense, the men's
broken oaths to scholarship, and the play's apparently broken trust
with the audience, may cause just as much pleasure, or more, than
had everything proceeded according to plan. The audience is asked
to join in a theatrical game as they recognize that the performance presented to them may succeed as a courteous jest precisely
through its presentation of a failure to convince of its authenticity.
Like a contemporary British pantomime that entertains by revel-
ing in its ostensible ineptitude, the play asks its audiences to ponder how to determine the line between a botched performance and
a savvy presentation of humility that is anything but. As spectators accustomed to thinking about the relationship between artifice
and social performance, Shakespeare's first audiences would have
been well prepared to wrestle with the multiple overlapping ways
in which *Love's Labour's Lost* presents exposed and hidden artfulness. The courteous performances of the four "brave conquerors"
of Navarre would seem to entail not so much a skilled display of
sprezzatura, but rather a complete bungling of their efforts. In presenting the failure of love's labors, however, the entire play also
delights its audiences with its own pleasingly self-deprecating performance of *sprezzatura* even as it exposes the techniques of its artifice. *Love's Labour's Lost* engages with the notion of *sprezzatura*
in a complicated way, revealing rather than hiding its artfulness in
metatheatrical moments, yet simultaneously teasing its audiences'
minds by presenting itself self-deprecatingly as a failure of a play,
requiring audience members to come to their own assessment of
it as they attempt to sort out the contradictory evidence that it
presents. The play refuses to be pinned down, oscillating between

pleasure and displeasure, courtesy and the failure of courtesy, and in doing so invites its audiences to consider the different possible relationships between courtesy and learning. Needless to say, that very reflection on the complexity and slipperiness of courtesy is in part what the play teaches. Spenser's explorations of instruction through spectatorship bring the audience *into* the fold as part of the poem's discipline; the poem encourages them to become students *like* Satyrane and Briana. Shakespeare's play, in contrast, proposes a rupture between the characters and audience. Armado's closing words, "You that way, we this way," if directed to the audience, may further reinforce the disconnect between player and spectators (5.2.919). Yet precisely by acknowledging the play's lack of a standard ending and the way in which it might have failed to satisfy its audience, the metatheatrical words of both Berowne and Armado also put them on the same page as the audience with their shared acknowledgement of a theatrical game.

Spenser's poem and Shakespeare's play take seriously Castiglione's proposition, which is also filtered through Ascham, that pedagogy based in pleasure is the most effective kind, with each offering critiques of that proposition for different purposes. In both, the movement from the coercion of the word (rules, precepts, oaths) gives way to an experimentation with forms of pedagogy that emphasize the refining force of theatrical spectatorship. While Spenser's poem suggests the efficacious role that such spectatorship can play in the movement toward moral discipline, Shakespeare's play instead offers a parody of the educational function of theater. Castiglione's text works hard to show that the courtier's self-promotion and recreational pursuits are not in conflict with his moral role as educator of the prince, whereas Shakespeare's *Love's Labour's Lost* insists on the difficulty of reconciling pedagogy and pleasure, showing that the four young men's desire for scholarly glory is incompatible with the more attractive pull toward recreation and romantic love. The play also offers less straightforward lessons for its audience about the importance of their own judgment. Castiglione's veneer of idealism is punctured for comic effect in Shakespeare's play at the same time that it punctures the epic aspirations of a pedagogical poem like Spenser's through its send-up of the Nine Worthies. Nonetheless, I want to underscore what *The Book of the Courtier*, *The Faerie Queene*, and *Love's Labour's Lost* have in common: they all work by enlisting readers and audience members in mental games, challenging them to think about their relationship to audiences depicted within the works, and all three also challenge readers and audiences to consider what their reading and viewing tell them about their own identities.

Notes

1 Rebecca Bushnell, *Culture of Teaching*, 17. More recently, Joe Moshenska has also called attention to how the experience of "play" in reading Spenser's text overlaps with serious reflection, as readers are encouraged to be aware of their own responses to the poem; they "both delight in it and wonder at their delight" ("Spenser at Play," 29).

2 Jane Grogan, *Exemplary Spenser*, 11.

3 Isabel MacCaffrey, *Spenser's Allegory*, 8. MacCaffrey insists that Spenser's allegory "is turned directly upon us, the readers, urging introspection into our own ways of knowing" (45).

4 Grogan, *Exemplary Spenser*, 12, 16, and 19.

5 A. Leigh DeNeef emphasizes the importance of the reader in arguing that "his reading is a metaphoric quest" (*Spenser and the Motives of Metaphor*, 142). While Castiglione's text offers in dialogue form a variety of perspectives on the best practices of social life, Spenser's poem requires the reader to grapple with contradictory and conflicting messages; as Paul Alpers argues, "The genius of Spenser's poetry is that it holds in focus a variety of moral truths, even when they might conflict if they were structured as a moral judgment" (*Poetry of* The Faerie Queene, 148). See also A. C. Hamilton, *Structure of Allegory*, and Jonathan Goldberg, *Endlesse Worke*.

6 Jeff Dolven, *Scenes of Instruction*, 3 and 8. On Spenser's increasing skepticism about examples, see 135–71; on the poem's "refusal to teach" (234), see 207–37.

7 Corey McEleney, *Futile Pleasures*, 4 and 121. For the full discussion of Book 6, see 102–26.

8 Jeff Dolven, *Scenes of Instruction*, 229–30.

9 McEleney, *Futile Pleasures*, 105 and 82.

10 Dolven, *Scenes of Instruction*, 233.

11 Dolven, *Scenes of Instruction*, 137.

12 Grogan, *Exemplary Spenser*, 68.

13 Criticism does, of course, acknowledge the possibility that Shakespeare's plays lead to learning. Robert Hapgood emphasizes

Shakespeare's "creative guidance" of his audience's responses, asserting that "responsive members of Shakespeare's audience, like his
characters, will *develop* in the course of the play" (*Shakespeare the
Theatre-Poet*, viii and 223). Darryll Grantley offers a wide-ranging
exploration of the "prominence of drama in social pedagogy" (*Wit's
Pilgrimage*, 5).

14 Judith Owens, *Emotional Settings*.
15 Lynn Enterline, *Shakespeare's Schoolroom*, 1.
16 Enterline, *Shakespeare's Schoolroom*, 25 and 40. Enterline connects
   the schoolboy's self-division to Berger's concept of the "internal audi-
   tor" as developed in his *Imaginary Audition*.
17 Dolven notes the frequency with which a Renaissance "poem is bound
   to the double business of staging a scene of instruction and instructing
   its reader" (*Scenes of Instruction*, 10).
18 Crucial to Grogan's argument is the reader's recognition of the poet's
   craft: "The narrative intelligence that Spenser tries to develop in his
   readers is one that is prepared to participate in these complex epis-
   temological structures, as well as notice the author's poetic contriv-
   ance of them" (*Exemplary Spenser*, 67).
19 Critics have differed in the extent to which they see Ascham as allied
   with the court, with Richard Helgerson (*Forms of Nationhood*,
   25–40) and Melanie Ord ("Classical and Contemporary Italy in
   Roger Ascham's *The Scholemaster* (1570)") emphasizing their
   differences and Linda Bradley Salamon emphasizing the overlap
   between Ascham's views and Castiglione's ("*The Courtier* and *The
   Scholemaster*").
20 I cite throughout the edition of *The Schoolmaster* edited by Lawrence
   V. Ryan. While Ascham's project involves some criticism of nobility ("and therefore ye deserve the greater blame that commonly the
   meaner men's children come to be the wisest counselors and greatest
   doers in the weighty affairs of this realm" [40]), it is important to note
   the limits to the egalitarianism of his educational model.
21 Ascham's discussion of the dangers of Italy takes place in close prox-
   imity to his warnings about chivalric romance, suggesting a link
   between the two. On Ascham's disdain for romance and the implications of this for Spenser's choice of genre, see Helgerson, *Forms of
   Nationhood*, 40–59.
22 Though Helgerson does not specifically link Castiglione and Ascham,
   he does note that "the deliberate fashioning of oneself and of others is
   what *The Schoolmaster* is all about" (*Forms of Nationhood*, 29).
23 See McEleney, *Futile Pleasures*, 70. Linda Salamon emphasizes that
   both Ascham and Castiglione are engaged in the project of civic
   humanism, suggesting the value to the state of a proper education

(*"The Courtier"*). As part of his longer project on "the erotics of male knowledge transactions," Alan Stewart argues that *The Schoolmaster* is "a book about the social assimilation of the pedagogic function and the pedagogic industry," considering how the text itself both documents and forms a part of social "transactions" (*Close Readers*, 116, 109, and 112). On the role of humanism in supporting a "new elite," see also Anthony Grafton and Lisa Jardine, *From Humanism to the Humanities*, xii–xvi.

24 Ian Smith cogently points out the imbrication of Ascham's elitist project and English imperialism: "we identify Ascham's polemic on the need for gentleness in instruction as a model of the benign pedagogue as benevolent colonial master" (*Race and Rhetoric*, 119).

25 As Owens aptly notes, in Ascham "the emphasis falls not on faults to be amended but on allurements to learning" (*Emotional Settings*, 37).

26 See also Melanie Ord, "Classical and Contemporary Italy," 212, on Ascham's caution in recommending Castiglione.

27 In Hotspur's recounting, the courtier is "neat and trimly dressed, / Fresh as a bridegroom" (*Henry IV, Part 1*, 1.3.33–34). Note that Ascham will also himself use the term "trimly" disparagingly, as when he criticizes mothers' preferences that their sons "live trimly" rather than be good counselors (40).

28 McEleney, *Futile Pleasures*, 71. On Ascham's "use of the word 'pleasure' in implicitly opposed contexts," see also Ord, "Classical and Contemporary Italy," 206.

29 McEleney, *Futile Pleasures*, 72–82.

30 On the shared emphasis on judgment in Castiglione and Ascham, see especially Salamon, *"The Courtier."*

31 Helgerson, *Forms of Nationhood*, 28–59.

32 Robert Matz, *Defending Literature*, 121–22. Greenblatt notes of the destruction of the Bower, "A pleasure that serves its own end, that claims to be self-justifying rather than instrumental, purposeless rather than generative, is immoderate and must be destroyed, lest it undermine the power that Spenser worships" (*Renaissance Self-Fashioning*, 176–77).

33 In two complementary articles, William A. Oram argues that Spenser's disappointed hopes for playing a role at court meant that after 1591 he sought readers other than "the queen and her court" ("Spenser's Audiences," 516), and also that Spenser was "forced to recognize that the audience for which he was writing was not listening, but to recognize as well his dependence on that audience," thus creating an "ambivalence about [*The Faerie Queene*'s] courtly audience" ("Spenser in Search of an Audience," 24 and 36). Michael Murrin suggests that Spenser "had in mind a larger, more variegated

audience than the aristocracy alone" ("Audience of *The Faerie Queene*," 9).

34 Jonathan Goldberg, *Endlesse Worke*, 28.

35 On Ascham and Elyot as owners and readers of *The Courtier*, see Peter Burke, *Fortunes of the* Courtier, 76–77 and 86.

36 I cite the edition of S. E. Lehmberg.

37 On the reader's role in following the examples of the text, and the complications that this may involve, see especially Timothy Hampton, *Writing from History*.

38 On the ways in which the first canto of the poem draws in the reader, see Judith H. Anderson, "'The Hard Begin,'" 41–48.

39 On the correspondence of Redcrosse and Sansjoy, see Maureen Quilligan, *The Language of Allegory*, 257.

40 On Spenser's juxtaposition of these three mountains, see Carol V. Kaske, *Spenser's Biblical Poetics*, 38–41. Kaske notes that the contrast between Mount Sinai and the Mount of Olives is a contrast between Mosaic law and the law written on the heart.

41 Frank Whigham notes the difficulty of distinguishing Calidore and Crudor in this episode, arguing that "moral disparity recedes before martial resemblance" (*Ambition and Privilege*, 79).

42 See also Dolven on Calidore's "sententious sermon" (*Scenes of Instruction*, 220). Dolven remarks on the strangeness of having a character named Crudor reform, and suggests that he is changed in the same way Briana is; my own reading emphasizes the difference between the two, which perhaps goes some way in explaining his name. Here too we might recall Patricia Akhimie's work on the creation of characters who are apparently beyond instruction. Paul Suttie draws attention to the importance of force in Calidore's conversion of Briana (*Self-Interpretation in* The Faerie Queene, 197–98).

43 See Northrop Frye, *Anatomy of Criticism*, 169. Frye specifically adduces the men's oath in *Love's Labour's Lost* as another example of an "absurd law."

44 Readers who have emphasized the parody at work in the play's presentation of both pedagogy and Christianity include Rosalie L. Colie, *Shakespeare's Living Art*, 32; Louis Montrose, "'Sport by Sport O'erthrown'"; and Charlotte Scott, *Shakespeare and the Idea of the Book*, 93–94. Darryll Grantley suggests that the aspirations of both the noble and the middle-class characters are the targets of satire (*Wit's Pilgrimage*, 188–94). My own emphasis is specifically on the vision of pedagogy as pleasure modeled by Castiglione and Spenser.

45 In his introduction to the Arden edition, H. R. Woudhuysen suggests a possible date range of 1594 to 1598, with 1594 being a strong but not certain possibility (59–61).

46 See Thomas M. Greene, "*Love's Labour's Lost*," especially 318–19; Montrose, "'Sport by Sport O'erthrown,'" 538; and Donatella Baldini, "The Play of the Courtier," 9.

47 All citations of *Love's Labour's Lost* are from the edition by H. R. Woudhuysen.

48 Montrose, "'Sport by Sport O'erthrown,'" 530. Montrose insists on the "reciprocal relation" between play and audience (531).

49 Robert Matz, *Defending Literature*, 111.

50 Burke, *Fortunes of the* Courtier, 71.

51 Patricia Akhimie, *Shakespeare and the Cultivation of Difference*.

52 See note to *Love's Labour's Lost* 1.1.72.

53 See Colie, *Shakespeare's Living Art*, 33, on the play's relationship to and divergence from Castiglione, including this scene. In the phrase from the play that gives her book its title, Colie notes an echo of the self-fashioning project outlined in *The Courtier*. Grantley also notes the characters' divergence from *sprezzatura* (*Wit's Pilgrimage*, 193–94). On the play's emphasis on the asceticism of study and depiction of breaches of decorum, see Tara Collington and Philip Collington, "'The Time When ....'"

54 Here we might also recall the "assehead" Bottom's aping of courtly discourse while he is waited on by the fairies in *A Midsummer Night's Dream* 3.1.

55 Charlotte Scott also notes the similarity (*Shakespeare and the Idea of the Book*, 84).

56 See Erika T. Lin, *Shakespeare and the Materiality of Performance*, 59, and Jeremy Lopez, *Theatrical Convention and Audience Response*, 2 and 34.

57 Lisa Zunshine, *Why We Read Fiction*, 47 and 50. Zunshine does note in passing that live performance, with its reliance on "the physical presence of actors," offers challenges to audience's theory of mind that differ from the novel (23).

58 Lukas Erne's *Shakespeare as Literary Dramatist* (14), drew my attention to this text. Erne also recounts Drummond's donation of his library to the University of Edinburgh (*Shakespeare and the Book Trade*, 195–96); I am grateful for the opportunity to consult the book on site.

59 This exchange was given special resonance in the 2015 production of the play at the Stratford Festival, in which Rosaline was portrayed by the Black actor Sarah Afful.

60 Yunah Kae has recently argued that this play "explores and advances a racialized theory of poesy as a masculine property of whiteness" ("'Light in Darkness Lies,'" 55).

61 Woudhuysen notes the echo of Romans 13.8, pointing to love as the fulfillment of the law.

62 On the women as instructors of the men, and the critique of gender roles that this entails, see Kathryn M. Moncrief, " 'Teach Us, Sweet Madam.' " Baldini notes the parallel between *The Courtier* and the play in their contradictory treatment of women's roles ("The Play of the Courtier," 13).

63 Greene also connects these two performances ("*Love's Labour's Lost*," 323).

64 Her reference to "merriment" here echoes her previous greeting to Marcadé: "thou interruptest our merriment" (5.2.712).

65 The poem is included in Woudhuysen's introduction to *Love's Labour's Lost*, 77.

66 Collington and Collington note that this poem shows "how individual perception reflects the reception of dramatic genre" (" 'The Time When ...,' " 787). Charles Whitney likewise emphasizes Tofte's personal response to the play (*Early Responses*, 142–44).

67 As David Ives' Vanda says in *Venus in Fur*, "Just hand out library cards, why dontcha."

3

Honorable action upstaged by theatrical wordplay in *The Faerie Queene* and *Much Ado About Nothing*

Immediately before presenting a tragic tale that may well have inspired Shakespeare, Spenser's *Faerie Queene* depicts a comic encounter between Belphoebe and Braggadocchio, the braggart warrior with a "flowing toung." Braggadocchio's primary concern is his reputation, and the "thought of honour" doesn't enter his mind as he steals Guyon's horse (2.3.4). This theft enables him to present himself as a "knight," causing Belphoebe to associate him with those who "honor haue pursewd / Through deeds of armes and prowesse martiall" (2.3.37). But Braggadocchio is a talker more than a doer; he is a "vaineglorious man" who believes that he can attain advancement "without desert of gentle deed" (2.3.10), and Belphoebe soon recognizes his true character when he responds to her attack on courtly frivolities by making a misguided pass at her. Guyon's stolen horse assesses his inferiority even more quickly, viewing Braggadocchio as a "base burden" (2.3.46). As the narrator comments, his poor horsemanship reveals that "he had not trayned bene in cheualree," as easily perceived by the stolen horse he rides, which exceeds him in virtue: "Which well that valiaunt courser did discerne" (2.3.46). The comic incongruity between Braggadocchio's words and deeds points toward two different understandings of honor: Belphoebe's view, in which honor is linked to effort in both battle and books ("Abroad in armes, at home in studious kynd / Who seekes with painfull toile, shal honor soonest fynd" [2.3.40]), and Braggadocchio's view, in which the mere trappings of honor, achieved through verbal impersonation, are adequate. As Robert Matz has noted, the link Spenser's Belphoebe makes between arms and study here is itself a provocative one, taking place at a time of "transition from a warrior to an educated civil elite."[1] David Quint has also argued that Spenser's Braggadocchio functions as a representative of "the newfangled vanity of the court" in contrast to an older model of chivalric honor such as Shakespeare's Hotspur; for a figure like Braggadocchio, Quint suggests, "clothes literally make the man."[2]

The contrast in *Faerie Queene* 2.3 between two related models of masculine honor—chivalry, in which valiant deeds that overcome all challenges are the primary source of approbation, and courtesy, in which reputations are maintained through constant attention to social self-presentation according to changing circumstances—is comic, but it also highlights how the discourse of courtesy organized itself around the idea of the impossibility of a stable identity. In his seminal reading of Book 2's conclusion, Greenblatt usefully emphasizes the tension between restraint and "excess" in the construction of contemporary masculinity, suggesting that "the fashioning of a gentleman ... depends upon the imposition of control over inescapable immoderate sexual impulses that ... must constantly recur: the discriminations upon which a virtuous and gentle discipline is based are forever in danger of collapsing."[3] In Greenblatt's model of Guyon's destruction of the Bower of Bliss, even "a triumphant act of virtuous violence" is insufficient, because "each self-constituting act is haunted by inadequacy and loss."[4] Additionally, Robert Matz has emphasized how the anxiety about pleasure and leisure in the Bower, which Greenblatt links to colonial projects, could also be a critique of a "courtly ethos of leisure and consumption."[5] Indeed, as we have seen in the previous chapter, both Spenser and Shakespeare display persistent interest in the relationship between pleasure and education. My reading of *Faerie Queene* 2.4 in this chapter in conversation with *Much Ado About Nothing* is designed to contribute to ongoing conversations about what Mark Breitenberg has aptly termed "anxious masculinity," placing special emphasis on how both Spenser's and Shakespeare's texts are preoccupied with the variable relationships between words and actions in contemporary expressions of courteous masculinity.[6]

While Spenser's Calidore blithely asserts in Book 6 that "seldome yet did liuing creature see, / That curtesie and manhood euer disagree" (6.3.40), the works of Spenser and Shakespeare nonetheless underscore that the relationship between courtesy and masculinity was a vexed one. In Spenser's satire *Prosopopoia: or Mother Hubberds Tale* (published in 1591), a mule offers cynical advice to an ape on how one should seek favor as a courtier: "with a good bold face, / And with big words, and with a stately pace, / That men may thinke of you in generall, / That to be in you, which is not at all" (645–48). The danger of a focus on the regard of others, achieved primarily through "big words," is the creation of a masculinity that is a series of apparently honorable impersonations with no authentic core. As Gavin Alexander has suggested, Spenser's prosopopoeia, in which an ape poses as a courtier, who is himself defined by his poses, provides a particularly useful illustration of the way in which "it may not be possible to distinguish selfhood from the words we speak."[7]

Faerie Queene 2.3 demonstrates the acute cultural awareness of performance at a time of increasing social emphasis on self-fashioning through courtly language. In doing so, it prepares the way for the following canto, in which Spenser's depiction of the tragic tale of Phedon and Claribell transforms Ariosto's account of chivalric action into a study of theatrical subterfuge. At the outset of Canto 2.4, the narrator both emphasizes and troubles the distinction between actions and verbal performance:

> In braue poursuitt of honorable deed,
>> There is I know not (what) great difference
>> Betweene the vulgar and the noble seed,
>> Which vnto things of valorous pretence
>> Seemes to be borne by natiue influence;
>> As feates of armes, and loue to entertaine,
>> But chiefly skill to ride seemes a science
>> Proper to gentle blood; some others faine
> To menage steeds, as did this vaunter; but in vaine. (1)

On the one hand, the narrator asserts a clear-cut difference both between "the vulgar and the noble seed" and between their actions and those of imposters, yet his reference to "things of valorous pretence" undercuts the distinction. As the *OED* notes, "pretence" can refer to "an intention, purpose, or design," which appears to be the narrator's primary meaning here, but it can also suggest the more familiar contemporary definition of "false, feigned, or hypocritical … show," and indeed the *OED* here cites a quotation from later in *The Faerie Queene* in reference to Braggadocchio's "boastfull vaine pretense" (4.5.23).[8] Even as the narrator suggests a clear-cut distinction between "feates of armes" and the vain, feigning vaunts of Braggadoccio, this binary is troubled by the question of performance. This is indeed apt for a society in which, as Jean Howard and Phyllis Rackin have noted, "If a man's place in the social hierarchy had to be achieved and secured by his own efforts, any claims to authority required that both social status and gender status had to be sustained in performance."[9] More generally, Judith Butler's argument that "gender identity … is performatively constituted by the very 'expressions' that are said to be its results" is an important reminder that the overlapping traditions of chivalry and courtesy both depend on the imitation of socially constructed models of masculinity.[10]

In this chapter, I will argue that Spenser's representation in *Faerie Queene* 2.4 of a masculinity defined by its reaction to others' role-playing significantly informs Shakespeare's depiction of Claudio and his milieu in *Much Ado About Nothing*. Both texts feature young men who falsely believe that they have witnessed scenes of sexual betrayal, and both use this plot device to explore the relationship between unstable masculine identity and social honor. As we have seen, Phedon's canto opens with a reference to honorable endeavor ("braue poursuitt of honorable deed" [2.4.1]), while at the outset of *Much Ado* Leonato states, "I find here that Don Pedro hath bestowed much honour on a young Florentine called Claudio" (1.1.9–11).[11] Even as these texts foreground the importance of masculine honor attained through deeds, they also present male characters who define themselves through words and their subjection to the feminine as they conceive it. Spenser's episode anticipates Shakespeare's concern with the relationship between identity and theatricality, portraying in Phedon's character an unrestrained vulnerability to misleading appearances, devoid of any "honorable deed," that is replicated to a great degree in *Much Ado About Nothing*. Indeed, as Shakespeare reworks Spenser's text, his own response to his sources continues even further the shift of focus from actions to words initiated by Spenser, but in both texts, acts of verbal deception and storytelling establish a culture of role-playing in which honor depends on the preservation of a persona amidst shifting circumstances. In depicting extreme forms of linguistic impersonation, Spenser and Shakespeare emphasize the close ties between role-playing and masculine honor, revealing the dangers of a society in which the perception of social performances shapes reality.

While Spenser's tragic tale of Phedon and Claribell in *Faerie Queene* 2.4 has long been acknowledged as one possible source of Shakespeare's *Much Ado About Nothing*, the connections between the two texts bear re-examination. Their relationship is admittedly complicated by a number of competing versions of the Claudio-Hero plot that Shakespeare is likely to have consulted, especially Ariosto's 1532 *Orlando Furioso* (translated by John Harington in 1591) and Bandello's 1554 *Novelle*. And some possible sources may be lost; most tantalizing of these is *Ariodante and Genevora*, performed by the Merchant Taylors' Boys in 1583.[12] Nonetheless, I argue that the available evidence in Spenser's and Shakespeare's texts reveals a sustained exploration of a masculine inability to act independently and claim ownership of one's actions. This critical depiction of a masculine lack of authenticity and agency distinguishes *Faerie Queene* 2.4 and *Much Ado* from other treatments of this tale.

As both authors adapt their sources, and especially as Shakespeare responds to Spenser, they trace the cultural movement away from chivalrous action and toward theatrical self-presentation, registering this common concern at the level of genre as well as in small details of imagery and phrasing. Crucially, Shakespeare's text converts some plot devices from *Faerie Queene* 2.4 into wordplay, showing a deep engagement with Spenser's tragic depiction of disavowed masculine agency and the replacement of heroic actions with words and subterfuge. I will take seriously J. B. Lethbridge's suggestion that "Shakespeare's borrowing is likely to be single-word intensive," examining the shared resonances of specific terms across both texts.[13] I argue that *Faerie Queene* 2.4 and *Much Ado About Nothing* persistently expose the loss of agency that afflicts male characters who see themselves as players, spectators, and the objects of others' actions, revealing the costs of maintaining the appearance of masculine honor in a culture obsessed with impersonation.[14] The unsettling aspects of the ostensibly comic *Much Ado About Nothing*, and especially its tendency to offer role-playing as a replacement for more decisive action, may well arise from

Shakespeare's engagement with Spenser's tragic parallel. Spenser's text emphasizes the tragic possibilities of theatrical models of masculine honor, while Shakespeare suggests both the costs and creative possibilities of lives composed of linguistic performance.

Phedon's tragic spectatorship

In his account of the "civilizing process," Norbert Elias traces a movement away from frequent violence and toward greater calculation and foresight through the formation and centralization of the courts. Through what Elias refers to as "the courtization of the warriors," subjects who were used to wielding violence as a means of maintaining their status found themselves in the position of competing through words and self-presentation.[15] More recently, Keith Thomas has likewise emphasized the shift in the early modern period toward "increasing readiness of the nobility and gentry to adopt the ethic of civility, and, later, of politeness as a way of modifying the more assertive notions of honor, military prowess, and superiority of lineage that had dominated aristocratic culture in earlier ages."[16] Still, even as courtesy books, by their very nature, emphasized the importance of self-creation through language, they registered the importance of ostensibly manly deeds, suggesting the tension in the early modern period between advancement through courtly and battlefield honor.

The Courtier insists throughout on the connection between manliness and action, at the same time emphasizing that action should be well controlled. In Book 1, Count Lodovico suggests that "feates of armes" should be "the principall and true profession of a Courtyer" (1.17), while in Book 2, Federico insists that a "gentleman that is of prowesse and well seene in armes" should engage in "little speaking, muche dooing" (2.7). He goes on to emphasize that the best sort of young man is "a man at armes" who has "a certayne sagenesse in him and few woordes," who, characterized by "mylde beehavyour," is "sturred, not of wrathe but of judgemente" (2.16). In Book 4, Ottaviano goes even further, explaining how the courtier's pursuits run the risk of being merely "lightnesse and vanitie" if all he is occupied with is "meerie talke and such other matters belonginge to enterteinment of women and love" which "womannish the mindes" (4.4). As explored in Chapter 1, in order for the courtier's efforts to avoid being "vaine" (4.4), he must engage his attention toward the manly end of the instruction of the prince in virtue, including acquiring "valiauntnesse of cour- age" (4.5). Ottaviano makes a close connection between temper- ance and manliness, asserting that "of temperance arrise manie other vertues: for whan a minde is in tune with this harmonie, by the meane of reason he easely receiveth afterward true manlinesse" (4.18) as he creates a model of "true manlines, which maketh the minde voide from all passions" (4.28). In Ottaviano's idealizing model, Aristotle serves as an example of a "perfect Courtier," one who made Alexander "most wise, most manlie, moste continent, and a true morall Philospher, not in woordes onelye, but in deedes" (4.47). Following J. L. Austin, we can recognize that the text's fre- quent distinction between words and deeds is too neat, as words may also be actions, and especially so in a dialogue that is obsessed with the idea of performative self-creation.[17] At the same time, the difference between words and actions is emphasized so frequently in this and other Renaissance texts that it was clearly a distinction that made sense and mattered to contemporary readers.

The prefatory materials to George Pettie's translation of Stefano Guazzo's *Civil Conversation* similarly insist on the importance of arms while also underscoring the value of the arts of language. Pettie's dedicatory letter to his translation praises the "manly prow- esse" of Lady Norris's sons, comparing them to Alexander the Great as they "seeke newe Countries, and newe worldes to shewe their valiancie in," and going on to praise the "valiaunt deedes" of the Norris family. And in the Preface to the Readers Pettie apolo- gizes, however formulaically, for the publication of a book by one whose "profession should chiefely be armes." He then goes on to offer a defense of the kind of training in the verbal arts his book will give to the gentleman warrior. Pettie's words offer a suitable preface to Guazzo's book as a whole, which emphasizes at the outset the value and even healing powers of human conversation in society, as well as its ostensible dangers—including that "a Carpet knight cor- rupteth & effeminateth a valiant man" (16v). As *The Book of the Courtier* and *Civil Conversation* demonstrate in complementary ways, contemporary treatments of courtesy continue to emphasize the importance of battlefield honor even as they are premised on theatrical self-creation—including, of course, the self-creation at work in literary authorship and the poses of book dedications.

As *The Faerie Queene* moves from Canto 2.3 to 2.4, the juxtaposition of Braggadocchio's comical performance of knightliness with Phedon's unwitting participation in a tragic drama demonstrates the vulnerability of masculine honor when it is based primarily on reaction to verbal impersonation rather than on goal-directed action. While the Phedon episode is framed with references to honor, in the embedded tale itself the term is exclusively used in Philemon's false accusation of Claribell: "That Lady whom I had to me assynd, / Had both distaind her honorable blood, / And eke the faith, which she to me did bynd" (22). In that sense, honor figures in this episode primarily by its lack, both in Phedon's fears about Claribell and in his intemperate response to those fears. Phedon's story reveals the difficulty of preserving a stable sense of self in a milieu saturated with both theatricality and latent rage. When Guyon and the Palmer first meet Phedon, he is being tormented by Furor, whose "force was vaine, and strooke more often wyde, / Then at the aymed marke, which he had eyde" (7). Guyon and Furor mirror one another through the poem's theatrical metaphors; Furor's "currish play" (8) is matched by Guyon's own efforts "to maintaine his part" (9), and it is only with the Palmer's help that this "madman" (6) is bound with "both his feet in fetters to an yron rack" (14). Furor, here compared to a "blindfold Bull" (7) in parallel to an emblematic tradition that portrayed him as wearing a blindfold,[18] anticipates the lack of focused, independent vision that will be central to Phedon's tale. Once Occasion and Furor have been subdued, Phedon recounts how his friend Philemon betrayed him with a manufactured spectacle of his beloved's infidelity.

In its allegorical portrait of raging misdirection, Phedon's tale creates a strong contrast with its source, Ariosto's *Orlando Furioso* 4.51–6.16, in which characters achieve social rewards by completing brave deeds. While the knights of *Orlando Furioso* are hardly immune to the passions of love or rage, as the poem's title indicates, Ariosto's depiction of the tale of Ariodante and Ginevra emphasizes an honor derived from a valorous masculinity that surmounts impediments in order to achieve its aims. Because this episode may not be familiar, I will lay out briefly how it depicts chivalric deeds leading to narrative resolution. In Scotland, the knight Rinaldo finds himself in the world of Lancelot and Arthur, where honor is won through action amidst constant risk: "Chi non ha gran valor, non vada inanti; / che dove cerca onor, morte guadagna [Who does not have great valor, let him not proceed; / since where he seeks honor, he will attain death]" (4.52).[19] Learning that the Princess Ginevra, whose name recalls Arthur's unfaithful Guinevere, has been accused of infidelity, he sets out to champion her in order to perform a "fatto eggregio [exceptional deed]" (4.55), not caring whether or not she has been unchaste, and indeed tending to believe that she is merely guilty of defying an unreasonable prohibition. In preserving Ginevra's "fama [reputation]" (4.57) and her father's "onor [honor]" (4.62), Rinaldo will increase his own "onor e fama" (4.61); his performance of chivalry is both idealistically unconcerned with the practical details of Ginevra's behavior and pragmatically attuned to the benefits of linking his honor with hers.[20] Ironically, it finds its meaning in the performance of valor rather than in the constraints of reality.[21] Embarked on his quest, Rinaldo happens upon Ginevra's handmaid Dalinda, whom he saves from being murdered. Dalinda then recounts how her lover Polinesso convinced her to dress up as Ginevra when he could not obtain the Princess's love. In the meantime, and unbeknownst to Dalinda, Polinesso promised Ginevra's true love, Ariodante, that he would be able to witness Ginevra's infidelity with his own eyes. This apparent proof of Ginevra's infidelity moved Ariodante, in the grip of "furore," to the brink of suicide, from which he was thwarted by his brother, Lurcanio, who demanded why he had "perduto l'intelletto [lost his mind]" over a woman (5.53). When Lurcanio later comes to believe that Ariodante has successfully committed suicide, he publicly denounces Ginevra, thereby creating the crisis in which Rinaldo is on his way to intercede.

At the same time that Ariosto's male characters perform with real attention to their social audience, they also see themselves as agents able to right wrongs through independent heroic deeds. After hearing Dalinda's story, Rinaldo arrives at the court of Ginevra's father, exposes and kills Polinesso, and prevents a battle between Lurcanio and a mysterious knight who has already arrived to defend Ginevra. The tale's resolution is made complete when this knight reveals that he is Ariodante himself, come to defend Ginevra *despite his continued doubts about her fidelity*: "convien ch'a dritto e a torto, per suo scampo / pigli l'impresa [It is fitting whether right or wrong that I take up the enterprise for her safety]" (6.10).[22] Though the unlucky victim Dalinda is relegated to a convent, the episode as a whole is comic, incorporating the victory over a rigid law ("L'aspra legge di Scozia, empia e severa" [4.59]) that Northrop Frye identifies with comedy as well as the humor of Rinaldo's defense of unchaste women (4.63–67).[23] Most importantly, honorable actions triumph as the ongoing narrative moves from past to present tense; Ariodante moves out of the control of furor to chart his own course of action, and he and Rinaldo both take part in events in progress in order to rescue Ginevra's reputation. Their readiness to perform self-sacrifice places them in an idealistic tradition of chivalrous generosity that nonetheless blurs the distinction between a courageous lack of concern with the facts about Ginevra's fidelity, and a blithe willingness to participate in the recuperation of her honor even at the risk of supporting a lie. The tale's happy ending—Ginevra is to all appearances faithful despite her name's allusion to Guinevere— keeps the focus on a celebration of male honor while acknowledging that this honor is a complex social construction.

Spenser alters his Ariostan source in *Faerie Queene* 2.4 by depicting a vengeful protagonist who is unable to claim his own actions, underscoring the costs of an honor defined principally by its defensive reaction to theatrical subterfuge rather than by self-motivated courageous deeds.[24] Contrary to what readers might expect, the episode's shift of first-person narrator from the handmaid to Phedon actually emphasizes how far this character is from being the author of his own destiny. Phedon reveals his strangely passive stance to his own life as he looks back at a story that has already effectively reached its conclusion. His narrative is embedded as a tale within a tale, with his "It was my fortune" (19) echoing the narrator's previous description of Guyon at the start of the canto ("It fortuned forth faring on his way" [3]). These formulaic references to "fortune" at the opening of a narrative underscore that telling one's own tale here serves as an inadequate substitute for masculine agency. Combining first and third person in his contorted syntax, Phedon demonstrates a lack of recognition of his own deeds; he paradoxically fashions an identity for himself that relies on a deflection of his own responsibility. Phedon makes fortune the driving force of his story when he passively exclaims to

Guyon: "Fayre Sir … what man can shun the hap, / That hidden lyes vnwares him to surpryse? / Misfortune waites aduantage to entrap / The man most wary in her whelming lap" (17). As he tells his tale, Phedon erases his personal involvement and presents himself as unmanned by feminine Fortune's control over his future, in contrast to those who physically subdue Misfortune in the iconographical tradition identified by David Burchmore as the source of Spenser's depiction of Occasion.[25]

Thus, even when he seems to assert ownership of his fortune in phrases such as "my fortune," Phedon still denies his own agency by assuming that he was at the mercy of that fortune. Robin Headlam Wells asserts that one ideal of Renaissance masculinity is the "defiance of fortune";[26] Phedon, in his subjection to the related figures of Occasion and Misfortune, fails to meet this ideal, resembling Ariosto's Dalinda more than Rinaldo or Ariodante. As the imagery of his being trapped in the "whelming lap" of Misfortune suggests, Phedon also anticipates other characters from Book 2 who lay down their arms and lose themselves in the luxurious lap of the enchantress Acrasia: both Cymochles (2.5.28, 36) and Verdant, who rests his "sleepie head" in Acrasia's lap while his arms hang in a tree (2.12.76, 80). Greenblatt has characterized this moment as depicting "a narcotic slumber" in which "all 'manly' energy, all purposeful direction, all sense of difference upon which 'civil' order is founded have been erased," connecting it to "what the Europeans perceived as the *pointlessness* of native cultures."[27] For Matz the image of Verdant in Acrasia's lap recalls Stephen Gosson's gendered critique of courtly indulgence as "wallowyng in Ladies laps."[28] In the case of Phedon, loss of self-control due to jealousy and rage sets him on a course that combines intemperate action prompted by theatrical display with desperate attempts at self-repair through narrative. As do these other allegorical figures, Phedon embodies a masculinity threatened by submission to passions closely associated with the feminine.[29]

Ariosto's chivalric arena is notably absent from Spenser's version, which is set instead in a smaller world in which a sense of theater suffuses social relationships.[30] There are occasional theatrical references in Ariosto's episode, such as Dalinda's calling the scene that she and Polinesso create for Ariodante a "rio spettacolo [wicked spectacle]" (5.51). In Spenser, however, the theatrical terminology is pervasive. The vocabulary of "parts" and "playing" employed in the scuffle between Guyon and Furor is echoed in Phedon's account of his friendship with Philemon; they were practically brothers, he says, joined in "league of vowed loue": "And for my part I vow, dissembled not a whitt" (18). Even as Phedon distinguishes his own actions from Philemon's deceptive performance, his use of the term "part" suggests, however unwittingly, the world of dramatic role-playing. Similarly, the way in which Philemon convinces Claribell's handmaid, Pryene, to wear her mistress's clothing by appealing to her sense of class entitlement—another Spenserian innovation—speaks to a culture both accustomed to, and anxious about, seeing the conventions of status and gender broken at the theater.[31]

As the canto continues, Phedon demonstrates an unstable mind-set in which reality is defined by dissimulation, and agency is reduced to observation and role-playing. Under Philemon's influence, he doubts his own feelings as "blind abused loue" (24) and substitutes his friend's vision for his own:

> The whiles to me the treachour did remoue
> His craftie engin, and as he had sayd,
> Me leading, in a secret corner layd,
> The sad spectatour of my Tragedie;
> Where left, he went, and his owne false part playd,
> Disguised like that groome of base degree,
> Whom he had feignd th'abuser of my loue to bee. (27)

Philemon's playing of a "false part" renders false the part that Phedon thought he played as a friend bound up to his other self in symmetrical loyalty; his account demonstrates his inability to determine his own place in the world. While readers have taken note of how the phrase "spectatour of my Tragedie" renders ambiguous whether Phedon plays an active or a passive role in that tragedy, it is certain in any case that he uses the word "my" only to lay claim to events in which his own role has been directed by others;[32] he has been placed as an observer by Philemon: "Me leading, in a secret corner layd." As Lauren Silberman argues, the effect of his spectatorship is that "Phedon distances himself" from his own responsibility.[33] Taking his identity from the parts he plays with others, Phedon sees himself as at the mercy of others' role-playing.

Feebly attempting to make sense of himself and his story, Phedon applies theatrical terms retrospectively. His words underscore his removal from and lack of control over his own lived experience:

> Eftsoones he came vnto th'appointed place,
>> And with him brought *Pryene*, rich arayd,
>> In *Claribellaes* clothes. Her proper face
>> I not descerned in that darkesome shade,
>> But weend it was my loue, with whom he playd.
>> Ah God, what horrour and tormenting griefe
>> My hart, my handes, mine eyes, and all assayd?
>> Me liefer were ten thousand deathes priefe,
> Then wounde of gealous worme, and shame of such repriefe. (28)

As he recalls how the lovers "playd," Phedon conflates sexual dalliance and theatrical performance, acknowledging that the source of his jealousy was merely show. Even though this performance has actual physical effects on him, tormenting the various parts of his body and leading him to commit real murder (of Claribell and Philemon), Phedon disconnects his actions from his own directed intentions. His "outrageous deede" (29) parallels the "outrageous talke" (5) of Occasion, and underscores his passive subjection to misfortune. The only consolation he can imagine is the hyperbolic experience ("priefe") of ten thousand annihilations of himself. While his reckless slaying of Claribell and poisoning of Philemon might well serve as arguments against his passivity, they are still the actions of a mind possessed by forces Phedon feels to be alien from himself. Unlike Ariosto's Ariodante, who independently chooses his own course of self-sacrificing action, Phedon overactively responds to the stimulation of others in a desperate, violent struggle, and he fails to the last to acknowledge his own culpability. Indeed, his reference to "hellish fury" (30) recalls Furor himself, serving as a useful reminder that in Spenser's allegory, Phedon's physical violence is also a vivid verbal portrait of an emotion, and Phedon himself an embodied representation of masculine weakness. As a tragic figure who loses everything because he loses himself, Phedon may seem to have little in common with the comic world of *Much Ado*; I suggest nevertheless that Phedon's juxtaposition with Braggadocchio underscores the dangers in Spenser's poem of equating masculine honor with verbal performance, and that his episode crucially informs Shakespeare's play.

Tragedy and courtesy in *Much Ado*

If Spenser's tale offers a tragic world in which reactive violence and theatrical impersonation replace idealized, goal-directed chivalry, *Much Ado About Nothing* offers an apparently celebratory depiction of a world in which courtesy is the predominant social value. Shakespeare's Claudio is a successful suitor who gets the happy ending of a comedy (however unmerited many have found his good fortune), and in this he resembles Ariosto's Ariodante or Bandello's Timbreo.[34] Readers have thus tended to see these sources as being primary for the play over Spenser's poem, which is often viewed as having a more limited influence, if any.[35] An important exception is Kasey Evans, who has asserted that "Spenser's theatricalization of the scene of misreading prepares the episode for its transition to the stage in *Much Ado*." Evans argues that *Much Ado*'s frequent metaphorical dissection of the body offers a "critique of the fantasy of corporeal integrity" that concludes with "a wholehearted embrace of misreading," which differentiates it from Spenser.[36] In my own focus on the play's critical exploration of how masculine honor may be deprived of its claim to authenticity, I diverge from Evans in asserting a strong textual and thematic continuity between Spenser's tragic tale and *Much Ado* that tempers the apparent festivity of the play's conclusion. Although it is true that there are other sources to which *Much Ado* is more similar in its plot, thematically it places very strong emphasis on the shift away from chivalrous action that is central to Spenser's narrative; Claudio resembles Spenser's Phedon both in his hapless passivity and in his difficulty taking responsibility for his actions.[37] I argue that as *Much Ado* further transforms the violent action of Spenser's episode into wordplay and emphasizes how a culture of role-playing may deprive honor of authenticity, it engages at a deep level with the tragic potential of disavowed masculine agency that is Spenser's contribution to this tale's history. Even as *Much Ado* celebrates the power of performance, that sense of festivity is tempered by its recognition of the costs of courtesy.

In contrast to his counterparts in Ariosto, Bandello, and others, but not to Phedon, Shakespeare's Claudio has difficulty taking ownership of the language through which he defines himself.[38] In his social world, verbal courtesy coexists in uneasy tension with aggressive protection of one's reputation, and for him the pursuit of honor is more about preserving himself from bad talk than about pursuing good deeds.[39] Although *Much Ado About Nothing* is often and rightly connected to the witty banter of Castiglione's *Courtier*, it is also profoundly suspicious of the verbal techniques of courtesy through which masculinity may present itself, which, in their constant attention to the demands of a social audience, require an artful self-presentation and a subservience to changing social circumstances that place the courtly gentleman in the ostensibly feminine position of pleasing others.[40] In Book 6 of *The Faerie Queene*, Spenser praises courtesy as the ability of knights and ladies "to beare themselues aright / To all of each degree, as doth behoue" (6.2.1). Yet as Spenser's own example of Calidore illustrates, courtesy runs the risk of being equivalent to social subterfuge. In contrast to *The Faerie Queene*'s often critical presentation of the courtier's theatricality (to be discussed further in Chapter 4), Shakespeare's play does suggest that aristocratic role-playing might have a creative and joyful function. In supplying frequent reminders of its tragic Spenserian source, however, *Much Ado* also acknowledges the threat to personal integrity posed by a culture of role-playing.

As the play portrays the shift from valorous action to courtesy, its characters emphasize the relationship between romantic love and the loss of self-control. Claudio's account of his feelings for Hero underscores both his removal from the battlefield and his submission to the feminine: "But now I am returned, and that warthoughts / Have left their places vacant, in their rooms / Come thronging soft and delicate desires, / All prompting me how fair young Hero is" (1.1.282–85). Yet even these words, which indicate that he is the object on which love acts and imply that he is like a player being prompted to speak, are taken from Claudio. Don Pedro cuts him off, telling him that he will be "like a lover presently / And tire the hearer with a book of words" (1.1.287–88), and also "Was't not to this end / That thou began'st to twist so fine a story?" (1.1.291–92). Like Phedon, Claudio is a storyteller, and, also like Phedon, he does not control his own narrative. Here he plays the part of a lover, taking on all the verbal aspects of that role as he leaves behind his identity as a soldier. Claudio's later assertion that "Beauty is a witch" (2.1.164), not to mention Benedick's semiserious promise to Beatrice that he will "die in thy lap" (5.2.93), also show how the male characters acknowledge their Acrasian vulnerability even as they create social identities through the tales that they speak and ascribe to each other.

When Claudio's match with Hero is finally formalized, Beatrice will have to remind him of his "cue" to speak (2.1.280), and here too he displays a troubling willingness to renounce his identity: "I give away myself for you, and dote upon the exchange" (2.1.283–84). Beatrice's reference to Claudio's missed cue complements his own words about the "desires" that are "prompting" him, and contributes to the play's larger pattern of theatrical language. Though this theatrical language is typical of Shakespeare's work, here it emphasizes how competitive courtly self-fashioning creates identities while simultaneously making it impossible to determine the authenticity of those identities. Claudio's reference to Benedick's need to "maintain his part" (1.1.221), a phrase that echoes Spenser's description of Guyon's own attempt to "maintaine his part" (2.4.9), shows that the men accept from the start the need for role-playing and saving face. Early on, Don Pedro casually offers to shift Claudio's identity from him: "I will assume thy part in some disguise / And tell fair Hero I am Claudio" (1.1.302–03).[41] Full of linguistic bravado, Don Pedro promises to acquire Hero by taking "her hearing prisoner with the force / And strong encounter of my tale" (1.1.305–06), substituting verbal actions for physical ones. In so doing, he anticipates his later assertion that tricking Benedick and Beatrice into admitting their love for one another will be the equivalent of one of "Hercules' labours" (2.1.337)—a possible allusion to the Globe's sign on Shakespeare's part, one that underscores all the more the prominence of theatricality in the play.[42] Impersonation takes precedence over heroic action, and the gulling scenes are also rich in theatrical references such as "scene," "dumb show," and "played their parts" (2.3.210–11, 3.2.70). Don Pedro's various prosopopoetic plans, which rely on his ability to impersonate Claudio and other characters' ability to personate versions of themselves, suggest the provisional nature of identity in the play. Despite Don Pedro's talk of heroic conquests, the main action that *Much Ado* depicts is theatrical acting.

Beatrice's gulling scene also offers a striking textual echo of *Faerie Queene* 2.4 that underscores how the play's characters have little ability to direct their own lives. As Hero anticipates the success of the scheme, she exclaims, "If it prove so, then loving goes by haps; / Some Cupid kills with arrows, some with traps" (3.1.105–06). Hero's commentary transforms an engineered, theatrical scene ("traps") into the fortuitous means by which Love operates ("haps"). Her rhyme on "hap" and "trap," which is unique in Shakespeare, recalls Phedon's words to Guyon: "what man can shun the hap, / That hidden lyes vnwares him to surprise? / Misfortune waites aduantage to entrap / The man most wary in her whelming lap" (2.4.17). Both Phedon and Guyon lament the disastrous consequences of engineered deceptions, just as Hero herself will soon have cause to do. Those who have paid attention to Don John's schemes in progress, seen the play before, or, indeed, read their Spenser, may be chilled by Hero's festive comment. Her improvised bit of proverb-making connects the two plots of the play even as it reminds the audience of the unaddressed implications of her formulation. Shakespeare's use of Spenser's words here both celebrates the power of theatrical wordplay and points to its dangers.

Claudio's own experiences with mistaken impressions and active, if benevolent, deception give him abundant reasons to be cautious, to "let every eye negotiate for itself, / And trust no agent" (2.1.163–64), and yet his concern for his reputation nonetheless leads him to succumb to Don John's bait. Shakespeare here depicts honor as something that can easily be lost in social interactions, rather than something to be acquired with self-directed action attentive to social expectations. Borachio's plan relies on a close link between Don Pedro's "honour" (2.2.21, 2.2.34) and Claudio's "reputation" (2.2.35), as both have been put at stake in the match with Hero. Like Spenser's Philemon, Don John offers to have Claudio "see" the proof of Hero's infidelity (3.2.107), and he stresses the vulnerability of Claudio's honor: "it would better fit your honour to change your mind" (3.2.104). The male characters in this scene assume that Claudio's honorable reputation depends on Hero's chaste name; her apparent infidelity means that Claudio must himself be inconstant, changing his mind as circumstances change. His response is thus in striking contrast to Ariosto's Ariodante, who decides on his own course of action even while believing Ginevra to be guilty. For Claudio, protecting his honor boils down to reacting to what others say about him, reinforcing the claim in Balthasar's song that men are "To one thing constant never" (2.3.63). His actions run quite contrary to Spenser's narrator's caution to a "young knight ... that dost armes professe" that he should "beware of fraud" that might lead him to "too lightly blame" his "deare loued Dame" (1.4.1). Castiglione's Giuliano de' Medici suggests that it is the duty of knights to "defende alwaies with weapon" women who are accused (3.38), with *The Courtier*'s Gaspare Pallavicino going still further in saying that even apparently guilty women should be defended: "I ... take it for great courtesy and honestie to cover some offence that by mishappe or overmuch love a woman is renn into" (3.39). At the same time that Claudio prioritizes his honorable reputation, then, he fails to live up to contemporary prescriptions for noble behavior.

As Borachio later recounts Claudio's deception, his narration both thematizes the problematic nature of gentlemanly agency and, in its revision of Spenser's Phedon episode, emphasizes the replacement of valorous actions with ostensibly feminized performances. Shakespeare omits Spenser's recounting of the maid's being convinced to wear fancy clothes, and replaces it with a strange, seemingly off-topic rant by Borachio about fashion's role as a "deformed thief" (3.3.120).[43] Despite the apparent digression, Borachio's words are actually central to the play's themes.[44] In Borachio's view, young men are controlled by a personified fashion. They are the objects on which fashion acts, turning them this way and that, making them resemble, among other things, "the shaven Hercules in the smirched worm-eaten tapestry, where his codpiece seems as massy as his club" (3.3.131–33). This image of Hercules with his powerful club invokes an ideal masculinity, depicted in emblem books as a model of choosing "heroic virtue" over "pleasure."[45] At the same time, Borachio's reference to a decaying image, a representation of an ideal that is already corrupt, underscores the extent to which masculinity in the play is a constant performative striving, destined to fall short, toward an abstract idea of honor. Shakespeare's reference to a fading, idealized Hercules here is quite relevant to debates about the value and place of linguistic labor. Borachio's discussion of shifting fashion as the controlling force in young men's lives also recalls Spenser's references to fortune in *Faerie Queene* 2.4. In Spenser, Philemon lures Pryene into impersonating her social superiors by telling her that "fortune" has wrongly kept her beauty hidden, not allowing it to "deface all others lesser light" (2.4.25). Shakespeare's focus on the deforming role of fashion likewise raises

the question of class difference, as Borachio's words are misinterpreted by the watchman, who sees this thief as a kind of noble
imposter: "I know that Deformed ... 'a goes up and down like a
gentleman" (3.3.121–23). The actual impersonation of gentility
that Spenser presents, with its tragic consequences, shows up in
Shakespeare as comic wordplay masking a sharp social critique.

Even as it suggests that gentlemanly identity is based on the imitation of an image, Borachio's report also shows how a social culture
defined by fiction and role-playing may deprive its participants of
agency. Borachio emphasizes his role as a narrator, albeit a disorgan-
ized one, when he says of Margaret: "she leans me out at her mistress' chamber window, bids me a thousand times good night—I tell
this tale vilely" (3.3.140–42). Not only does Borachio speak of his
actions as a "tale," but his account includes a conspicuous reference to the balcony scene in *Romeo and Juliet*.[46] His blunt prose
description, a parody of the idealizing poetry of *Romeo and Juliet*,
suggests the staged quality of the deception that Claudio has witnessed, which Borachio is already in the process of packaging into
narrative. Like Phedon, the "spectatour" of a "Tragedie," Claudio is
also the spectator of a scene that makes a prominent allusion to one
of Shakespeare's own tragedies.[47] And, again like Phedon, he has
failed to understand what he has seen. Still, while Phedon describes
himself as witnessing "my Tragedie" (2.4.27) in his extended narration of his own tale, Claudio is described here in the third person
in Borachio's "tale." Claudio's inability to finish his own "story"
earlier in the play makes him vulnerable to becoming a character in
someone else's narrative.

In the interrupted marriage ceremony that soon follows, Claudio
indulges in his own verbal outburst, yet here too he receives needed
support from Don Pedro. Claudio's false assertion that Hero is
"but the sign and semblance of her honour" (4.1.31) is comple-
mented by Don Pedro's erroneous testimony: "Upon mine honour,
/ Myself, my brother and this grieved count / Did see her, hear her,
at that hour last night, / Talk with a ruffian at her chamber window" (4.1.88–91). There is a strong irony in the fact that Claudio
and Don Pedro lay claim to honor even as they discredit themselves
with their false words. The bitter sarcasm with which Leonato later
addresses the pair makes the disjunction between their verbal performances and their cowardly nature clear: "Here stand a pair of

honourable men ... I thank you, princes, for my daughter's death; / Record it with your high and worthy deeds" (5.1.256–59).

In light of the play's increasing insistence on the emptiness of masculine oaths, Beatrice's early assertion that she "had rather hear my dog bark at a crow, than a man swear he loves me" (1.1.125–26) emerges as a critique of the way apparently honorable masculinity is created primarily by verbal subterfuge. Beatrice's direct command to Benedick that he "kill Claudio" is thus not the prelude to action; the audience may respond with laughter, and Benedick in any case instantly dismisses the proposal.[48] Beatrice's rejected demand spurs her to exclaim that honor has been reduced to theatrical dissimulation: "O that I were a man for his sake! Or that I had any friend would be a man for my sake! But manhood is melted into curtsies, valour into compliment, and men are only turned into tongue ... He is now as valiant as Hercules that only tells a lie and swears it" (4.1.315–20).[49] Despite Don Pedro's previous equation of linguistic impersonation with Herculean labor, the figure of Hercules is here used to attack the dissembling courtesy of contemporary masculinity, as Beatrice laments the lack of a figure such as Ariosto's Rinaldo who can step in and truly do something. (Indeed, it is striking that every other use of the term "valiant"—which is such a key term in translations of Castiglione and Guazzo—is ironic in some way, from Beatrice referring to Benedick as a "valiant trencher-man" [1.1.48], to her desire not "to be overmastered with a piece of valiant dust" [2.1.53–54], to Claudio's reference to Benedick as "valiant" in the gulling scene, to which Don Pedro preposterously responds, "As Hector, I assure you" [2.3.183–84].) Beatrice's unknowing rejoinder to Don Pedro's comparison of his cohort to Hercules recalls the contrast Spenser's Belphoebe makes between courtesy and valorous action; the men around Beatrice, made of "tongue," are no better than Braggadocchio.[50] I would therefore argue that the critical commonplace that Benedick is the "antithesis" of Claudio is an overstatement.[51] It is Benedick, after all, not Claudio, who is the recipient of these cutting words. The difference between Benedick and Claudio matters, to be sure—Benedick is repeatedly referred to as a "man" in the play, in contrast to Claudio, and by the end of the scene he does display a theoretical willingness to do as Beatrice asks and "use" his hand "some other way than swearing by it"—but both characters rely on a verbal self-presentation that the play critiques (4.1.323–24).

The events that follow bear out Beatrice's accusation, revealing men who prefer words to physical actions. When he does come to challenge Claudio, Benedick may, for example, throw down a glove (as Benjamin Curns did in the 2012 American Shakespeare Center production), but in the end his challenge, however genuinely offered, amounts to copious words rather than deeds. Leonato and Antonio offer similarly ineffective challenges to Claudio (5.1.58–99). In Ariosto's version, in contrast, the offer to prove an accusation with arms is the prelude to physical engagement between both Lurcanio and Ariodante (5.65, 5.79) and between Rinaldo and Polinesso (5.86).[52] Even Claudio's eventual change of heart is portrayed in figurative terms. Horrified to hear Borachio reveal Hero's innocence, Don Pedro asks Claudio, "Runs not this speech like iron through your blood?" to which Claudio responds: "I have drunk poison whiles he uttered it" (5.1.235–36). Claudio's answer takes its cue from the imagery of Don Pedro's question; his repentance takes the form of a metaphor. While Philemon and Romeo both drink real poison, Claudio lives his life at a distance, neither truly murderous nor suicidal, but substituting words for action. Especially through Claudio, but to a degree through all of its male characters, the play confronts the possibility that courteous manhood is just Braggadocchio's bluster.

Claudio's rage and guilt remain contained in metaphor in contrast to Phedon's rash physical action, yet he resembles Phedon in his inability to see himself as the agent controlling his own life. In contrast to Ariosto's Ariodante, Claudio never shows a willingness to defend a Hero who may be guilty. When first confronted with Hero's supposed death, Claudio simply disclaims responsibility, as he disclaims the first person, asking doubtfully, "My villainy?" (5.1.72). Even when he acknowledges his role in what has happened, Claudio's contorted syntax shows his desire to keep personal guilt at a distance: "Impose me to what penance your invention / Can lay upon my sin. Yet sinned I not / But in mistaking" (5.1.263–65). Claudio remains the object of Leonato's actions throughout the rest of the play, including being stage-managed by him in the concluding wedding scene. Strikingly, after he performs his penance at Hero's supposed tomb, Claudio hopes for "luckier issue" in his next marriage (5.3.32). Like Phedon, Claudio conceives of himself to the end as someone who has been led astray by misfortune, and, ironically, his way of making amends is to continue to be the object of others' plans.[53] Claudio's character reveals the weakness of a courtly honor based on role-playing and constant attention to the threats of shifting appearances. It is not hard to imagine that he could be tricked again.

Words, words, words

As Spenser's episode and Shakespeare's play move toward conclusions that seem designed to be dissatisfying, both take up the theme of counsel, a topic that allows them to lament the unmooring of language from lived experience. This connection between the two texts underscores their shared meditation on the changing nature of honor and their characters' diminished sense of agency. In Spenser, the theme of counsel frames Phedon's embedded tale; bad "counsell" initiates its plot, and misguided counsel serves as its moral and conclusion. At the beginning of his story, Phedon reveals how he suffered "gnawing anguish" because of Philemon's "sad speach" to him, and therefore sought his false friend's "counsell" (2.4.23). And the narration itself of Phedon's tale prompts the Palmer and Guyon to do some inept moralizing, as Harry Berger Jr. has shown.[54] The Palmer repeats three times a formulaic list of the emotions from which Phedon should simply separate himself, but it is not at all clear how Phedon will do so, or that doing so will help him. Guyon goes on to describe Phedon as an "vnlucky Squire," telling him to "guyde thy waies with warie gouernaunce, / Least worse betide thee by some later chaunce" (2.4.36). Even as Phedon is encouraged toward temperance, then, Guyon acknowledges the role that chance has played and may yet still play in Phedon's life, pointing toward the difficulties in Phedon's self-direction in the same stanza in which his identity as a descendant of "famous *Coradin*, / Who first to rayse our house to honour did begin" is revealed (2.4.36). Readers' views of the episode's concluding tone have varied. Paul Alpers notes Phedon's "restored humanity" as he reveals his name and claims that "the climax of the episode is not an action at all, but a rhetorical scheme, a formal arrangement of words—precisely a stanza of poetry and nothing else."[55] In response to Alpers, Berger also notes the emphasis on language itself, but argues that the "effect" of the moralizing "is to mark the rhetorical cure as a conspicuous allegorical whitewash."[56] The restoration of Phedon's name and lineage comes at precisely the moment in which the hollowness of words (in the form of misguided counsel) is most on display, and the contrast between Phedon and his honor-seeking ancestor is clear.

In *Much Ado*, Antonio's attempt to console his brother is similarly fruitless, and Leonato begs him, "cease thy counsel" (5.1.3). While the dismissal of pat advice does occur frequently in Shakespeare,[57] it is nonetheless tempting to read the specific imagery of Leonato's attack on Antonio's words as Shakespeare's response to Spenser. Both Spenser's Palmer and Shakespeare's Antonio speak in formulaic terms about how grief may act as a force attacking someone from the outside; Antonio insists to Leonato, "If you go on thus you will kill yourself, / And 'tis not wisdom thus to second grief / Against yourself" (5.1.1–3). Leonato, however, rejects the possibility that one can "patch grief with proverbs" (5.1.17), suggesting that to do so is as foolish as to "give preceptial medicine to rage, / Fetter strong madness in a silken thread, / Charm ache with air and agony with words" (5.1.24–26). As Leonato rails against hearing simplistic advice from someone who hasn't experienced what he has, his imagery recalls and revises the depiction of Guyon's attempt to subdue Furor in *The Faerie Queene*: "And both his hands fast bound behind his back, / And both his feet in fetters to an yron rack" (2.4.14). Leonato's imagery underscores the absurdity of the glib kind of advice that the Palmer and Guyon offer to Phedon. Words, especially the canned words of precepts, will not assuage his grief, any more than a "silken thread" can contain fury. Leonato here hints at a rage that is largely beneath the surface of the play; though its latent violence is ultimately smoothed over by the "silken thread" of fancy clothes and entertaining talk, its dangers are imperfectly contained. Even as *Much Ado* revels in the pleasure of language and its power to feign reality through the medium of theater, it also reminds the audience of the troublesome tension between words and reality in the society it presents.

In *Faerie Queene* 2.3, the talker Braggadocchio is insistently associated with "vanity"; the narrator describes him as "puffed vp with smoke of vanity" (2.3.5), and Trompart's plan to manipulate him is to "vphold / His ydle humour with fine flattery, / And blow the bellowes to his swelling vanity" (2.3.9). Spenser's poem in 2.3 and 2.4 takes a dim view of a courtly society composed by the vanity of speech. In *Much Ado About Nothing*, by contrast, it is Dogberry who dismisses the language arts: "To be a well-favoured man is the gift of fortune, but to write and read comes by nature ... and for your writing and reading, let that appear when there is no need of such vanity" (3.3.14–16, 20–21). On the one hand, the ill-spoken Dogberry's muddled reference to literacy is comical. On the other hand, it suggests the play's vexed engagement with the power of words. To dismiss them as frivolous is absurd, and yet to make them the foundation of human relationships is dangerous. But what other option is there?

The numerous connections between Spenser's episode and Shakespeare's play, many of which indicate a heightened awareness of the loss of heroic action and masculine self-ownership, suggest that the witty banter of *Much Ado About Nothing* should be understood in something other than a purely festive sense. It is striking that the jokes of the play continue even when they are least appropriate—notably when both Claudio and Don Pedro make wisecracks about Leonato and Antonio immediately after they learn of Hero's supposed death in 5.1. In re-presenting a tragic sensibility in the guise of comedy, Shakespeare's play points toward a disjunction between inner nature and outward expression that gets to the heart of contemporary concerns about the authenticity of a masculine courtly honor based on verbal self-presentation. Indeed, the happy ending of *Much Ado* may well seem as slapped on to the text as Guyon's moralizing.[58] That is not to suggest that Spenser's Phedon and Shakespeare's Claudio are equivalent, or that the two texts treat the vexed question of honor with the same tone. Most important, of course, is that the further movement from action to words in Shakespeare's play allows for second chances: Spenser's Claribell dies, but Hero, in mimicking death (through her faint) and then feigning death, is able to "die to live" (4.1.253), paying a smaller price than Claribell does for her lover's mistakes, yet recalling her literary predecessor in her metaphorical death. An absence of murder in Shakespeare's play is not actually to be lamented, and the creation of society through language that it offers in its place suggests the powerful possibilities of linguistic play. Words are something to celebrate in Shakespeare's text, but the festivity of its ending is tempered by its recognition that the honor by which the characters define themselves is fundamentally unstable and that the "happy" ending has been supplied by chance rather than deriving from the merit of its male protagonists, who are themselves trapped by a code of honor that offers a dismal choice between pointless violence and empty words. The separation from himself that Spenser's Phedon initiates when he regards his own life as a tragic play is explored to the fullest in *Much Ado*'s Claudio as the play marks what is gained and lost in the movement away from Shakespeare's more action-oriented sources.

Taken together, Chapters 2 and 3 reveal the multivalent role that courtesy can play in both Spenser and Shakespeare, spurring different kinds of learning, and leading to both tragic and comic outcomes. The chapter that follows will continue to argue for the challenges that courtesy offers to readers and audiences in the development of their judgment as I explore a play that even more problematically suggests a too-easy comic resolution to the social questions that it raises.

Notes

1 Robert Matz, *Defending Literature*, 111. Matz's work on Sidney and Spenser usefully notes the ambivalence that both authors feel positioning themselves with reference to the Renaissance binary that opposed, on the one hand, masculine action on the battlefield, and, on the other hand, feminine language in the court (*Defending Literature*, 56–127).

2 David Quint, "Bragging Rights," 414–15. On contemporary "schematic oppositions between an idealized masculine past and a degraded effeminate present," see also Jean E. Howard and Phyllis Rackin, *Engendering a Nation*, 147. Louis Montrose sees in this encounter between Belphoebe and Braggadocchio a critique of Elizabeth's court ("Spenser and the Elizabethan Political Imaginary"). On the tensions between crown and aristocracy that played out in the realm of chivalry, see Richard C. McCoy, *Rites of Knighthood*; McCoy sees Spenser as particularly successful in "confronting the contradictions at the heart of Elizabethan chivalry" (127).

3 Stephen Greenblatt, *Renaissance Self-Fashioning*, 177.

4 Greenblatt, *Renaissance Self-Fashioning*, 179.

5 Matz, *Defending Literature*, 95.
6 On the ways in which "anxiety" was "an inevitable part of a discourse of masculinity," see Mark Breitenberg, *Anxious Masculinity*, 6. Alexandra Shepard argues that there was "enormous variation in men's experiences and assertions of male identity" in the early modern period (*Meanings of Manhood*, 17). On Renaissance masculinity, see also Bruce R. Smith, *Shakespeare and Masculinity*, and Robin Headlam Wells, *Shakespeare on Masculinity*.
7 Gavin Alexander, "Prosopopoeia," 105–06 and 112.
8 *OED*. "pretence" n. 5a.
9 Howard and Rackin, *Engendering a Nation*, 142.
10 Judith Butler, *Gender Trouble*, 25.
11 All quotations of *Much Ado About Nothing* are from the edition by Claire McEachern.
12 On *Much Ado About Nothing* and its sources, see Charles T. Prouty, *The Sources of* Much Ado About Nothing, and Geoffrey Bullough, *Narrative and Dramatic Sources of Shakespeare*, Vol. 2. Alwin Thaler was an early advocate of a close relationship between Spenser's and Shakespeare's versions of the tale, though his argument focuses particularly on the role of the handmaid ("Spenser and *Much Ado about Nothing*"). On "gendered misreading" (272) in three versions of the *Much Ado* story, see Kasey Evans' perceptive "Misreading and Misogyny." Evans is also concerned to explore the relationship between "theatricality" and a "threatened sense of masculinity" in Spenser and Shakespeare (262), though not to establish the same textual connections and influence I assert here. On Shakespeare's changes to Ariosto and Bandello in portraying the relationship between Leonato and Hero, and his related critique of patriarchy, see Claire McEachern, "Fathering Herself."
13 J. B. Lethbridge, *Shakespeare and Spenser*, 20.
14 On the relationship between the stage and gender, see Stephen Orgel, *Impersonations*.
15 See Norbert Elias, *Civilizing Process*, 363–435 and passim. Elias also notes the possibility of "competition" through "polished social conduct" (422).
16 Keith Thomas, *In Pursuit of Civility*, 24.
17 J. L. Austin, *How to Do Things with Words*.
18 See "Fury" in Cesare Ripa, *Iconologia*, 30. See also "Virtuti sapientia comes" in Otto Vaenius, *Q. Horatii Flacci Emblemata*.
19 All quotations of *Orlando Furioso* are from the edition by Lanfranco Caretti. Translations from the Italian are my own, though I have also benefited from the translation of Guido Waldman.

20 On Rinaldo as the author of his own narrative, see Kasey Evans, "Misreading and Misogyny," 264–70. Evans goes further than I do in suggesting the self-aggrandizing nature of Rinaldo's quest; my argument places particular emphasis on the link between Rinaldo and Ariodante in not having their actions determined by Ginevra's apparent guilt.

21 Borrowing Butler's phrasing from another context, we might call it "a kind of persistent impersonation that passes as the real" (*Gender Trouble*, x).

22 Indeed, in the following stanza Ariodante suggests that he knows that he is defending an unjust cause (6.11).

23 Northrop Frye, *Anatomy of Criticism*, 169.

24 In his comparative treatment of Spenser and Ariosto, Paul Alpers emphasizes how Spenser converts Ariosto's emphasis on "external dramatic action" into a focus on the narration of Phedon's psychological transformation (*Poetry of* The Faerie Queene, 54–69). Lawrence Rhu emphasizes the problem of interpretation in different versions of the tale ("Agons of Interpretation"). On the handmaid figure in various versions of the tale, see Tracey Sedinger, "Working Girls." On Spenser's use of Ariosto's enchantress/hag figure in the play, see Melinda Gough, " 'Her Filthy Feature Open Showne.' " On critique and crisis in Ariosto, see Albert Ascoli, *Ariosto's Bitter Harmony*.

25 David Burchmore, "Medieval Sources of Spenser's Occasion Episode." My reading here agrees with Harry Berger's treatment of Phedon's passivity and his relationship to Fortune; while Berger's focus is on the question of "rhetorical performance" (18) by Phedon and in the poem as a whole, my own emphasis is on how Phedon's troubled masculinity is adapted by Shakespeare ("Narrative as Rhetoric," especially 17–22). On the misogyny present in Guyon's defeat of Occasion, see also Evans, "Misreading and Misogyny," 270–72.

26 Robin Wells, *Shakespeare on Masculinity*, 2.

27 Greenblatt, *Renaissance Self-Fashioning*, 182–83.

28 Matz, *Defending Literature*, 94.

29 On Phedon's name as deriving from a young man whom Socrates delivered from sexual slavery and thus offering a "warning against the subjection of reason to passion," see David W. Burchmore and Susan C. Burchmore, "Occasion." Phaedo was the author of the lost dialogue *Zopyrus* in which Socrates admits he possesses sexual appetite, but claims to have overcome it through discipline subjected to reason (Cicero, *Tusculan Disputations* 4.37.80), thus avoiding *akrasia* (incontinence). On how other details of the episode bring out

Phedon's "sense of his feminized position," see Evans, "Misreading and Misogyny," 273. For an argument that "the capacity to be vulnerable to experience" and "to pleasure" (467) is presented positively in Book 2 as part of Spenser's critique of the "ethos of heroic masculinity" (481), see Joseph Campana, "Boy Toys and Liquid Joys."

30 Readers who have explored the theatrical themes of this episode include Paul Alpers (*Poetry of* The Faerie Queene, 54–69) and Kasey Evans, who notes that it "stag[es], in an explicitly theatrical way, the problems of misreading" ("Misreading and Misogyny," 272).

31 On the ambitions of the handmaid figure, see Tracey Sedinger, "Working Girls"; on contemporary anxiety about the effeminizing role of the theater, see Laura Levine, *Men in Women's Clothing.*

32 On this line as referring to Phedon as both spectator and actor, see Alpers, *Poetry of* The Faerie Queene, 63; for the more active role that Phedon takes as "*author* of this tragedy" despite his attempts to deny responsibility, see Berger, "Narrative as Rhetoric," 26. Evans emphasizes that Phedon experiences both the "emasculation and passivity" of the spectator and the "masculine privilege" of the "playwright" ("Misreading and Misogyny," 273–76), while Susanne Lindgren Wofford takes a positive view of Phedon's spectatorship (*Choice of Achilles*, 250).

33 See Lauren Silberman, "*The Faerie Queene*, Book II and the Limitations of Temperance," 13.

34 Though he takes a more positive view of Claudio, Charles Prouty does refer to a "general critical agreement in regarding Claudio as an unpleasant young man who behaves very badly" (*Sources*, 41); more recently, Claire McEachern asserts "Claudio is far more of a cad than his counterparts" (*Much Ado*, 19).

35 McEachern agrees with both Prouty and Bullough in suggesting that Shakespeare would have encountered in Spenser a tale that simply shows "the dangers of intemperate action" and in describing Spenser's story as "a warning against lack of moderation" (*Much Ado*, 7). See also Prouty, *Sources*, 26, and Geoffrey Bullough, *Narrative and Dramatic Sources*, Vol. 2, 73.

36 See Evans, "Misreading and Misogyny," 274, 277, 284, and 286.

37 Jennifer A. Low's analysis of masculinity in the play offers an insightful treatment of its depiction of "the disintegration of the warrior ethic" (30); see *Manhood and the Duel*, 27–39. Jennifer C. Vaught also pays useful attention to the shift from warrior to court culture in Book 6 of *The Faerie Queene*; see *Masculinity and Emotion*, 136–55. Cristina León Alfar sees the play as offering, especially through Beatrice, an "interrogation of manhood" (*Women and Shakespeare's Cuckoldry Plays*, 103–34).

38 In the English versions of the tale that owe the most to Ariosto's plot, there is an emphasis on heroic action even as the vocabulary of the theater is augmented. Peter Beverley's *Ariodanto and Jenevra* (ca. 1565–66) is set in a courtly and theatrical atmosphere, yet it also moves beyond "play" in depicting male action leading to narrative resolution. John Harington's 1591 translation of *Orlando Furioso* also makes use of more performance terminology than Ariosto's original, but follows its predecessor in including chivalrous action in addition to impersonation.

   Bandello's Novella 22 (1554) resembles Shakespeare's play more directly in its movement away from action; though its characters are described as knights, they too do all their fighting before the story begins. But as his tale moves toward a resolution, Bandello's Timbreo differs from Claudio in actively admitting and righting his wrongs. On the loss of Bandello's "chivalric high-mindedness" (229) in Shakespeare's play, see Leo Salingar, "Borachio's Indiscretion." Laurie E. Osborne suggests that Shakespeare would have been interested in the "dangerous powers of dramatic play" (168) depicted in Ariosto and Bandello, but does not explore what is, in my view, the greater relevance of Spenser on these topics ("Dramatic Play in *Much Ado about Nothing*"). John Traugott likewise leaves Spenser to the side in his argument that Shakespeare's play offers a reaction against the violent possibilities in chivalric romance ("Creating a Rational Rinaldo").

39 On the "susceptibility of Messina" and its "Men's Club" (311), see Harry Berger Jr., "Against the Sink-a-Pace." Carol Cook also analyzes the "pervasive masculine anxiety" and "fear of the feminine" at work in the play ("'Sign and Semblance of Her Honor,'" 186 and 189).

40 See Mary Augusta Scott, "*Book of the Courtyer*," and, more recently, Philip D. Collington, "'Stuffed with All Honourable Virtues.'" On the influence of Castiglione and the importance of "linguistic performance" (1398) in the play, see also Stephen Greenblatt, Introduction to *Much Ado About Nothing*, 1395–1402. Joan Kelly famously suggests that Castiglione depicts a courtier who must "adopt 'woman's ways' in his relations to the prince" ("Did Women Have a Renaissance?," 44).

41 Jean E. Howard explores how the play naturalizes "theatricality as a vehicle for the exercise, by aristocratic males, of power" (*Stage and Social Struggle*, 69).

42 On the Globe's sign as a source of metatheatrical reference, see Tiffany Stern, *Making Shakespeare*, 14–17.

43 Thomas Moisan notes the substitution of this discussion for the actual presentation of apparent betrayal ("Deforming Sources," 173).

44 John A. Allen has argued that Borachio's comments about "fashion" offer a critique of Messina's courtly atmosphere ("Dogberry"). Jonathan Walker sees in Borachio's references to "the conspicuous consumption of gallants" a criticism of Claudio and Don Pedro's misogynistic interpretation of Hero based on outward signs (*Site Unscene*, 75).

45 See Cesare Ripa's emblem of "Heroic Virtue" (*Iconologia*, 79) and Geoffrey Whitney, *Choice of Emblemes*, 40. McEachern notes the tension between "actual strength" and "representation" in her commentary on these lines (*Much Ado*, 244); F. H. Mares notes their connection to emblem books in his edition of the play. Matz has persuasively argued that the contrast in Sidney's *Defense* between the "warrior activity" of Hercules and his "feminine activity of spinning cloth" is linked to anxiety about the value of "courtly poetry" (*Defending Literature*, 74).

46 McEachern remarks on the connection in her notes to the play (*Much Ado*, 245). Moisan suggests that presenting this scene as a recounted tale rather than directly onstage is a nod to Shakespeare's narrative sources ("Deforming Sources," 170).

47 On the repeated scenarios of spectatorship in *Much Ado*, see especially Nova Myhill, "Spectatorship in/of *Much Ado about Nothing*."

48 Traugott sees this scene as crucial for the play's "parody of the code of romance" and as part of its assembly of "braggadochio charades" ("Creating a Rational Rinaldo," 169).

49 Alfar argues for the importance of Beatrice's speech in encouraging Benedick's adoption of a new model of manhood (*Women and Shakespeare's Cuckoldry Plays*, 126).

50 Abbie Findlay Potts also connects Benedick to Braggadocchio (*Shakespeare and* The Faerie Queene, 51–54).

51 Bullough claims that Benedick is the "antithesis" of Claudio (*Narrative and Dramatic Sources*, 74). However, Benedick may also display a comic lack of self-control, becoming flummoxed by Beatrice and love. In the 2012 production at the American Shakespeare Center, Benjamin Curns' Benedick made use of a combination of mock-heroic gestures and over-the-top girlish bashfulness; he was sympathetic, but hardly heroic.

52 Jennifer Low asserts that Benedick's "challenge to Claudio brings acts and words into consonance for Messina, a society so involved in ceremonial discourse that words no longer necessarily correspond to reality" (*Manhood and the Duel*, 28); while I agree strongly with her suggestion about the divorce between "words" and "reality" in Shakespeare's Messina, I am more convinced by Moisan's argument

that in this scene the play moves "into a parodic tangency with the chivalric ethos of Ariosto and his imitators" because no physical trial results ("Deforming Sources," 177). Considering the mediating role between Ariosto and Shakespeare of Spenser's Phedon episode allows us to recognize the loss that is registered by the insistent wordiness of Shakespeare's play.

53 Cf. Jean Howard's assertion that the wedding with Hero is "a lesson in having faith in the authority of social superiors, a lesson to which Claudio is already predisposed" (*Stage and Social Struggle*, 70).

54 Berger, "Narrative as Rhetoric," 28–31. See also Silberman on "the inadequacies of Guyon's approach" ("*The Faerie Queene*," 15). On the problem of instructional examples in Book 2 as a whole, see Jeff Dolven, *Scenes of Instruction*, 154–65.

55 Alpers, *Poetry of* The Faerie Queene, 69.

56 Berger, "Narrative as Rhetoric," 30. As part of his argument that Spenser is not a "dramatic" or "expressivist" poet, Lethbridge also offers a critique of Alpers' and Berger's reading of this episode ("Poetry of *The Faerie Queene*," 202–08).

57 See, for example, *The Merchant of Venice* 1.2 and *Othello* 1.3. On *Much Ado*'s critique of "sententiousness" and "counsel," see Moisan, "Deforming Sources," 169.

58 Here I agree with other readers who have taken a dim view of the play's apparently happy ending; see Berger, "Against the Sink-a-Pace," 313, and Carol Cook, "'Sign and Semblance of Her Honor,'" 200. The performance directed by Tim Ocel at Saint Louis University in March 2011 offered a conclusion in which Claudio and Benedick continued their alienation, a possibility that Alfar also emphasizes in her reading of the play (*Women and Shakespeare's Cuckoldry Plays*, 127).

4

Courteous competitions: blood, gold, and outward shows in *Nennio*, Spenser's Book of Courtesy, and *The Merchant of Venice*

In his commendatory sonnet in praise of Thomas Hoby's translation of Castiglione, Thomas Sackville offers two opposing definitions of gold:

> These royall kinges, that reare up to the skye
> Their Palaice tops, and decke them all with gold:
> With rare and curious woorkes they feed the eye:
> And showe what riches here great Princes hold.
> A rarer work and richer far in worth,
> Castilios hand presenteth here to the,
> No proud ne golden Court doth he set furth
> But what in Court a Courtier ought to be.
> The Prince he raiseth houge and mightie walles,
> Castilio frames a wight of noble fame:
> The kinge with gorgeous Tyssue claddes his halles,
> The Count with golden vertue deckes the same,
> Whos passing skill lo Hobbies pen displaise
> To Brittain folk, a work of worthy praise.[1]

Sackville's sonnet offers an implicit critique of showy, glittering riches that "feed the eye," contrasting the actual gold of palaces with the "golden vertue" of both Castiglione's text and the counseling courtier. His text thus suggests the importance of the true riches of character that deserve the title of "noble fame." At issue in his sonnet is not only the relationship of the courtier to the prince, but also the question of whether nobility primarily derives from material or moral wealth, the latter of which is closely associated with the "golden vertue" of the mind acquired through the study of the right books. In this chapter, I explore how competing definitions of nobility uneasily map onto competitions in courtesy in both Spenser and Shakespeare's *Merchant of Venice*. Both Book 6 of *The Faerie Queene* and Shakespeare's play consider the stakes in attributing nobility to wealth, inherited blood, or moral worth, and neither text defines what it means to be noble conclusively. Beginning by discussing the Italian dialogue *Nennio*, which offers an explicit debate about the nature of true nobility, I then consider *Faerie Queene* 6.9 in the context of other moments from Book 6 when Spenser's multifaceted examinations of nobility, rhetorical deception, greed, and generosity require readers to be alert to connections and willing to refine their judgments. I argue that, in contrast to *Nennio's* relatively straightforward presentation of the victory of nobility of mind, the intertwined narratives of *The Faerie Queene's* Book of Courtesy require readers to exercise discernment as they negotiate the poem's presentation of the relationship between courtesy and "outward shows." Likewise, in *The Merchant of Venice*, Bassanio's denigration of "outward shows" when rejecting the golden casket is, I contend, crucial to the play's call for audience judgment. Undoubtedly both Spenser's and Shakespeare's texts contribute to a harmful process of reifying aristocratic difference, of which the practice of courtesy forms a central part. Yet, in prompting audiences to evaluate the competitions they stage, these texts also spur explicit attention to the kinds of judgment courtesy fosters, thus allowing for the possibility of critique as well. As all three of these texts probe the instrumentality of courteous generosity, they provide readers and audiences with tools not only to distinguish courtesy's contradictions, but also to engage in the kind of judgment that is itself fundamental to the practice of courtesy.

As Spenser and Shakespeare portray the machinations through which ostensibly noble blood retains its hegemony, their works also provide the material for readers and audiences to recognize the pretenses on which aristocratic virtue depends. Both works support the theoretical superiority of gentle blood while simultaneously undermining its premises. For example, Spenser's readers must particularly attend to the opening lines of Book 6, canto 3 of *The Faerie Queene*, which present conflicting claims about the true nature of gentility as though it were a seamless whole.[2] The canto opens with the simplistic assertion "True is, that whilome that good Poet sayd, / The gentle minde by gentle deeds is knowne," which Spenser credits to Chaucer, and invites readers to question precisely by insisting on its obvious truth. This formulation asserts that actions reflect a noble state of mind, and it echoes the Wife of Bath's claim (in the persona of the old woman to the knight) that "gentil dedes" characterize the "gentil man" (1115–16), as opposed to anything that is inherited ("For, God it woot, men may wel often fynde / A lordes son do shame and vilenye" [1150–51]) or possessed ("genterye / Is nat annexed to possessioun" [1146–47]).[3] And yet, immediately after citing Chaucer's criticism of nobility tied to blood and wealth, the narrator turns about, suggesting the obvious worth of inherited gentle blood:

> For a man by nothing is so well bewrayd,
> As by his manners, in which plaine is showne
> Of what degree and what race he is growne.
> For seldome seene, a trotting Stalion get
> An ambling Colt, that is his proper owne:
> So seldome seene, that one in basenesse set
> Doth noble courage shew, with curteous manners met.

> But euermore contrary hath bene tryde,
> That gentle bloud will gentle manners breed. (6.3.1–2)[4]

The logical evidence that the narrator seems to offer with the conjunction "for" at the start of this quotation actually stands in contrast to the claim about the "gentle minde" being known "by gentle deeds" that precedes it; one statement points toward the mind's reflection in noble deeds, and the other points toward the physicality of noble inheritance through "gentle bloud." In giving equal weight to two contradictory statements about the relationship between blood and race, on the one hand, and manners and deeds, on the other, the narrator provokes his readers to notice the discrepancy and reflect upon the relation between these conflicting assertions and the tale that follows, to be discussed later in this chapter.[5]

The Spenserian narrator here puts forward for his readers' consideration a link between race, blood, and class that replicates an accepted notion of gentility in the early modern period. As Dennis Austin Britton and Kimberly Anne Coles assert, "To speak of race in Spenser … is to speak the language that Spenser and his contemporaries used to denote and understand the significance of human difference."[6] Jean Feerick argues that early modern systems of social differentiation were based in part on a view of a "sanguinary nature of race" that relied upon inherited aristocratic blood; for Feerick, "in English literature of the late sixteenth and early seventeenth centuries, race is most frequently used and understood as a mode of social differentiation that naturalizes a rigid social hierarchy within a polity."[7] Andrew Hadfield likewise claims that in the early modern period "theories of race and class cannot easily be separated because discourses of racial identity were inextricably bound to those of social standing."[8] And Ania Loomba similarly argues, "All over Europe, the nobility were often understood as a 'race' distinct from ordinary folk."[9] Loomba later claims, "Anxieties about skin colour, religious identity, and female sexuality all overlap; they also all hinge on the relationship between inner and outer being, between what is fixed or natural, and what is artificial and changeable."[10] As this chapter explores, the discourse of courtesy is especially concerned with both decoding and troubling the relationship between "inner and outer being."

In staging lively debates about the nature of nobility and the related question of how to interpret "gentle manners," Spenser's and Shakespeare's texts contributed to contemporary discussions about the connections between courtesy and aristocratic identity, and critics have shown how the works of both authors replicate as well as critique systems of racialized prejudice. Both Feerick and Hadfield credit Spenser with questioning the contemporary linking of blood inheritance and gentility in the presentation of the Ruddymane episode in Book 2 of *The Faerie Queene*;[11] in this chapter, I examine a similar troubling at work in Book 6. Patricia Akhimie's foundational work on "the imbrication of race, class, and conduct" underscores that Shakespeare's plays could be a place of resistance as well as containment:

> A careful reading ... reveals a recurrent critique of the conduct system voiced, for example, by malcontents and social climbers such as Iago and Caliban, and embodied in the struggles of earnest strivers such as Othello, Bottom, Dromio of Ephesus, and Dromio of Syracuse. Though these characters are neither rewarded for their insights, nor freed by those insights from the confines of that system, their complaints introduce audiences to the ironies ... inherent in the conduct system without endorsing out-and-out reform. It is no coincidence that the characters who identify injustice are those whose bodies are bruised, pinched, blackened, and otherwise indelibly marked as uncultivatable.[12]

Akhimie's work demonstrates the ongoing power of racialized oppression; as she aptly notes in her discussion of how *Merchant*'s Prince of Morocco is denigrated for his "complexion," "in a culture of conduct, the power of judgment resides with the dominant group."[13] Akhimie further argues that Shakespeare's plays offer a "chance to view a system of social differentiation under scrutiny, under pressure, laid open to critique," arguing that this "anatomy of naturalized social difference" can provide material for "antiracist critique and activism" alongside the ways in which the plays also perpetuate social discrimination.[14] Her assertion that "systems of social differentiation" are supported by "opposing ideas about a malleable, performative self, and a natural and immutable self that is essential or biological"[15] reinforces the importance of attending to the contradictions in how early modern texts present the performance of courtesy.

This chapter aims to extend this important work on social differentiation by exploring literary presentations of status competitions in *Nennio*, Book 6 of *The Faerie Queene*, and *The Merchant of Venice*. I claim that in presenting competitions with explicit winners and losers, Spenser and Shakespeare associate noble blood with virtue but also demonstrate both the hollowness and costs of noble characters' victories. While these texts present moments of judgment such as contests and court decisions, their depictions of courtesy may also heighten critical judgment in readers and audiences. Both *The Faerie Queene* and *The Merchant of Venice* claim that true courtesy is inured to economic advantage. At the same time that these texts represent an idealistic view of courtesy, however, they also convey to readers and audiences the means to reflect on courtesy as a technique of self-advancement, dependent upon the rhetorical coloring and masked intentions it disavows. Noble blood is thereby closely linked with a generosity that is revealed to be frequently self-promoting. In the case of Spenser, I argue, Calidore's pastoral interlude offers an inconsistent case for the definition of nobility, both demystifying and bolstering the value of Calidore's brand of courtesy as he takes on the role of a lowly shepherd, cynically outperforms a rustic rival, and yet also acts with real heroism. Shakespeare's play, by juxtaposing mercantile and courtly economies, goes even further in representing an empty victory for courteous nobility. Taking as its touchstone the device of paradiastole, or the rhetorical relabeling of vice as virtue, *The Merchant of Venice* proposes that the problem of "outward shows" is ultimately intractable; the ostensible inscrutability of the Jewish "others" in the play appears alongside Christian adeptness at hiding motives, provoking audience reflection on how apparent distinctions between social groups both come to exist and are maintained.

Spenser and *Nennio*

Readers of Book 6 of Spenser's *Faerie Queene* are familiar with Calidore's competition with Coridon in Canto 9. A pastoral setting provides leisure for conversation and recreation. Two men of different social stations compete for the favor of a lovely woman. One of them finally gains victory over the other in part due to his insistent generosity. Less familiar is another passage perfectly described in these same terms: the parallel conclusion to the dialogue *Nennio, or A Treatise on Nobility*. *Nennio*, originally written in Italian by Giovanni Battista Nenna, was published in Venice in 1542; in 1595, William Jones brought out an English translation that included commendatory sonnets by Spenser and others.[16] While there is no critical consensus about Spenser's familiarity with the dialogue, there is at least a reasonable possibility that he studied *Nennio* before completing the 1596 *Faerie Queene*. Spenser's praise of the translation's accuracy in his commendatory sonnet even implies that he read the text in both English and Italian.[17]

Nennio and Book 6 of *The Faerie Queene* not only share a common vocabulary but also a sense that competitions in generosity may help in defining nobility. In *Nennio*, when a group sets out to avoid plague and war, the noble Lady Virginia visits their idyllic place of recreation. Before she departs, she leaves a ring with the company, saying: "I doe bestow this ring upon him that is the most noble of you two, whom I incharge to weare it in remembrance of me" (B3r).[18] Possidonio, a wealthy man of noble blood, and Fabricio, a man of noble learning, both lay claim to the ring. In the remainder of the dialogue, they make their cases until Nennio, their judge, decides in favor of Fabricio (the representative of learning), who then unexpectedly gives the ring to Possidonio (the representative of noble birth).

Spenser's commendatory sonnet to *Nennio* points out readers' need for accurate insight when choosing between the dialogue's two forms of nobility, which are reflected in the rival characters' names. In *Nennio*, Fabricio's self-created nobility of mind triumphs over Possidonio's inherited nobility of blood (closely connected to nobility based on wealth), and though Spenser does not declare his own preference directly, he strongly hints at it when he contrasts "painted shewes & titles vaine" to "true Nobility":

> Who so wil seeke by right deserts t'attaine
>   unto the type of true Nobility,
>   And not by painted shewes & titles vaine,
>   Derived farre from famous Auncestrie,
> Behold them both in their right visnomy
>   Here truly pourtray'd, as they ought to be,
>   And striving both for termes of dignitie,
>   To be advanced highest in degree.
> And when thou doost with equall insight see
>   the ods twixt both, of both them deem aright
>   And chuse the better of them both to thee,
>   But thanks to him that it deserves, behight:
> To *Nenna* first, that first this worke created,
>   And next to *Jones*, that truely it translated.[19]

Spenser here asks the reader to regard the two kinds of nobility and "behold them both in their right visnomy,"[20] to look at them "with equall insight," and to "chuse the better of them both"—yet he also offers clues so heavy-handed as to foreordain the proper decision. Further, his emphasis falls on making a *correct* decision, rather than on achieving a higher level of thinking. Spenser praises the justness of the dialogue's portraits of nobility ("truly pourtray'd, as they ought to be") even as he lauds Jones's translation's accuracy rather than a more creative aspect of his writing. Spenser here presents readers with a simple choice, and even steers them invariably toward it. Indeed, by criticizing inherited nobility explicitly at the outset of the dialogue, he takes for granted the victory of nobility of mind. While the dialogue's moderator gives at least some credit to the value of titles, Spenser here brushes them aside.

Possidonio and Fabricio's conflict contributes to an ongoing debate over the definition of nobility that was especially pressing in Spenser's time.[21] Spenser's sonnet's assertion that defining nobility

is about making a simple choice is belied by his own extended treatment of noble virtue in Book 6 of *The Faerie Queene*, which at
times supports the view of Possidonio, that nobility is physically
inherited, and at other times supports the view of Fabricio, that
"true and perfect nobilitie, doth consist in the vertues of the minde"
(H4v).[22] Readers, understandably, have divided interpretations over
what this sonnet reveals regarding Spenser's own attitude, with previous generations of critics underscoring his support for the aristocracy of blood. A. C. Judson acknowledges that Spenser shows
here a "democratic" sympathy, yet believes that he may merely be
indulging Jones and the "conclusions" reached in *Nennio*.[23] Millar
MacLure goes further, claiming that Spenser is "at one" with
Possidonio's view that aristocratic grace is a gift from God.[24] Louis
Montrose and John Huntington identify a greater willingness on
Spenser's part to agree with *Nennio*'s critique of nobility of blood,
though even Huntington, who provides the most thorough attention to this sonnet, sees Spenser's endorsement of *Nennio*'s ideas
as tepid. Huntington views Spenser as agreeing with the dialogue
primarily on "moral" grounds without really recognizing its "social
implications."[25] I bring *Nennio* into conversation with Book 6 of
The Faerie Queene, especially Canto 9, in order to afford additional
insight into Spenser's method of open-ended literary argument, despite our inability to establish definitively whether he read *Nennio*
early enough to influence his treatment of courtesy in *The Faerie
Queene*.[26] *Nennio* paints a portrait of generous nobility that has
much in common, on its face, with that of Calidore's liberality, but
the dialogue also provides a lens through which Spenser's reader
may view Calidore's techniques critically, in an exercise requiring
something other than outright acceptance or dismissal.

Nennio's debate

Though *Nennio* is structured as a debate, both Nenna and his translator foreshadow its outcome in their front matter.[27] The dialogue's
pastoral setting presents an ideal social world toward which Nenna
gestures in his dedicatory letter to the Duchess of Bari. This letter
expresses a longing for a golden age unspoiled by the strife that
accompanies riches, honor, and nobility, even as it contradicts this

sentiment when addressing the Duchess herself as someone who encompasses "le vere qualità della perfetta nobiltade."[28] Jones does not include a translation of the dedication, though he may well have been informed by its spirit. His own front matter—a dedication to the Earl of Essex and a Letter to the Courteous Reader—is also contradictory on the topic of nobility, although Jones ultimately makes his preference clear. In his dedicatory letter to the Earl of Essex, Jones insists on the modesty of his own achievement as well as on the perfections of the Earl; referring to the dialogue's debate between "Nobilitie by descent" and "Nobilitie, purchased by vertue," Jones asserts that Essex exemplifies both. Furthermore, he insists that Essex's noble blood "is well knowne to all men" and that his "perfections can well witnesse" his nobility of virtue (A2r). Should Essex wish for an example of perfect nobility, he may gaze in a mirror rather than read the book (A2v). While Jones's address to the Earl sidesteps nobility's complexity, the Letter to the Courteous Reader undermines the notion of nobility of blood by claiming all people descend from "one Stocke" and that uncertain family fortunes mean that nobles "have smal reason to bragge so much of their Nobility" (A3r). One wonders what the flattered Essex would have made of this. Jones next anticipates the dialogue's resolution with further criticism of mere inherited titles, suggesting that "without vertue, it [nobility] is as a ring of gold, wanting the ornament of some pretious stone" (A3v–A4r). Even as Nenna and Jones effusively praise their dedicatees, they nonetheless indicate that the dialogue itself will favor nobility of mind.

As the debate over whose nobility is superior begins, the aristocrat Possidonio is unwilling to recognize that any real question will be decided, foreshadowing his ultimate loss. It makes sense that Possidonio would be "desirous to be the first that should enter into the listes" (B4r); his opinion that his case is obvious closely connects to his lack of deference to his competitor. For Possidonio, nobility is akin to an inherited physical trait, for which he uses the example of skin color: "if a man be white, the child shal likewise be participant of his whitenes: if he be blacke, he shall be partaker of his blacknes" (D2v). He argues further that it is "a general and common custome" to see nobility as synonymous with inheritance in this way, and that disagreeing is equivalent to using "sophisticall arguments, to make men deeme, that white is black" (D4v). Possidonio's rhetoric is far from neutral; not only does it add further support to Feerick's argument about how the concept of inherited gentility was itself a racialized discourse, it also recalls the early modern trope of "the whitewashed Ethiopian," explored by Kim F. Hall as "a ubiquitous image in Renaissance literature, appearing often in emblem books and proverbs as a figure of the impossible."[29] And, as Hall's foundational work demonstrates, White aristocratic identity in the Renaissance was often defined against a Black "other."[30] Possidonio sees the superiority of his own inherited nobility as a manifest truth, and he therefore disdains Fabricio's acquired nobility of learning as artifice not nature (F3v), just as he mocks Fabricio's case as derived from the colors of rhetoric rather than the legitimacy of a natural, physical truth.

Proving something that is self-evident ends up being more of a challenge than Possidonio anticipates. As the dialogue progresses, Fabricio points out the problems with a mode of thinking that asserts that thought is not necessary. Though Fabricio too considers his case to be self-evident, he looks forward to the *argument*, contending that he will "plainly" reveal Possidonio's "manifest error" (Ir) and claiming, "let everie one of them alleadge the most pregnant and strong reasons they can, for I shall not want courage sufficient to confute them all" (E3v). Fabricio makes his case at greater length than Possidonio, posing a number of pointed questions: Who now knows about the descendants of such ancient nobles as the Scipios (I2v)? What about the fact that ignoble children can come from noble blood (I3r–v)? Don't we all descend from Adam anyway (I2r)? He provides new interpretations of Possidonio's examples alongside his own counterexamples, such as Moses' disavowal of Pharaoh's "royall blood" and Jesus' preference for disciples "of base estate" (L2v, Lv). In contrast to Possidonio's insistence on the physical manifestation of nobility, Fabricio anticipates Spenser's claim that "vertues seat is deepe within the mynd" (6.Proem.5) when he asserts that true nobility "consisteth in the vertues of the mind, whither the sight of our outward eies cannot pierce" (I3r). In a similar vein, Fabricio takes on Possidonio's claim that nobility is inherited like skin color:

> I saie that his similitude is not worth a rushe: In asmuch as blacknesse, or whitenesse, are demonstrative dispositions of the body; but Nobilitie is a hidden propertie of the minde, in regard that it

proceedeth of vertue: So that a painter may by arte easily alter either the whitenesse or blacknesse of man: but he can never paint forth with his pensill, the nobilitie of the mind, as being a thing not subiect unto the sight of bodily eyes. (I4v)

Fabricio makes a case for a more nuanced understanding of worth than Possidonio's view that art is simply inferior to nature, masterfully reworking the terms of Possidonio's mocking suggestion that he will attempt to reverse white and black through the distortions of his argument. Here Fabricio concedes that apparently fixed physical characteristics may be more readily manipulated through art than may the interior worth of the truly noble person be depicted or conceived of. Nobility of mind, Fabricio argues, cannot be appreciated with physical eyes, nor does it lend itself to the rhetorical coloring that Possidonio claims.

Most crucially, Fabricio denigrates riches in order to assert the superior value of learning, insisting that wealth, like skin color, is external to the true self and thus the cause of more harm than good. Comparing the rich man to Tantalus, Fabricio asks, "Who is then so unadvised to terme such a one rich?" (L4v). Insisting on the deceptive quality of inherited nobility, Fabricio maintains that the sight of riches paralyzes the judgment and makes discernment of true nobility impossible:

riches ... is a thing most deformed, wearing on the naturall visage thereof, a masque of most fine gold, denoting thereby, that it is faire in apparence, but foule within: wherefore they who travell so many Countries, and take such paines to seeke it, are enamoured with the outward shewe, which blindeth the eyes of the understanding: so that they can hardly discerne how hurtfull the inward deformitie thereof is. (Mv)

In its condemnation of the "faire ... apparence" and "outward shewe" of deceptively glittering surfaces, Fabricio's image both anticipates the golden casket of *The Merchant of Venice* and resonates with Spenser's claims that the contemporary practices of courtesy lead others to "thinke gold that is bras" (6.Proem.5) and that "learnings threasures ... doe all worldly riches farre excell" (6.Proem.2). In his defense of learning over riches, Fabricio adduces such examples as Philip of Macedon and his son, Alexander the Great. Philip's hiring of Aristotle as tutor for Alexander shows that he saw "learning and science, as treasures of far more inestimable

value, then his nobilitie" (M3v). Fabricio further recounts how
Alexander, presumably having learned well from Aristotle, also
valued learning over riches. Having conquered Darius of Persia,
Alexander found a beautiful golden casket decorated with precious stones. He used this casket not for ointments, as Darius had
done, but for Homer's poetry. Fabricio describes Alexander as
"imagining he had not in al his treasure, a jewell of greater value"
than these "poeticall workes" (O4v). Fabricio's many examples
coalesce toward evincing the greater importance of inner essence
over appearance as well as the fundamental role of scholars and
poets. Clearly, Spenser too holds these values dear. Also, needless
to say, the smug and entitled Possidonio's arguments falter against
Fabricio's intellectual assault.

The resolution of the dispute between Possidonio and Fabricio
depends on the judgment of Nennio, who is daunted by the task.
He initially avoids a decision altogether, declaring that both sides
have made arguments that appear "probable," and that therefore
it "scarsely ... may be discerned, which of them draweth nearer the
troth" (S3v). Still, Nennio reveals his fundamental sympathy for
Fabricio's position when he compares a noble man without virtue
to a marble and gold sepulcher, an analogy worth quoting at length:

> For a noble man by bloud, who is deprived of vertue, is made no
> otherwise, then as a sepulchre of white marble, inriched with fine
> gold, which at the first shewe is pleasant to the sight of those, that
> behold it: but considering afterwards the rotten body, and filthy
> stinch, that is within it, it seemeth unto them hideous and horrible.
> Such a one is hee who is descended of noble bloud, for at the first
> sight he seemeth gratious, & pleasing, but looking afterwards to the
> foule corruption of his maners, and to the default of the gifts of his
> mind, by which he shuld become worthie, neither this grace, nor the
> pleasure which was found therein, is anie more seene, but in steede
> thereof basenesse, and deepe contempt. Whereof hee may be called
> noble in apparance by the which the common people (whose eyes are
> blinded, that they cannot see the trueth) doe lightly judge, and holde
> him as a nobleman, which is farre different from him, whose minde
> is fraught with vertues, because that hee holdeth not an apparance of
> true Nobilitie, but the verie essence thereof. (Xr–v)

The image of the golden sepulcher recalls Fabricio's argument
about the hollowness of "outward shewe."[31] Though the slapdash

judgment of the multitude is criticized here, Nennio also points to the possibility of correcting one's initial evaluation of what seems obvious, moving beyond the surface to consider the true nature of things. Perhaps, too, the legacy of nobility based on an inheritance from the dead is questioned through the gruesome imagery of the decaying body. In any case, Nennio underscores the need to reflect before coming to a proper decision about the worth of noble blood when it lacks virtue. His view, like Spenser's commendatory sonnet, emphasizes accurate judgment; it may not be easy to decide at first, but there is indeed a right way to see things. Nennio does not completely discount the value of nobility of blood, however, precisely because of its practical value in influencing the opinions of the crowd, who are taken in by surface appearances. He therefore invents another possibility, "compounded nobility," which combines material riches and learning (S3v). This "compounded" form is clearly his preference; he declares, "The nobility of bloode then, and noblenesse of the minde, when they concur togither in one subject, surely both the vulgar sort, and men of wisedome, will hold such a one to be most noble" (Bbv).[32] Yet only one person can wear a ring, and when Nennio must ultimately decide between the two competitors, he awards the ring to Fabricio. Fabricio's decision to pass the contested ring on to Possidonio demonstrates his mastery of generous savoir faire. In performing this noble act, Fabricio makes use of modesty for self-aggrandizing purposes, carrying out an action that Possidonio himself had only sarcastically expressed a willingness to do were the terms of the debate changed so that the prize would go to the "most unworthy" (Hr). Yet Fabricio too changes the terms of the debate by his apparently magnanimous transfer of the ring.

Fabricio has already paved the way for his renunciation of material goods through his insistence that the truly noble reject riches just as Pompey the Great refused to touch the treasure of the temple of Jerusalem (Mv–M2r). His gesture of generosity to Possidonio therefore cements his superior status even as it adds support to his own definition of nobility, causing their competition to shift from a debate to a kind of potlatch. Marcel Mauss's now classic account of the potlatch, which he describes as "above all a struggle among nobles to determine their position in the hierarchy," shows how the giving or even the scorning of goods may be one way of indicating

superiority.[33] Critics have paid much fruitful attention to the instrumentality of generosity in early modern literature, especially to
how gifts, both literary and otherwise, augment the status of the
giver as much as, or more than, the receiver.[34] Versions of Mauss's
model of the potlatch were theorized *avant la lettre* in the early
modern period; as Stefano Guazzo writes (in George Pettie's translation), "the more loftie we are placed, the more lowly wee ought
to humble our selves: which is in deed, the way to ryse higher"
(44v). While Possidonio credits the importance of liberality in contributing to "a glorie farre exceeding al other" (G3v), making it
part of his argument for the importance of riches,[35] Fabricio, in
contrast, exhibits a metaphorical understanding of generosity. Just
as Fabricio insists that scripture must be read with attention to its
figurative rather than to its literal meaning (T4v–Vr), his gift of the
ring to Possidonio reveals the true meaning of his contention that
"nobilitie is nothing else, but an excellencie, by the which things
that are most worthy, do take place before those that are lesse
worthy" (P3v). Winning the physical prize but conferring it on his
opponent becomes how Fabricio affirms his superiority on a higher
level, encouraging readers to recall the recent assertion of one of
the interlocutors that "gifts of the mind" are "not easie to be trans-
ported from one body to another" (Bb3r). His gift thus changes the
meaning of the contested token; as Fabricio ever so graciously rubs
it in, asking Possidonio to be a "partaker" of the "sentence" that
has just judged him unworthy, he also instructs Possidonio to wear
the ring in remembrance of *him*, rather than the lady Virginia. With
Fabricio's supremacy confirmed, the whole group prevails upon
Possidonio to take the ring as a "signe of brotherlie friendship"
(Ddr). Possidonio, who has spent the whole dialogue loudly trum-
peting his superiority, is finally compelled to accept the condes-
cension of his proclaimed inferior. Fabricio, for his part, receives a
crown of olive leaves, a plant associated with peace as well as with
Minerva's learning, that he is to wear as a "signe of victorie" (Ddv).
The narrator does offer faint praise of Possidonio's contributions
to the argument as "no weake reasons" (Ddv), but there is no real
advocacy in the remainder of the text for nobility based on blood
and wealth. While one reader of *Nennio* has suggested that its end
reveals an "Elizabethan love of compromise,"[36] that view discounts
the extent to which the competing views of nobility are not so much

reconciled as left to stand in tension. As Huntington notes, "this is a text that seems intent on voicing a critique but at the same time achieving deniability."[37] Still, though *Nennio*'s positive gestures toward inherited nobility may make the dialogue's scathing critique of its vices more palatable, the mere fact that nobility of blood is being offered a consolation prize demonstrates just how much it has suffered over the course of the dialogue. Although it is true that readers of Nenna's dialogue must weigh the merits of differing views, these readers, like those of Spenser's commendatory sonnet, have not been given a very challenging task.

Nobility and courtesy in *The Faerie Queene*

In many ways, *The Faerie Queene* follows the humanist emphasis on active virtue over inherited nobility, while also making it impossible to regard that virtue as straightforwardly as *Nennio* does. The Spenserian narrator postulates in Book 6 *both* that "gentle bloud will gentle manners breed" (6.3.2) *and* that "vertues seat is deepe within the mynd, / And not in outward shows, but inward thoughts defynd" (6.Proem.5).[38] In offering such apparently simple—and contradictory—statements about the nature of noble virtue, the narrator encourages readers to *test* these varying assertions rather than to adopt any one of his claims as definitive.

Even as the proem to Book 6 suggests a close relationship between nobility and courtesy, then, it points to the work that will be required of readers in interpreting this link:

> Amongst them all growes not a fayrer flowre,
>   Then is the bloosme of comely courtesie,
>   Which though it on a lowly stalke doe bowre,
>   Yet brancheth forth in braue nobilitie,
>   And spreds it selfe through all ciuilitie:
>   Of which though present age doe plenteous seeme,
>   Yet being matcht with plaine Antiquitie,
>   Ye will them all but fayned shows esteeme,
> Which carry colours faire, that feeble eies misdeeme. (4)

In his attack on contemporary expressions of courtesy and nobility (here tightly connected), the narrator insists that his readers perform the mental exercise of imaginatively contrasting the world around them with the world portrayed in his book. Here the narrator addresses readers directly, speaking of their own thought processes: "*Ye* will them all but fayned showes esteeme" (emphasis mine). Having been counseled to be suspicious of assumptions based on visual evidence, not to mention the "colours faire" of rhetoric, these readers are also in a good position to evaluate the narrator's own claims, including his association of courtesy with "nobilitie," a term that he declines to define specifically. While the description "noble" is frequently used in the first few cantos of Book 6, it appears quite sparingly in the later cantos. Book 6 increasingly emphasizes the movement from inherent nobility as a personal attribute to nobility characterizing an *action* that may admit of more than one interpretation.

In *Nennio*, readers' judgments likely accord with that of the dialogue's characters. In Book 6 of *The Faerie Queene* there are multiple possibilities for the readers' sympathy, as the differing assessments of Calidore, ranging from master manipulator to hero, in the past decades of scholarship attest.[39] Calidore, identified as a knight on Book 6's 1596 title page, could be seen as *Nennio*'s ideal of compounded nobility, linking him to the Earl of Essex, but it is not at all clear that his character blends inherited nobility, as represented by Possidonio, and acquired nobility, as represented by Fabricio, in equal measure. The narrator describes Calidore early in Canto 1 as having a "naturall" "gentlenesse of spright" to which he can "add" the learned art of "gracious speach" which is able to "steale mens hearts away" (2). Though the narrator goes on to say that Calidore "loued simple truth" (3), this description points toward the nuanced relationship between "speach" and "truth" in the poem rather than clarifying Calidore's character. Readers know much more about what Calidore does than what he thinks, rendering decisive judgment of him impossible. In the end, the poem emphasizes his courteous techniques rather than his ability to epitomize one form of nobility over another. The poem's valuing of "inward thoughts" over "outward shows" thus makes it necessary for readers to consider how outward shows—at their best, benevolent actions rather than subterfuge, though the distinction will prove difficult to maintain—serve as imperfect guides to a character's motivations and virtue.

The opening cantos of Book 6 demonstrate the troublesome nature of the link between courtesy and nobility on which the narrator insists in the proem. In Canto 1, Calidore himself connects the two concepts in his criticism of those who "defame / Both noble armes and gentle curtesie" (26), but readers may share Briana's initial disgust with his indiscriminate violence and her sense that these ideals do not combine as neatly as he claims, despite the resolution of that episode (discussed in Chapter 2). Canto 2's depiction of Tristram seems to illustrate the process by which courtesy moves from occupying a modest place to bursting onto the scene in the full-blown expression of nobility, yet in so doing, it invites an interrogation of its own terms.[40] This canto contains an explosion of instances of the word "noble," insisting on how Tristram's inherited gentle blood shines through despite his appearance; he is referred to as or associated closely with the term "noble" no fewer than eleven times in this canto, many more times than any other character in Book 6. Tristram's claim to true nobility is complicated, however, by his grasping relationship to material goods, revealed by his intense interest in the spoils of the knight he has vanquished.

Jeff Dolven argues convincingly that the greed Tristram shows here is part of Book 6's "creeping anxiety about proof"; I would add that his display of greed also encourages readers to evaluate Calidore's thought process in determining Tristram's nobility.[41] Having been told *twice* in parallel lines that Calidore views Tristram's nobility as certain ("That sure he deem'd him borne of noble race" [6.2.5] and "That sure he weend him borne of noble blood" [6.2.24]), Spenser's readers are now well placed to judge just what is meant by this confident label. As they watch how Tristram "long fed his greedie eyes with the faire sight / Of the bright mettall" (39), they may connect his ostensibly assured nobility of birth to the problems with counterfeit courtesy, especially its ability to "please the eies of them, that pas," and make one "thinke gold that is bras" (6.Proem.5). Tristram is here subjected to a "triall of true curtesie" (6.Proem.5)—a trial requiring readers' discrimination and work to bring together different parts of Book 6—and, with his disordered values, it is not at all clear that he passes. As readers begin to wonder if Tristram's golden character may actually be brass, the bond between apparent nobility and true courtesy becomes more and more suspect. While the Tristram episode is cited by Richard Helgerson as part of his claim that Spenser's poem "entertains no … doubts concerning the aristocratic myth of natural, inborn superiority," it may well raise more questions about the nature of inherited nobility than it answers.[42] Tristram's desire to supplement his ostensible natural superiority with the "faire sight" of gleaming metal underscores the degree to which the aristocracy relies on external support.

Book 6's ongoing conflict between presenting nobility as something genuine and inborn—transmitted through the blood—on the one hand, and socially constructed—indeed, fabricated—on the other, continues in Canto 3. This canto is introduced, as we saw earlier in this chapter, with contradictory claims about the causal relationships among the "gentle minde," "gentle deeds," "gentle bloud," and "gentle manners" (6.3.1–2). As Canto 3's episode unfolds, characters demonstrate their mastery of the concept that inherited gentility is closely linked to outward manners. This means, however, that they actively seek to preserve the *appearance* of a quality that the narrator insists is natural. As Calidore comes to the aid of Priscilla and Aladine, illicit, socially unequal lovers, he both reinstates a conservative social system and shows the deception and contradiction at its heart. While sneaking out on a tryst with Priscilla, Aladine—a lesser-born knight who is not Priscilla's father's preferred match for her—has been wounded by the discourteous knight who has since been slain by Tristram. Calidore responds to this bloody scene in which Aladine's "many wounds full perilous and wyde ... all his garments, and the grasse in vermeill dyde" (6.2.40) by doing his best to help cure Aladine's wounds and prevailing upon Priscilla to accept the "base" burden of helping to carry her lover to the safety of his father's castle, where they stay overnight as Aladine recovers (6.2.47–6.3.11). This leads to a potentially reputation-damaging delay in her return home, and both Priscilla and Aladine scramble to avert harm to the honor of her "noble blood" (6.3.11), again with Calidore's help.

Melissa Sanchez's reading of this episode persuasively emphasizes how it works to restore a White patriarchy that is dependent on female chastity, one that links "whiteness, nobility, and sexual purity."[43] Sanchez argues that "slander and courtesy work in tandem to help preserve and naturalize the superiority of Whiteness as both sign and foundation of civilization as such" and that "the regulation of female sexuality is foundational to racial hierarchies"; without the reliability of female chastity, the supposed inheritance

of nobility through the blood to which Spenser refers at the outset of Canto 6.3 becomes impossible.[44] On the one hand, this episode shows the characters at work to preserve the appearance of
unblemished chastity; Priscilla seeks to maintain her reputation
with "coloured disguize," and Calidore thinks in similar terms: "He
can deuize this counter-cast of slight, / To giue faire colour to that
Ladies cause in sight" (6.3.8, 16). Sanchez notes the irony at work
here: "The 'coloured disguize' that Priscilla seeks will restore the
'faire colour' of white, unspotted chastity."[45] Thus, I stress, readers are also provided with a "behind the scenes" view of what is
required to preserve the apparent close, naturalized link between
chastity and inherited noble blood, with courtesy serving as the
effortful means of creating a convincing performance rather than
a natural expression of blood worth. In "coloring" the tale that he
will tell Priscilla's father, Calidore demonstrates his skill in precisely
those contemporary practices of rhetoric that the narrator criticizes
as "fayned showes ... which carry colours faire, that feeble eies
misdeeme" (6.Proem.4).[46]

Readers may well agree that Calidore's methods are dubious,
while also being spurred to question the aim toward which he
employs them—the maintenance of the façade of noble blood that
is shown by episode's end to be neither trustworthy nor particularly valuable. In the classic conflict of young lovers against old
fathers, could the position of Priscilla's father really attract much
sympathy, especially when Spenser tips the balance by emphasizing that Aladine's father is "courteous ... to euery wight" (6.3.3)
and himself a "good old Knight" who is readily able to "temper
his griefe" and convincingly moralize about the "tickle ... state of
earthly things" and the resultant foolishness of envying "the state
of Keasars and of kings" (6.3.5–6)? Priscilla, too, is represented as
caring more about the moral character of her lover Aladine than
the wealth of her father's proposed match; the "meaner borne"
Aladine is nonetheless "full of valour," leading her to "th'others
riches scorne" (6.3.7). In short, the values and choices of the apparent protagonists of this story are the same ones that Spenser and
his narrator elsewhere validate, suggesting that the smooth face
superimposed upon Priscilla's restored chastity and her protected
bloodline are more of a lip-service concession to the values of the
blocking character than a sincere testament to the importance of

inherited noble blood. Indeed, the fact that Calidore *severs the head* of the knight killed by Tristram ("the necke thereof did cut in twaine, / And tooke with him the head, the signe of shame"), which he then offers to Priscilla's father as "witnesse" of his misleading story about her absence (6.3.17–18), suggests that the concept of inherited nobility, preserved through chastity, is in practice much more messy and suspect than the narrator's blithe claim at the outset of the canto that "gentle bloud will gentle manners breed" (6.3.2). Even as this episode depicts the restoration of the patriarchal order, then, it also provides a critical commentary on the hollow nature of the nobility that the characters work to preserve; readers have themselves witnessed unrefuted counterarguments against the value of inherited nobility, and the costs of keeping up appearances are on full bloody display.

Similarly, when readers encounter the narrator's assertion, "O what an easie thing is to descry / The gentle bloud, how euer it be wrapt" at the outset to Canto 5 (1), they will recall the tale that has immediately preceded it: Calepine's satisfaction of Matilde's desire for a "noble *chyld*" with a foundling who will go on to accomplish "right noble *deedes*" (6.4.33, 38; emphasis mine). The characterization of nobility here has shifted toward outward action, and, furthermore, it has been supplemented by Calepine's speech suggesting that proper *training* forms "more braue and noble knights" than being "dandled in the lap" (6.4.35–36). Here too, the very confidence with which both Calepine and the narrator speak invites readers' attention.

Similarly, though the narrator introduces Canto 5 with the assertion that the Salvage Man who rescues Calepine and Serena from the Blatant Beast is a source of obvious proof for the ease with which "gentle bloud" manifests itself ("That plainely may in this wyld man be red … For certes he was borne of noble blood" [6.5.2]), readers have already received abundant cautions to be skeptical of such evidence. As the account of the Salvage Man proceeds, the narrator's claim for his *obvious* nobility is complicated. He is misunderstood by Arthur and Timias when they first approach him (6.5.25), and his displays of violence, though aimed in the proper direction, are unsettlingly animalistic, such as when, lion-like, he attacks Turpine's groom and "him rudely rent, and all to peeces tore" (6.6.22), when he is "found enuironed about /

With slaughtred bodies" (6.6.38), and when, in his attack on Enias, "he flew vpon him, like a greedy kight / Vnto some carrion offered to his sight" (6.8.28). The Salvage Man may indeed contribute to the poem's portrait of gentility—the lion is a noble beast—but his verbal associations with rudeness, slaughter, and greed undermine the correspondence between "gentle bloud" and "sparkes of gentle mynd" (6.5.1) as well as the link between "noble armes and gentle curtesie" (6.1.26). When readers of Book 6 reflect on these early examples of nobility in action, they may be inclined to feel that its definition is not so obvious.

Calidore's generous courtesy

In the latter cantos of Book 6, the term "noble" falls away almost completely, and beginning in Canto 9, Calidore's pastoral sojourn asks readers to consider instead how his courtesy may be both troubling and efficacious. As Louis Montrose has highlighted in drawing from Puttenham's *Art of English Poesy*, the pastoral mode is well suited to the deception of courtly expression; making use of Puttenham's formulation that the device of pastoral allows the poet "under the vaile of homely persons, and in rude speeches to insinuate and glaunce at greater matters," Montrose asserts that "Puttenham's courtier dissembles most cunningly when he is masked as a gentle shepherd."[47] Calidore's strategic poses of deference while among the shepherds—including posing as a shepherd himself—have varying degrees of success, offering readers the tools to consider courtesy from a variety of angles. Both *Nennio* and Canto 6.9 depict contests between noble and lower-born characters, and both texts position the reader as judge in these contests, yet they also differ in important ways. Although *Nennio*'s Possidonio and Fabricio openly compete with one another, and readers are directed to prefer one over the other, Calidore deals with others in ways that admit of less definitive judgments. By restaging Calidore and Coridon's rivalry in Cantos 10 and 11, Spenser requires his readers to revise their conclusions and resist simple distinctions.

Calidore reveals himself in Canto 9 as susceptible to genuine, overwhelming emotion, but also as adept at self-mastery and ready to use speech to manipulate. After being caught by Cupid and "surprisd in subtile bands," Calidore is unable to do much more than gaze at Pastorella (11, 12). When he masters himself again, however, he has the presence of mind to orchestrate the conversation with the shepherds in his favor, drawing it out "to worke delay," and speaking to the shepherds but aiming his words at Pastorella's "fantazy" (12). Having gained a dinner invitation to Pastorella's house, Calidore chooses a post-prandial topic of discussion designed to appeal to his hosts. The narrator describes him in this moment as "the gentle knight, *as* he that did excell / In courtesie, and well could doe and say" (18; emphasis mine). While "gentle" describes Calidore directly, his courteous actions are distanced from him by the term "as," which suggests that he performs *like* a courteous person in his pose, rather than simply *being* courteous. Despite his supposed courteous skill, Calidore is at cross-purposes with Meliboe, Pastorella's foster father. It may well be that they are speaking in different genres: what Calidore seems to intend as pleasing after-dinner *talk* becomes, in Meliboe's responses, a *debate* about the way to live one's life, with Meliboe insisting on the value of withdrawal from the world of commerce. Calidore's expression of envy for Meliboe's low station in life, which may be no more than making conversation, meets with serious rebuke by Meliboe and a lesson about the true nature of contentment. When Meliboe speaks without interruption for six stanzas, Calidore is yet again left to gaze, and yet again left with divided attention, affected by both the sound of Meliboe's speech and the sight of Pastorella. His "greedy eare" suggests a link to Tristram, though the "double rauishment" he feels is not due to gold, but to the myriad attractions of a pastoral world to which he does not really belong (26).

Even as he experiences a real desire to become part of Pastorella's world, Calidore reveals his outsider status by using techniques resembling those of rich show-offs like Possidonio or even Mammon.[48] In an echo of Guyon's words to Mammon ("To them, that list, these base regardes I lend" [2.7.33]), Meliboe asserts to Calidore the importance of rejecting ambition and its attendant spectacles, saying "To them, that list, the worlds gay showes I leaue, / And to great ones such follies doe forgiue" (22).[49] Calidore appears to share this condemnation, declaring, "Now surely syre, I find, / That all this worlds gay showes, which we admire, / Be but vaine shadowes to this safe retyre / Of life, which here in lowlinesse ye lead" (27), but his audience here includes Pastorella. The narrator explains that Calidore condemns the court in order "to occasion meanes, to worke his mind, / And to insinuate his harts desire" (27), lines that echo the narrator's previous description of how Calidore banters with the shepherds simply to create delay.[50] Calidore's carefully chosen words suggest the "painted shewes" of Spenser's commendatory sonnet to *Nennio* despite his attempt to distance himself from court life. Calidore's show may not be completely insincere, but neither is it completely convincing to Meliboe or the reader. When Calidore goes too far in wishing for the shepherd's life, Meliboe offers him a sententious rebuke, calling into question the judgment of the many and telling him "It is the mynd, that maketh good or ill, / That maketh wretch or happie, rich or poore" (29, 30).[51] Meliboe's emphasis on retirement is misinterpreted by Calidore, however, who immediately sees in his assertion that "each vnto himselfe his life may fortunize" the possibility of an active self-fashioning (30, 31).

With his focus on the mind and on the need for proper judgment, Meliboe resembles Fabricio,[52] while Calidore in turn resembles Possidonio when he offers to repay Meliboe for his hospitality. Although Calidore's gesture may seem generous, it suggests a misplaced esteem for wealth that conflicts with what he has just heard Meliboe say about internal contentment. Here Spenser rewrites Tasso's *Gerusalemme Liberata*, his source for this exchange, in an important way. In Tasso, Erminia, the outsider guest who is Calidore's counterpart, shows that she has understood the words of her host by *not* offering the money adored by the vulgar crowd; she only acknowledges that she would have been willing to do so.[53] In contrast, Calidore actually produces the gold and thrusts it toward Meliboe: "forth he drew much gold, and toward him it driue" (32). In offering a "recompense" to Meliboe (32), one of a series of humble hosts in Book 6, Calidore potentially deprives him of the means to enact courtesy, while also demonstrating that he ignored Meliboe's scorn for the time when he sold his services (24). Further, Calidore shows an uncomfortable resemblance to Turpine, who himself uses a disguise of courtesy "to cloke the mischiefe" when he offers a "goodly meed" to Enias and his companion (6.7.4).[54] Meliboe, for his part, practically recoils: "Sir knight, your bounteous proffer / Be farre fro me, to whom ye ill display /

That mucky masse, the cause of mens decay" (33). Meliboe's allit-
eration turns Calidore's attempt to "golden guerdon giue" (32) into
an emphatic rejection of the "mucky masse," which he wants to
be "farre ... farre" from him. Not only is Meliboe's scorn another
echo of Guyon to Mammon, as Judith Anderson has noted,[55] it also
condemns Calidore's sensibilities; Meliboe criticizes both Calidore's
decision to offer him money and his doing so through "display." As
Fabricio asserts in his own critique of Possidonio's view of liberality, "true liberalitie springeth not from riches, but from the love
of the minde" (M2v). Spenser's characterization of courtesy as
"forgerie" in the proem to Book 6 is well illustrated by Calidore's
practice of it here; Meliboe rejects his offers just as Guyon rejects
Philotime's "art and counterfetted shew" (2.7.45).[56] Readers must
judge whether Calidore and Meliboe engage in a competition of
values or merely of courteous one-upmanship in this conversation,
but in any case, Meliboe emerges victorious, in a victory of the
mind's treasures over the power of golden speech and golden gold.

Spenser's readers must continue to exercise discernment in evaluating Calidore's decision to present himself as a shepherd the better
to woo Pastorella, who has also rejected his "courteous guize" in
another alliterative series ("His layes, his loues, his lookes she did
them all despize" [35]). Spenser writes of Calidore that "who had
seene him then, would haue bethought / On *Phrygian Paris*" (36),
a suggestion that Calidore's garb could provoke a critical response.
The association of the Judgment of Paris with a bad choice of life
paths was conventional;[57] Book 2 of *Nennio* begins with an allegorical reading of the myth as proving the greater value of the contemplative life over the active life or the life of pleasure, indicating the
narrator's own sympathy for the case that Fabricio will make about
the nobility of Pallas Athena's domain of learning, and foreshadowing the end of the debate. This reading of the Judgment of Paris in
Nennio also provides a useful lens for viewing Calidore, who, with
his shepherd's garb and lovesickness, may be likened to the Paris of
poor choices.[58] Indeed, readers may remember, yet again, Spenser's
description of the Cave of Mammon, which includes the golden
apple of discord among the fruits of Proserpina's garden and a reference to "partiall *Paris*" in the same position in the stanza as the
reference to "*Phrygian Paris*" in Book 6 (2.7.55). While the term
"Phrygian" may connote effeminacy, the word "partiall" clearly

disparages and evokes faulty judgment. Crucially, Spenser does not just compare Calidore to Paris, he represents the *thought process* of those who might see him in this condition ("who had seene him then, would haue bethought"). Spenser's readers are thus implicitly included among those who would have been *reminded* by Calidore's dubious disguise of a Paris whom they know to be prejudiced and foolhardy. Nonetheless, by pointing to a connection that Calidore's costume might cause others to make, rather than simply declaring Calidore to be *like* Paris, the narrator also hints that the similarity need not be the whole story. The reader's associations also form part of the tale.

As the disguised Calidore goes on to compete with Coridon for Pastorella's love, his insistent deference involves him in another competition in generosity which Coridon loses even as readers must interpret Calidore's courtesy. The narrator clearly describes Coridon's disposition and actions as both base and ineffective; he scowls, pouts, lowers, frowns, and repeatedly bites his lip (38, 39, 41), and he sets up a wrestling contest expressly to embarrass Calidore ("t'auenge his grudge, and worke his foe great shame" [43]). Coridon is unpleasant company. Yet, at the same time that Coridon's motives are made explicit, readers must conjecture about Calidore's thoughts, being told merely that his actions arise from "courteous inclination" (42). Calidore's generosity could derive from ingrained disposition, calculated technique, or a combination of the two. The narrator simply reveals how Calidore's actions *appear* to others, that he "did *seeme* so farre / From malicing, or grudging his good houre, / That all he could, he graced him with her, / Ne euer *shewed* signe of rancour or of iarre" (39; emphasis mine). Calidore's gifts to Coridon call into question his motives even further. Recalling Fabricio's gesture to Possidonio, Calidore places a "flowry garlond" (42) that Pastorella has given him on Coridon's own head.[59] Calidore must lighten his fall to prevent breaking Coridon's neck, but he downplays his success: "Then was the oaken crowne by *Pastorell* / Giuen to *Calidore*, as his due right; / But he, that did in courtesie excell, / Gaue it to *Coridon*, and said he wonne it well" (44). Calidore devalues the gift by saying that Coridon is the rightful recipient of this token of victory; as Stanley Stewart has noted, this only serves to turn the crown into a "token of defeat."[60] Precisely by shifting the crown from his own head to Coridon's, Calidore underscores the fact that what makes him noble, his generous courtesy, *cannot* be shifted to another.

Performing as a shepherd, Calidore typifies the savvy courtliness that operates both through self-deprecation and the genre of pastoral, itself a deceptively humble genre. As Montrose has argued in linking *sprezzatura* and pastoral, "In its essence an art that conceals art, Puttenham's pastoral is a cultural form ideally suited to the strategies of graceful dissimulation recommended in Castiglione's book and practiced in Elizabeth's court."[61] The more Calidore downplays his own efforts in a classic display of *sprezzatura*, the more he can win over his rivals; the narrator's very suggestion that Calidore *excels* in courtesy reveals the nature of courtesy as a means of achieving success in public competition, rather than being an inward disposition. The narrator comments that "courtesie amongst the rudest breeds / Good will and fauour" (45), using a hereditary metaphor that could mean that courtesy is recognized *even* "amongst the rudest," but which also suggests that the rustic crowds who witness Calidore's courteous performance lack the critical judgment of Meliboe, who knows to reject a display of generosity motivated, at least in part, by self-interest. Even if Calidore's generosity dupes the pastoral audience, readers who have witnessed his prior bumbling encounter with Meliboe may well have a more complicated reaction; having seen the rebuke of his previous ostentatious generosity, they have the tools to evaluate his performance of both pastoral impersonation and courtly self-deprecation with a more critical eye. While *Nennio*'s Fabricio shows a certain shrewdness in passing on the ring to Possidonio, he does so as the winner of a contest with explicit terms, making the meaning of the gift explicit. Calidore, in contrast, doesn't reveal the motivation of his generosity, nor does Spenser tell readers directly what to think of it. When Coridon envies Calidore leading the dance, the narrator recounts that Calidore kindly "set him in his place" (42); the double meaning of the line perfectly captures the ambiguity of Calidore's action.

While Spenser's Calidore appears suspiciously adept at manipulating his gifts to secure public favor, he also appears to have a real instinct for generous courage, as subsequent cantos reveal. In Canto 10, his *teleological* desire for the "guerdon" of Pastorella's love (2) stands in tension with the vision of the Graces on Mount

Acidale, who represent the ideal *circulation* of generosity.[62] Calidore is overcome by Colin Clout's explication of the vision just as he is by Meliboe's talk and Pastorella's beauty in Canto 9; he feeds "his greedy fancy," and "his sences" are "rauished" (30). It is tempting to imagine that Calidore learns from this vision, and the narrator does describe him as "voide of thoughts impure" when he resumes his pursuit of Pastorella (32). Soon after he gives her the gift that really wins her over: the head of the tiger from which he has just saved her (36–37). In this moment of unhesitating bravery and self-sacrifice, which Maurice Evans likens to "put[ting] on the mantle of the good shepherd," Calidore distinguishes himself clearly from Coridon and his "cowherd feare" (35).[63] Nonetheless, Calidore immediately follows this deed with actions that underscore his showiness and questionable sincerity, taking the odd step of "hewing off" the tiger's head, presumably with his "shepheards hooke," rather than attending to the more pressing needs of the "scarcely" recovered Pastorella (36).[64] Although killing the tiger should speak for itself, Calidore adds a superfluous proof of his bravery for which Pastorella is bound to repay him with "a thousand" thanks (36). In this, Calidore seems more courtier-like than Christ-like, supplementing actual sacrifice with performative flourishes. A reader who pauses to imagine this messy scene will appreciate the messiness of courtesy itself; as in Canto 3, when Calidore makes use of another head, the actual practice of courtesy contrasts with the narrator's idealizing formulations. Calidore's display of a tiger's head here is strange rather than deceptive, but it does suggest that readers should connect the two moments from Book 6, and even more so when the narrator refers to Calidore's use of rhetorical coloring in the very next stanza. In perhaps the narrator's most critical words so far, readers are told: "Yet *Calidore* did not despise him [Coridon] quight, / But vsde him friendly for further intent, / That by his fellowship, he colour might / Both his estate, and loue from skill of any wight" (37). Calidore's adaptability to the changing demands of his situation, a fundamental attribute of the courtier, means that he can take on the tiger *and* continue to use others. Book 6 as a whole neither utterly rejects nor utterly condones the notions of blood-borne courtesy with which it flirts.

Canto 11 also insists on the practical value of Calidore's courtesy, and even, perhaps especially, his craftiness in deploying it.

Though Calidore may be associated with a vocabulary of use and greed, he also saves Pastorella from the worst examples of such forces by rescuing her from the brigands to whom, as Douglas A. Northrop and Heather Dubrow note, he bears some resemblance.[65] If Spenser's narrator suggests that readers pass judgment against Calidore's efficacious manipulation in Canto 9, the narrator also requires them to revisit that judgment in Canto 11, when the idealistic Meliboe is summarily "slaine" (18),[66] when Calidore must use his ability to influence Coridon with both "meed" and "words" to locate Pastorella (35), and when Calidore's disguise as a shepherd and his willingness to let the brigands "hyre" him enables him to save Pastorella (36, 40). When Calidore acquires the "victors meed" after his battle with the brigands,[67] he passes on the best of the treasure to Pastorella, his primary concern, while giving all the recovered flocks to Coridon (51). Readers who have seen how both Calidore's courage and his grief at Pastorella's apparent death (41) exceed Coridon's may well be inclined to feel that he is the proper victor despite their lingering reservations, reservations not provoked by the conclusion of *Nennio*. By presenting more than one version of the competition between Calidore and Coridon, Spenser calls upon his readers to contemplate the issues at stake from several angles, and to recognize that the text's definition of nobility in action eludes clarification. The noxious tug of courtesy defined as superior birth remains in the poem even as it suggests the serious problems with this definition.

When Calidore captures the Blatant Beast at the end of Book 6, the narrator calls him "noble" for the first time, a word that he has not used since Arthur's defeat of Disdaine in Canto 8 (12.36). Though the appellation underscores Calidore's achievement, it also hints at its precarity; Book 6's series of *agones* has taught readers to suspect the term "noble" as definitive. In rendering Calidore's victory over Coridon in Canto 9 hollow while going on to convey how Calidore's various acts of generosity comprise craftiness, display, *and* courage, Spenser declines to direct the argument of his poetry toward a clear-cut definition of nobility or a simplistic evaluation of courtesy. With his nuanced consideration of Calidore's goal-directed actions, Spenser suggests a different possibility for his own poetry: readers must take time in assessing competing values, recognizing the stakes inherent to a question rather than answering it definitively. Even as Spenser praises accurate decision-making in the commendatory sonnet to *Nennio*, in his own poem he suggests that Calidore's generous virtue derives from a combination of inward thoughts and outward shows that is impossible to untangle, provoking his readers to adopt a view of courtesy that moves beyond simple choices. While the readers of today will be even more skeptical of the case for inherited gentility, Spenser's poem sows the seeds for a thoughtful critique of its own terms.

Courtesy, judgment, and the audience in *The Merchant of Venice*

Like Spenser's *Faerie Queene*, *The Merchant of Venice* investigates courteous generosity by similarly instigating audience awareness of the power of their own judgments; the word "judgment" appears more in this Shakespeare play than any other.[68] As discussed in Chapter 1, the courtier must attend to both his own faculty of judgment, by deploying discretion, and to his peers' verdicts on his social performances. In presenting a variety of competitions, *The Merchant of Venice* closely examines how courteous characters present themselves during several judging moments, both building up to and beyond its notorious courtroom scene. The "triall[s] of true curtesie" (*FQ* 6.Proem.5) presented in the play, I contend, not only demystify the generosity and mercy on which the Christian characters pride themselves, but go further than Spenser in calling upon the audience to explore the radically unstable distinction between virtue and vice in a society founded on courtesy. By employing the device of paradiastole, or the rhetorical redescription of vice as virtue—which is itself concerned with judgment—the play challenges audiences to evaluate critically both the techniques of courtesy and their underlying assumptions about those who are and are not worthy of it.

While other critics have commented on the play's lack of a clear resolution,[69] my argument focuses especially on how courteous relations function as both a structure and a theme in the play, requiring the audience to assess the value of the social transactions it presents. *The Merchant of Venice* constantly raises questions about rhetorical disguise and the shifting meanings of words as it not only depicts characters who are deeply invested in the courteous technique of self-deprecation, but also explores the problems with a world of courtesy in which economic interest is denied.[70] René Girard has said of the play that "it is characteristic of the Venetians that they look like the very picture of disinterestedness at the precise moment when their sly calculations cause the pot of gold to fall into their lap."[71] Harry Berger Jr., who also critiques the role of self-interested generosity in the play, suggests that the Christian characters' "negative usury" allows them to emerge victorious, pointing to the Christians' "shiny displays of self-sacrifice and gift giving" that run contrary to their self-interested motives.[72] In contrasting Shylock's single-minded pursuit of judgment with the flexible judgment revealed by the courteous Christian characters, *The Merchant of Venice* confers an apparent victory for Christian courtesy within the play that may nonetheless provoke audiences to produce varying judgments of their own.

In many ways, *The Merchant of Venice* is a drama of choice; characters are tested, and the right answers provided: "lead" or "mercy." Both "right" answers correspond to what courtesy, with its emphasis on savvy self-deprecation and generosity, dictates. But the play also encourages the audience to see matters as more complicated and to determine on its own the meaning of events. Contemporary stagings of *Merchant* highlight the play's openness to varied judgments. A 2009 performance of the play at the Brooklyn Academy of Music, directed by Edward Hall, began and ended with the words, "Which is the Christian and which the Jew?"—a question that, in framing the main action of the play, was directed to the audience as much as to anyone else.[73] In a 2011 Theatre for a New Audience production, directed by Darko Tresnjak, during the trial scene the Duke's voice boomed overhead as if coming from the audience, placing the audience in the position of judges. Such performance choices are reasonable responses to a play that, like *The Faerie Queene*, depicts true judgment as considering the complexity of a situation more than arriving at a single correct and final answer. In this, *The Merchant of Venice* reveals its indebtedness to the rhetorical tradition of argument *in utramque partem* (argument on both sides of the question) that, as Joel Altman demonstrates, privileges investigating issues from a variety of perspectives rather than determining definitive responses.[74] In *The Merchant of Venice*, this ambiguity raises the unsettling possibility that audiences will approve of the Christians' hypocritical and hateful treatment of Shylock. Nonetheless, the play also provides the tools to criticize this treatment by showing the efforts required to maintain the appearance of an aristocratic Christian virtue that the text both naturalizes and interrogates.[75]

In querying the treatment of the Jewish "other," *The Merchant of Venice* also probes the nature of a Christian aristocratic identity that was uneasily defined, in part, through a superseding of Judaism. Britton has demonstrated the crucial role of theology in contemporary ideologies of race, arguing that " 'infidel' and 'Christian' became racial categories in early modern England."[76] Shakespeare's original audiences would have been familiar with antisemitic bigotry and could well have connected it to the tradition in courtesy literature of scorn for the outsider. Stefano Guazzo, for example, hatefully lumps Jews in with those who "cary a marke in their forehead, and are intollerable":

> Those who for notable cause are hated of the worlde, as some for suspition of heresie, some for theft, some for vsurie, & other for other misdéedes, to whom wée must adde ruffians, harlots, flatterers, dicers, cooseners, and such, who for the basenesse of their condition, and trade of their life, are holden for infamous, as Sergeants, Hangmen, Tormentours. Besides such as differ from vs in religion as *Iewes, Turkes, &c.* (24v–25r)

And yet in Shakespeare's London, converted Jews were not so simple to identify, at least from their Christian neighbors' perspective; as Janet Adelman asserts, "The conversos were troubling partly because they demonstrated the impossibility of knowing what is within."[77] For Adelman, early modern Christians' suspicion about the supposed duplicity of converted Jews is closely related to "anxieties about the difference between Christian and Jew," anxieties that *The Merchant of Venice* explores alongside its pervasive examination of deceptive surfaces.[78] Adelman's rich argument suggests that "the relation between Christian and Jew in *Merchant* turns crucially on blood"; in her analysis of Bassanio, whose machinations my own work is particularly concerned to explore, she notes, "When Bassanio tells Portia that all the wealth he has runs in his veins (3.2.253–54), he makes a claim to inner riches—and to an aristocratic blood difference—that legitimizes his claim to her, despite his outer poverty."[79]

Important readings of the play by Adelman, M. Lindsay Kaplan, and Lara Bovilsky emphasize how it, in Adelman's words, "racializes both 'gentle' and 'Jew.'"[80] In her examination of the play's punning on gentle and gentile, seen in Gratiano's obnoxious reference to Jessica as "a gentle, and no Jew" (2.6.52),[81] Bovilsky argues that the ideology of blood in the play crucially defines both Jews and Christians:

> The word "gentle" itself echoes through the play, nearly always marking or strengthening divisions between characters and serving to encode the values the play endorses. These values permit the absorption of Jewish qualities considered desirable, such as wealth. At the same time, "gentleness" is far more leery of sharing its privileges, or bloodlines, with outsiders.[82]

Although the play's Christian characters profit from their relationships with Shylock and Jessica, as Bovilsky makes clear, they are also at pains to disavow these connections. As Adelman shows in her reading of *Merchant*'s trial scene, however, the play also undermines the notion of a difference between Christian and Jewish blood even as it shows the Christian characters' anxiety to maintain this difference.[83]

While *The Merchant of Venice* makes available pernicious readings of its Jewish characters, then, it concurrently interrogates how Christian aristocratic identity is constructed in part through strained and racialized othering.[84] Shakespeare's play shows courtesy at work against Shylock and those who could be explicitly excluded from the aristocratic, Christian ranks, both insisting on the difference between Christian and Jewish characters and troubling that distinction. *The Merchant of Venice* thus suggests that nobility cannot be neatly defined by lineage, wealth, or character. In presenting multiple and conflicting ways of reading blood, gold, and virtue, the play prompts audiences to consider how the Christian characters' senses of self depend on smoothing over the self-interest at work in their deployment of self-deprecation and generosity, offering audiences further choices about how to interpret courtesy's apparent victories.

Paradiastole and thrift

Merchant repeatedly refers to and also undermines courtesy, rendering readers and audiences potentially skeptical of this apparent ideal. Nerissa describes Bassanio as "a scholar and a soldier" (1.2.107), suggesting that he fulfills the dictates of Castiglione's *Courtier* in pursuing both the active and the contemplative life.[85] Yet the play provides no evidence whatsoever that Bassanio excels as scholar or soldier, thus asking us what difference it makes that he is *described* in this way. Indeed, soon after Nerissa offers this courteous characterization of Bassanio, she downplays both herself and her judgment: "He, of all the men that ever my foolish eyes looked upon, was the best deserving a fair lady" (1.2.112–14). While there is no doubt the requisite courteous self-deprecation in Nerissa's reference to her "foolish eyes," her words also recall Spenser's description of contemporary courtesy as presenting "colours faire, that feeble eies misdeeme" (6.Proem.4). The evaluation of courteous merit in both works is closely connected to a discourse in which fairness is claimed, yet also revealed as deceptive.

Antonio is also characterized as an exemplary figure of courtesy, in contrast to the apparent greed and bloodthirstiness of Shylock, in an opposition that the play both reinforces and critiques. Bassanio calls Antonio "the kindest man, / The best-conditioned and unwearied spirit / In doing courtesies" (3.2.291–93), even as Shylock points to Antonio's rudeness and dehumanizing treatment of him in the Venetian marketplace, sarcastically asking if he should speak to him in the following way: "Fair sir, you spat on me on Wednesday last, / You spurned me such a day; another time, / You called me dog: and for these courtesies, / I'll lend you thus much moneys" (1.3.121–24). As Shylock's irony makes clear, both "fair" and "courtesies" are labile terms, amenable to denoting their apparent opposites despite their use in the text to reify difference.[86] His irony underscores the duplicity of courtesy itself.

In its depiction of the confrontations between Shylock and the Christian characters, *The Merchant of Venice* explicitly problematizes the relationship between rhetoric and moral judgment. It does so especially in its employment and meditation on the device of paradiastole—the technique of rhetorical redescription in which vice may be presented as virtue. Rhetorical redescription is we   ⋅⁼ᵗᵉᵈ to considering complicated issues from more than one   tive, which, as Quentin Skinner has observed, connects it of argument *in utramque partem* (identified by Altmar to Renaissance drama).[87] Puttenham describes paradia discussion of ornament as a figure useful to both poets and courtiers, which involves "when we make the best of a bad thing": "as, to call an unthrift, a liberal gentleman; the foolish-hardy, valiant or courageous; the niggard, thrifty; a great riot or outrage, a youthful prank; and such like terms, moderating and abating the force of the matter by craft and for a pleasing purpose" (3.17). While Henry Peacham disparagingly explains that "this figure is used, when vices are excused" (N4v), Daniel Javitch aptly notes, "By the *Arte*'s standards, the fact that the figure makes a veil of language and thereby conceals meaning is what constitutes its virtue."[88] Indeed, it is striking that Peacham's definition reveals the contradiction at the heart of Puttenham's defense of poetry. Although Puttenham claims that poets played a primary role in the development of civilized society, asserting that they "made the first differences between virtue and vice" (1.4), what Peacham's terms reveal is that poets also have methods that *obscure* this difference. The fact that Peacham can criticize a technique of which Puttenham approves shows how paradiastole requires readers' judgment. For example, in Castiglione, paradiastole is explored in a discussion of the variability of human judgment that recognizes that what is appropriate in one situation may not be appropriate in another: "In everye thynge it is so harde a matter to knowe the true perfeccion, that it is almoste unpossible, and that by reason of the varietie of judgementes" (1.13). For Count Lodovico, the device of paradiastole demonstrates this variety: "And thus dooeth everye man prayse or dysprayse accordynge to hys fansye, always coverynge a vyce with the name of the next vertue to it, and a vertue with the name of the nexte vice" (1.13). For Castiglione, paradiastole (not mentioned by name, but clearly defined) points to the instability of human judgment. Lodovico connects it closely to human uncertainty, saying of his own "smal judgement": "Neither will I (for all that) stand stiffe that mine is better than yours, for not onelye one thynge maie seme unto you, and an other to me, but also unto my self it may appere sometime one thing, sometime another" (1.13). In explicitly engaging with paradiastole, *Merchant* not only dissects courtesy's relationship to judgment, it also, like *The Faerie Queene*, encourages the audience to see how the colors of rhetoric are deployed to defend ostensibly natural aristocratic identity.

In Puttenham's examples of paradiastole, cited above, the root "thrift," which is absent in Castiglione's own definition, strikingly occurs twice. Puttenham's examples suggest something suspicious about both liberality and thrift—either appellation may shift one's interpretation of less flattering situations. Indeed, in Shakespeare the term "thrift" may be negative even without the prefix "un," such as in the suggestion of *Hamlet*'s Player Queen that the only motivation for a "second marriage" is "base respects of thrift" (3.2.176–77). In *The Merchant of Venice*, both Bassanio and Shylock refer to "thrift" for their own diverging purposes. Bassanio first does so as he seeks Antonio's aid, garrulously telling him of the "fair" lady in Belmont, "nothing undervalued / To Cato's daughter," with hair like a "golden fleece," who is sought by "many Jasons" (1.1.162, 165–66, 170, 172). He finally winds around toward asking Antonio for money: "had I but the means / To hold a rival place with one of them, / I have a mind presages me such thrift / That I should questionless be fortunate" (1.1.173–76). As critics have frequently noted, Bassanio's pursuit of Portia is bound up in this early speech with dreams of monetary gain as well as victory in a competition over other men.[89] But Bassanio's speech, with its indirect means of asking for Antonio's money, also functions as a paradiastole. Though Bassanio has failed to act responsibly with Antonio's money in the past, what he points out is not his previous lack of thrift, but his chances for future success. At the same time, his description of Portia's particular beauty—her golden hair—conceals while revealing his financial interest in her love.[90]

Shylock's use of "thrift" invokes paradiastole even more explicitly as he defends his practice of charging interest, revealing his own rhetorical powers as he seeks to defend himself from Antonio's dehumanizing treatment. Shylock recognizes that there is more than one way to define his economic activities, but he suggests in an aside that Antonio is the one who is distorting the truth: "my well-won thrift, / Which he calls 'interest'" (1.3.46–47). Later in conversation with Antonio (in his extended comparison of his profit-making to Jacob's crafty, successful sheep breeding) he again makes clear his view that what Antonio considers to be "interest," he considers "thrift."[91] Skinner suggests that Shylock's use of the term "thrift" as a rhetorical redescription would be "unsympathetically ... viewed even by the rhetoricians themselves" of Shakespeare's time, an assertion supported by Antonio's blunt dismissal of Shylock: "Mark you this, Bassanio, / The devil can cite Scripture for his purpose. /

An evil soul producing holy witness / Is like a villain with a smiling cheek, / A goodly apple, rotten at the heart. / O, what a goodly
outside falsehood hath!" (1.3.93–98).[92] Indeed, the play certainly
allows for the possibility that audiences will identify with this antisemitic characterization of Shylock. Antonio's disgust with Shylock
accords with what Geraldine Heng has traced as a long history in
England of viewing Jews as both economically rapacious and "figures of absolute difference."[93] This disgust is seconded by Bassanio,
who concludes their discussion by expressing his doubts about the
"merry bond": "I like not fair terms and a villain's mind" (1.3.169,
175), echoing both the moral and class-based insult "villain," as
well as implying by contrast that Shylock himself is far from "fair."
In doing so, Bassanio invokes a whole discourse that associates
Jews with dark skin in contrast to supposed Christian fairness,
articulated by critics such as Kaplan and Britton and Coles.[94] Most
recently, Ian Smith traces the echoes of "fair" throughout the play
in order to cogently argue that this scene is crucial to its construction of Whiteness as well as Blackness, underscoring that what the
"merry bond" will potentially bestow on Shylock is Antonio's "fair
flesh," and saying of it: "In Shakespeare's Venice, Shylock's negotiated bond is a thoughtful, subtle, and strategic political act of
resistance to the oppressive systematic whiteness that marginalizes
and blackens him relentlessly through Antonio's cultural agency."[95]
I would add to this important reading that Shylock's deployment
of the same device that underpins Antonio's self-serving rhetoric is
another way he seeks to deflate his rival and construct their moral
equivalence, revealing to the audience the shared economic interest
that connects him to the Christian characters.

   While Bassanio and Antonio work to reinforce the supposed distinction between themselves and Shylock, then, the play also suggests their resemblance; both Christian characters adeptly present
the "goodly outside" they criticize in Shylock when desired, which
is typically when they are performing generosity for their own in-
group. An audience that has previously been engaged by Bassanio's
own self-serving description of his romantic pursuit of Portia as
the path toward "thrift" is primed to consider the conflict—and
connection—between Bassanio and Shylock as making vivid a
debate rather than presenting an obvious villain. Even as it traf-
fics in pernicious stereotypes about Shylock, then, the dialogue

adjudicating the bond also problematizes the Christians' own self-defining claims to plain-dealing fairness.[96]

Indeed, as it continues, *Merchant* suggests that one of the crucial differences between Shylock and the Christian characters is not the latter's freedom from subterfuge, but rather their aptitude for deploying deception. The fact that both Bassanio and Shylock make use of the term "thrift" creates a textual link between them that is hard to discount. In contrast to Shylock, however, Bassanio is skillful at taking on new poses and even new identities that will help him to acquire the rewards he seeks. Despite his need to borrow money from Antonio and his economic interest in Portia, Bassanio presents himself throughout the play as a figure of courteous liberality, instantly ready to grant the requests of Gratiano and Lancelot.[97] He is able, at once, both to protest that he will act more responsibly in the future and to keep up the same habit of ostentatious generosity that presumably caused him trouble in the first place.[98] Shylock, however, maintains a more single-minded view of his thrift; it is not just something that he will *acquire*, but part of what he *is*. This is underscored by the fact that even in the privacy of his home (and so apart from any need to put on a public face), he repeats for his daughter Jessica a saying that itself is repetitive: " 'Fast bind, fast find.' / A proverb never stale in thrifty mind" (2.5.52–3). Shylock does not merely seek rhetorical cover with his use of the term "thrift"; he claims it as a description of his very nature.

Outward shows and fair ornament

The play dramatically takes up the question of paradiastole and "outward shows" in the scene when Bassanio rejects the golden casket, thereby winning Portia. While Bassanio's speech denigrates the use of rhetorical redescription, it does so for its own rhetorical purposes. In scorning the golden casket and in refusing to praise himself as his rivals do, Bassanio demonstrates the modest self-deprecation that is central to the performance of aristocratic identity in the Renaissance, following Castiglione's dictate that "yet ought a man alwaies to humble himself somewhat under his degree, and not receive favour and promocions so easilye as thei be offred him, but refuse them modestlye" (2.19). An audience cognizant that

Bassanio seeks both Portia and her cash is positioned to interpret Bassanio's speech as both a kind of potlatch and a pose of courteous deference rather than true modesty. Even the name "Bassanio" suggests the low humility with which he presents himself to others as he works toward self-advancement.

Before the casket test itself, audiences receive multiple reminders to be on their guard; just as Bassanio chooses between different caskets, they must choose between different views of Bassanio. An audience that laughs at Portia's exclamation "Go, Hercules!" (3.2.60), as they tend to do, is primed to consider the stark difference between Bassanio and Hercules. The song that precedes Bassanio's choice-making speech points to the problems with "fancy" generated in the "eye," a cerebral process less weighty than judgment, even as it may cause audiences to be wary about whether Bassanio is being given an explicit hint about which casket to pick or not (3.2.63–71).[99] Most crucially, audiences already know the answer to the casket test by process of elimination, and their sense of dramatic convention must also make Bassanio's correct choice seem like a foregone conclusion. If they are not in suspense about the outcome, however, they may well be curious as to how the feckless Bassanio will achieve it. As he makes his choice, Bassanio exhibits his *sprezzatura* by having at the ready a long, polished speech that ostensibly relates his impromptu thinking, but that seems out of character for his scattered and self-indulgent personality.[100]

As Bassanio makes vivid his purported reasons for choosing the lead casket, then, he demonstrates his courteous savoir faire as he scorns the kind of rhetorical self-presentation of which he is a master. Central to Bassanio's argument in support of the lead casket is his rejection of ornament. For Castiglione, "ornament" is a word with a strongly positive valence; the courtier's "grace," for example, is "an ornament to frame and accompanye all his actes, and to assure men in his looke, suche a one to bee woorthy the companye and favour of every great man" (1.14). While, in a telling metaphor, Puttenham openly endorses the "richest attire" for poetry over "simple apparel" (3.1), Bassanio makes the denigration of poetic ornament the theme of his speech:

> So may the outward shows be least themselves,
> The world is still deceived with ornament.
> In law, what plea so tainted and corrupt,

But, being seasoned with a gracious voice,
Obscures the show of evil? In religion,
What damned error but some sober brow
Will bless it and approve it with a text,
Hiding the grossness with fair ornament?
There is no voice so simple but assumes
Some mark of virtue on his outward parts. (3.2.73–82)

Bassanio's lengthy speech criticizes many facets of society: "law," "religion," brave men, and beautiful women. The entire speech obsesses over the problem of how to distinguish truth from fiction, nature from art, and in so doing it takes aim at the foundations on which Bassanio's own character is built; as Patricia Fumerton underscores, apparently trivial ornaments were crucial to the self-definition of the aristocracy.[101] Here Bassanio criticizes the very ornament that he formerly manipulated with panache as he considered his self-presentation. Having been instructed by Antonio to show "fair ostents of love / As shall conveniently become you there" (2.8.44–45), Bassanio now both employs and disavows "fair ornament," all in the service of pursuing a woman whom the text insistently associates with fairness.[102] Even as Bassanio presents a display of spontaneous aristocratic superiority, the text's recurrent, shifting use of the term "fair" renders ironic his ostensibly natural gentleness of blood.

Although Bassanio strives to keep his distinctions neat, the strict contrast that he asserts between interior and exterior is problematic. When Bassanio asks "In law, what plea so tainted and corrupt, / But, being seasoned with a gracious voice, / Obscures the show of evil?," the location of the actual evil is difficult to pin down. The question begins by referring to a "tainted and corrupt" "plea," but by its end the "gracious voice" is "obscur[ing] the show of evil"; the voice articulating the plea seems to be both "corrupt" and "gracious," raising the troubling possibility that there is no clear foundation for either virtue or vice, but that they are determined by "shows" that create different impressions and effects. The problem of interpreting verbal performances is underscored when Bassanio asserts, "There is no voice so simple but assumes / Some mark of virtue on his outward parts" (3.2.81–82). The Arden editor retains the word "voice" used in early editions of the play; the Second Folio supplied the word "vice" here for "voice," a correction also accepted by other editors, including those of the Oxford and Riverside editions.[103] I would propose that the verbal echoing of "vice" and "voice" need not be definitively resolved, but that we should take note of how two words that would have had close auditory echoes in performance link vice with pleasing speech, doing so in a speech that is itself pleasing. As well, whether we accept later editors' emendations of "voice" to "vice" or not, Bassanio's assertion that "there is no voice so simple but assumes / Some mark of virtue on his outward parts" and his reference to "hiding the grossness with fair ornament" also suggest very strongly the device of paradiastole, as Skinner has noted.[104] Though Bassanio's words point toward the need for authenticity, they also reveal a courteous disposition at work, one ready to *show* his best self to his current audience. The monologue thus provides the audience with additional ways to take the measure of Bassanio's own selective self-presentation. Tellingly, for example, he criticizes "cowards" who wear "beards of Hercules and frowning Mars," a reference that may make the audience recall Portia's ludicrous comparison of him to Hercules. Bassanio's lecture places him in the false position of objective observer of a social system in which he himself is implicated. While Spenser's and Shakespeare's texts both present the interpretation of courtesy as a difficult problem to be explored from a variety of angles, Bassanio's speech offers instead a smug and self-serving dismissal of performance that is itself part of a calculated performance.

Though he presents himself as the opponent of "outward shows," Bassanio also reveals himself to be vulnerable to these shows, or at least puts on a show of being vulnerable; he underscores the stark difference between what is authentic and what is not, but his subsequent words and actions trouble that distinction. When the opening of the casket indicates that he has won the competition, Bassanio quickly follows up his criticism of gold with praise of the golden hair shown in "fair Portia's counterfeit," acknowledging its ability to trap men and showing himself trapped by it (3.2.115). Bassanio's effusions over Portia's hair, lips, and eyes render even more ironic both his previous words and those that he will shortly read from the scroll ("*You that choose not by the view*" [3.2.131]). His praise for the "counterfeit" is specifically praise for an artistic recreation that has the ability to seem genuine; recall Puttenham's approving assertion that the poet "is both a maker and a counterfeiter" (1.1). Bassanio here proclaims, "What demigod / Hath come so near creation?" (3.2.115–16), pointing to the counterfeit's convincing realism even as he acknowledges the work of the "painter" who has "woven / A golden mesh t'entrap the hearts of men" (3.2.121–22). While he earlier criticizes the power of "gaudy gold" "to entrap the wisest" (3.2.101), here Bassanio applauds this power. In both Bassanio's speech and Portia's portrait, art masquerades as nature, allowing audiences to read in Bassanio's rhetorical praise of the portrait either his emotional helplessness, or his *sprezzatura*, or indeed both at once.

A further echoing of words in the scene ("praise" and "prize") underscores the degree to which Bassanio's rhetorical self-presentation is linked to the reward that he seeks in Portia: "Yet look how far / The substance of my *praise* doth wrong this shadow / In under*priz*ing it, so far this shadow / Doth limp behind the substance" (3.2.126–29; emphasis mine). The verbal echo of "praise" and "prize" repeats in Bassanio's extended simile: "Like one of two contending in a *prize* / That thinks he hath done well in people's eyes, / Hearing applause and universal shout, / Giddy in spirit, still gazing in a doubt / Whether those peals of *praise* be his or no" (3.2.141–45; emphasis mine). Though this extended simile is often cut in performance, it is an important place for a reader or audience member to pause, think, and judge, as Bassanio compares what he has just done to a social performance and competition. The simile underscores the difference between the Bassanio who can present himself as a wise judge while speaking in defense of the lead casket and the Bassanio who seems to have lucked out in his proper choice and acquisition of Portia; his self-deprecation also masks the courtly savvy that determined his choice of casket. Bassanio's selection of the lead casket is a downplaying of himself that allows his suit to emerge victorious, and he imagines his victory as a defeat of his rivals in a social setting, one that has earned him "applause" and high estimation "in people's eyes," even if he won't be fully convinced of this until his victory is sealed with Portia's kiss (3.2.141–48). He can afford to act uncertain so that others must crown his victory, thus lending it more authority. Like Calidore savvily competing against Coridon, Bassanio triumphs precisely through his practiced self-deprecation, displaying his vulnerability as he exhibits the dawning awareness that he has won the game. Before the scene is over, Bassanio's scorn for the golden casket, and his attestation of Antonio's courtesies, have earned him from the golden-haired Portia "gold / To pay the petty debt twenty times over" (3.2.305–06). Bassanio's performance is largely effective to the other characters in the play, but the audience, possessed of a "behind the scenes" view of what brings him to Belmont, may well have a different reaction. Just as Spenser's readers see the messy efforts that Calidore puts into preserving Priscilla's spotless reputation, so too do Shakespeare's audiences witness the stumbling Bassanio before he appears on stage at Belmont.

The casket test, appearing to determine Bassanio a superior suitor, permits audiences insight into how aristocratic identity depends on contradictory displays of courtesy; explicit reflection on the device of paradiastole, treated as a topic in Bassanio's speech, invites further thought, too, about the self-serving rhetoric that constructs the nobility. As in Spenser's Book of Courtesy, true nobility also undergoes a "triall of true curtesie" in *Merchant* as characters who are *called* noble are put to the test. Bassanio's first appearance in the play coincides with a bland reference to his nobility: "Here comes Bassanio, your most noble kinsman" (1.1.57). Yet this apparently clear-cut reference is soon undercut by Bassanio's own description of himself as having "disabled" his "estate / By something showing a more swelling port" than he was able to maintain, leading him to be "abridged / From such a noble rate" (1.1.123–24, 126–27). Rather than being an intrinsic quality of Bassanio, his "aristocratic standard of living," as Drakakis glosses "noble rate," is something that can be lost. Indeed, in the casket scene Bassanio stages a miniature version of the debate about inherited gentility when he says to Portia, "When I did first impart my love to you, / I freely told you all the wealth I had / Ran in my veins—I was a gentleman— / And then I told you true. And yet, dear lady, / Rating myself at nothing, you shall see / How much I was a braggart" (3.2.252–57). Bassanio's description of the worth of noble blood turns rather quickly to the suggestion that, in practical terms if nothing else, as a debtor and a spendthrift he is worth less than "nothing." Other references to nobility in the play underscore its emptiness as a signifier; Portia calls both the Prince of Morocco and the Prince of Arragon "noble prince" (2.7.2 and 2.9.4) as they prepare to make their choice of caskets, a task in which both show an inflated sense of self-worth. Morocco is dismissed by Portia with a racist reference to his appearance ("Let all of his complexion choose me so" [2.7.79]) and Arragon—who makes a reasonable case that honor should be determined by merit, despite his being otherwise a buffoon—is dismissed as a fool (2.9.36–48, 79). Finally, Portia's nobility of character is probed, too. Initially complimented by Lorenzo as one who has "a noble and a true conceit / Of godlike amity" (3.4.2–3), she is also effusively praised by Shylock for her role at his trial scene, twice called a "noble judge" (4.1.242, 249) in words that the audience cannot take at face value. When Shylock addresses Portia with "O noble judge! O excellent young man!" (4.1.242), the audience can see the irony at work because Portia dissembles as both a judge and a man, thus undermining the epithet "noble" as well. Shylock unknowingly suggests here just how much the definition of nobility in the play has been left to the audience's judgment, a question that becomes increasingly urgent given Portia's imminent participation in his punishment.

Shylock and judgment

Bassanio deploys judgment by adapting his performances to circumstances; in this way he contrasts with Shylock, who takes a stricter view of judgment, especially in the courtroom conflict. Just as the casket challenge is a judging moment for the audience as well as the characters, so too is the play's trial scene. Audiences with any sense of the conventions of comedy will not doubt that Antonio's life will be spared, but, as with the casket test, they may well wonder *how* the desired outcome will be achieved. As it contrasts dexterous Christian courtesy with ostensible Jewish rigidity, the play reifies the differences between the characters and yet debates the basis for that distinction. (Here it is especially useful to recall Akhimie's insight that the conduct book tradition also served to exclude many, which she aptly characterizes as "the fact of immobility despite the promise of betterment through cultivation."[105]) In the case of *Merchant*, the Christian characters' bigoted dismissal of Shylock as a lost cause closely connects to the presentation of his immobility of character. The Duke explicitly links the bestowing of mercy to "offices of tender courtesy" (4.1.32), but Shylock refuses to follow the suggestion that he act as the Christians request. Other characters refer to him offensively in terms suggesting rigidity and obstinacy, such as calling him an "impenetrable cur" (3.3.18) or a "stony adversary" (4.1.3), but Shylock also claims his own immobility as stability, speaking of his "lodged hate" and "certain loathing" (4.1.59). For Shylock, judgment should serve justice, as he makes clear in assertions such as "What judgement shall I dread, doing no wrong?" (4.1.88), and "I stand for judgement" (4.1.102). By repeatedly asking for one simple unchanging thing, Shylock is vulnerable to being outfoxed by the Christian characters who are so adept at changing the terms of the argument. Just as Shylock wants his motto "fast find, fast bind" always in the forefront of his mind, he also rigidly pursues the letter of the "sentence" (4.1.294 and 300) against Antonio.

Given the Duke's connection of mercy with courtesy, it may be tempting to equate Portia's famous courtroom defense of mercy as exemplifying courtesy at its self-sacrificing best, and indeed, in popular culture the speech is frequently taken out of context to suggest just such an idealistic view of mercy. However, even in her monologue Portia points to the instrumental dimension of mercy, describing it as something that blesses both the receiver and the giver, and is "becom[ing]" to a king (4.1.184); here we might recall Calidore's words to Briana's seneschal: "Who will not mercie vnto others shew, / How can he mercy euer hope to haue?" (6.1.42). More than that, Portia's lauding of mercy also recalls Bassanio's praise of the lead casket, in that it seems more designed to provoke audience reflection than to provide a coherent addition to Portia's character. Both the casket test and the trial scene have a fairytale, "riddle" quality to them as they lead the audience through the steps of seeing how the counter-intuitive answer is the "right" one, while also displaying the risks of being smugly satisfied with one answer.[106] In any case, Portia readily abandons her espousal of mercy when it is time to judge Shylock, refusing him any leeway from his requests in telling him that he shall have "merely justice" (4.1.335). Thus, Portia reveals her expertise in courtesy in this scene most of all in her ability to *make use* of the doctrine of mercy, and then to discard it when it no longer serves her, ensuring her success before the social audience of the courtroom.[107]

I add my reading of the courtroom scene, with its emphasis on the demystification of courtesy, to an important tradition of seeing it as a place of potential critique. Adelman's reading of this trial scene connects the possibility that Shylock will literally expose Antonio's heart to the play's concern with the problem of hidden interiority. Her argument underlines the way in which the play ends up being as much about the difficulties of interpreting the Christian characters as about Shylock, suggesting, "Though it creates a monstrous Jew as it reproduces the threat of circumcision and crucifixion in 4.1, it also allows us to see what needs that creation fulfills, for its characters as well as its audience."[108] For Adelman, "Portia manages to reinforce something like a Belmont-style xenophobia even in Venice itself ... her rescue of Antonio depends crucially not only on the niceties of Venetian law but on her reinstating of the distinctions—between Christian and Jew, citizen and alien—that Venetian law had initially seemed immune to."[109] In his reading of the courtroom scene, Ian Smith points out that Portia's clever condition that Shylock not spill any of Antonio's blood connects to the play's presentation of racialized blood, exposing how the Christian characters in the play—coded as White—are uniting to defend themselves against Shylock's possession of Antonio's "fair flesh"; for Smith this demonstrates "Shakespeare's critique of whiteness."[110] Thus, while the play ends with a victory over Shylock, the work of both Adelman and Smith clarifies the extent to which it also unmasks the effort required to support the categories of Christian and White. In extending these important arguments, I would emphasize here just how much *Merchant* also invites audiences to take the play's demystification of courtesy as a spur to their own judgment. Bassanio's *sprezzatura* and easy generosity, together with Portia's performative mercy, may be held up as ideals, but the audience has also seen behind the curtain.

Portia's substitution of brutal justice for apparent mercy despite her own claim that "earthly power doth then show likest God's / When mercy seasons justice" thus proves apt Bassanio's suggestion that courts of law are places where what is "tainted and corrupt" is "seasoned with a gracious voice" (4.1.192–93, 3.2.75–76). The audience has been given the vocabulary to critique the Christians' hypocrisy through Bassanio's own account of "outward shows," suggesting, in its treatment of paradiastole, that their victory has more than one interpretation. When the Duke and Antonio do bestow apparent mercy on Shylock in order that he might "see the difference of our spirit" (4.1.364)—reducing his fine on the condition that he convert—the audience is empowered to criticize a mercy revealed as a *display* of courtesy that more closely resembles revenge. In *A Discourse of Civill Life*, Lodowick Bryskett describes the magnanimous man in this way:

> knowing right well that whoso offereth iniury to another, cannot be rightly called Magnanimous, he abstaineth from doing any: and if any man haue offered him iniurie, he holdeth it for the greatest and honorablest reuenge to forgiue, though he haue the partie in his power, & maye satisfie himselfe; and thinketh that the greatest displeasure he can worke to his enemy, is to shew himselfe euermore garnished with vertue. (232)[111]

Bryskett's account highlights the disguised competition—even hostility—that might be expressed through apparent generosity. As Bryskett's account of revenge disguised as forgiveness suggests, virtue may be no more than an ornament of the courteous man who is "garnished with vertue" rather than possessing it as a fundamental part of his character. In its culminating presentation of mercy, then, *Merchant* also presents the radical instability of courtesy, revealing it, like poetry, to be both a force for civilization and a means of rendering hypocritical that civilization, a means of differentiating vice from virtue and a means of obscuring that difference.[112]

Though the Christian community successfully ostracizes Shylock, Shakespeare's play also provides ample material to critique that apparent victory; the audience may well wonder if the marvelously flexible contrasts to Shylock are any better, or indeed as good. Close to the beginning of the play, as I have noted, Shylock speaks with bitter irony of the "courtesies" that Antonio has inflicted upon him; one of his last lines of the play is also suffused with the irony of defeat as he is forced by Portia's mercy to say, "I am content" (4.1.389). As before, he draws attention to the contrast between the Christians' actions and their supposed values as he suggests the coercive power of courteous renaming. A 2010–11 production of the play, directed by Daniel Sullivan for the Public Theater and on Broadway, hid nothing about what Shylock's imposed conversion entailed, presenting a baptism in which his head was dipped three times, and lingering on the last dunking long enough to suggest that his head might be kept under water—that forced baptism would give way to drowning. This disturbing moment underscored the violence and cruelty at work in the imposition of the Christians' ostensibly merciful sentence. Even as the play definitively excludes Shylock, it also points to the antisemitic discrepancy between the words and actions of the Christian characters.[113]

In their presentations of contests in courtesy that appear to have clear winners, Spenser's Book of Courtesy and Shakespeare's *Merchant of Venice* spur further reflection on how nobility is defined and maintained. While nobility of blood is acknowledged to have obvious practical advantages in both works, both also deem problematic the techniques by which noble blood insists on its difference from others. As they demystify the techniques of courtesy—which are also the techniques of the poet's craft, namely rhetorical colors and ornament—*Faerie Queene* Book 6 and *The Merchant of Venice* reveal the variable nature of the relationships between inherited nobility and outward shows, demonstrating just how much terms such as nobility, courtesy, and generosity resist simple definition; blood and gold are both equated and placed into opposition with one another, as characters who pride themselves on their supposedly innate courtesy employ the tools of rhetoric to protect their social position. Readers and audience members watch characters both create successful pretenses and make judgments, and they are also implicitly invited to refine their own judgments in dialogue with those of the texts. The painful history of discrimination in which these works participate is also called into question by them. In the following chapter, I will continue to explore how nobility is recognized, showing how both Spenser and Shakespeare critique aristocratic identity-fashioning by prompting reflection on their own artistry.

Notes

1 Cited in Cox's edition of *The Book of the Courtier.*
2 On the complicated relations between the narrator's precepts and his text, see especially Harry Berger, "Narrative as Rhetoric." For the narrator's ability to provoke with an "overly neat syllogism," see

Richard Neuse, "Book VI as Conclusion to *The Faerie Queene*," 341. See also Jane Grogan, *Exemplary Spenser*, 65, and Isabel MacCaffrey, *Spenser's Allegory*, 52.

3 The speech goes on at some length, placing a strong emphasis on "gentillesse" as a gift from God (1162–63). It also specifically credits Dante for this emphasis on Christian virtue (1125–30). As the *Riverside Chaucer* notes explain, the speech is also indebted to Boethius's *Consolation of Philosophy*, which Chaucer translated. Note, for example, Chaucer's translation of Philosophy's words: "Certes dignytees ... aperteignen properly to vertu, and vertu transporteth dignyte anoon to thilke man to whiche sche hirself is conjoigned" (3.Prosa 4.37–40).

4 Note that Fabricio mocks Possidonio for implying a similar connection between human and animal breeding (*Nennio*, I3v).

5 On Spenser's distortions of Chaucer, see also A. C. Judson, "Spenser's Theory of Courtesy," 123–24.

6 Dennis Britton and Kimberly Coles, "Spenser and Race," 4.

7 Jean Feerick, *Strangers in Blood*, 10 and 6.

8 Andrew Hadfield, "In the Blood," 56. Hadfield also notes the importance of analogies of horse breeding in the Renaissance.

9 Ania Loomba, *Shakespeare, Race, and Colonialism*, 7. As Loomba also notes, "what we call race does not indicate natural or biological divisions so much as social divisions which are characterized as if they were natural or biological" (3); on the equation of race and class in the period, as seen in Polixenes' famous discussion of the crossbred flowers in *The Winter's Tale*, see also Loomba, *Shakespeare, Race, and Colonialism*, 32–35.

10 Loomba, *Shakespeare, Race, and Colonialism*, 63.

11 See Feerick, *Strangers in Blood*, 25–54.

12 Patricia Akhimie, *Shakespeare and the Cultivation of Difference*, 2 and 29.

13 Akhimie, *Shakespeare and the Cultivation of Difference*, 3.

14 Akhimie, *Shakespeare and the Cultivation of Difference*, 35.

15 Akhimie, *Shakespeare and the Cultivation of Difference*, 13.

16 Raffaele Girardi includes a brief biography and discussion of the dialogue in the introduction to his edition of the text (*Il Nennio*, v–xxxii). Jones published translations of Lipsius and Guicciardini in 1594 and 1595 with Spenser's publisher Ponsonby. For the scant bibliographical information available on Jones, see Leslie Shepard's biographical note in Alice Shalvi's facsimile edition of the 1595 *Nennio*, xiv, as well as Franklin B. Williams Jr., "Commendatory Sonnets." The other commendatory sonnets to Jones's *Nennio* were written by Samuel Daniel, George Chapman, and Angel Day.

17 Willy Maley notes that Sonnet 80 of the *Amoretti*, which claims that
   The Faerie Queene is complete, was entered in the Stationers' Register
   in November 1594 (*Spenser Chronology*, 62). But Hugh MacLean
   and Anne Lake Prescott allow for the possibility that it was revised
   before itself being entered in the Stationers' Register in January 1596
   (*Edmund Spenser's Poetry*, 619). A French translation of the dialogue
   was published in 1583. Shalvi also notes the accuracy of Jones's translation, an assessment with which I concur (*Nennio*, xii).

18 *Nennio, or A Treatise of Nobility: Wherein is discoursed what true
   Nobilitie is, with such qualities as are required in a perfect Gentleman.*
   I have appreciated the opportunity to consult the 1595 edition and
   the original 1542 Italian edition in the Folger Library.

19 The poem is printed after A4; John Huntington notes that the commendatory sonnets were "clearly a late edition" (*Ambition, Rank,
   and Poetry*, 168n. 14). See also the sharply critical characterization of
   inherited nobility found in Spenser's *Teares of the Muses*: "But they doo
   onely strive themselves to raise / Through pompous pride, and foolish
   vanitie; / In th'eyes of people they put all their praise, / And onely boast
   of Armes and Auncestrie: / But vertuous deeds, which did those Armes
   first give / To their Grandsyres, they care not to atchive" (91–96).

20 The use of "visnomy," or physiognomy, is interesting in this context,
   as it points to a relation between the exterior and the interior that is
   especially complicated in *The Faerie Queene*.

21 For the Italian tradition of this debate, both primary texts and intro-
   ductions, see Albert Rabil Jr., *Knowledge, Goodness, and Power*.
   Rabil locates the beginning of the Italian debate in Dante's *Convivio*,
   which emphasizes virtue over wealth (3, 12). Quentin Skinner in
   Foundations of Modern Political Thought notes that "the equation
   between virtue and nobility became a humanist commonplace" (82),
   though he also emphasizes the conservative attitude toward the aristocracy held by many northern humanists (238). On the topic of
   nobility in Spenser, see Lila Geller, "Spenser's Theory of Nobility,"
   an article that places more emphasis on the importance of aristocratic
   blood than I believe the text warrants. William A. Oram also makes
   brief reference to *Nennio* as well as to the different definitions of
   nobility of which Spenser's Dedicatory Sonnets make use ("Seventeen
   Ways of Looking at Nobility," 106–07 and 110).

22 Nenna here uses the term *animo*. Jones makes use of the term "mind"
   to translate both *anima* and *animo*, though he will also at times translate *anima* as "soul," as on N3v when he translates both *anima* and
   animo in the same passage.

23 Alexander Judson, "Spenser's Theory of Courtesy," 123.

24 Millar MacLure, "Nature and Art in *The Faerie Queene*," 16.

25 John Huntington, *Ambition, Rank, and Poetry*, 75. On Spenser's agreement with Fabricio in this sonnet, see also Louis Montrose, "Spenser and the Elizabethan Political Imaginary," 922–23. For the view that Spenser is sympathetic to the possibility of social mobility in this sonnet, see also Arthur F. Marotti, " 'Love is Not Love,' " 418 and Christopher Ivic, "Spenser and the Bounds of Race," 166–67.

26 My sense of Spenser as an author who insists on examining the nuances of his subject matter despite the risk of contradiction has been influenced by critics such as Paul Alpers, who characterizes Spenser as an author who "makes us see a moral question from all sides" ("How to Read *The Faerie Queene*," 334). Other critics who emphasize Spenser's tolerance for tension and open-endedness in his poem include A. Bartlett Giamatti (*Play of Double Senses*); Bill Nestrick ("Virtuous and Gentle Discipline"); James Nohrnberg (*Analogy of The Faerie Queene*); and Jonathan Goldberg (*Endlesse Worke*). See also Jeff Dolven, *Scenes of Instruction*, 229–30.

27 On Jones's front matter, including the other commendatory sonnets, see Huntington, *Ambition, Rank, and Poetry*, 69–76.

28 Girardi edition, 6. At the end of his dialogue, Nenna also includes a letter to his readers that addresses criticism of his text's language and topic (though not its actual argument). See Shalvi, *Nennio*, for a translation, xvii–xix.

29 Kim Hall, *Things of Darkness*, 114. Dennis Austin Britton also explores this trope as one in which Ethiopians are associated with sinfulness, and so-called "infidels" such as "Ethiopians, Moors, Turks, and Jews" are created as "racialized subjects" (*Becoming Christian*, 5). See also Loomba, *Shakespeare, Race, and Colonialism*, 55–59.

30 In *Things of Darkness*, Hall observes the involvement of the English aristocratic class in joint-stock companies, and argues, "discourses of fairness were by and large shaped by this aristocratic class, which may have been anxious over its novel involvement in mercantile adventure" (18); she later notes "the association of aristocratic identity with the Elizabethan cult of fairness" (222).

31 The image also recalls the House of Pride, whose "golden foile" obscures its adjacent "Donghill of dead carcases" (1.4.4, 1.5.53).

32 Compounded nobility is also proclaimed the ideal in Castiglione, though not of course without the dissension characteristic of that work (*Book of the Courtier*, 1.16).

33 Marcel Mauss, *The Gift*, 1–4.

34 For theories on the paradoxical nature of the gift, see Pierre Bourdieu, *Practical Reason*, 75–91. I find Bourdieu's formulation of how groups such as the nobility may have an "interest in disinterestedness" (85)

especially compelling. See also Jacques Derrida, *Given Time*. On the contradictions in early modern gift-giving, see Natalie Zemon Davis, *Gift in Sixteenth-Century France*; Alison V. Scott, *Selfish Gifts*; and Louis Montrose, "Gifts and Reasons." For gift-giving in Spenser, see Patricia Fumerton, *Cultural Aesthetics*, 29–66. See also Patricia Wareh, "Humble Presents."

35 Cf. Mammon's argument to Guyon about the usefulness of money for chivalry (2.7.11). In her discussion of the contested meanings of the categories of nobility and gentility in the English Renaissance, Ruth Kelso notes that "liberality, one of the chief distinguishing virtues of the gentleman and Christian, was not possible without wealth" (*Doctrine of the English Gentleman*, 28).

36 Shalvi, *Nennio*, xi.

37 Huntington, *Ambition, Rank, and Poetry*, 74.

38 On courtesy as a virtue that "must eventually manifest itself in society and public life," see Anthony Low, *Georgic Revolution*, 45. Low takes a positive view of the character of Calidore but also sees a "criticism" of court culture in Book 6 through its emphasis on the value of work over aristocratic leisure (67). John D. Staines argues for Spenser's "dissatisfaction with a pastoral fantasy where poetry and virtue are isolated from action" ("Pity and the Authority of the Feminine Passions," 150).

39 For a reading of Book 6 that emphasizes the cynicism in its depiction of Calidore, see especially Richard Neuse, "Book VI as Conclusion to *The Faerie Queene*." Other accounts that emphasize the negative portrayal of courtesy in Book 6 include Montrose, "Gifts and Reasons"; Dolven, *Scenes of Instruction*, 207–37; Bruce Danner, "Courteous *Virtù* in Book 6 of *The Faerie Queene*"; Jacqueline T. Miller, "Spenser's Anatomy of Allegory"; and Michael Schoenfeldt, "Poetry of Conduct."

For more positive readings of Calidore and courtesy in Book 6, see Lila Geller, "Spenser's Theory"; Donald Cheney, *Spenser's Image of Nature*, 176–238; Kathleen Williams, *Spenser's World of Glass*, 189–223; Mark Archer, "The Meaning of 'Grace' and 'Courtesy'"; Debra Belt, "Hostile Audiences and the Courteous Reader"; and P. C. Bayley, who calls Calidore "a paragon, almost the apotheosis, of the virtues Spenser has displayed in earlier books" ("Order, Grace, and Courtesy," 195).

Critics who deal with the tensions at work in Book 6 include Maurice Evans, who takes issue with some of Calidore's decisions but underscores the "redemption" at work in Book 6 as a whole (*Spenser's Anatomy of Heroism*, 209–28); Humphrey Tonkin

(*Spenser's Courteous Pastoral*); Nohrnberg, who emphasizes Book 6's treatment of "questions of essential and feigned sincerity" (*Analogy of The Faerie Queene*, 668); Maureen Quilligan, who explores Book 6's questioning of the link between courtesy and the court (*Language of Allegory*, 47–51); Derek Alwes ("'Who Knowes Not Colin Clout?,'" 31 and passim); and Douglas A. Northrop ("The Uncertainty of Courtesy"). See also Grogan, *Exemplary Spenser*, 137–75. Grogan observes that, with his emphasis on "interior virtue, Spenser gives courtesy a rigorous and well-nigh impossible brief: to be a virtue that defies expression" (149). Rebecca Wiseman emphasizes Book 6's presentation of aesthetic training as a supplement to nobility of birth ("Courtesy, Cultivation, and the Ethics of Discernment"). Richard Z. Lee emphasizes the "dialectical character" of courtesy ("Wary Boldness," 5). On the contradictions in the definition of courtesy in Book 6, see also Catherine Bates, *Rhetoric of Courtship*, 151–72. On Book 6 as a place for reflection, see Gordon Teskey, "'And Therefore as a Stranger Give it Welcome.'"

40 See also Hamilton's note on the link between 6.2.35 and Book 6's proem (*Structure of Allegory*).

41 Dolven, *Scenes of Instruction*, 219–23.

42 See Richard Helgerson, *Forms of Nationhood*, 57, and note 63.

43 Melissa Sanchez, "'To Giue Faire Colour,'" 246; see also 262–68. Sanchez's important argument emphasizes "the cultural and material association of chastity, rank, and race" (264), building on Hall's groundbreaking work exploring the period's racialized understanding of "fairness" as both an aesthetic and moral category in contrast to Blackness; see Hall, *Things of Darkness*, especially 8–9 and 62–122 for an exploration of how fairness has "moral, sexual, and ethical implications that apply specifically to women" (70).

44 Sanchez, "'To Giue Faire Colour,'" 248 and 249.

45 Sanchez, "'To Giue Faire Colour,'" 267.

46 Tonkin also remarks on this echo in his discussion of Priscilla and Aladine, though for somewhat different purposes (*Spenser's Courteous Pastoral*, 45–48). Critics who have commented on Calidore's deception in this canto include Neuse ("Book VI as Conclusion to *The Faerie Queene*"); Bruce Danner ("Courteous *Virtù* in Book 6"); and Grogan, who sees Calidore as an "accomplished storyteller" (*Exemplary Spenser*, 156–57).

47 Louis Montrose, "Of Gentlemen and Shepherds," 435–39.

48 On Calidore's problematic relationships with Meliboe and Coridon, see also Donald Cheney, *Spenser's Image of Nature*, 218–27, and Tonkin, *Spenser's Courteous Pastoral*, 115–23.

49 Judith Anderson also notes how Meliboe echoes Guyon, though she does not treat this particular instance (*Reading the Allegorical Intertext*, 91–105).

50 Michael Schoenfeldt also notes the connection, and draws a similar conclusion ("Poetry of Conduct," 157).

51 On Meliboe's *sententiae*, see Anderson, *Reading the Allegorical Intertext*, as well as the notes by A. C. Hamilton.

52 Cf. Fabricio: "And that his felicity is greater ... whose mind resteth contented with povertie, then his happines, who hath attained to the height of worldly welth, and lordly authoritie" (Q3v).

53 "Ché se di gemme e d'or, che 'l vulgo adora/ sí come idoli suoi, tu fossi vago, / potresti ben tante n'ho meco ancora, / renderne il tuo desio contento e pago" (7.16, *Gerusalemme Liberata*, ed. Lanfranco Caretti). On the relation between this scene and Tasso, see Jason Lawrence, "Calidore *fra i pastori*," and Cheney, *Spenser's Image of Nature*, 219–22. Lawrence does not explore Spenser's alteration of Tasso in Calidore's offer, though Cheney does (221).

54 Schoenfeldt also connects the economic vocabulary of Canto 7 with this discussion in Canto 11 ("Poetry of Conduct," 162–63).

55 Anderson, *Reading the Allegorical Intertext*, 101–02. Anderson's comparison of Meliboe to Guyon is for a different purpose; she is particularly interested in pointing out the problems with Meliboe's idealism rather than in comparing Calidore to Mammon.

56 Cf. as well Guyon's rejection of Mammon's "ydle offers" and "vaine shewes" (2.7.39).

57 On Spenser's poetic choices and the Judgment of Paris tradition, see especially Stanley Stewart, "Spenser and the Judgment of Paris." Montrose also sees this passage as describing a "choice among life patterns" ("Gifts and Reasons," 434).

58 On the troubling implications of Calidore's costume, see Stanley Stewart, "Sir Calidore and 'Closure,'" 78–79. On Calidore's connection to the Trojan Paris, see also Cheney, *Spenser's Image of Nature*, 223–25, and Tonkin, *Spenser's Courteous Pastoral*, 274–80.

59 In her brief connection of these two moments, Lila Geller sees Fabricio's action as "a gesture that anticipates Calidore's gentle removal of the sting of Coridon's defeat by passing the victor's garland to him" ("Spenser's Theory of Nobility," 55). An important part of my own argument is that Spenser's account of the episode as a whole makes descriptions of it as simply "gentle" impossible.

60 For Calidore's self-interested courtesy in Canto 9, see, for example, Neuse, "Book VI as Conclusion to *The Faerie Queene*," 347–49; Nohrnberg, *Analogy*, 709–10, and Stewart, "Sir Calidore and

'Closure,' " 79–80. Stewart makes use of Spenser's commendatory sonnet to *Nennio* to hint, very briefly, at Calidore's bad behavior. Schoenfeldt comes closest to my own argument in asserting that Spenser in Book 6 "exposes the brutal economy of exchange buried within courtesy's terminology of disinterested gift giving"; he also notes that Book 6 "oscillates between a definition of courtesy as an internal moral virtue and as a repertoire of shrewd social practices" ("Poetry of Conduct," 152 and 151).

61 Montrose, "Of Gentlemen and Shepherds," 444–45.

62 The maidens of the vision dance in a "ring" that is also compared to a "girlond" (6.10.11, 12), recalling the circular shape of the contested tokens in both *Nennio* and *The Faerie Queene*, 6.9. On the "circulation" of courtesy, see also 6.Proem.7 as well as Patricia Fumerton, *Cultural Aesthetics*, 31–36.

63 Maurice Evans, *Spenser's Anatomy of Heroism*, 223.

64 A. C. Hamilton also notes the oddness of this detail in his edition.

65 See Douglas Northrop, "Uncertainty of Courtesy," 226–27, and Heather Dubrow, " 'A Doubtfull Sense of Things.' " Dubrow rightly cautions readers to see Calidore and the brigands as being "compared," not "equated" (207).

66 For Meliboe's lack of efficacy, see also Low, *Georgic Revolution*, 43.

67 The similes with which this battle is described also complicate Calidore's character; his comparison to a beast swatting flies recalls an image used in 6.1.24, as Hamilton notes, and his comparison to a lion further recalls the Salvage Man at 6.6.22. In both cantos indiscriminate killing and generosity are combined.

68 Harry Morris also emphasizes the importance of judgment in the play, but he does so in order to argue that the play offers a Christian allegory—a matrix I find unpersuasive. See "Judgment Theme in *The Merchant of Venice*."

69 See, for example, Madeleine Doran, *Endeavors of Art*, 318, and Richard Horwich, "Riddle and Dilemma in *The Merchant of Venice*."

70 David Nirenberg takes note of Bassanio's economic vocabulary to observe in the play "a confusion of profit and passion that is precisely the kind of reversal of values the audience would have associated with Judaism" ("Shakespeare's Jewish Questions," 85). Both René Girard and Stephen Greenblatt take up the question of how apparent Christian virtues may serve as a covering for economic interest. See Girard, " 'To Entrap the Wisest,' " and Greenblatt, "Marlowe, Marx, and Anti-Semitism." Lars Engle takes Girard as a point of departure in order to explore how "love and money reflect and express each other in the play" (*Shakespearean Pragmatism*, 78). David Landreth

argues that "the disavowal of coinage will prove to be not aberrant but foundational to the commonwealth that the play depicts," going on to claim that Bassanio's correct choice of the lead casket is what establishes him as "a true gentleman" (*Face of Mammon*, 151 and 176). In her exploration of the play's two overlapping definitions of credit (economic credit and personal trustworthiness), Jill Phillips Ingram takes a generally positive view of Bassanio as a character who can be rehabilitated (*Idioms of Self-Interest*, 99–115). Amanda Bailey argues that the play is particularly concerned with exploring the complexities of debts, bonds, and forfeits rather than usury ("Shylock and the Slaves"). In "*The Merchant of Venice* and the Value of Money," Peter Holland emphasizes both Bassanio's ostentatious spending and the play's presentation of different systems of value. See also Walter Cohen, "*The Merchant of Venice* and the Possibilities of Historical Criticism," and Walter S. H. Lim, "Surety and Spiritual Commercialism in *The Merchant of Venice*."

71 Girard, "'To Entrap the Wisest,'" 103. Harold C. Goddard suggests that in the trial scene "Portia is the golden casket" because her exemplary self-presentation is at odds with her concealed interest in the case (*Meaning of Shakespeare*, 112).

72 Harry Berger Jr., *Fury in the Words*, 19 and 28. Berger's discussion is particularly attentive to Portia's ultimate victory in her competition with Antonio. Janet Adelman points to the "ambiguous triumphalism" of *Merchant* (*Blood Relations*, 24).

73 In her discussion of the play's presentation of the English anxieties contributing to the "racialization of Jews," Loomba suggests that this question "touches an exposed cultural nerve" (*Shakespeare, Race, and Colonialism*, 150–51). Nirenberg argues for a "systematically staged confusion of Christian and Jew in the play" as the means by which it considers "a crucial question: how can a society built upon 'Jewish' foundations of commerce, contract, property, and law consider itself Christian?" ("Shakespeare's Jewish Questions," 82). And Carole Levin and John Watkins begin *Shakespeare's Foreign Worlds* with a discussion of this question as well (1–2), going on to point out that "in Shakespearean drama, every hero internalizes aspects of his or her antagonists" (9). In "'Which is the Merchant Here, and Which the Jew?,'" Anna Carleton Forrester "argue[s] that Antonio's sadness manifests as a malady born out of recognizing spiritual, physical and intellectual similitude with Shylock, the Jewish usurer of Venice, despite Antonio's active insistence upon their absolute difference" (37).

74 Joel Altman notes that "the habit of argument *in utramque partem* permeated virtually all areas of intellectual life" (*Tudor Play of Mind*,

34). As Altman puts it, Renaissance "plays did not merely raise questions ... but literally were questions" (2–3). From a different perspective, Bridget Escolme has argued that the practice of direct address to
the audience, a fundamental part of Renaissance theatrical practice
sometimes employed on the stage today, may help in escaping "the
ease of judgment that an audience is permitted when the extremities
and inconsistencies of the early modern dramatic figure are explained
away through consistent characterization," as well as in avoiding "a
single perspective from which truths about humanity are revealed, not
questioned" (*Talking to the Audience*, 50).

75 See, for example, Girard: "He can stage a scapegoating of Shylock
entirely convincing to those who want to be convinced, and simultaneously undermine that process with ironic touches that will reach only
those who can be reached" (" 'To Entrap the Wisest,' " 109). For a critical reading of Girard that explores the risk that " 'anti-anti-Semitism'
turns out in many ways to be the mirrored inversion of anti-Semitism,
which raises the (possibly unanswerable) question of whether it is
anti-Semitism's antagonist or equivalent" (162), see Richard Halpern,
Shakespeare Among the Moderns, 159–84. Steven Mullaney aptly
notes that the play "prompts unsavory responses from some in the
audience" at the same time that it "prompts and induces distractions,
discomforts, and ironies" (*Reformation of Emotions*, 92–93).

76 Dennis Britton, *Becoming Christian*, 8.

77 Adelman, *Blood Relations*, 6.

78 Adelman, *Blood Relations*, 36.

79 Adelman, *Blood Relations*, 37 and 125.

80 Adelman, *Blood Relations*, 75; M. Lindsay Kaplan, "Jessica's
Mother"; and Lara Bovilsky, *Barbarous Play*, 73. Kaplan underscores
the link the play makes between gentility and Christianity (22).

81 Citations of *The Merchant of Venice* are from the edition of John
Drakakis.

82 Bovilsky, *Barbarous Play*, 80; for her full discussion of the play's troubling of gentility, see 67–102. Bovilsky also notes that the "competitive generosity" which will distinguish Bassanio has been funded by
"Shylock's Jewish wealth" (85 and 92). Like Adelman, she underscores the difficulty the play shows in accepting Jessica's conversion
(88–89). Kaplan argues, in contrast, that misogynistic notions of
women's biological inferiority make Jessica's conversion more plausible ("Jessica's Mother," especially 19–30).

83 See Adelman, *Blood Relations*, 125–28.

84 In addition to Adelman, on the racializing of Jewishness in the early
modern period, see Britton, *Becoming Christian*.

85 Drakakis also connects this moment to the ideal of courtliness expressed in Castiglione (*Merchant*, 199).

86 Ian Smith aptly notes that Shylock's use of the phrase "fair sir" here "exposes white violence as normative and self-justifying" (*Black Shakespeare*, 90).

87 See Quentin Skinner, "Paradiastole: Redescribing the Vices as Virtues," 158. Skinner's chapter offers a useful view of the term's history and usage in the early modern period.

88 See Henry Peacham, *Garden of Eloquence*, and Daniel Javitch, *Poetry and Courtliness*, 63. For another study that explores Shakespeare's use of paradiastole, see John Roe, *Shakespeare and Machiavelli*. For the relationship between courtly conversation and paradiastole, in addition to Javitch, see also Frank Whigham, *Ambition and Privilege*, 40–42.

89 See, e.g., Goddard, *Meaning of Shakespeare*, 85, and Walter Lim, "Surety and Spiritual Commercialism," 361.

90 Bassanio's competing definitions of gold in this passage thus resonate with what Hall has traced as a "dynamic contest" (*Things of Darkness*, 73) in English sonnet sequences between discourses of fairness and Blackness, as well as between mercantile and natural systems of value (*Things of Darkness*, 62–122). Hall, building on Tzevetan Todorov, contends that "the desire for the mistress's golden hair over actual gold, then, masks a pan-European avarice" (*Things of Darkness*, 84). Of Portia in particular, Hall argues elsewhere: "Portia is the focal point of the Venetian economy and its marriage practices: it is through her that money is recirculated to the Christian males and difference is excluded or disempowered" ("Guess Who's Coming to Dinner?," 103). Eric Song observes the tensions in golden hair as a "literary and racial signifier" with "idolatrous" potential in his account of Spenser's Una and Milton's Eve ("Maybe She's Born with It," 218).

91 In "Race, Natality, and the Biopolitics of Early Modern Political Theology," Urvashi Chakravarty explores Shylock's metaphorical references to breeding as a site for considering "difference as spectacular rather than sanguineal" (155), arguing that "Shylock's story reminds us, ultimately, both of the reproducibility of blackness, and of the ways in which it can be generated quite apart from lineage. That is, it deliberately disaggregates blood from the emergence of marked bodies, rendering marked difference both more arbitrary and more unknowable, more uncontrollable and more dangerous" (159). Marc Shell makes adroit use of the puns in this exchange to explore the "verbal usury" at work in the play's presentation of rhetorical

ornament, enabling him to note Bassanio's hypocrisy in the casket scene (*Money, Language, and Thought*, 49, 60).

92 Skinner, "Paradiastole," 160–61.

93 On antisemitic associations of Jews with economic greed and the racialization of Jews in medieval England, see Geraldine Heng, *Invention of Race*, 55–81. As Heng aptly notes, "The creation of England's Jews as racial subjects, *and* as racial subalterns, are mutually constitutive moments" (75). See also her *England and the Jews*. In *Shakespeare and the Jews*, James Shapiro offers an important account of both the English racialization of Jews and the ways in which "ideas about race, nation, and religion are inextricably and hopelessly intertwined" (170); he thus seeks to explore how "the English turned to Jewish questions in order to answer English ones" (1), especially in *The Merchant of Venice* (113–93).

94 Kaplan, "Jessica's Mother," 4–10. In their introduction to a special issue of *Spenser Studies* on Spenser and race, Britton and Coles explore the ways in which "darkness had become the racialized inscription of those whose religion was suspect throughout the medieval period" (6), noting the "long established connections between white skin and Christianity" (9). On the resonances of "villain" as both "low-born base-minded rustic" and "unprincipled or depraved scoundrel," see *OED*, "villain," n. 1. John Drakakis observes, "Bassanio's reservation … suggests that the Jew is associated with an inner 'blackness' that reinforces his position as an outsider" (*Merchant*, 221).

95 Smith, *Black Shakespeare*, 83 and 92. On Shylock's use of the story of Jacob, insulted by Antonio, Smith claims, "Shylock's Jacobean construction of blackness is coterminous with ingenuity, resilience, and tactical surety that resists cooption and disputes the valorization of whiteness as transcendent" (88).

96 As Adelman notes, "Despite its ostentatious theological triumphalism, *The Merchant of Venice* persistently troubles the distinction between Christian and Jew, and not only in the domain of the economic, where the distinction between usurer and merchant was increasingly difficult to maintain: theologically, the knowledge that *Merchant* simultaneously gestures toward and defends against is that the Jew is not the stranger outside Christianity but the original stranger within it" (*Blood Relations*, 4).

97 Urvashi Chakravarty aptly suggests that Bassanio's "generosity" is "framed as a racial and religious virtue" (*Fictions of Consent*, 27).

98 Harry Berger, who also observes this contradiction in Bassanio, aptly declares, "Part of what makes *The Merchant of Venice* a richly

embarrassing play is that one of Shakespeare's most accomplished heroines engages herself to one of his sleaziest protagonists" (*Fury in the Words*, 41–42).

99 Drakakis cites John Weiss, *Wit and Humour in Shakespeare*, 312, as an early entrant into this debate.

100 Bridget Escolme writes convincingly of how "fictional figures" might have "theatrical intentions" (*Talking to the Audience*, 41); I would like to consider, from a related perspective, how features of a play might have effects on audiences that are closely tied to the meaning and experience of a play without necessarily contributing to a coherent character.

101 Fumerton, *Cultural Aesthetics*.

102 See 1.1.162, 1.1.182, 1.2.113, 2.7.43, 2.7.47, 3.2.115, 3.2.139, 3.2.146, 5.1.242.

103 Drakakis suggests that the substitution in the Second Folio could have arisen "because the two words were homophones" (*Merchant*, 298).

104 Skinner, "Paradiastole," 159.

105 Akhimie, *Shakespeare and the Cultivation of Difference*, 9.

106 Sigmund Freud links the casket test to the Cinderella story in "Theme of the Three Caskets," 154.

107 For an interpretation that emphasizes Portia's deception rather than her equity, see Thomas C. Bilello, "Accomplished with What She Lacks."

108 Adelman, *Blood Relations*, 112, and Chapter 4 as a whole.

109 Adelman, *Blood Relations*, 21. As Hall aptly notes of Portia, "her subversiveness is severely limited, for her strongest verbal abilities are only bent toward supporting a status quo which mandates the repulsion of aliens and outsiders" ("Guess Who's Coming to Dinner?," 104).

110 Smith, *Black Shakespeare*, 104–08.

111 I cite the edition of J. H. P. Pafford.

112 Cf. Girard's characterization of Shakespeare's Venice as "a world in which even the difference between revenge and charity has been abolished" (" 'To Entrap the Wisest,' " 107). Berger coins the term "mercifixion" to describe the combination of penalty and mercy here: "you punish by mercifying" (*Fury in the Words*, 20).

113 Britton has argued that conversion plays such as *The Merchant of Venice* "ask playgoers to consider the authenticity of the conversions"; of Shylock's required conversion he writes, "Shylock's gender, Protestant theology, and a distrust of Jews in early modern England would all conduce to the view that Shylock remains a Jew at the end

of the play. Shylock is thus bracketed from the comedic ending of the play" (*Becoming Christian*, 143, 149). Hall likewise underscores Shylock's exclusion, suggesting that "The comic resolution of the play is not merely the proper pairing of male and female, but the redistribution of wealth from women and other strangers to Venice's Christian males" ("Guess Who's Coming to Dinner?," 99).

5

Literary mirrors of aristocratic performance: readers and audiences of *The Faerie Queene* and *The Winter's Tale*

Act 3, scene 2, of Shakespeare's *Winter's Tale* ends with Leontes' terrible recognition of what his jealous imagination has cost him, and it also initiates the play's movement into the world of fairytale. The 2011 Royal Shakespeare Company production directed by David Farr included a dramatic demonstration of this shift: the towering bookshelves that had flanked the stage as part of a realistic regal dining hall in the first half of the play came crashing down as the ruined Leontes (played by Greg Hicks) exited, and the fallen bookshelves, together with the piles of spilled books, remained onstage for the rest of the play, physically emphasizing the fictional composition of everything taking place. The green world in which much of the play's second half occurs was strewn with book pages at intermission, and the fictionality of the setting was further emphasized by using book pages as the material for the leaves of trees, for the costumes of the satyrs, and for the life-size puppet of the famous bear. These staging choices underscored an important theme of the play: the fanciful, extravagant artfulness that makes possible the improbable recovery of both Perdita and Hermione.

In *The Winter's Tale*, moments of recognition—here Leontes' new tragic understanding, and later the realization that Perdita and Hermione are alive—make the literariness of the play overt, both connecting the play to literary tradition and suggesting a correspondence between watching the play and reading a book.[1] With its very title *The Winter's Tale* points to its own fictionality, encouraging in its audience a "consciousness of artifice"[2] especially in its recognition scenes. The recognition of Perdita in particular not only prompts the audience to become aware of its own participation in the drama, but also, as I will argue here, reproduces the literary self-consciousness of a parallel moment in *The Faerie Queene*. While the self-referential nature of Spenser's insistently fictional poem has been frequently explored,[3] it has not yet been fully appreciated how the metapoetic treatment of Pastorella's recognition encourages readers to see the relationship between the author's fashioning of the text and the fictions at work in aristocratic identity. In so doing, I suggest, it serves as an important example for Shakespeare. Though Robert Greene's 1588 *Pandosto* more closely anticipates the *plot* of *The Winter's Tale*, *The Faerie Queene* shares with Shakespeare's play a preoccupation with simultaneously creating and debunking the case for the superiority of inherited nobility, making it a more fundamental source than has been previously acknowledged. Especially in the Book of Courtesy, which has clear textual connections to *The Winter's Tale*, the readers' interrelated tasks of decoding courteous self-presentation, recognizing nobility, and teasing out the relationship between ostensibly natural gentility and literary artfulness come to the fore. As Spenser's narrator depicts the recognition of Pastorella at the end of Book 6, he too acknowledges the conventionally literary nature of his plot, drawing attention to the fictions at work in contemporary courtiership as well as anticipating Shakespeare's own socially aware recourse to outrageous artfulness in Perdita's reported recognition in *The Winter's Tale*. The recognitions of Pastorella and Perdita are, I argue, opportunities for both Spenser and Shakespeare to show the difficulty of establishing noble identity by pointing toward their own authorial roles as fiction-makers. In self-consciously presenting fictions about the obviousness of gentle blood, they evoke the English elite's awareness of how supposedly natural noble identity may problematically depend on artifice. And just as Spenser and Shakespeare point toward their own artistry in metapoetic and metatheatrical moments, their texts spur readers and audiences to question their own relationship to the story and to recognize how their responses render the work meaningful. This chapter thus continues the previous chapter's emphasis on the active judgment of readers and audiences while also drawing attention to the importance of literary convention (both the genre of pastoral and recognition scenes) as a prompt for reflection. I argue that even as recognition scenes emphasize the fictional nature of the text, they also denaturalize gentle identity by encouraging readers and audiences to make a connection between the texts' literary performances and aristocratic role-playing.

My aim in this chapter, then, is to explore the significant parallel in how *The Faerie Queene* and *The Winter's Tale* make use of literary convention as a vehicle of social critique. Patrick Cheney has argued that Shakespeare, through his appropriation of the Spenserian pastoral in *The Winter's Tale*, "both *pays homage* to Spenser as England's national poet and *critiques* Spenser's laureate self-presentation" as he follows his own "principle of self-concealment."[4] Like Cheney, I am concerned with how the intertextual connections between Pastorella and Perdita might comment on Spenser's and Shakespeare's artistry; however, I also see *The Winter's Tale* as calling attention to its author's hand, especially in its over-the-top reporting of Perdita's recognition after she has fled from a fictional, pastoral Bohemia. As both Spenser and Shakespeare provide pastoral interludes in their works, they make use of a genre that is ostensibly about the country, but that is really, as Louis Montrose has argued, more about literary tradition and the court.[5] While Montrose's link between pastoral and the courtier's hidden art of *sprezzatura*, touched on in the previous chapter, is well taken, it is *also* the case that pastoral offers overt artifice. As William Empson puts it in his classic study, pastoral combines "humility" and the "absurdly artificial."[6] Empson's definition anticipates Stephen Greenblatt's characterization of Spenser as a poet who "deeply distrusts" *sprezzatura* and who brings into *The Faerie Queene* "an art that constantly calls attention to its own processes, that includes within itself framing devices and signs of its own createdness."[7] For Greenblatt, however, this leads to a poem that "does not lead us to perceive ideology critically," a suggestion that may well also recall Empson's suggestion that "the essential trick of the old pastoral, which was felt to imply a beautiful relation between rich and poor, was to make simple people express strong feelings ... in learned and fashionable language ... From seeing the two sorts of people combined like this you thought better of both."[8] My readings of Spenser and Shakespeare in this chapter, in contrast, will explore how both call attention to the pretenses at work in the construction of the class system.

I suggest that in allowing readers and audiences to take varied stances to their works, including both absorption and critical distance, Spenser and Shakespeare prod them to critique the artifice that goes into constructing social identities even as they may be engrossed in the narrative. For Montrose, "Elizabethan pastoral forms may have worked to mediate differential relationships of power, prestige, and wealth in a variety of social situations, and to have variously marked and obfuscated the hierarchical distinctions—the symbolic boundaries—upon which the Elizabethan social order was predicated."[9] Montrose thus offers a reading of pastoral that emphasizes the variety of social roles it may perform. Here I will especially attend to how both Spenser and Shakespeare make use of exposed artifice (including but not limited to the pastoral genre) as a spur to the critical consideration of ideological questions about the nature of gentility. Readers or viewers of pastoral depictions would be aware of the text's artfulness, rather than its realism, and in *The Faerie Queene* and *The Winter's Tale* this artfulness is especially explicit in the conventional recovery of the lost daughter of gentle birth. Even as these texts offer apparent proof of the importance of gentle lineage, drawing in readers and audiences with gripping tales of recovery, they also prompt reader and audience reflection on the literary and social construction of aristocratic identity.[10]

The two texts do point toward their fictionality for different purposes, however. *The Faerie Queene* directs readers' attention to their involvement in an implausible story as it abruptly calls them up short, asking them to reconsider what it means to read a romance fiction that claims to offer an education in gentility. *The Winter's Tale* encourages audiences to remain involved in a theatrical game that they know to be an improbable fiction, yet it also draws them in by overtly acknowledging and sharing this awareness of artifice with them. In making a claim for *The Faerie Queene*'s social application that he eventually subverts, Spenser challenges readers to be skeptical of the artifice in contemporary social practices at the same time that they critically engage with the text's literary artifice. Shakespeare's *Winter's Tale* instills pleasure as the play pokes fun at contemporary social fictions, prompting in its audiences a heightened awareness of how aristocratic pretensions may be a source of comedy without letting them forget their destructive potential. By contrasting the metapoetics at the end of *The Faerie Queene* with the metatheatricality of *The Winter's Tale*, we appreciate more fully how much Spenser's poem ultimately antagonizes its readers as a means of engaging their critical faculties, whereas Shakespeare's play collaborates with its audiences even as it increases their consciousness of literary and social constructions. Both texts, however, spur readers and audiences to recognize their artfulness, despite the differences in tone with which they instill a critical thoughtfulness. The kinds of responses to poetry *as poetry* and to theater *as theater* that these texts facilitate must be taken into account if we are to have a complete picture of how they explore the socially constructed nature of aristocratic identity.[11] In examining their own reactions to poetic and theatrical works, I suggest, Renaissance readers and audiences were given the tools to take a skeptical attitude toward the cultural fiction of inherited gentility and the social performance of courtesy that supported it, even as they might derive enjoyment from texts that offered both a support and a critique of contemporary aristocracy. In their treatments of courtesy in Book 6 of *The Faerie Queene* and *The Winter's Tale*, Spenser and Shakespeare provoke readers and audiences to consider critically the relationships between art and nature, between literary and social fictions, and between the writer's artifice and the courtier's. Their texts' metapoetic presentations of recognition prompt an awareness not only of the text as a literary object but also of the reader or audience member's own self-creative performances and practices. While Spenser's narrator ultimately suggests how different he is from his readers, goading them toward self-criticism, Shakespeare's play encourages a feeling of pleasurable collaboration between players and audience that nonetheless allows audience members to recognize their own role in the social construction of gentility.

Sprezzatura and fictions of nobility

As they staged the debate about the relative importance of noble blood, Renaissance authors depicted the proper relationship between inherited titles and individual achievement in a variety of ways. As we have seen in Chapter 4, Spenser, in his commendatory sonnet to *Nennio, or A Treatise on Nobility*, sharply rejects the relevance of "painted shewes & titles vaine" to "true Nobility." Although most writers of courtesy manuals accepted the value of "noble blood" to a greater or lesser degree, precisely in debating the relative value of a gentle lineage they suggest a growing cultural doubt even when the importance of noble ancestry is defended. In Annibale Romei's dialogue *Courtiers Academie* (published in English translation in 1598), Signor Varrani insists that nobility depends on "the vertue of our progenitors" (196), but he also presents the opposing view, championed by "philosophers," that nobility of birth is irrelevant (187–89). In John Ferne's 1586 dialogue *The Blazon of Gentrie*, Paradin the Herald privileges a combination of gentle lineage and earned merit (15) while criticizing those who would prefer a wicked man with noble blood to an upstart virtuous man. He refers dismissively to the sole reliance on "bare and rude title of noblenesse" as he asserts that individual worth should take precedence over those who "can but onely shew vs a long succession of their name" (19). Even as Paradin emphasizes the value of an aristocratic bloodline, he denigrates the sufficiency of bloodline alone, with other characters, such as Columell the Plowman, going further in saying that aristocratic blood is unimportant. In *The Winter's Tale*, Polixenes expresses a view similar to Ferne's Paradin when he tells Camillo, "As you are certainly a gentleman, thereto / Clerk-like experienced, which no less adorns / Our gentry than our parents' noble names, / In whose success we are gentle" (1.2.387–90).[12] To varying degrees, all of these writers bring into question the relationship between inherited family gentility and individual virtue; ancient family histories do not have a definitive correspondence to current identities.

The "notorious" work of the College of Heralds in devising fictitious coats of arms for sale,[13] and the selling of titles under James,[14] also contributed to undermining the value of gentle blood and encouraging the association of it with artifice. Although he says it for his own rhetorical purposes, *The Duchess of Malfi*'s Bosola is expressing a culturally available viewpoint when he asks the Duchess, "Will you make yourself a mercenary herald, rather to examine men's pedigrees than virtues?" (3.2.261–62). Bosola goes on to dismiss "these shadows / Of wealth and painted honors" (3.2.277–78); his words align closely with the Duchess's view that virtue derives from actions rather than gentle birth (4.1.120–22).[15] In his dedication to *The Duchess of Malfi*, John Webster likewise proclaims that "the ancient'st nobility" is "but a relic of time past," echoing and exceeding John Ferne's earlier assertion that "it sufficeth not, that Gentlemen should thinke themselues of perfect Gentrie, if they can produce the auncient patron of their house" (20). The market in coats of arms and titles was a crucial and contestable part of a society in which, as Lawrence Stone has observed, social "mobility ... is hastily made respectable by the fiction of gentle birth."[16] Indeed, Shakespeare himself participated in this market, acquiring a coat of arms for his father in 1596, the legitimacy of which would subsequently be cast into doubt.[17] The debates about the authenticity and value of aristocratic honors had interested parties on all sides, who would have been attuned to the possibilities and dangers offered by falsification. In short, Spenser's readers and Shakespeare's audiences would have been acutely alert to the different ways that artfulness, including the self-serving family histories of times gone by as well as creative self-fashioning, could play a crucial role in constructing aristocratic identity.

As discussed in Chapter 1, a fundamental aspect of aristocratic artfulness is that it is hidden. In his account of *sprezzatura*, Castiglione's Lodovico places special emphasis on the need for concealment, declaring, "Therfore that may be said to be a very art that appeereth not to be art, neyther ought a man to put more diligence in any thing then in covering it: for in case it be open, it loseth credit cleane and maketh a man litle set by" (1.26). The courtier's hidden artfulness "maketh great wonder [maraviglia]" in his social audience (1.26).[18] In his discussion of wonder as a response to paradox, Rebhorn aptly emphasizes its connection to "mystification and revelation."[19] I would emphasize here that Castiglione's use of the term *maraviglia* is especially resonant for the stage as well as literature, both of which may inspire wonder. And, too, though Castiglione's text counsels the aspiring courtier to avoid affectation ("preciseness" in Hoby, 1.27), "affectation" was also a common feature of the Renaissance stage.[20] Indeed, the theatrical genre most concerned with wonder—romance—is also the genre in which artfulness is made most *explicit*. At the same time that *The Book of the Courtier* suggests that social art should be hidden, then, the imaginative texts of Spenser and Shakespeare make a point of calling attention to their artistry in their explorations of courtesy. Book 6 of *The Faerie Queene* foregrounds the narrator's vexed relationship with his readers, while *The Winter's Tale* has an abundance of metatheatrical moments in which characters make direct reference to the stage as a place of fictional art. In their willingness to discard the techniques of *sprezzatura*, both Spenser and Shakespeare create metapoetic moments in which their own literary creation is the primary focus, yet they do so with some difference in tone and effect.

The Faerie Queene and *The Winter's Tale*—both written by authors who had relatively modest backgrounds as well as frequent interactions with the aristocracy—deal with questions of how nobility is recognized and how courtesy is interpreted even as they form part of their authors' bids for "social capital," which for Bourdieu is connected to "possession of a durable network of more or less institutionalized relationships of mutual acquaintance and recognition—or in other words, to membership in a group."[21] As Montrose asserts, "In a culture in which pastoral forms have become associated with a refinement of the self beyond the capacity of the multitude—a culture in which the humble pastoral form has acquired a paradoxical prestige—merely to write a pastoral is to make a symbolic claim to membership within society's charmed circle."[22] Although literary texts might support an aristocratic social system, they could also question this system's foundation in the inheritance of gentle blood and its expression in theatricalized courtesy. Reflection on the overt literary artfulness with which Spenser and Shakespeare depict aristocratic characters may be a spur to considering the artificial nature of nobility itself; self-awareness is prompted by literary awareness. Despite their use of recognizable literary conventions that demonstrate their cultural sophistication and belonging, then, both Spenser and Shakespeare render problematic the mutual recognitions by which the elite define themselves, encouraging readers and audiences to recognize the artifice at work in these ostensibly natural mutual recognitions.

Pastorella's recognition and Spenser's readers

Renaissance readers of Book 6 of *The Faerie Queene* would have experienced the pleasures of fiction at the same time that they were asked to consider the place of social fictions in a courtesy book culture; though the text offers to instruct them, it also takes them to task, provoking them to consider how they themselves might support the construction of an aristocracy in which identity and artifice are closely linked. Even while composing a text that could "with the greatest purchas[e] greatest grace" (6.1.3.5), Spenser demonstrates that the recognitions on which the courtly elite bases its identity involve something besides straightforward reading of an unequivocal truth. As I asserted above and now will argue in detail, Pastorella's recognition at the end of Book 6 places special demands on the poem's readers as the narrator underscores the implausible nature of the episode as a prelude to distancing himself from them. Spenser's metapoetic treatment of aristocratic identity spurs readers to engage critically with the poem itself, and especially its propositions about the defining role of gentle blood. At the same time, it also encourages their critical awareness of their participation in a culture of artifice. As I have begun to explore in Chapter 4, in *Faerie Queene* 6.9 Calidore encounters Pastorella, living among shepherds and unaware of her gentle birth. From one perspective, the treatment of Pastorella is relatively uncomplicated. Her natural superiority among the rustics provides seemingly straightforward proof of the narrator's claims at the beginnings of Cantos 3 and 5 that gentle blood will always manifest itself; she is first presented wearing "a crowne / Of sundry flowres" (7) and "placed / Higher then all the rest" (8), even though her origins are unknown to those around her. As Pastorella effortlessly creates the "wonder" associated both with dazzling courtiership and literary romance, her position as a "soueraine goddesse" (9) suggests that noble blood inevitably leads to social superiority. The shepherds who surround her "oft for wonder shout" (8), and Calidore in particular takes note of how she excels those around her: "he in his mind her worthy deemed, / To be a Princes Paragone esteemed" (11).

Early on, the narrator also hints at Pastorella's status as a fictional character when he corrects the "common" assumption that Meliboe is Pastorella's father: "Yet was not so, but as old stories tell / Found her by fortune, which to him befell" (14). Even as the narrator emphasizes Pastorella's social superiority, then, he also makes clear that she is an artistic creation, derived from the fictions of "old stories." Just as her name gestures to the genres of pastoral and pastourelle, so too does the conclusion of her tale, in which she is recognized as noble, reveal a strong debt to the romance tradition.[23] As the narrator explains at the start of Canto 12, Pastorella's parents Claribell and Bellamour were married in secret despite the wishes of Claribell's father, and the discovery led to their imprisonment; they therefore felt forced to abandon a daughter conceived and born in captivity. Pastorella was given to a handmaid, "that for hyre / She should it cause be fostred vnder straunge attyre" (6), and the baby was left in a field, abandoned to the elements. This means—naturally!—that she has been recovered by the shepherd Meliboe. Because Pastorella has a distinguishing birthmark (shaped, rather improbably, like a "rose" unfolding its leaves [7]), the handmaid is able to recognize her with confidence many years later when fate returns her to the home of Claribell and Bellamour, who are now respectable castle-dwellers. Spenser's narrator describes the recognition as moving from observation to consideration to confidence in a new reality. First the handmaid notices the birthmark, and then she begins to reflect: "Which well auizing, streight she gan to cast / In her conceiptfull mynd, that this faire Mayd / Was that same infant" (16). She quickly becomes confident of the "most certaine markes" (18) in telling Claribell of her discovery, and Claribell verifies the "very certaine signes" (20). From one perspective, Claribell's identification of her daughter shows the obviousness of nobility of blood. True, her recognition of her daughter is instant—but only once she knows what she is looking for:

> The matrone stayd no lenger to enquire,
>   But forth in hast ran to the straunger Mayd;
>   Whom catching greedily for great desire,
>   Rent vp her brest, and bosome open layd,
>   In which that rose she plainely saw displayd.
>   Then her embracing twixt her armes twaine,
>   She long so held, and softly weeping sayd;
>   And liuest thou my daughter now againe?
> And art thou yet aliue, whom dead I long did faine? (19)

Claribell's identification of Pastorella as her daughter leads to an immediate sympathy with her; Pastorella is no longer a "straunger," but someone with whom she feels an intense familial connection. The narrator's depiction of certain proof *within* the narrative makes the story less plausible to the reader *outside* the text, however, rendering more obscure the larger social issues that the narrative addresses through Pastorella. The text thus participates in contemporary debates about the nature of aristocratic identity by addressing them directly *and* by turning away from them toward an insistently *literary* narrative. In doing so, it encourages readers to examine the relationship between the text's literary construction of aristocratic identity and the artfulness that attaches to aristocratic identity in the society in which they live.

The narrator thus creates an artistic fiction that is both plausible and implausible: plausible to characters in its construction of a clear-cut, physical case to establish Pastorella's aristocratic parentage, and implausible to readers who are prodded to recognize that this case depends on unrealistic artistic conventions for its proof. Terence Cave has argued about recognition more generally that while on the one hand it involves "a shift from ignorance to knowledge," it is also "a shift *into* the implausible."[24] A crucial source for Cave's view of recognition comes from Chapter 16 of the *Poetics*, in which Aristotle criticizes the kind of recognition that is based on "external signs" such as birthmarks or jewelry, preferring instead "one that arises from the incidents themselves, striking us ... with astonishment through the very probability of their occurrence ... Such recognitions, alone, are accomplished without contrived signs and necklaces."[25] Spenser's readers, whether or not they had Aristotle in mind, would very likely rely on their own common sense and previous reading experience in viewing the physical proof of Pastorella's identity (the birthmark) as contrived and unlikely, however convincing to Claribell and the handmaid within the narrative itself. Despite the Spenserian narrator's previous claim that it is "easie ... to descry / The gentle bloud" (6.5.1), the poem here demonstrates the ostensible ease with which gentle blood is determined with a recognizably fictional, and implausible, romance convention, one that Spenser's readers could well have encountered in other popular fictions such as Heliodorus's influential *Aethiopica*.[26] This literary motif can hardly strike the reader as proving the obviousness of nobility of blood in the real world, and, indeed, as the narrator continues, he underscores his lack of interest in doing so. Instead, the recourse to a literary formula suggests that the real emphasis of the text is on considering critically the relationship between artfulness and identity rather than on reinforcing a simplistic view of the formative power of gentle blood.

Immediately after Pastorella is recognized, the narrator shifts the terms of his treatment of "proof" in order to suggest the limits of the text, asserting that the true pathos of the recognition scene can only be felt by one who has already *experienced* such an event. While the characters in Spenser's poem are described as "wondring long at those so straunge euents" (20), the reader is abruptly cut off from that sensation of wonder by being further reminded of its status as a fiction: "Who euer is the mother of one chylde, / Which hauing thought long dead, she fyndes aliue, / Let her by *proofe* of that, which she hath fylde / In her owne breast, this mothers ioy descriue: / For other none such passion can contriue / In perfect forme, as this good Lady felt" (21; emphasis mine). The reader who finds her own experience mirrored in this episode, then, will feel the sympathy of instantaneous recognition, just as Claribell does when realizing the identity of her daughter. It will, however, be a rare reader indeed who recognizes herself in this episode; for others, the sympathetic "proof" of common experience is lacking, and cannot be supplied by the narrative itself. Readers are explicitly told of the narrative's inability to instill in them an emotion equal to Claribell's, and of their own inadequacy to "contriue" a commensurate experience, despite the artistic contrivances of the text.[27] What the text encourages here, then, is a decisive break between the experience of the readers and the experience of the characters. Still, even if readers do not recognize their own life stories in the narrative, they will almost certainly have recognized the literary device of the birthmark employed there. Indeed, the conventional nature of the plot is much more likely to provoke the pleasure of recognition on the part of the reader, a recognition of the traditional components of romance literature. Jeff Dolven has argued that the resolution of Book 6 offers "a perfect romance wish fulfillment" that should provoke the reader's "skepticism," if not disgust.[28] I would emphasize that the Spenserian narrator's own commentary on Pastorella's recognition is what seems specifically geared to provoke such a reaction. At the same time, readers still have the option to savor the pleasure of both the text and the romance fantasy, and indeed they need not absolutely choose between the two options. What Pastorella's recognition demonstrates above all is a capriciousness in the narrator's fiction that offers no readily discernible model for the reader's own action. It may, however, remind the reader of other real-life examples in which artifice supports the creation of social identity. If the world of the court is based on mutual recognition of identities formed through concealed artistry,

Spenser's text, at its conclusion, insists on unmasking that artifice. In requiring readers to concede the problem with their vicarious identification with its characters, *The Faerie Queene* also requires them to reflect on their relationship to fiction.

Perdita's recognition and Shakespeare's audience

The Winter's Tale was first performed at the Globe Theatre in 1611 before a relatively socially diverse audience,[29] and in many ways the play addresses just such an audience, both reaffirming the value of aristocratic courtesy and bringing it into question. Ann Jennalie Cook's view that Shakespeare's audience members were predominantly privileged still allows for quite a degree of variety among them.[30] Thus, audience members could well have had a stake both in challenging elite privilege and confirming it, and may indeed have had complicated feelings about the social system whatever their place in it; as Jeffrey Knapp has argued, "For Shakespeare, the mixed audience of the commercial theater encouraged a view of individuals as mixed, and the cohesive public that he hoped to make of his disparate spectators were theatergoers who could consistently relish a dramaturgy of heterogeneous effects."[31] The play itself was performed by actors whom Montrose has described as having "shifting identifications" with a variety of social stations, aristocratic as well as working class,[32] and it offers both a literary example of the value of gentle blood *and* the means to view that blood as a socially constructed fiction. Like Book 6 of *The Faerie Queene*, *The Winter's Tale* explores the relationship between courtesy and performance.[33] It differs from that text, however, in never claiming a pedagogical purpose; continuously performed in a group setting, the play allowed no time to pause the action (except in moments of distraction), or to add one's own words to the text in a marginal note. While in this way the play induced the audience to be caught up in the action, it nonetheless also facilitated critical responses, aided by the fact that the reactions of audience members were visible to others in the universal lighting of the Renaissance stage, marking the onstage action as a fiction.[34] Paul Yachnin has suggested that one of the main pleasures offered audiences by the early modern English theater was the "opportunity to play at being their social 'betters' and a limited mastery of the system of social rank itself," which involves a "recognition of rank as a kind of theatrical artifice."[35] And, too, some members of the audience might be men who had done school exercises in Latin translation that, as Paul Sullivan has demonstrated, would have asked them to impersonate the elite and thus "to regard social rank as the performance of roles."[36] In making explicit the connections between courtesy and social performance, *The Winter's Tale* encouraged audience reflection both on its own fictional practices and on the social fictions that it represented.

The first half of *The Winter's Tale* presents a courtly milieu in which characters both engage in artful self-presentation and, especially in the case of Hermione, undermine it. The opening exchange between Archidamus and Camillo shows a combination of hyperbole and self-deprecation at work. To Archidamus's "We will give you sleepy drinks, that your senses, unintelligent of our insufficience, may, though they cannot praise us, as little accuse us," Camillo returns his own courteous formula: "You pay a great deal too dear for what's given freely" (1.1.13–18). This mildly amusing competition in courtesy is soon replayed between Leontes and Hermione with disastrous results; while Leontes' displacement as host is certainly not an adequate explanation for his jealous fit, it must be added to the list of other insufficient rationales.[37] The fact that Hermione pokes fun at the game of gentlemanly self-deprecation, implicitly refusing to minimize her own social skills ("What? Have I twice said well?" [1.2.90]) does not help matters, although of course her gently mocking banter reveals more her sophistication at playing the game of courtesy than her wholesale rejection of this game. The social techniques at work in Leontes' court lead naturally to questions about authenticity, and in Leontes' confused mindset, his wife's role of courteous hostess maps all too readily on to other identities, including cuckolding wife and theatrical player.[38] When Leontes confidently asserts that he has "drunk, and seen the spider" (2.1.45), he suggests a world of disguised realities that he has failed to understand despite his claims to heightened sensitivity.

Leontes' diseased state of mind arises out of this atmosphere of courtly self-presentation and is closely associated with the false knowledge of which he feels so confident. The accused Hermione looks ahead to his recovery of true understanding through recognition as she asks him, "How will this grieve you / When you shall come to clearer knowledge, that / You thus have published me?" (2.1.96–98). The word "knowledge" appears more in this play than in any other work of Shakespeare, an indication of its concern with how characters process the world around them as well as with what constitutes that world (whether art or nature).[39] Even as the play emphasizes knowledge, however, it also provokes uncertainty in characters and audience alike about what it means to know something is true. The more characters and audience are asked to examine the bases for their knowledge, the more that knowledge ebbs away from them. In particular, Leontes' mad jealousy suggests that the related concepts of female fidelity and reliable bloodlines, ostensibly rooted in physical facts, also depend on what people *think* about the performances of others. In his view, calling Hermione by the name she truly deserves would upend the social order, creating a precedent that would end "mannerly distinguishment ... Betwixt the prince and beggar" (2.1.86–87).[40] (Here the audience may well perceive an irony in that these lines about the power of words and mental fantasies to create social disruption are themselves spoken by an actor impersonating a king.) Leontes' "weak-hinged fancy" (2.3.117) renders strange to him what he has every reason to know: that his newborn daughter is his own. He puts his child at a distance, twice making use of a term associated with the wonder of romance: "As by *strange* fortune / It came to us, I do in justice charge thee, / On thy soul's peril and thy body's torture, / That thou commend it *strangely* to some place / Where chance may nurse or end it. Take it up" (2.3.177–81; emphasis mine). On the one hand, the character Leontes shows an inability to see reality. On the other hand, as Shakespeare echoes Robert Greene's *Pandosto* ("seeing (as he thought) it came by fortune, so he would commit it to the charge of fortune" [166]), Leontes' words recall his own *literary* lineage through an allusion to the extremely popular prose romance that was Shakespeare's main source for the plot of the play.[41] For Leontes the recuperation of his daughter will involve discovering a new way of seeing things, and the resolution of the play will depend upon its shift toward overt fictionality and away from the verisimilar depiction of courtly pretense.

In its movement toward pastoral at the end of Act 3, *The Winter's Tale* replicates the shift of focus in Book 6 of *The Faerie*

Queene. Both works make use of a simpler, yet decidedly artful, landscape as they continue to treat the question of aristocratic self-presentation. The play's explicit engagement with literary tradition, especially but not exclusively Spenser, significantly informs its audience's reaction to the recognition scenes that bring *The Winter's Tale* to its conclusion. The reactions from the audience that the play solicits through its use of intertextuality and metatheater must be taken into account when considering how *The Winter's Tale* participates in Renaissance debates about aristocratic identity.

Even as *The Winter's Tale* provokes reflection on the costs of the courtier's hidden arts by depicting how a culture of *sprezzatura* may lead to tragedy, it also makes use of metatheatrical moments, especially in Perdita's reported recognition, in order to enlist the audience in the collaborative pleasure of recognizing the play's artfulness. References to the stage prompt audiences to be acutely attuned to the fictionality of the performance itself and to their own willing participation in that fiction. As Jeremy Lopez notes, the "self-conscious" theater of the period "demanded an equal self-consciousness from its audience"; T. G. Bishop has similarly explored Shakespearean wonder as "a site for the complex modulation of audience identification and detachment."[42] In spurring its audiences to experience conflicting thoughts and emotions about the nature of the play, *The Winter's Tale* offers an especially strong example of how metatheater may prompt critical attention even as it increases audiences' involvement, encouraging them to recognize with enjoyment the fictional nature of Perdita's character at the same time that it prods them to consider the relationship between the play's fictive art and their own social practices. Thus Shakespeare's play courts the audience members' communal laughter, which Jeremy Lopez associates with their being "happily complicit,"[43] and eventually their approving applause. While Spenser's narration of the Pastorella episode initiates a break between the readers and the poem, Shakespeare's play follows in the theatrical tradition of players who "strive to please you every day,"[44] though it does so in part by prompting the audience members to laugh at the social conventions in which they also variously participate, speaking to aristocratic insiders as well as to aspirers and the working class. The pleasure that the play instills in its audiences is tinged with an increased recognition of the potential for danger in contemporary practices of courtesy.

As *The Winter's Tale* moves from despair to resolution through the recognition of the abandoned Perdita, the world of gentility becomes the matter for comedy again. In the second half of the play, true nobility, especially as exhibited by Perdita, shines through in an apparent validation of the importance of inherited gentle blood; in this Perdita has a strong resemblance to Spenser's Pastorella. Perdita easily attracts the love of Prince Florizel, whose praises of her include the compliment that all her "acts are queens" (4.4.146). In a similar vein, Polixenes says of her, "Nothing she does or seems / But smacks of something greater than herself, / Too noble for this place" (4.4.157–59). Perdita is described by Time as having the fundamental characteristic of courtliness—she has "grown in grace / Equal with wondering" (4.1.24–25)—but in the discussion of the cross-bred gillyflowers, she roundly dismisses the disguised Polixenes' argument that art is a legitimate (and even natural) supplement to nature (4.4.79–108).[45] Like her mother, she speaks out against courteous exaggeration, gently criticizing Florizel for overpraising her (4.4.147) and for having a "poor lowly maid, / Most goddess-like pranked up" (4.4.9–10). Simpler and rougher around the edges than the refined Hermione, however, Perdita appears at first glance to be the voice for nature in the play.

Yet Shakespeare's text also resembles Spenser's and exceeds it in offering frequent reminders of Perdita's status as an artistic creation. The "unusual weeds" (4.4.1) that she wears are not only the festive garments of a character in a play, but also the costume of a working boy actor on the stage. "Methinks I play as I have seen them do / In Whitsun pastorals" (4.4.133–34), Perdita tells Florizel, underscoring her role in a *theatrical* performance. Perdita's reference to the pastoral, reinforced by Camillo's description of her as "the queen of curds and cream" (4.4.161), further points to her status as both a humble, natural beauty, and an artful representation of what is really an aristocratic genre.[46] After their discovery by Polixenes, Perdita laments, "This dream of mine / Being now awake, I'll queen it no inch farther, / But milk my ewes and weep" (4.4.453–55). Her statement, which links dreaming to theatrical performance as Shakespeare did in *A Midsummer Night's Dream*, reminds the audience that her role as a queen is just that, a role. In so doing, it puts Florizel's assertion that her "acts are queens" in a new light, further underscoring her theatricality. A Renaissance audience hearing Perdita say that she would go back to her "real" position as a shepherdess might also recall that that character, too, is a role, both because she is "really" a lost princess and because she is, still more "really," an obvious impersonation brought to life by a boy who would indeed go back to his real identity after the performance. Leontes may have been on to something after all when he doubted that Perdita was his flesh and blood; as the play increasingly emphasizes, she is not flesh and blood at all, but a fictional creation.[47]

So, while Perdita's character seems on the one hand to indicate the defining importance of noble blood, the ease with which she distinguishes herself from the rustics who surround her also reveals her *literary* heritage, and especially her debts to Fawnia in Robert Greene's *Pandosto* (whose "natural disposition did bewray that she was born of some high parentage" [176]) and Pastorella in Spenser's *Faerie Queene*. Like Spenser, Shakespeare makes Perdita's gentle identity over-determined. Despite the fact that everything in her bearing shows Perdita's regal nature, she will still rely on conventional romance tokens of recognition to establish her identity. *The Winter's Tale*, then, does suggest in an apparently verisimilar manner that there is something in Perdita's innate character that demonstrates her nobility, but it also emphasizes the play's divorce from reality and movement into the world of tale-telling. In considering Perdita's relationship to *sprezzatura*, Martine van Elk argues that her "courtesy outdoes that of Castiglione's courtier in that it is not a product of performance but a grace derived from birth,"[48] but because van Elk's useful reading of the play does not deal with Perdita's reported recognition, it overlooks the ways in which she owes her apparently *natural* superiority to her *literary* lineage. Indeed, before Perdita has been identified, Paulina suggests that her return would be "monstrous to our human reason" (5.1.41); though the audience *does* know that Perdita is alive, they still do not have any ready intellectual framework (outside of storybooks) for understanding her recognition. As the play proceeds, it insists more and more overtly on its divergence from reality, explicitly drawing attention to the preposterousness of the case it makes for the formative role of gentle blood, and in this it resembles Spenser more than Greene.

In reminding audience members of its links to romance fiction, *The Winter's Tale* invites them to share a recognition of its artifice even as they are wrapped up in its narrative pleasures. Before Perdita's actual recognition as Leontes' daughter, Florizel offers a falsified story about her lineage that is also at least momentarily convincing to other characters: she is the daughter of the Libyan Smalus, and has come "from him whose daughter / His tears proclaimed his, parting with her" (5.1.158–59). John Pitcher in his notes to these lines suggests that "the racial joke may have brought the house down."[49] At the same time, this unfunny "joke" also underscores the ways in which White aristocratic identity was defined through the othering of those with dark skin, as Kim F. Hall has argued. I would add that Florizel's story about the White daughter of an African lord may well have reminded some audience members of Heliodorus's Chariclea, who was long kept from her Ethiopian father because of the concerns about paternity her fair skin would raise.[50] Florizel's tale contains a compact story about how paternity is established (in this case, by the emotions of the father) that would be immediately recognizable to the audience as an implausible fiction despite the fact that Leontes appears to take it seriously; it sets the stage for the offering of another implausible fiction that the play will allow to pass for truth, even as it fashions an audience who may regard such truths with a more skeptical eye.

While *The Winter's Tale* features metatheatrical moments throughout,[51] the reporting of Perdita's recognition by minor courtiers is particularly crowded with ostensible vouchers about its truthfulness that instead underscore its fictionality. These characters' speech is characterized not by the courtly technique of hidden art, *sprezzatura*, but by the playwright's technique of exposed artfulness. Perdita's actual recognition takes place offstage, and the scene's many references to the notion of wonder ("amazedness," "admiration," and "wonder" itself twice) further indicate experiences removed from the audience's vicarious identification.[52] Moving the ostensibly main action offstage shifts the focus to how that action is recounted and to the nature of the text itself, just as Spenser's tale of Pastorella's recognition shifts to an emphasis on the narrator's commentary. The difference here is that the play encourages the audience to see itself as in on the joke and to take delight in the narrative's implausibility. The characters' descriptions of Perdita's recognition reinforce that words alone cannot do it justice at the same time that they heavy-handedly offer nothing besides artful words. Instead of actually giving the audience a scene of wonder here, astounding it with his ability to make art seem natural, Shakespeare presents instead a readily recognizable performance of an inadequate performance. Rogero's comments form part of the scene's ironic self-referentiality; he suggests that what has happened defies expression as well as interpretation ("ballad-makers cannot be able to express it" [5.2.24–25]) and goes on to say, "This news which is called true is so like an old tale that the verity of it is in strong suspicion" (5.2.27–29).[53] These remarks underscore the implausibility of a scene that is told by the accumulated details of entering characters. An arriving steward reinforces the point when he tells both the onstage characters and (indirectly) the audience, "Then have you lost a sight which was to be seen, cannot be spoken of," and "I never heard of such another encounter, which lames report to follow it, and undoes description to do it" (5.2.41–42, 55–57), lines that invite the audience's laughter. The steward also echoes Rogero's phrase in describing the fate of Antigonus: "Like an old tale still, which will have matter to rehearse though credit be asleep and not an ear open—he was torn to pieces with a bear" (5.2.60–62). The repetition of "old tale" underscores the point for the listening audience, and the reference to sleeping "credit" provides the opportunity for the player to sympathize with the audience and place himself on its side in any doubts it may have. The more the characters *within* the play insist on its implausible verity, the more the audience may share with the players the recognition that it is knowingly collaborating to create an engrossing, enjoyable, and utterly fictional pretense of belief; the moment-by-moment interactions among players and audience members form an important part of the play's meaning as they witness one another's skepticism and delight.

The scene thus incites audience members to recognize the over-the-top storytelling in the account of Perdita's recognition, including its use of what Aristotle called "contrived signs" such as "the mantle of Queen Hermione's; her jewel about the neck of it" (5.2.32–33), which they would very likely have encountered in other romance fictions.[54] In pairing these romance tokens with the apparently naturalistic proofs of Perdita's appearance and disposition, Shakespeare, like Spenser, enables the audience to consider the artificiality of nobility itself. An audience that has laughed at Perdita's outrageously implausible recovery will likely view the steward's references to "the majesty of the creature, in resemblance of the mother; the affection of nobleness which nature shows above her breeding, and many other evidences" (5.2.35–37) as all part of the fiction, and, in so doing, may well consider how "nature" is socially constructed in the contemporary discourses about nobility. When a Gentleman further comments that "the dignity of this act was worth the audience of kings and princes, for by such was it acted" (5.2.78–79), many in the audience may have been prompted to think how far both they and the players were from being royalty, especially if the Gentleman took the opportunity to gesture ironically to the audience as he spoke the lines; paradoxically, perhaps, the audience's awareness of how it is largely excluded from the milieu depicted onstage may increase the delight that it takes in the absurdity of the pretense. The audience members' pleasure is in recognizing this artfulness and collaborating with it in full view of each other and the players, rather than completely losing themselves in the fiction. If *The Winter's Tale* sets the characters at a distance, I suggest, it nonetheless offers the audience a chance to identify with the players and to achieve a heightened awareness of its own relationship to impersonation.

Shakespeare's comical reporting of Perdita's recognition echoes the discovery of Spenser's Pastorella in that it asks the audience to consider how this scene's obvious artifice relates to the play's engagement with courtesy and noble identity throughout; it differs from Spenser, however, in encouraging that audience to persist in its enjoyment even after this realization. While Spenser's narrator presents the mother and child reunion directly, only to distance his readers immediately from it, Shakespeare moves from the second-hand version of Perdita's recovery to an onstage presentation of Perdita and Hermione's reunion in which the audience is invited to participate fully, as knowing witnesses addressed by the players and aware of one another's spectatorship, in creating a make-believe theatrical moment that nonetheless may be tinged with awe. The light touch with which Perdita's recognition scene is treated leaves the audience with some energy for the final revelation of a living Hermione, which is offered with a more serious

tone even as it too revels in its fictionality.[55] Hermione's statue is
described as a perfect "ape" of "Nature" (5.2.97), showing "the
life as lively mocked as ever" (5.3.19), but the claim of verisimili-
tude is rendered ironic, if not in the moment, at least by the retro-
spective thinking that the revelation might stimulate. Paulina's
metatheatrical comment "That she is living, / Were it but told you,
should be hooted at / Like an old tale" (5.3.115–17) echoes, yet
again, the phrase "old tale" used by both Rogero and the steward in describing Perdita's recognition, encouraging the audience
to connect the two scenes despite the jokiness of the one and the
high seriousness of the other.[56] The phrase "old tale" also recalls
Spenser's reference to Pastorella's part in a tradition of "old stories" (6.9.14), further connecting this recognition scene with its
conventional artistic lineage.

Moreover, Paulina's words spur the audience to consider the
relationship between drama on the stage and fiction on the page.
While Paulina is contrasting "real events" with fictional gossip
that could be readily ignored, the audience is also asked to contrast theatrical performance with words-only forms of conveying
fiction; the difference may be not so much in their believability,
but in the way in which a theatrical spectacle involves more of the
audience's bodily participation. Thus, members of the audience
may share with each other and the actors on the stage the visceral
joy of the concluding scene, even as the fact that they are observing the reactions of others encourages them also to recognize their
shared spectatorship of an overt fiction. Though Leontes suggests
that he has been "mocked with art" (5.3.68), the audience has been
encouraged instead to regard the characters from the playwright's
knowing perspective at the same time that it shares in the delight
of engagement.[57] As she awakens the statue, Paulina commands it
to "strike all that look upon with marvel" (5.3.100), a request that
also draws in the onlooking audience,[58] asking it to join with the
characters' awe *and* to notice that it is, however temporarily, playing along. That Leontes bizarrely reacts to Hermione's reawaken-
ing by immediately marrying off Paulina and Camillo provides the
audience with the happy ending of a comedy which it recognizes
as all part of the fun, and which the play encourages it to accept,
in the moment, despite any misgivings it may have.[59] The arbitrary
comedic closure offered by the marriage satisfies the members of the

audience without insulting them, allowing them to laugh together and to congratulate themselves for being in the know.

Conclusion: Gentlemanly imposters

In performance, *The Winter's Tale* is composed of onstage impersonation, but it also *represents* impersonation, offering an "authentic" Perdita as well as the thief Autolycus, who falsely and ludicrously presents himself as a courtier. Autolycus's exaggerated performance of a "courtier cap-à-pie" (4.4.740), convincing primarily to the Shepherd and his son, makes the other performances in the play seem "convincing" by contrast, but it might also challenge the audience to consider what real difference there is between the two. Surely audiences will want to see themselves as being more sophisticated than these rustics in cultivating a sense of suspicion about the nature of courtliness. By having fun with the theatrical conventions of wonder, *The Winter's Tale* also demystifies the artificial category of nobility, a tendency of the play that is reinforced by the comments of the Shepherd and his son that they have been "gentlemen born" for the past "four hours" (5.2.125, 134); in addition to being logically confused, their words remind the audience of the dubious contemporary market in coats of arms and titles. The Clown's description of this new state of affairs as "preposterous" not only provides a gloss on the action of the play as a whole, it also offers an opportunity for the audience to consider both the exaggerations that accompany the performance of noble virtue and the fictions that might be at work in the pretense to gentle blood.[60] Despite the humor of these characters' situation, the audience is unlikely to have forgotten that Leontes' tragic jealousy arises out of an atmosphere of courtly performance. The turn that *The Winter's Tale* makes toward overt literary playfulness allows for more generous responses from Leontes, while also reminding its audience of the artificiality of the solutions it offers.

   With different tones, then, both *The Winter's Tale* and Book 6 of *The Faerie Queene* critically engage with the technique of *sprezzatura*, overturning it with their own explicit artfulness. In their parallel recognition scenes, both also require readers and audiences to reflect on the dangers of courtesy and on the fictions at work in aristocratic identity, a reflection that is prompted by their attention to the literary text itself. Far from inspiring his readers to identify with his poem at the culminating moment of Pastorella's recognition, Spenser's narrator jarringly points out the distance between his fiction and his readers' experience. His refusal to allow readers to relate the poem to their own lives, together with his insistence that they reflect on the discrepancy, forms part of his critique of a feigned courtesy that relies on art passing for nature. Shakespeare, at the parallel moment of Perdita's recognition, creates a different kind of distance between his audience and the events of his play. While Spenser's narrator will shortly end the poem by calling attention to his own artistry as he criticizes his pleasure-seeking readers and asserts the futility of his poetic project (a moment I will address further in the Conclusion), Shakespeare's play encourages its audiences to be aware of their submission to the delightfulness of its art even as they too gain a heightened awareness of their own complicity with a culture of role-playing. If Shakespeare's text ultimately offers a more accepting attitude toward the aristocracy, it nonetheless also demystifies social privilege in making it the subject of comedy and in showing the tragic potential of a culture of courteous masking. Readers and audiences of both works are thus spurred by metapoetic commentary to ask themselves how their relationship to a literary text fits in with their own self-creating performances, and what of their own experiences, literary and otherwise, they may recognize in recognition scenes. In their different ways, then, both of these Renaissance texts presuppose that their meanings will be formed by the reactions that they engender from readers and audiences. Even as the end of *The Winter's Tale* emphasizes the pleasure of pure artfulness, audiences will remember the costs of the art that infects courtesy as well as the ways in which the entire concept of noble blood is rendered preposterous. In the 2011 RSC *Winter's Tale*, the bleaker side of court society was indicated by the exclusion of the imposter Autolycus (played by Brian Doherty) from the concluding festivities. While the other characters had exited and their revelry could still be heard, Autolycus was left on stage, literally out in the cold: confetti snowflakes came down on him as he pulled closer the ill-fitting coat from the royal Florizel. Here Autolycus acted as a reminder of the world's real outcasts, perhaps—but he also offered the audience a knowing wink and a shrug.

Notes

1 Indeed, *The Winter's Tale* is one of Terence Cave's first examples in his study of anagnorisis; he points to the reported recognition of Perdita as showing the play's own recognition that it has "the character of an old tale" (*Recognitions*, 3).

2 Stephen Miko, "Winter's Tale," 263. On the play's obvious artifice, see also Rosalie Colie, *Shakespeare's Living Art*, 266; Christopher J. Cobb, *Staging of Romance*, 160; and Andrew Gurr, "The Bear, the Statue, and Hysteria," 420–25.

3 See Introduction, note 33.

4 Patrick Cheney, "Romance of Literary Form," 124–25. Martin Butler says of the 1609 printing of *The Faerie Queene* that "traces of Spenser in *The Winter's Tale* suggest that its reissue affected Shakespeare profoundly" (Introduction to *Cymbeline*, 11, cited in Patrick Cheney, "Romance of Literary Form," 126).

5 Louis Montrose, "Of Gentlemen and Shepherds."

6 William Empson, *Some Versions of Pastoral*, 12.

7 Stephen Greenblatt, *Renaissance Self-Fashioning*, 189–90. Daniel Javitch argues that Spenser's artistry involves "a dissociation of his poetic practices from those of the courtier" (*Poetry and Courtliness*, 137), while Jacqueline T. Miller asserts a parallel between Calidore's practices and those of the poet that enables him to "expos[e] ... the deceptive artifice that lies at the heart of his allegory" ("Courtly Figure," 64).

8 Empson, *Some Versions of Pastoral*, 11. Paul Alpers characterizes Empson as believing that pastoral "has a unifying social force, is a means of bridging differences and reconciling social classes" ("Empson on Pastoral," 101).

9 Montrose, "Of Gentlemen and Shepherds," 418.

10 Cf. Paul Suttie, "The Legend of Courtesy, then, is playing a double game, at once exposing the basis in art of various systems of natural ethics, and artfully investing its own ethical commitments in just such a naturalizing fiction" (*Self-Interpretation in* The Faerie Queene, 204).

11 On the importance of the relationship between "literary pleasure" and "ideological efficacy" in Renaissance texts, see Genevieve Guenther, *Magical Imaginations*, 3.

12 All citations of *The Winter's Tale* are from the edition of John Pitcher.

13 See Ruth Kelso, *Doctrine of the English Gentleman*, 26, and Lawrence Stone, *Crisis of the Aristocracy*, 68. On the cultural awareness of the practice of "forging genealogies," see also J. F. R. Day, "Primers of Honor," especially 94–96.

14 Stone, *Crisis of the Aristocracy*, 71–82.
15 I cite the edition by David Bevington et al.
16 Stone, *Crisis of the Aristocracy*, 65.
17 See Katherine Duncan-Jones, *Shakespeare: An Ungentle Life*, 94–119.
18 I do not, of course, mean to imply that *sprezzatura* was always successfully hidden, or that the concept could not itself be a spur to consider the constructedness of nobility. Jennifer Richards, for example, has suggested that Castiglione's concept of *sprezzatura* "enables the 'outsider' to realise his native nobility" and thus offers a potential "critique" of "the idea that 'nobility' and 'courtliness' are the inherited gifts of the nobly born" (*Rhetoric and Courtliness*, 48 and 51–52). On the link between *sprezzatura* and wonder, and the many resonances of "maraviglia," see especially Wayne Rebhorn, *Courtly Performances*, 47–51.
19 Rebhorn, *Courtly Performances*, 49. Rebhorn draws here from Puttenham's *Art of English Poesy*, which refers to paradox as "the wonderer."
20 Andrew Gurr, *Shakespearean Stage*, 133.
21 Pierre Bourdieu, "Forms of Capital," 248. On contemporary rhetorical strategies for indicating membership in a group, see also Frank Whigham, *Ambition and Privilege*, 63–87.
22 Montrose, "Of Gentlemen and Shepherds," 447–48.
23 On Pastorella's name and her connection to romance, see Richard Neuse, "Pastorella," 533.
24 Cave, *Recognitions*, 1.
25 Aristotle, *Poetics*, trans. Leon Golden, 27–29. See also Cave, *Recognitions*, 1–54.
26 On the influence of the *Aethiopica*, first printed in English translation in 1577, see Steve Mentz, *Romance for Sale*, 47–71.
27 My reading of this often overlooked stanza is in broad agreement with Barbara L. Estrin's; she too comments on the "formulaic" and "conventional" nature of the plot in order to say of Spenser, "detaching himself from his characters, the poet alienates himself from his audience as well" (*Raven and the Lark*, 101).
28 Jeff Dolven, *Scenes of Instruction*, 233–34. For a more optimistic reading of Pastorella's reintegration with her family that compares it to the return of the Biblical prodigal son, see Kenneth Borris, "Pastorella's Allegorical Homecoming."
29 While Alfred Harbage emphasizes the working class's participation in the audience (which he identifies as a factor in the greatness of the period's theater) and Ann Jennalie Cook that of the "privileged playgoers," there is general agreement that different social classes

would have been represented. See Harbage, *Shakespeare's Audience*, and Cook, *Privileged Playgoers*. Gurr also emphasizes the range of social classes in attendance (*Playgoing*, 58–94). See also Cyndia Susan Clegg, *Shakespeare's Reading Audiences*, 1–21.

30 On the wide social variation among the privileged, see Cook, *Privileged Playgoers*, 11–51.

31 Jeffrey Knapp, "Shakespeare's Pains to Please," 267. Knapp here convincingly responds to Richard Helgerson's argument that Shakespeare's theater was increasingly attentive to the well-educated and wealthy members of its audience, arguing, "suppose that Shakespeare's theater did indeed constitute 'a school for social advancement' as Helgerson claims. Why should we conclude that the gentry were the only spectators capable of learning its lessons?" See Helgerson, *Forms of Nationhood*, 193–245, and Knapp, "Shakespeare's Pains to Please," 259. Darryll Grantley, like Helgerson, emphasizes the construction of an elite audience through their "sophisticated response" to plays (*Wit's Pilgrimage*, 131).

32 See Louis Montrose, *Purpose of Playing*, 208.

33 Martine van Elk has noted that *The Winter's Tale* depicts a court in which "social identity is constructed through public, rhetorical performance," and Jennifer Richards has called attention to the play's critical attitude toward both courtly speech and the concept of "innate nobility." See van Elk, " 'Our Praises are Our Wages,' " 431, and Richards, "Social Decorum in *The Winter's Tale*," especially 88–91.

34 Here I rely on my experiences at the American Shakespeare Center, which seeks to recreate the conditions of Shakespeare's Blackfriars Playhouse; attending their productions has been a tremendous aid to me in formulating this argument.

35 While Yachnin underscores the "pleasurable submission to the system of rank," however, my own argument emphasizes the possibility of critique. See Dawson and Yachnin, *Culture of Playgoing*, 41 and 44. Yachnin's co-author Anthony B. Dawson voices a similar idea in connecting "theatrical representation" with "the subversive idea that rank itself is nothing but display" (*Culture of Playgoing*, 89). Erika T. Lin also notes the potential for theatrical impersonation to raise complicated questions about the interpretation of bodies in a system of patrilineage (" 'Lord of Presence,' " 113–33).

36 See Paul Sullivan, "Playing the Lord," 179.

37 Paul Alpers has noted the "courtly habit of hyperbole that is implicated in the tragedy of the first three acts" (*What is Pastoral?*, 205–06). Van Elk also importantly points to Hermione's victory in a "rhetorical

competition" as a source for Leontes' jealousy (" 'Our Praises are Our Wages,' " 439–40).

38 On these overlapping concerns in the play, see also Graham Holderness, "*The Winter's Tale*," 195–235. John Roe in "A Niggle of Doubt" suggests that the courtly displays of both Hermione and Desdemona raise questions about interiority that leave these women particularly vulnerable. Note also Katharine Eisaman Maus's suggestion that there is a parallel between the cuckold and the theatrical spectator, both of whom must make conclusions based on the incomplete evidence of their eyes ("Horns of Dilemma," 561–83). In a different context, Michael Slater argues that Desdemona's role as court lady in *Othello* renders her particularly vulnerable to accusations of infidelity ("Desdemona's Divided Duty").

39 I am aided in making this observation by the concordance at www. opensourceshakespeare.org. Cave observes that recognition is a "vehicle for themes of knowledge" (*Recognitions*, 4).

40 John Pitcher notes the ambiguity of "creature of thy place," suggesting that it can refer either to the low position Hermione has earned in Leontes' eyes, or to her former high rank (*The Winter's Tale*, 192).

41 I cite Paul Salzman's edition of *Pandosto*. Pitcher characterizes *Pandosto* as an "Elizabethan bestseller" and notes that "it was reprinted more than a dozen times before 1642" (*The Winter's Tale*, 94).

42 See Jeremy Lopez, *Theatrical Convention*, 2, and T. G. Bishop, *Shakespeare and the Theatre of Wonder*, 41. Dawson and Yachnin emphasize the importance of metatheater in creating "a conscious awareness in audience members of their position as spectators" (which they also associate with "pleasure") and facilitating the "sounding of cultural dissonances" (Introduction to *Culture of Playgoing*, 7), and Montrose has also offered a cogent analysis of metatheater as a means "by which Shakespeare shapes a dialectic between his profession and his society" (208). See Montrose, *Purpose of Playing*, especially 179–211.

43 Lopez, *Theatrical Convention*, 174.

44 *Twelfth Night*, 5.1.394.

45 Polixenes himself goes on to reject the implications of his argument that the "baser" should conceive from the "nobler" (4.4.94–95) when he condemns the relationship between the "baser" Perdita and the "nobler" Florizel. See also Northrop Frye, *Fables of Identity*, 113. On the connection between Perdita's rejection of the gillyflowers and Puttenham's suggestion that art should be concealed, see Frances E. Dolan, "Taking the Pencil out of God's Hand," 226–28.

46 Perdita also shows pastoral's function in criticizing the court when she says that she would have liked to tell Polixenes that "the selfsame sun that shines upon his court / Hides not his visage from our cottage" (4.4.449–50).

47 While this assertion may seem too postmodern for Shakespeare, we should bear in mind that Beaumont's *Knight of the Burning Pestle* had already been performed in 1607; this play calls attention still more overtly to its fictionality by including players who pose as audience members and are part of the play's obviously feigned presentation of impromptu audience–player interaction.

48 Van Elk, "'Our Praises are Our Wages,'" 444.

49 Pitcher, *The Winter's Tale*, 322.

50 On the racial politics of Heliodorus's Chariclea, see Sujata Iyengar, *Shades of Difference*, 19–43. On the connection between Heliodorus's novel and *The Winter's Tale*, see Simon Reynolds, "Pregnancy and Imagination." Both Reynolds and Iyengar discuss the role of maternal impression in Heliodorus, with Reynolds linking it to Shylock's account of Jacob and his ewes (436) and emphasizing its connection to *The Winter's Tale*'s interest in the imagination. Noémie Ndiaye suggests that stage adaptations of the *Aethiopica* in both England and France "contributed to the racialization of blackness" (161) in the period, and that the novel's interest in the question of biological inheritance would have been of particular interest to "courtly aristocratic circles" (162); see "'Everyone Breeds in His Own Image.'"

51 These include Leontes' disgust with playing "so disgraced a part" and his accompanying hints about cuckolds in the audience (1.2.187–95), Hermione's assertion that her sadness "is more / Than history can pattern, though devised / And played to take spectators" (3.2.34–36), and Perdita's own comment, "I see the play so lies / That I must bear a part" (4.4.659–60).

52 Here I agree with both Richards, who suggests that "this distance from the action should prompt us to reflect on the attitudes of the gentlemen, and, indeed, on our own unwavering perception of Perdita's nobility" ("Social Decorum," 89), and Miko, who explores the way in which the "erupting emotion" of the scene "was very deliberately set at a distance" ("Winter's Tale," 271).

53 On the place of tales in the play, and the way in which this scene "points to its own profound implausibility" (535), see Mary Ellen Lamb, "Engendering the Narrative Act," 532–37. For Lamb this does not undermine the scene's credibility but rather leads to a sense of child-like "wonder" on the part of the audience (535). Northrop Frye has also noted, "There is little plausibility in *The Winter's Tale*, and

a great deal of what is repeatedly called 'wonder'"; like Lamb, he specifically calls attention to the links between Perdita's recognition scene and popular entertainments such as ballads (*Fables of Identity*, 113–14).

54 In Heliodorus, for example, Chariclea is recognized by a fascia with her mother's handwriting, jewels from her mother, a ring from her father, and a mole on her left arm (*An Aethiopian Historie*, 138v–141v).

55 As it was in the 1998 Royal Shakespeare Company production directed by Gregory Doran, for example, as well as in the 2011 RSC production.

56 Andrew Gurr sees the statue scene in similar terms, arguing, "as a stage appearance it is only apparent life, not a reality. It is of a piece with the rest of the tale, a myth. As with the bear, we are being reminded that what we see is a fiction" ("The Bear, the Statue, and Hysteria," 425). On the "emphatic metatheatricality" of the statue scene, see also Gina Bloom, "'Boy Eternal,'" 356.

57 In Ovid's version of Pygmalion, a source for this scene, the vivid statue is described in terms that anticipate Castiglione's *sprezzatura*: "Ars adeo latet arte sua" or "Art lies hidden by its own art" (*Metamorphoses* 10.252; translation mine). In Shakespeare the emphasis is on something very different from hidden artistry. T. G. Bishop notes the contrast between Ovid and Shakespeare here, but not the connection to Castiglione (*Shakespeare and the Theatre of Wonder*, 173).

58 Here I agree with Dawson's argument that this scene brings together the onstage and offstage audiences as both are "enjoined to see and enjoy" (*Culture of Playgoing*, 106). Bishop also emphasizes the audience's intense imaginative participation in the scene; his argument does not take Perdita's reported recognition into account, however (*Shakespeare and the Theatre of Wonder*, 161–75).

59 In this sense, while *The Winter's Tale* addresses audience members with diverse relationships to social and sexual structures of power, it also encourages them to come together in their knowing enjoyment of the play's conclusion. It may well not succeed in all cases; it would be reasonable to take offense at Leontes' casual manipulation of Paulina, a character whose ability not to be constrained by Renaissance conceptions of female decorum has been noted by Laurie Shannon, who emphasizes her role as a dispenser of counsel (*Sovereign Amity*, 199–222), and Mario DiGangi, who emphasizes her likeness to the sexual type of the tribade (*Sexual Types*, 84–87). Yet it may be that the play's overt fictionality also encourages audiences to accept, in the moment, actions that they might otherwise find offensive, just as they are

willing to go along with the play's improbable plot. Valerie Traub has said that plays such as *The Winter's Tale* "enact the *process* of female objectification *as* the dramatic process. Inviting our complicity with this process as the very terms of their intelligibility, these plays seduce us with the promise of theatrical pleasure" (*Desire and Anxiety*, 26 and 42–49). I would add that the pattern of metatheatricality I have traced in *The Winter's Tale* also encourages audiences to recognize the "complicity" they have temporarily enacted.

60 On the relationship between the "preposterous" in Shakespeare's works and the suspicions cast on Shakespeare's own claim to gentility, see Patricia Parker, *Shakespeare from the Margins*, 20–55, especially 21–23.

Conclusion: courteous farewells in Spenser and Shakespeare

In the special space of the theater, nothing is worse for an audience than when an actor unintentionally breaks character. There they are, nervous and awkward, grasping for a line, and we in the audience feel their shame and embarrassment as our own. Time slows as we rejoice in our distance from the perspiring player even as we cringe in sympathy and identify with their awkwardness.

And yet, nothing is better than when an actor breaks character. There they are, cracking up at the joke they just can't manage to deliver deadpan, and we are laughing along with them, caught up in the moment together at the same time that we are enjoying the fracturing of the performer's pose.

Whatever their effects, breaks in character offer audiences opportunities to connect in new ways with a performer on stage. And, as we know, the staging conventions of Shakespeare's theater especially lent themselves to establishing such direct connections with audiences. For Castiglione, Spenser, and Shakespeare, moments of rupture particularly invite reflection about the relationship between aesthetic pleasure and identity; readers and audiences, because they are prompted to consider explicitly the courteous poses of texts, narrators, characters, and players, are left with a productive uncertainty that I have argued is characteristic of courtesy. In my own concluding thoughts here, I want to suggest by way of Castiglione how the final moments of the 1596 *Faerie Queene* and *The Tempest* encourage attention on the part of readers and audiences to the relationships between courtesy, artistic craft, and their present moment. Spenser's narrator ultimately takes a critical view of the link between courtesy and aesthetic pleasure, in contrast to *The Tempest*, which encourages audiences to mindfully play along.

The Faerie Queene glances backward in its final negative outlook on contemporary society, while Shakespeare's text emphasizes the value of what is now even as it marks loss. Nonetheless, readers and audiences who are mindful of how courtesy may speak with more than one voice will recognize their own agency to respond to these provocative moments.

Castiglione and the pleasures of the past

At the same time that it offers many possibilities for self-fashioning and reader identification, Castiglione's *Book of the Courtier* also encourages readers to see the idealized conversations of the courtiers as distinct from their own experience, emphasizing that these conversations are irretrievably removed in time from the reader's own milieu (a fact that would of course be accentuated in the experience of its English readers). Despite being full of nostalgia, Castiglione's text also criticizes the age-old instinct of the has-been to find fault with the present. At the outset of Book 2, Castiglione sketches this perennial temptation, comparing the conditions of life to the limitations of a sea-going vessel:

> and we with the vessell of mortalitye flying away, go one after an other through the tempestuous sea that swaloweth up and devoureth al thinges, neither is it graunted us at any time to come on shore again, but alwaies beaten with contrary windes, at the end we break our vessell at some rocke. Because therefore the minde of old age is without order subject to many pleasures, it can not taste them. (2.1)

The inability to access the pleasures of youth and the resultant dis-enchantment are part of the typical life cycle, figured as the inevitable succumbing to storm and shipwreck, as we are borne back ceaselessly into the past. Shakespeare's world-weary Prospero—an expert on tempests who stands just on the verge of this predicament of old age—exemplifies this in his jaded response to Miranda's exclamation about the "brave new world" in which she finds herself: "'Tis new to thee" (5.1.184).[1]

Even as Castiglione's text both recognizes and participates in the human cycle of disenchantment, it also offers another model of ongoing aspiration. The elusive drive toward future perfection is suggested by the purpose of the dialogue itself (the framing of an ideal courtier)

as well as in its concluding presentation of the path toward divine
beauty, as voiced by Pietro Bembo: "Let us therefore bende all oure
force and thoughtes of soule to this most holye light, that showeth
us the waye which leadeth to heaven ... let us clime up the stayers
... and there shall we fynde ... a most sure haven in the troublesome
stormes of the tempestuous sea of this life" (4.69). Bembo's repeated
use of the pronoun "us" here incorporates both his immediate audience within the dialogue and Castiglione's readers, joining them in a
unified vision of heavenly aspiration. When Bembo's idealistic rap-
tures have gone as far as they can go, the moment is punctured: "the
LADY EMILIA ... tooke him by the plaite of hys garment and pluck-
inge hym a litle, said: Take heede (M. Peter) that these thoughtes
make not your soule also to forsake the bodye" (4.71). The spell is
certainly broken, yet it's an interruption that prompts ongoing reflection: "and every one thought he felt in his minde (as it were) a certein
sparkle of that godlye love that pricked him, and they all coveted to
heare farther" (4.71). The text ends with a hopeful tone, emphasizing the "wonder" the interlocutors feel in recognizing how they were
all lost in the pleasure of the moment:

> Then everie man arrose upon his feete with much wonder, bicause
> they had not thaught that the reasoninges had lasted lenger then the
> accustomed wont, savinge onelye that they were beegon much later,
> and with their *pleasantnesse* had deceived so the Lordes mindes, that
> they wist not of the going away of the houres. (4.73; emphasis mine)

There is also the plan of continued discussion that evening—the
kind of promise of ongoing storytelling that concludes so many of
Shakespeare's plays. The ending of *The Book of the Courtier* does
little to undermine the suggestion of Book 4 as a whole that the
pleasure the good courtier will employ in the education of the prince
is a valuable thing; even as the dialogue as a whole is full of tension,
its suggestion of the redemptive value of pleasure is left intact.

Scolding the reader in Spenser

While Castiglione's text gestures toward a unity of pleasure and
pedagogy that incorporates both the characters and the readers
of the dialogue, Spenser's 1596 *Faerie Queene* ultimately points
out the great gulfs both between pleasure and virtue and between

the narrator and his readers. Though much of the narrative links proper pleasure and pedagogy, in the final moments of the text there is a break with the readers that has been anticipated by the alienation of Pastorella's recognition, explored in Chapter 5. In *The Faerie Queene* as a whole, conclusions to the individual books tend to emphasize not so much the completion of a quest, but the continued shared enterprise of the narrator and his readers. And the conclusion to Book 3 in the 1590 *Faerie Queene* especially emphasizes unity, with Amoret and Scudamour locked in a hermaphroditic embrace, and the reader's gaze blending together with that of the onlooking Britomart: "Had ye them seene, ye would haue surely thought, / That they had beene that faire *Hermaphrodite*" (3.12.46).[2] The narrator also anticipates continued engagement with his readers after his respite:

> But now my teme begins to faint and fayle,
> All woxen weary of their iournall toyle:
> Therefore I will their sweatie yokes assoyle
> At this same furrowes end, till a new day:
> And ye faire Swayns, after your long turmoyle,
> Now cease your worke, and at your pleasure playe;
> Now cease your worke; to morrow is an holy day. (3.12.47)

"Now," the narrator tells us three times, it is time for a regenerating pause. This conclusion to the 1590 *Faerie Queene* presents a positive view of leisure and pleasure as the appropriate conclusion to the labors of the author. And therefore it makes sense that its readers could turn the page at the end of Book 3 and see the letter to Raleigh, with its linking of pleasure and instruction in Spenser's suggestion that he has designed his work to be both "plausible and pleasing."

The abrupt conclusion to the 1596 *Faerie Queene* offers a sharp contrast to its predecessor, emphasizing instead rupture and discontent. However briefly, the conclusions to Books 1 to 5 of the poem all promise more, creating an implicit bond between the narrator and readers—putting them on the same page. But the conclusion to Book 6 takes an apparently very different tone, as the narrator most directly addresses his book itself rather than his readers, connecting the impossibility of finally containing the Blatant Beast—that discourteous figure of indecorum who is described as having "broke his yron chaine" (6.12.38)—with the slanders he has received as a poet. The narrator thus turns away from his readers, directly addressing the poem itself on how to please those he scorns as part of contemporary society:

> Ne may this homely verse, of many meanest,
>> Hope to escape his venemous despite,
>> More then my former writs, all were they clearest
>> From blamefull blot, and free from all that wite,
>> With which some wicked tongues did it backebite,
>> And bring into a mighty Peres displeasure,
>> That neuer so deserued to endite.
>> Therfore do you my rimes keep better measure,
> And seeke to please, that now is counted wisemens threasure.
> (6.12.41)

The book format of the 1596 edition further emphasizes the text's break with its readers. It concludes with this final stanza of Book 6, with none of the paratextual material from the 1590 edition. For reasons of space, the word "threasure" is hyphenated and crammed into the line above, and the stanza is followed by FINIS, also emphasizing the decisiveness of the ending. (This word also marks the conclusion to Book 3 in the 1590 *Faerie Queene*, yet its reference to the pause of a "holy day" and the addition of subsequent pages all mitigate the apparent finality of the ending.[3])

The concluding couplet to the 1596 *Faerie Queene* produces much more of a rupture than the conclusion to Castiglione's text. While in form the narrator admonishes his poetry ("seeke to please"), in practice he takes readers and their society to task. Even as the poem as a whole frequently anticipates its readers' possible responses, here it insistently turns away from readers. "Now," as opposed to the narrator's idealized vision of the past, pleasure is paramount, and, in a fittingly economic metaphor, it passes for the highest good—but only because cynicism has replaced true wisdom. This couplet challenges readers to recall the lessons of *The Faerie Queene* as a whole, asking themselves how well they are able to distinguish an apparent good from its evil twin, or to recognize when a pleasing exterior is rotten at its core. It demands that they consider where they stand in relation to the poem: with the pleasure-seekers who are chastised here, or with those who seek true wisdom. Perhaps if they identify with the latter category, they still have a chance of being part of the narrator's intellectual in-group. The narrator's parting shots also raise complicated questions about Spenser's own self-positioning, in his claim to have cynically thrown his lot in with the crowd at the same time that he separates himself from them with his critique.[4] Castiglione suggests that "old men" are prone to a common "errour": "all of them commend the times past, and blame the times present" (2.1). If it is an error, it is one into which Spenser's narrator ostentatiously plunges himself, going well beyond Castiglione's elegiac tone to indignant cynicism about the courtly world. In forging a relationship with his readers that ends by provoking rather than pacifying, the Spenserian narrator here performs the role of gruff pedagogue, prompting them to ask more questions of both themselves and the text. The poem's lack of resolution may create a fruitful tension in its readers, a consequence of the self-awareness it induces.

Prospero's broken staff

As *The Tempest* moves toward its conclusion, it similarly provokes the audience to respond to the rupture of its theatrical magic.[5] Although it is crucial and conventional to consider Prospero in his epilogue as a figure of the retiring playwright, it is just as crucial to consider how he provides a model for the audience, guiding their responses to the conclusion of the play by creating a model of spectatorship that combines courtesy, empathy, and mercy. Prospero "starts suddenly" (4.1, stage direction) in the midst of the masque he has commandeered for Ferdinand and Miranda, going on to offer them conflicting advice about how they should respond emotionally to this break; he tells Ferdinand to "be cheerful" (4.1.147) while at the same time acknowledging his own "vexed" (4.1.158) state of mind. In effect, he counsels Ferdinand not to respond empathetically to his distressed state ("Be not disturbed with my infirmity" [4.1.160]), implying that it would in fact be quite natural for Ferdinand to take his emotional cues from Prospero's mood.

Prospero's magical, theatrical labors make him an active audience member as well as a stage-managing playwright. He tells Ariel, "At this hour / Lies at my mercy all mine enemies. / Shortly shall all my labours end" (4.1.262–64), underscoring the power that he has over his usurping brother and his entourage. Ariel will also go on to underscore this power: "They cannot budge till your release"

(5.1.11). Ariel emphasizes just how much the suffering of his enemies will affect Prospero: "Your charm so strongly works 'em /
That, if you now beheld them, your affections / Would become tender" (5.1.17–19). In Ariel's formulation, Prospero participates in
a mutually constitutive relationship with his prisoners: he is their
playwright/director as well as their audience, and his spectatorship
will effect a sea-change in his character. (Ariel specifically associates
the sympathy Prospero might feel with his humanity: "Mine would,
sir, were I human" [5.1.20]).[6] Prospero's sympathetic, humane
response to the captured men will cause him to extend the kind of
generous mercy that is so often connected to courteous superiority: "The rarer action is / In virtue than in vengeance" (5.1.27–
28). Of course, as we know from the discussion of mercy in *The
Merchant of Venice*, the bestowal of mercy can go hand in hand with
the consolidation of power. Prospero's seeming willingness to let go
of the power of his art, based in his sympathetic humanity, is what
will allow the captives to be more fully their human selves: "My
charms I'll break; their senses I'll restore; / And they shall be themselves" (5.1.31–32). That is to say, with some metatheatrical irony,
that the captives will return to their true characters, as personated
by the actors on the stage. Prospero's gestures of rupture ("But
this rough magic / I here abjure" [5.1.50–51]; "I'll break my staff"
[5.1.54]) both expose the tools of his art and continue the theatrical game, as Prospero not only continues to dominate his captives,
but also seeks to conduct the audience's response.[7] The sympathetic
spectatorship—the tendering of the affections—that Ariel associates with humanity remain saturated with theatricality, as Prospero
speaks to the semi-charmed Gonzalo: "Mine eyes, ev'n sociable to
the show of thine, / Fall fellowly drops" (5.1.63–64). Prospero's
reflection of Gonzalo is a moving presentation of human sympathy,
but his reference to the "show" of Gonzalo's eyes also recalls the
blurry distinction between authenticity and performance.[8]

In the play's epilogue, we see yet another breaking of boundaries, as the actor playing Prospero now speaks in something like
their own voice. It is conventional to see Prospero's epilogue as the
replacement of the character by the actor, and there is certainly truth
in the idea that the actor's pose has been broken: "*Now* my charms
are all o'erthrown, / And what strength I have's mine own, / Which
is most faint" (5.Epilogue.1–3; emphasis mine). At the same time,
the actor maintains a courteous pose of self-deprecation as they

speak to the audience—perhaps we might say that they are now playing the part of the gentle actor, just as Spenser plays the part of the curmudgeonly narrator at the close of *The Faerie Queene.* And yet Shakespeare's Prospero differs importantly in his invocation of the "now." However jaded and world-weary his character is, he nonetheless opens his epilogue with a word that has a new, contemporary referent in every performance, offering a fresh celebration of the shared imaginative labors of players and audiences even as it marks their imminent dissolution.

The player personating the player personating Prospero also presents a show of courtly deference as he emphasizes the power of the audience:

> Let me not,
> Since I have my dukedom got
> And pardoned the deceiver, dwell
> In this bare island by your spell;
> But *release* me from my bands
> With the help of your good hands.
> Gentle breath of yours my sails
> Must fill, or else my project fails,
> Which was to *please.* Now I want
> Spirits to enforce, art to enchant;
> And my ending is despair,
> Unless I be relieved by prayer,
> Which pierces so that it assaults
> Mercy itself, and frees all faults.
> As you from crimes would pardoned be,
> Let your indulgence set me free. (5.Epilogue.5–20; emphasis mine)

Prospero's prior action of mercy within the play is now a model for the audience's own benevolence; just as he has previously served as an audience member and released the prisoners under his power, now he encourages his own audience to play along with his courtly self-deprecation and commend the performance. To respond to the play with "gentle breath," Prospero suggests, is to join a mutually reinforcing dialogue of gentleness. Heather Kerr suggests that Prospero here "invites the audience to resolve the play's impasse by an act of human kindness," even as Jeffrey Knapp underscores the tension between Prospero's mistreatment of others throughout the play and his claim to only want to please: "By having Prospero wed an obsequious appeal for pardon with the galling suggestion that we think on our own 'crimes' ... Shakespeare transfers the trials of courtesy to us."[9] I would add that in his acknowledgment of the audience's power, Prospero here recognizes the limits of both theatrical coercion and seduction as he lets go of his ability to "enforce" and "enchant," instead recognizing his spectators' agency to respond at the same time that they, like the players, are bound by their shared expectations about playhouse decorum. So, as much as Shakespeare's play here suggests a breaking of character and a breaking of the fiction, it also prolongs the courteous role-playing and invites the knowing audience to join in; the audience may be spurred to criticize the deployment of power in the play and also to come to terms with its own power to generate meaning. Shakespeare's gentler approach here offers a striking contrast to Spenser's final takedown of his readers; Shakespeare here both lays bare the terms of the courtly game even as he invites the audience to participate, suggesting the positive value of their being pleased. If Spenser ultimately insults the value that his shallower readers place on what is pleasing, Shakespeare recuperates it while still encouraging his audience to regard it with a discerning eye.

Courtesy, fundamentally concerned with the judgment of human interactions and the creation of social identities, ultimately resists simplifying definitions; both Spenser and Shakespeare put it to varied uses as they create texts that flatter, teach, challenge, alienate, please, and even define their readers and audiences. As Spenser and Shakespeare engaged readers and audiences through the discourses of courtesy, they offered them pathways to forge new social identities and to grasp new understandings of their own agency to determine the meaning of texts. With their kaleidoscopic overlaps and divergences, Spenser's and Shakespeare's shared use of courtesy as a lens for approaching readers and audiences continues, I trust, to allow for the possibility of new readings in our own era of disruption.

Notes

1 Citations of *The Tempest* are from the revised edition of Virginia Mason Vaughan and Alden T. Vaughan.
2 Drawing on Lauren Silberman's account of the scene's "complex combination of engagement and detachment" (*Transforming Desire*, 68), Joe Moshenska explores how this passage "challenges the reader

both to look beyond, and to dwell delightedly with, the intense passion of this embrace" (*Feeling Pleasures*, 121). In its attention to both Amoret and Britomart as "reader surrogates" (58), Silberman's work offers an incisive account of Spenser's provocations.

3 The 1596 edition is also radically different from the 1609 publication, in which Book 6 is immediately followed by the Mutabilitie Cantos and then the paratexts of the 1590 version (the Letter to Raleigh and the dedicatory and commendatory verses). If the reader of the 1596 edition of the poem is forced to terminate their reading with the narrator's challenge, the reader of the 1609 edition of the poem has the option of hardly lingering over it at all.

4 For the view that these lines contain an instructional message about the value and power of the poet's work, see also Derek Alwes, " 'Who Knowes Not Colin Clout?,' " 41–42. Maureen Quilligan, in contrast, sees in this final stanza Spenser's admission of "deep failure" (*Language of Allegory*, 169). See also Richard Helgerson on the significance of these lines for the poet's sense of his project (*Self-Crowned Laureates*, 92).

5 Here I am less concerned with Shakespeare's specific debts to Spenser than with a comparison of how they view their poetic projects. On the former topic, see John Roe, "*The Tempest* and *The Faerie Queene*," which emphasizes their shared interest in the strange or wondrous.

6 On Ariel's prompting of Prospero's empathy, see Leah Whittington, "Shakespeare's Vergil," 114–15. See also Heather Kerr, " 'Sociable' Tears in *The Tempest*," 164–71.

7 For a discussion of how this speech gestures toward Shakespeare's involvement with print culture, see Patrick Cheney, *Shakespeare's Literary Authorship*, 1–4.

8 Prospero's account of his reaction to Gonzalo neatly anticipates Bruce McConachie's explorations of how "mirror neurons" facilitate audience empathy (*Engaging Audiences*, 65–120). Kerr reads "shared tears as evidence of common humanity" in the play, linking them to its "transition from revenge to reconciliation" (" 'Sociable' Tears," 164).

9 See, respectively, Kerr, " 'Sociable' Tears," 169, and Jeffrey Knapp, "Shakespeare's Pains to Please," 268. Jennifer Low and Nova Myhill also remark that this epilogue gives the audience "freedom of choice ... to determine the success or failure of the internal action of the play" (*Imagining the Audience*, 6).

Bibliography

Primary Works

Ariosto, Ludovico. *Orlando Furioso.* Ed. Lanfranco Caretti. Turin: Einaudi, 1966.

—. *Orlando Furioso.* Trans. John Harington. Ed. Robert McNulty. Oxford: Oxford University Press, 1972.

—. *Orlando Furioso.* Trans. Guido Waldman. Oxford: Oxford University Press, 1974.

Aristotle. *Nicomachean Ethics.* Trans. Terence Irwin. Indianapolis, IN: Hackett, 1985.

—. *Nicomachean Ethics.* Trans. Martin Ostwald. Indianapolis, IN: Library of Liberal Arts, 1962.

—. *Poetics.* Trans. Leon Golden. Tallahassee: University Presses of Florida, 1981.

Ascham, Roger. *The Schoolmaster.* Ed. Lawrence V. Ryan. Ithaca, NY: Cornell University Press, 1967.

Bandello, Matteo. *La prima parte de le novelle del Bandello.* Trans. Geoffrey Bullough. *Narrative and Dramatic Sources of Shakespeare,* Vol. 2. London: Columbia University Press, 1958.

Beverley, Peter. *The Historie of Ariodanto and Jenevra. The Sources of Much Ado About Nothing.* Ed. Charles Tyler Prouty. New Haven, CT: Yale University Press, 1950.

Bryskett, Lodowick. *Literary Works.* Ed. J. H. P. Pafford. Farnborough, UK: Gregg International, 1972.

Castiglione, Baldassare. *The Book of the Courtier.* Trans. Thomas Hoby. Ed. Virginia Cox. London: Everyman, 1994.

—. *The Book of the Courtier: A Norton Critical Edition.* Trans. Charles Singleton. Ed. Daniel Javitch. New York: W. W. Norton, 2002.

—. *Il libro del Cortegiano.* Ed. Giulio Carnazzi. Milan: Biblioteca Universale Rizzoli, 1987.

Chaucer, Geoffrey. *The Riverside Chaucer,* 3rd edn. Ed. Larry D. Benson. Boston, MA: Houghton Mifflin, 1987.

Cicero. *Tusculan Disputations*. Trans. J. E. King. Loeb Classical Library 141. Cambridge, MA: Harvard University Press, 1927.

Della Casa, Giovanni. *Galateo, Overo dei Costumi e Modi che si Debbono Tenere o Schifare nella Commune Conversatione*. Venice, 1558.

Elyot, Thomas. *The Book Named The Governor*. Ed. S. E. Lehmberg. New York: Everyman, 1962.

Ferne, John. *The Blazon of Gentrie*. London, 1586. Accessed through Early English Books Online.

Gosson, Stephen. *The Schoole of Abuse*. London, 1579. Accessed through Early English Books Online.

Greene, Robert. *Pandosto: The Triumph of Time. An Anthology of Elizabethan Prose Fiction*. Ed. Paul Salzman. Oxford: Oxford University Press, 1987.

Guazzo, Stefano. *The Civil Conversation*. Trans. George Pettie. London, 1581. Accessed through Early English Books Online.

Harington, John. *A Briefe Apologie of Poetrie* [Preface to translation of *Orlando Furioso*]. London, 1591. Accessed through Early English Books Online.

Heliodorus. *An Aethiopian Historie*. Trans. Thomas Underdowne. London, 1606. Accessed through Early English Books Online.

Heywood, Thomas. *An Apology for Actors*. London, 1612. Accessed through Early English Books Online.

Horace. *Satires, Epistles, and the Art of Poetry*. Trans. H. Rushton Fairclough. Loeb Classical Library 194. Cambridge, MA: Harvard University Press, 1978.

Lucretius. *De Rerum Natura*. Ed. William Ellery Leonard and Stanley Barney Smith. Madison: University of Wisconsin Press, 1942.

Nenna, Giovanni Battista. *Il Nennio*. Ed. Raffaele Girardi. Rome: Laterza, 2003.

—. *Nennio, or A Treatise of Nobility*. Trans. William Jones. London, 1595. Accessed through Early English Books Online.

—. *Nennio, or A Treatise of Nobility*. Trans. William Jones. Ed. Alice Shalvi. Jerusalem: Israel Universities Press and H. A. Humphrey, 1967.

Ovid. *Metamorphoses*. Ed. William S. Anderson. Norman: University of Oklahoma Press, 1972.

Peacham, Henry. *The Garden of Eloquence*. London, 1577. Accessed through Early English Books Online.

Plato. *The Republic*. Trans. Tom Griffith. Ed. G. R. F. Ferrari. Cambridge: Cambridge University Press, 2000.

Puttenham, George. *The Art of English Poesy*. Ed. Frank Whigham and Wayne A. Rebhorn. Ithaca, NY: Cornell University Press, 2007.

Ripa, Cesare. *Iconologia: or, Moral Emblems*. London, 1709. Accessed at the English Emblem Book Project.

Romei, Annibale. *The Courtiers Academie*. Trans. I. K[epers]. London, 1598. Accessed through Early English Books Online.

Shakespeare, William. *As You Like It. The Norton Shakespeare*, 3rd edn. Ed. Stephen Greenblatt et al. New York: W. W. Norton, 2016.

—. *Hamlet.* Ed. Ann Thompson and Neil Taylor. London: Arden Shakespeare, 2006.

—. *Henry IV, Part 1. The Norton Shakespeare*, 3rd edn. Ed. Stephen Greenblatt et al. New York: W. W. Norton, 2016.

—. *Henry V.* Ed. Gary Taylor. Oxford: Oxford University Press, 1994.

—. *Love's Labour's Lost.* Ed. H. R. Woudhuysen. Walton-on-Thames, UK: Arden Shakespeare, 1998.

—. *The Merchant of Venice.* Ed. John Drakakis. London: Arden Shakespeare, 2010.

—. *A Midsummer Night's Dream.* Ed. Peter Holland. Oxford: Oxford University Press, 1994.

—. *Much Ado About Nothing.* Ed. Claire McEachern. London: Arden Shakespeare, 2007.

—. *The Norton Facsimile: The First Folio of Shakespeare.* Prepared by Charlton Hinman. New York: W. W. Norton, 1968.

—. *Romeo and Juliet. The Norton Shakespeare*, 3rd edn. Ed. Stephen Greenblatt et al. New York: W. W. Norton, 2016.

—. *The Tempest.* Ed. Virginia Mason Vaughan and Alden T. Vaughan. London: Bloomsbury Arden Shakespeare, 2011.

—. *Twelfth Night. The Norton Shakespeare*, 3rd edn. Ed. Stephen Greenblatt et al. New York: W. W. Norton, 2016.

—. *The Winter's Tale.* Ed. John Pitcher. London: Arden Shakespeare, 2010.

Sidney, Philip. *An Apologie for Poetrie.* London, 1595. Accessed through Early English Books Online.

—. *The Major Works.* Ed. Katherine Duncan-Jones. Oxford: Oxford University Press, 2002.

Spenser, Edmund. *The Faerie Queene.* Revised 2nd edn. Ed. A. C. Hamilton, Hiroshi Yamashita, and Toshiyuki Suzuki. London: Routledge, 2013.

—. *Yale Edition of the Shorter Poems of Edmund Spenser.* Ed. William A. Oram et al. New Haven, CT: Yale University Press, 1989.

Tasso, Torquato. *Gerusalemme Liberata.* Ed. Lanfranco Caretti. Turin: Einaudi, 1971.

Vaenius, Otto. *Q. Horatii Flacci Emblemata.* Antwerp, 1612. Accessed at the Emblem Project Utrecht.

Webster, John. *The Duchess of Malfi. English Renaissance Drama: A Norton Anthology.* Ed. David Bevington et al. New York: Norton, 2002.

Whitney, Geoffrey. *A Choice of Emblemes.* Leyden, 1586. Accessed at the English Emblem Book Project.

Secondary Works

Adelman, Janet. *Blood Relations: Christian and Jew in* The Merchant of Venice. Chicago: University of Chicago Press, 2008.

Akhimie, Patricia. *Shakespeare and the Cultivation of Difference: Race and Conduct in the Early Modern World*. New York: Routledge, 2018.

Albury, W. R. *Castiglione's Allegory: Veiled Policy in* The Book of the Courtier *(1528)*. Farnham, UK: Ashgate, 2014.

Alexander, Gavin. "Prosopopoeia: The Speaking Figure." *Renaissance Figures of Speech*. Ed. Sylvia Adamson et al. Cambridge: Cambridge University Press, 2007, 97–112.

Alfar, Cristina León. *Women and Shakespeare's Cuckoldry Plays: Shifting Narratives of Marital Betrayal*. London: Routledge, 2017.

Allen, John A. "Dogberry." *Shakespeare Quarterly* 24.1 (1973): 35–53.

Alpers, Paul. J. "Empson on Pastoral." *New Literary History* 10.1 (1978): 101–23.

—. "How to Read the *Faerie Queene*." *Essential Articles for the Study of Edmund Spenser*. Ed. A. C. Hamilton. Hamden, CT: Archon Books, 1972, 334–46.

—. *The Poetry of* The Faerie Queene. Princeton, NJ: Princeton University Press, 1967.

—. *What is Pastoral?* Chicago: University of Chicago Press, 1996.

Altman, Joel B. *The Tudor Play of Mind: Rhetorical Inquiry and the Development of Elizabethan Drama*. Berkeley: University of California Press, 1978.

Alwes, Derek. " 'Who Knowes not Colin Clout?': Spenser's Self-Advertisement in *The Faerie Queene*, Book 6." *Modern Philology* 88.1 (1990): 26–42.

Anderson, Judith H. " 'The Hard Begin': Entering the Initial Cantos." *Approaches to Teaching Spenser's* Faerie Queene. Ed. David Lee Miller and Alexander Dunlop. New York: Modern Language Association of America, 1994, 41–48.

—. *Reading the Allegorical Intertext: Chaucer, Spenser, Shakespeare, and Milton*. New York: Fordham University Press, 2008.

Archer, Mark. "The Meaning of 'Grace' and 'Courtesy': Book VI of *The Faerie Queene*." *Studies in English Literature 1500–1900* 27.1 (1987): 17–34.

Ascoli, Albert Russell. *Ariosto's Bitter Harmony: Crisis and Evasion in the Italian Renaissance*. Princeton, NJ: Princeton University Press, 1987.

Attridge, Derek. "Puttenham's Perplexity: Nature, Art, and the Supplement in Renaissance Poetic Theory." *Literary Theory/Renaissance Texts*. Ed. Patricia Parker and David Quint. Baltimore: Johns Hopkins University Press, 1986, 257–79.

Austin, J. L. *How to Do Things with Words*. Cambridge, MA: Harvard University Press, 1962.

Avila, Carmela Nocera. *Tradurre il* Cortegiano: The Courtyer *di Sir Thomas Hoby*. Bari: Adriatica Editrice, 1992.

Bailey, Amanda. "Shylock and the Slaves: Owing and Owning in *The Merchant of Venice*." *Shakespeare Quarterly* 62.1 (2011): 1–24.

Baldini, Donatella. "The Play of the Courtier: Correspondences between Castiglione's *Il libro del Cortegiano* and Shakespeare's *Love's Labour's Lost*." *Quaderni d'italianistica* 18.1 (1997): 5–22.

Barish, Jonas. *The Antitheatrical Prejudice.* Berkeley: University of California Press, 1981.

Bate, Jonathan. *Soul of the Age: A Biography of the Mind of William Shakespeare.* New York: Random House, 2009.

Bates, Catherine. *The Rhetoric of Courtship in Elizabethan Language and Literature.* Cambridge: Cambridge University Press, 2006.

Bayley, P. C. "Order, Grace, and Courtesy in Spenser's World." *Patterns of Love and Courtesy: Essays in Memory of C. S. Lewis.* Ed. John Lawlor. Evanston, IL: Northwestern University Press, 1966, 178-202.

Bednarz, James P. "Imitations of Spenser in *A Midsummer Night's Dream.*" *Renaissance Drama* 14 (1983): 79-102.

Belt, Debra. "Hostile Audiences and the Courteous Reader in *The Faerie Queene,* Book VI." *Spenser Studies* 9 (1988): 107-35.

Berger Jr., Harry. *The Absence of Grace:* Sprezzatura *and Suspicion in Two Renaissance Courtesy Books.* Stanford, CA: Stanford University Press, 2000.

—. "Against the Sink-a-Pace: Sexual and Family Politics in *Much Ado About Nothing.*" *Shakespeare Quarterly* 33 (1982): 302-13.

—. *A Fury in the Words: Love and Embarrassment in Shakespeare's Venice.* New York: Fordham University Press, 2013.

—. *Imaginary Audition: Shakespeare on Stage and Page.* Berkeley: University of California Press, 1989.

—. "Narrative as Rhetoric in *The Faerie Queene.*" *English Literary Renaissance* 21.1 (1991): 3-48.

Bergeron, David M. Introduction to *Reading and Writing in Shakespeare.* Ed. David M. Bergeron. Newark: University of Delaware Press and Associated University Presses, 1996, 11-24.

Bilello, Thomas C. "Accomplished with What She Lacks: Law, Equity, and Portia's Con." *Law and Literature* 16.1 (2004): 11-32.

Biow, Douglas. *In Your Face: Professional Improprieties and the Art of Being Conspicuous in Sixteenth-Century Italy.* Stanford, CA: Stanford University Press, 2010.

Bishop, T. G. *Shakespeare and the Theatre of Wonder.* Cambridge: Cambridge University Press, 1996.

Bloom, Gina. "'Boy Eternal': Aging, Games, and Masculinity in *The Winter's Tale.*" *English Literary Renaissance* 40.3 (2010): 329-56.

Booth, Stephen. *Precious Nonsense: The Gettysburg Address, Ben Jonson's Epitaphs on His Children, and* Twelfth Night. Berkeley: University of California Press, 1998.

Borris, Kenneth. "Sub Rosa: Pastorella's Allegorical Homecoming and Closure in the 1596 *Faerie Queene.*" *Spenser Studies* 21 (2006): 133-80.

Bourdieu, Pierre. *Distinction: A Social Critique of the Judgement of Taste.* Trans. Richard Nice. Cambridge, MA: Harvard University Press, 1984.

—. "Forms of Capital." *Handbook of Theory and Research for the Sociology of Education.* Trans. Richard Nice. Ed. John G. Richardson. New York: Greenwood, 1986, 241-58.

—. *Practical Reason: On the Theory of Action*. Trans. Randall Johnson. Stanford, CA: Stanford University Press, 1998.

Bovilsky, Lara. *Barbarous Play: Race on the English Renaissance Stage*. Minneapolis: University of Minnesota Press, 2008.

Breen, Katharine. *Imagining an English Reading Public, 1150–1400*. Cambridge: Cambridge University Press, 2010.

Breitenberg, Mark. *Anxious Masculinity in Early Modern England*. Cambridge: Cambridge University Press, 1996.

Britton, Dennis Austin. *Becoming Christian: Race, Reformation, and Early Modern English Romance*. New York: Fordham University Press, 2014.

Britton, Dennis Austin, and Kimberly Anne Coles. "Spenser and Race: An Introduction." *Spenser Studies* 35 (2021): 1–19.

Bryson, Anna. *From Courtesy to Civility: Changing Codes of Conduct in Early Modern England*. Oxford: Clarendon, 1998.

Bullough, Geoffrey. *Narrative and Dramatic Sources of Shakespeare*, Vol. 2. London: Columbia University Press, 1958.

Burchmore, David W. "The Medieval Sources of Spenser's Occasion Episode." *Spenser Studies* 2 (1981): 93–120.

Burchmore, David W., and Susan C. Burchmore. "Occasion." *The Spenser Encyclopedia*. Ed. A. C. Hamilton et al. Toronto: University of Toronto Press, 1990.

Burke, Peter. *The Fortunes of the* Courtier: *The European Reception of Castiglione's* Cortegiano. University Park: Pennsylvania State University Press, 1995.

Bushnell, Rebecca. *A Culture of Teaching: Early Modern Humanism in Theory and Practice*. Ithaca, NY: Cornell University Press, 1996.

Butler, Judith. *Gender Trouble: Feminism and the Subversion of Identity*. New York: Routledge, 1990.

Butler, Martin. Introduction to *Cymbeline*. Cambridge: Cambridge University Press, 2005.

Campana, Joseph. "Boy Toys and Liquid Joys: Pleasure and Power in the Bower of Bliss." *Modern Philology* 106.3 (2009): 465–96.

Cave, Terence. "The Mimesis of Reading in the Renaissance." *Mimesis: From Mirror to Method, Augustine to Descartes*. Ed. John D. Lyons and Stephen G. Nichols Jr. Hanover, NH: University Press of New England, 1982, 149–65.

—. *Recognitions: A Study in Poetics*. Oxford: Clarendon Press, 1988.

Chakravarty, Urvashi. *Fictions of Consent: Slavery, Servitude, and Free Service in Early Modern England*. Philadelphia: University of Pennsylvania Press, 2022.

—. "Race, Natality, and the Biopolitics of Early Modern Political Theology." *Journal for Early Modern Cultural Studies* 18.2 (Spring 2018): 140–66.

Cheney, Donald. *Spenser's Image of Nature: Wild Man and Shepherd in* The Faerie Queene. New Haven, CT: Yale University Press, 1966.

Cheney, Patrick. "Perdita, Pastorella, and the Romance of Literary Form: Shakespeare's Counter-Spenserian Authorship." *Shakespeare and Spenser: Attractive Opposites.* Ed. J. B. Lethbridge. Manchester: Manchester University Press, 2008, 121–42.

—. *Shakespeare, National Poet-Playwright.* Cambridge: Cambridge University Press, 2004.

—. *Shakespeare's Literary Authorship.* Cambridge: Cambridge University Press, 2008.

—. *Spenser's Famous Flight: A Renaissance Idea of a Literary Career.* Toronto: University of Toronto Press, 1993.

Clegg, Cyndia Susan. *Shakespeare's Reading Audiences: Early Modern Books and Audience Interpretation.* Cambridge: Cambridge University Press, 2017.

Cobb, Christopher J. *The Staging of Romance in Late Shakespeare.* Newark: University of Delaware Press, 2007.

Cohen, Walter. "*The Merchant of Venice* and the Possibilities of Historical Criticism." *ELH* 49.4 (1982): 765–89.

Coldiron, A. E. B. *Printers Without Borders: Translation and Textuality in the Renaissance.* Cambridge: Cambridge University Press, 2015.

Colie, Rosalie Littell. *Paradoxia Epidemica: The Renaissance Tradition of Paradox.* Princeton, NJ: Princeton University Press, 1966.

—. *Shakespeare's Living Art.* Princeton, NJ: Princeton University Press, 1974.

Collington, Philip D. " 'Stuffed with All Honourable Virtues': *Much Ado About Nothing* and *The Book of the Courtier.*" *Studies in Philology* 103.3 (2006): 281–312.

Collington, Tara, and Philip Collington. " 'The Time When … The Place Where': Chronotopes and Chronologies in *Love's Labour's Lost.*" *Studies in Philology* 111.4 (2014): 786–820.

Cook, Ann Jennalie. *The Privileged Playgoers of Shakespeare's London, 1576–1642.* Princeton, NJ: Princeton University Press, 1981.

Cook, Carol. " 'The Sign and Semblance of Her Honor': Reading Gender Difference in *Much Ado about Nothing.*" *PMLA* 101.2 (1986): 186–202.

Correll, Barbara. *The End of Conduct:* Grobianus *and the Renaissance Text of the Subject.* Ithaca, NY: Cornell University Press, 1996.

Cox, Virginia. *The Renaissance Dialogue: Literary Dialogue in its Social and Political Contexts.* Cambridge: Cambridge University Press, 1992.

Craik, Katherine A. *Reading Sensations in Early Modern England.* London: Palgrave Macmillan, 2007.

Danner, Bruce. "Courteous *Virtù* in Book 6 of *The Faerie Queene.*" *Studies in English Literature 1500–1900* 38.1 (1998): 1–18.

Davis, Natalie Zemon. *The Gift in Sixteenth-Century France.* Madison: University of Wisconsin Press, 2000.

Davis, Philip. *Shakespeare Thinking.* London: Continuum, 2007.

Dawson, Anthony B., and Paul Yachnin. *The Culture of Playgoing in Shakespeare's England.* Cambridge: Cambridge University Press, 2001.

Day, J. F. R. "Primers of Honor: Heraldry, Heraldry Books, and English Renaissance Literature." *Sixteenth Century Journal* 21.1 (1990): 93–103.

DeNeef, A. Leigh. *Spenser and the Motives of Metaphor.* Durham, NC: Duke University Press, 1982.

Dent, R. W. *Shakespeare's Proverbial Language.* Berkeley: University of California Press, 1981.

Derrida, Jacques. *Given Time: I. Counterfeit Money.* Trans. Peggy Kamuf. Chicago: University of Chicago Press, 1992.

DiGangi, Mario. *Sexual Types: Embodiment, Agency, and Dramatic Character from Shakespeare to Shirley.* Philadelphia: University of Pennsylvania Press, 2011.

Dolan, Frances E. "Taking the Pencil out of God's Hand: Art, Nature, and the Face-Painting Debate in Early Modern England." *PMLA* 108.2 (1993): 224–39.

—. *True Relations: Reading, Literature, and Evidence in Seventeenth-Century England.* Philadelphia: University of Pennsylvania Press, 2013.

Dolven, Jeff. *Scenes of Instruction in Renaissance Romance.* Chicago: University of Chicago Press, 2007.

—. "Spenser and the Troubled Theaters." *English Literary Renaissance* 29.3 (1999): 179–200.

Doran, Madeleine. *Endeavors of Art: A Study of Form in Elizabethan Drama.* Madison: University of Wisconsin Press, 1954.

Dubrow, Heather. "'A Doubtfull Sense of Things': Thievery in *The Faerie Queene* 6.10 and 6.11." *Worldmaking Spenser: Explorations in the Early Modern Age.* Ed. Patrick Cheney and Lauren Silberman. Lexington: University Press of Kentucky, 2000, 204–16.

Duncan-Jones, Katherine. *Shakespeare: An Ungentle Life.* London: Methuen Drama, 2010.

Eagleton, Terry. *The Ideology of the Aesthetic.* Oxford: Basil Blackwell, 1990.

Elias, Norbert. *The Civilizing Process: Sociogenetic and Psychogenetic Investigations.* Trans. Edmund Jephcott. Rev. edn. Ed. Eric Dunning et al. Oxford: Blackwell, 2000.

Empson, William. *Some Versions of Pastoral.* Ed. Seamus Perry. Oxford: Oxford University Press, 2020.

Engle, Lars. *Shakespearean Pragmatism: Market of His Time.* Chicago: University of Chicago Press, 1993.

Enterline, Lynn. *Shakespeare's Schoolroom: Rhetoric, Discipline, Emotion.* Philadelphia: University of Pennsylvania Press, 2012.

Erne, Lukas. *Shakespeare and the Book Trade.* Cambridge: Cambridge University Press, 2013.

—. *Shakespeare as Literary Dramatist.* Cambridge: Cambridge University Press, 2003.

Escolme, Bridget. *Talking to the Audience: Shakespeare, Performance, Self.* New York: Routledge, 2005.

Esler, Anthony. *The Aspiring Mind of the Elizabethan Younger Generation.* Durham, NC: Duke University Press, 1966.

Estrin, Barbara L. *The Raven and the Lark: Lost Children in Literature of the English Renaissance.* Lewisburg, PA: Bucknell University Press, 1985.

Evans, Kasey. "Misreading and Misogyny: Ariosto, Spenser, and Shakespeare." *Renaissance Drama* 36/37 (2010): 261–92.

Evans, Maurice. *Spenser's Anatomy of Heroism: A Commentary on* The Faerie Queene. Cambridge: Cambridge University Press, 1970.

Falvo, Joseph D. *The Economy of Human Relations: Castiglione's* Libro del Cortegiano. New York: Peter Lang, 1992.

Feerick, Jean. *Strangers in Blood: Relocating Race in the Renaissance.* Toronto: University of Toronto Press, 2010.

Ferguson, Margaret W. *Trials of Desire: Renaissance Defenses of Poetry.* New Haven, CT: Yale University Press, 1983.

Finucci, Valeria. *The Lady Vanishes: Subjectivity and Representation in Castiglione and Ariosto.* Stanford, CA: Stanford University Press, 1992.

Fish, Stanley. *Is There a Text in This Class?: The Authority of Interpretive Communities.* Cambridge, MA: Harvard University Press, 1980.

—. *Surprised by Sin: The Reader in* Paradise Lost. London: Palgrave Macmillan, 1967.

Forrester, Anna Carleton. "'Which is the Merchant Here, and Which the Jew?': Alterity, Sameness and Irony in Venice." *European Judaism* 51.2 (2018): 36–43.

Foucault, Michel. *The History of Sexuality*, Vol. 1. Trans. Robert Hurley. New York: Vintage, 1980.

Freud, Sigmund. "The Theme of the Three Caskets." Trans. James Strachey. *The Merchant of Venice: A Norton Critical Edition.* Ed. Leah S. Marcus. New York: W. W. Norton, 2006, 152–60.

Frye, Northrop. *Anatomy of Criticism: Four Essays.* Princeton, NJ: Princeton University Press, 1957.

—. *Fables of Identity: Studies in Poetic Mythology.* New York: Harcourt Brace, 1963.

Fumerton, Patricia. *Cultural Aesthetics: Renaissance Literature and the Practice of Social Ornament.* Chicago: University of Chicago Press, 1991.

Garin, Eugenio. *Italian Humanism: Philosophy and Civic Life in the Renaissance.* Trans. Peter Munz. Oxford: Basil Blackwell, 1965.

Gaylard, Susan. "Castiglione vs. Cicero: Political Engagement, or Effeminate Chatter?" *Italian Culture* 27.2 (2009): 81–98.

—. *Hollow Men: Writing, Objects, and Public Image in Renaissance Italy.* New York: Fordham University Press, 2013.

Geller, Lila. "Spenser's Theory of Nobility in Book VI of *The Faerie Queene.*" *English Literary Renaissance* 5.1 (1975): 49–57.

Ghinassi, Ghino. *Fasi dell'elaborazione del* Cortegiano. Florence: Sansoni, 1967.

Giamatti, A. Bartlett. *Play of Double Senses: Spenser's* Faerie Queene. Englewood Cliffs, NJ: Prentice-Hall, 1975.

Girard, René. "'To Entrap the Wisest': A Reading of *The Merchant of Venice*." *Literature and Society*. Ed. Edward Said. Baltimore: Johns Hopkins University Press, 1980, 100–19.

Girardi, Raffaele. Introduction to *Nennio*. Ed. Raffaele Girardi. Rome: Laterza, 2003.

Goddard, Harold C. *The Meaning of Shakespeare*, Vol. 1. Chicago: University of Chicago Press, 1951.

Goffman, Erving. *The Presentation of Self in Everyday Life*. New York: Anchor, 1959.

Goldberg, Jonathan. *Endlesse Worke: Spenser and the Structures of Discourse*. Baltimore: Johns Hopkins University Press, 1981.

—. "The Print of Goodness." *The Culture of Capital: Property, Cities, and Knowledge in Early Modern England*. Ed. Henry S. Turner. New York: Routledge, 2002, 231–54.

—. *The Seeds of Things: Theorizing Sexuality and Materiality in Renaissance Representations*. New York: Fordham University Press, 2009.

Gough, Melinda. "'Her Filthy Feature Open Showne' in Ariosto, Spenser, and *Much Ado about Nothing*." *Studies in English Literature 1500–1900* 39.1 (1999): 41–67.

Grafton, Anthony, and Lisa Jardine. *From Humanism to the Humanities: Education and the Liberal Arts in Fifteenth- and Sixteenth-Century Europe*. Cambridge, MA: Harvard University Press, 1986.

Grantley, Darryll. *Wit's Pilgrimage: Drama and the Social Impact of Education in Early Modern England*. Aldershot, UK: Ashgate, 2000.

Greenblatt, Stephen. Introduction to *Much Ado About Nothing*. *The Norton Shakespeare*, 3rd edn. Ed. Stephen Greenblatt et al. New York: W. W. Norton, 2008.

—. "Marlowe, Marx, and Anti-Semitism." *Learning to Curse: Essays in Modern Culture*. New York: Routledge, 1990, 40–58.

—. *Renaissance Self-Fashioning: From More to Shakespeare*. Chicago: University of Chicago Press, 1980.

—. *Will in the World: How Shakespeare Became Shakespeare*. New York: W. W. Norton, 2004.

Greene, Thomas M. "*Il Cortegiano* and the Choice of a Game." *Castiglione: The Ideal and the Real in Renaissance Culture*. Ed. Robert W. Hanning and David Rosand. New Haven, CT: Yale University Press, 1983, 1–15.

—. "*Love's Labour's Lost*: The Grace of Society." *Shakespeare Quarterly* 22.4 (1971): 315–28.

Grogan, Jane. *Exemplary Spenser: Visual and Poetic Pedagogy in* The Faerie Queene. Farnham, UK: Ashgate, 2009.

Guenther, Genevieve. *Magical Imaginations: Instrumental Aesthetics in the English Renaissance*. Toronto: University of Toronto Press, 2012.

Gurr, Andrew. "The Bear, the Statue, and Hysteria in *The Winter's Tale*." *Shakespeare Quarterly* 34.4 (1983): 420–25.

—. *Playgoing in Shakespeare's Early Modern England*, 3rd edn. Cambridge: Cambridge University Press, 2004.

—. *The Shakespearean Stage, 1574–1642*, 4th edn. Cambridge: Cambridge University Press, 2009.

Hackel, Heidi Brayman. "The 'Great Variety' of Readers and Early Modern Reading Practices." *A Companion to Shakespeare.* Ed. David Scott Kastan. Oxford: Blackwell, 1999, 139–57.

Hadfield, Andrew. "In the Blood: Spenser, Race, and Identity." *Spenser Studies* 35 (2021): 47–68.

Hall, Kim F. "Guess Who's Coming to Dinner? Colonization and Miscegenation in *The Merchant of Venice.*" *Renaissance Drama* 23 (1992): 87–111.

—. *Things of Darkness: Economies of Race and Gender in Early Modern England.* Ithaca, NY: Cornell University Press, 1995.

Halpern, Richard. *The Poetics of Primitive Accumulation: English Renaissance Culture and the Genealogy of Capital.* Ithaca, NY: Cornell University Press, 1991.

—. *Shakespeare Among the Moderns.* Ithaca, NY: Cornell University Press, 1997.

Hamilton, A. C. *The Structure of Allegory in* The Faerie Queene. Oxford: Clarendon, 1961.

Hampton, Timothy. *Writing from History: The Rhetoric of Exemplarity in the Renaissance.* Ithaca, NY: Cornell University Press, 1990.

Hapgood, Robert. *Shakespeare the Theatre-Poet.* Oxford: Clarendon, 1988.

Harbage, Alfred. *Shakespeare's Audience.* New York: Columbia University Press, 1941.

Helgerson, Richard. *The Elizabethan Prodigals.* Berkeley: University of California Press, 1976.

—. *Forms of Nationhood: The Elizabethan Writing of England.* Chicago: University of Chicago Press, 1992.

—. *Self-Crowned Laureates: Spenser, Jonson, Milton, and the Literary System.* Berkeley: University of California Press, 1983.

Heng, Geraldine. *England and the Jews.* Cambridge: Cambridge University Press 2019.

—. *The Invention of Race in the European Middle Ages.* Cambridge: Cambridge University Press, 2018.

Hieatt, A. Kent. "William Shakespeare." *The Spenser Encyclopedia.* Ed. A. C. Hamilton et al. Toronto: University of Toronto Press, 1990.

Hobgood, Allison P. *Passionate Playgoing in Early Modern England.* Cambridge: Cambridge University Press, 2014.

Holderness, Graham. "*The Winter's Tale*: Country into Court." *Shakespeare: Out of Court.* Ed. Graham Holderness, Nick Potter, and John Turner. New York: St. Martin's Press, 1990, 195–235.

Holland, Norman N. *The Dynamics of Literary Response.* New York: Norton Library, 1975.

Holland, Peter. "*The Merchant of Venice* and the Value of Money." *Cahiers Élisabéthains: A Journal of English Renaissance Studies* 60.1 (2001): 13–31.

Horwich, Richard. "Riddle and Dilemma in *The Merchant of Venice*." *Studies in English Literature 1500–1900* 17.2 (1977): 191–200.

Howard, Jean E. *Shakespeare's Art of Orchestration: Stage Technique and Audience Response*. Urbana: University of Illinois Press, 1984.

—. *The Stage and Social Struggle in Early Modern England*. London: Routledge, 1993.

Howard, Jean E., and Phyllis Rackin. *Engendering a Nation: A Feminist Account of Shakespeare's English Histories*. London: Routledge, 1997.

Huntington, John. *Ambition, Rank, and Poetry in 1590s England*. Urbana: University of Illinois Press, 2001.

Ingram, Jill Phillips. *Idioms of Self-Interest: Credit, Identity, and Property in English Renaissance Literature*. New York: Routledge, 2006.

Iser, Wolfgang. *The Act of Reading: A Theory of Aesthetic Response*. Baltimore: Johns Hopkins University Press, 1978.

Ivic, Christopher. "Spenser and the Bounds of Race." *Genre* 32.3 (1999): 141–74.

Iyengar, Sujata. *Shades of Difference: Mythologies of Skin Color in Early Modern England*. Philadelphia: University of Pennsylvania Press, 2005.

Javitch, Daniel. "*Il Cortegiano* and the Constraints of Despotism." *Castiglione: The Ideal and the Real in Renaissance Culture*. Ed. Robert W. Hanning and David Rosand. New Haven, CT: Yale University Press, 1983, 17–28.

—. *Poetry and Courtliness in Renaissance England*. Princeton, NJ: Princeton University Press, 1978.

—. Preface to *The Book of the Courtier*. New York: W.W. Norton, 2002, vii–xvi.

Judson, Alexander. "Spenser's Theory of Courtesy." *PMLA* 47.1 (1932): 122–36.

Kae, Yunah. "'Light in Darkness Lies': Poesy, Love, and Whiteness in *Love's Labour's Lost*." *Shakespeare Studies* 50 (2022): 54–62.

Kahn, Victoria. *Rhetoric, Prudence, and Skepticism in the Renaissance*. Ithaca, NY: Cornell University Press, 1985.

Kaplan, M. Lindsay. "Jessica's Mother: Medieval Constructions of Jewish Race and Gender in *The Merchant of Venice*." *Shakespeare Quarterly* 58.1 (2007): 1–30.

Kaske, Carol V. *Spenser's Biblical Poetics*. Ithaca, NY: Cornell University Press, 1999.

Kastan, David Scott. *Shakespeare and the Book*. Cambridge: Cambridge University Press, 2001.

Keilen, Sean. *Vulgar Eloquence: On the Renaissance Invention of English Literature*. New Haven, CT: Yale University Press, 2006.

Kelly, Joan. "Did Women Have a Renaissance?" *Women, History, and Theory: The Essays of Joan Kelly*. Chicago: University of Chicago Press, 1984, 19–50.

Kelso, Ruth. *The Doctrine of the English Gentleman in the Sixteenth Century*. Urbana: University of Illinois Press, 1929.

Kerr, Heather. "'Sociable' Tears in *The Tempest*." *Shakespeare and Emotions*. Ed. R. S. White, Mark Houlahan, and Katrina O'Loughlin. New York: Palgrave Macmillan, 2015, 164–72.

Kinney, Arthur. *Continental Humanist Poetics: Studies in Erasmus, Castiglione, Marguerite de Navarre, Rabelais and Cervantes*. Amherst: University of Massachusetts Press, 1989.

Kintgen, Eugene R. *Reading in Tudor England*. Pittsburgh, PA: University of Pittsburgh Press, 1996.

Knapp, Jeffrey. "Shakespeare's Pains to Please." *Forms of Association: Making Publics in Early Modern Europe*. Ed. Paul Yachnin and Marlene Eberhart. Amherst: University of Massachusetts Press, 2015, 256–71.

Kolsky, Stephen. "Learning Virtue, Teaching Politics: Some Notes on Book Four of the *Cortegiano*." *Forum Italicum* 34.1 (2000); reprinted in *Courts and Courtiers in Renaissance Northern Italy*. Aldershot, UK: Ashgate Variorum, 2002.

—. "Making and Breaking the Rules: Castiglione's *Cortegiano*." *Renaissance Studies* 11 (1997); reprinted in *Courts and Courtiers in Renaissance Northern Italy*. Aldershot, UK: Ashgate Variorum, 2002.

Lamb, Mary Ellen. "Engendering the Narrative Act: Old Wives' Tales in *The Winter's Tale*, *Macbeth*, and *The Tempest*." *Criticism* 40.4 (1998): 529–53.

Landreth, David. *The Face of Mammon: The Matter of Money in English Renaissance Literature*. Oxford: Oxford University Press, 2012.

Lawrence, Jason. "Calidore *fra i pastori*: Spenser's Return to Tasso in *The Faerie Queene*, Book VI." *Spenser Studies* 20 (2005): 265–76.

Lee, Richard Z. "Wary Boldness: Courtesy and Critical Aesthetics in *The Faerie Queene*." *Spenser Studies* 33 (2019): 1–34.

Lerner, Ross. "Allegory and Racialization in *The Faerie Queene*." *Spenser Studies* 35 (2021): 107–32.

Lethbridge, J. B. Introduction to *Shakespeare and Spenser: Attractive Opposites*. Ed. J. B. Lethbridge. Manchester: Manchester University Press, 2008, 1–53.

—. "The Poetry of *The Faerie Queene*." *Spenser in the Moment*. Ed. Paul J. Hecht and J. B. Lethbridge. Madison, NJ: Fairleigh Dickinson University Press, 2015, 169–216.

Levin, Carole, and John Watkins. *Shakespeare's Foreign Worlds: National and Transnational Identities in the Elizabethan Age*. London: Cornell University Press, 2009.

Levine, Laura. *Men in Women's Clothing: Anti-theatricality and Effeminization, 1579–1642*. Cambridge: Cambridge University Press, 1994.

Lim, Walter S. H. "Surety and Spiritual Commercialism in *The Merchant of Venice*." *Studies in English Literature 1500–1900* 50.2 (2010): 355–82.

Lin, Erika T. "'Lord of Thy Presence': Bodies, Performance, and Audience Interpretation in Shakespeare's *King John*." *Imagining the Audience in Early Modern Drama, 1558–1642.* Ed. Jennifer A. Low and Nova Myhill. New York: Palgrave Macmillan, 2011, 113–33.

—. *Shakespeare and the Materiality of Performance.* New York: Palgrave Macmillan, 2011.

Loomba, Ania. *Shakespeare, Race, and Colonialism.* Oxford: Oxford University Press, 2002.

Lopez, Jeremy. *Theatrical Convention and Audience Response in Early Modern Drama.* Cambridge: Cambridge University Press, 2003.

Lovett, Frank. "The Path of the Courtier: Castiglione, Machiavelli, and the Loss of Republican Liberty." *The Review of Politics* 74 (2012): 589–605.

Low, Anthony. *The Georgic Revolution.* Princeton, NJ: Princeton University Press, 1985.

Low, Jennifer A. *Manhood and the Duel: Masculinity in Early Modern Drama and Culture.* New York: Palgrave Macmillan, 2003.

Low, Jennifer A., and Nova Myhill. Introduction to *Imagining the Audience in Early Modern Drama, 1558–1642.* Ed. Jennifer A. Low and Nova Myhill. New York: Palgrave Macmillan, 2011, 1–17.

Lyne, Raphael. *Shakespeare, Rhetoric and Cognition.* Cambridge: Cambridge University Press, 2011.

MacCaffrey, Isabel Gamble. *Spenser's Allegory: The Anatomy of Imagination.* Princeton, NJ: Princeton University Press, 1976.

MacLean, Hugh, and Anne Lake Prescott, eds. *Edmund Spenser's Poetry*, 3rd edn. New York: W.W. Norton, 1993.

MacLure, Millar. "Nature and Art in *The Faerie Queene.*" *ELH* 28.1 (1961): 1–20.

Maley, Willy. "Shakespeare and Spenser: Bards of a Feather?" *Early Shakespeare, 1588–1594.* Ed. Rory Loughnane and Andrew J. Power. Cambridge: Cambridge University Press, 2020, 180–99.

—. *A Spenser Chronology.* London: Macmillan, 1994.

Mares, F. H. Notes to *Much Ado About Nothing.* Ed. F. H. Mares. Cambridge: Cambridge University Press, 1988.

Marotti, Arthur F. " 'Love is Not Love': Elizabethan Sonnet Sequences and the Social Order." *ELH* 49.2 (1982): 396–428.

Matz, Robert. *Defending Literature in Early Modern England: Renaissance Literary Theory in Social Context.* Cambridge: Cambridge University Press, 2000.

Maus, Katharine Eisaman. "Horns of Dilemma." *ELH* 54.3 (1987): 561–83.

Mauss, Marcel. *The Gift: Forms and Functions of Exchange in Archaic Societies.* Trans. Ian Cunnison. New York: W.W. Norton, 1967.

McConachie, Bruce. *Engaging Audiences: A Cognitive Approach to Spectating in the Theatre.* New York: Palgrave Macmillan, 2008.

McCoy, Richard C. *The Rites of Knighthood: The Literature and Politics of Elizabethan Chivalry.* Berkeley: University of California Press, 1989.

McEachern, Claire. "Fathering Herself: A Source Study of Shakespeare's Feminism." *Shakespeare Quarterly* 39.3 (1988): 274–80.

McEleney, Corey. *Futile Pleasures: Early Modern Literature and the Limits of Utility*. New York: Fordham, 2017.

Mentz, Steve. *Romance for Sale in Early Modern England: The Rise of Prose Fiction*. Aldershot, UK: Ashgate, 2006.

Miko, Stephen J. "Winter's Tale." *Studies in English Literature 1500–1900* 29.2 (1989): 259–75.

Miller, Jacqueline T. "The Courtly Figure: Spenser's Anatomy of Allegory." *Studies in English Literature 1500–1900* 31.1 (1991): 51–68.

Moisan, Thomas. "Deforming Sources: Literary Antecedents and Their Traces in *Much Ado About Nothing*." *Shakespeare Studies* 31 (2003): 165–83.

Moncrief, Kathryn M. " 'Teach Us, Sweet Madam': Masculinity, Femininity, and Gendered Instruction in *Love's Labor's Lost*." *Performing Pedagogy in Early Modern England: Gender, Instruction, and Performance*. Ed. Kathryn M. Moncrief and Kathryn R. McPherson. London: Routledge, 2016, 113–28.

Montrose, Louis. "Of Gentlemen and Shepherds: The Politics of Elizabethan Pastoral Form." *ELH* 50.3 (1983): 415–59.

—. "Gifts and Reasons: The Contexts of Peele's *Araygnement of Paris*." *ELH* 47.3 (1980): 433–61.

—. *The Purpose of Playing: Shakespeare and the Cultural Politics of the Elizabethan Theatre*. Chicago: University of Chicago Press, 1996.

—. "Spenser and the Elizabethan Political Imaginary." *ELH* 69.4 (Winter 2002): 907–46.

—. " 'Sport by Sport O'erthrown': *Love's Labour's Lost* and the Politics of Play." *Texas Studies in Literature and Language* 18.4 (1977): 528–52.

Morini, Massimiliano. "The Superiority of Classical Translation in Sixteenth-Century England: Thomas Hoby and John Harington." *Philological Quarterly* 98.3 (2019): 273–95.

Morris, Harry. "The Judgment Theme in *The Merchant of Venice*." *Renascence* 39.1 (1986): 292–311.

Moshenska, Joe. *Feeling Pleasures: The Sense of Touch in Renaissance England*. Oxford: Oxford University Press, 2014.

—. "Spenser at Play." *PMLA* 133.1 (2018): 19–35.

Mowat, Barbara A. "The Theater and Literary Culture." *A New History of Early English Drama*. Ed. John D. Cox and David Scott Kastan. New York: Columbia University Press, 1997, 213–30.

Mullaney, Steven. *The Place of the Stage: License, Play, and Power in Renaissance England*. Chicago: University of Chicago Press, 1988.

—. *The Reformation of Emotions in the Age of Shakespeare*. Chicago: University of Chicago Press, 2015.

Murakami, Ineke. " 'The Fairing of Good Counsel': Allegory, Disgust, and Discretion in Jonson's *Bartholomew Fair*." *Disgust in Early Modern Literature*. Ed. Natalie K. Eschenbaum and Barbara Correll. London: Routledge, 2016, 145–63.

Murray, Peter B. *Shakespeare's Imagined Persons: The Psychology of Role-Playing and Acting*. Lanham, MD: Barnes & Noble, 1996.

Murrin, Michael. "The Audience of *The Faerie Queene*." *Explorations in Renaissance Culture* 23.1 (1997): 1–22.

Myhill, Nova. "Spectatorship in/of *Much Ado about Nothing*." *Studies in English Literature 1500–1900* 39 (1999): 291–311.

Ndiaye, Noémie. "'Everyone Breeds in His Own Image': Staging the *Aethiopica* across the Channel." *Renaissance Drama* 44.2 (2016): 157–86.

Nestrick, William V. "The Virtuous and Gentle Discipline of Gentlemen and Poets." *ELH* 29.4 (1962): 357–71.

Neuse, Richard. "Book VI as Conclusion to *The Faerie Queene*." *ELH* 35.3 (1968): 329–53.

—. "Pastorella." *The Spenser Encyclopedia*. Ed. A. C. Hamilton et al. Toronto: University of Toronto Press, 1990.

Nirenberg, David. "Shakespeare's Jewish Questions." *Renaissance Drama* 38 (2010): 77–113.

Noble, Greg, and Megan Watkins. "So How Did Bourdieu Learn to Play Tennis? Habitus, Consciousness and Habituation." *Cultural Studies* 17.3–4 (2003): 520–39.

Nohrnberg, James. *The Analogy of* The Faerie Queene. Princeton, NJ: Princeton University Press, 1976.

Northrop, Douglas A. "'The Ende Therfore of a Perfect Courtier' in Baldassare Castiglione's *The Courtier*." *Philological Quarterly* 77.3 (1998): 295–305.

—. "The Uncertainty of Courtesy in Book VI of *The Faerie Queene*." *Spenser Studies* 14 (2000): 215–32.

Oram, William A. "Seventeen Ways of Looking at Nobility: Spenser's Shorter Sonnet Sequence." *Renaissance Historicisms: Essays in Honor of Arthur F. Kinney*. Ed. James M. Dutcher and Anne Lake Prescott. Newark: University of Delaware Press, 2008, 103–19.

—. "Spenser in Search of an Audience." *Spenser Studies* 20 (2005): 23–47.

—. "Spenser's Audiences, 1589–91." *Studies in Philology* 100.4 (2003): 514–33.

Ord, Melanie. "Classical and Contemporary Italy in Roger Ascham's *The Scholemaster* (1570)." *Renaissance Studies* 16.2 (2002): 202–16.

Orgel, Stephen. "The Book of the Play." *From Performance to Print in Shakespeare's England*. Ed. Peter Holland and Stephen Orgel. London: Palgrave Macmillan, 2006, 13–54.

—. *Impersonations: The Performance of Gender in Shakespeare's England*. Cambridge: Cambridge University Press, 1996.

Osborne, Laurie E. "Dramatic Play in *Much Ado about Nothing*: Wedding the Italian *Novella* and English Comedy." *Philological Quarterly* 69.2 (1990): 167–88.

Ossola, Carlo. *Dal "Cortegiano" all' "Uomo di mondo": Storia di un libro e di un modello sociale*. Turin: Giulio Einaudi, 1987.

Owens, Judith. *Emotional Settings in Early Modern Pedagogical Culture*: Hamlet, The Faerie Queene, *and* Arcadia. London: Palgrave Macmillan, 2020.

Oxford English Dictionary. www.oed.com.

Pangallo, Matteo A. *Playwriting Playgoers in Shakespeare's Theater*. Philadelphia: University of Pennsylvania Press, 2017.

Parker, Patricia. *Shakespeare from the Margins*. Chicago: University of Chicago Press, 1996.

Partridge, Mary. "Thomas Hoby's English Translation of Castiglione's *Book of the Courtier*." *Historical Journal* 50.4 (2007): 769–86.

Peters, Julie Stone. *Theatre of the Book, 1480–1880: Print, Text, and Performance in Europe*. Oxford: Oxford University Press, 2000.

Pollard, Tanya. *Shakespeare's Theater: A Sourcebook*. Malden, MA: Blackwell, 2004.

Posner, David. *The Performance of Nobility in Early Modern European Literature*. Cambridge: Cambridge University Press, 1999.

Potts, Abbie Findlay. *Shakespeare and* The Faerie Queene. Ithaca, NY: Cornell University Press, 1958.

Prouty, Charles Tyler. *The Sources of* Much Ado About Nothing. New Haven, CT: Yale University Press, 1950.

Quilligan, Maureen. *The Language of Allegory: Defining the Genre*. Ithaca, NY: Cornell University Press, 1979.

Quint, David. "Bragging Rights: Honor and Courtesy in Shakespeare and Spenser." *Creative Imitation: New Essays on Renaissance Literature in Honor of Thomas M. Greene*. Ed. David Quint et al. Binghamton, NY: Medieval & Renaissance Texts & Studies, 1992, 391–430.

Quondam, Amedeo. *"Questo povero Cortegiano": Castiglione, il Libro, la Storia*. Rome: Bulzoni, 2000.

Rabil Jr., Albert. *Knowledge, Goodness, and Power: The Debate over Nobility among Quattrocento Humanists*. Binghamton, NY: Medieval & Renaissance Texts & Studies, 1991.

Rebhorn, Wayne A. *Courtly Performances: Masking and Festivity in Castiglione's Book of the Courtier*. Detroit, MI: Wayne State University Press, 1978.

Reid, Robert Lanier. *Renaissance Psychologies: Spenser and Shakespeare*. Manchester: Manchester University Press, 2017.

Reynolds, Simon. "Pregnancy and Imagination in *The Winter's Tale* and Heliodorus' *Aithiopika*." *English Studies* 84.5 (2003): 433–47.

Rhu, Lawrence. "Agons of Interpretation: Ariostan Source and Elizabethan Meaning in Spenser, Harington, and Shakespeare." *Renaissance Drama* 24 (1993): 171–88.

Richards, Jennifer. *Rhetoric and Courtliness in Early Modern Literature*. Cambridge: Cambridge University Press, 2003.

—. "Social Decorum in *The Winter's Tale*." *Shakespeare's Late Plays: New Readings*. Ed. Jennifer Richards and James Knowles. Edinburgh: Edinburgh University Press, 1999, 75–91.

Roberts, Sasha. *Reading Shakespeare's Poems in Early Modern England*. Basingstoke, UK: Palgrave, 2003.

Roe, John. "A Niggle of Doubt: Courtliness and Chastity in Shakespeare and Castiglione." *Shakespeare and the Italian Renaissance: Appropriation, Transformation, Opposition.* Ed. Michele Marrapodi. Farnham, UK: Ashgate, 2014, 39–56.

—. *Shakespeare and Machiavelli.* Cambridge: D. S. Brewer, 2002.

—. "*The Tempest* and *The Faerie Queene*: Shakespeare's Debt to Spenserian Strangeness." *Critical Survey* 34.2 (2022): 24–38.

Ryan, Lawrence V. "Book Four of Castiglione's *Courtier*: Climax or Afterthought?" *English Studies in the Renaissance* 19 (1972): 156–79.

Saccone, Eduardo. "*Grazia, Sprezzatura, Affettazione* in the *Courtier.*" *Castiglione: The Ideal and the Real in Renaissance Culture.* Ed. Robert W. Hanning and David Rosand. New Haven, CT: Yale University Press, 1983, 45–67.

—. "The Portrait of the Courtier in Castiglione." *Italica* 64.1 (1987): 1–18.

Salamon, Linda Bradley. "*The Courtier* and *The Scholemaster.*" *Comparative Literature* 25.1 (1973): 17–36.

Salingar, Leo. "Borachio's Indiscretion." *The Italian World of English Renaissance Drama: Cultural Exchange and Intertextuality.* Ed. Michele Marrapodi. Newark: University of Delaware Press, 1998, 225–38.

—. "Jacobean Playwrights and 'Judicious' Spectators." *Renaissance Drama* 22 (1991): 209–34.

Sanchez, Melissa E. " 'To Giue Faire Colour': Sexuality, Courtesy, and Whiteness in *The Faerie Queene.*" *Spenser Studies* 35 (2021): 245–84.

Schoenfeldt, Michael. "The Poetry of Conduct: Accommodation and Transgression in *The Faerie Queene*, Book 6." *Enclosure Acts: Sexuality, Property, and Culture in Early Modern England.* Ed. Richard Burt and John Michael Archer. Ithaca, NY: Cornell University Press, 1994, 151–69.

Scott, Alison V. *Selfish Gifts: The Politics of Exchange and English Courtly Literature.* Madison, NJ: Fairleigh Dickinson University Press, 2006.

Scott, Charlotte. *Shakespeare and the Idea of the Book.* Oxford: Oxford University Press, 2007.

Scott, Mary Augusta. "*The Book of the Courtyer*: A Possible Source of Benedick and Beatrice." *PMLA* 16.4 (1901): 475–502.

Sedinger, Tracey. "Working Girls: Status, Sexual Difference, and Disguise in Ariosto, Spenser, and Shakespeare." *The Single Woman in Medieval and Early Modern England: Her Life and Representation.* Ed. Laurel Amtower. Tempe: Arizona Center for Medieval and Renaissance Studies, 2003, 167–92.

Shalvi, Alice. Introduction to *Nennio, or A Treatise of Nobility.* Jerusalem: Israel Universities Press and H. A. Humphrey, 1967.

Shannon, Laurie. *Sovereign Amity: Figures of Friendship in Shakespearean Contexts.* Chicago: University of Chicago Press, 2002.

Shapiro, James. *Shakespeare and the Jews.* New York: Columbia University Press, 1996.

Shell, Marc. *Money, Language, and Thought: Literary and Philosophic Economies from the Medieval to the Modern Era*. Baltimore: Johns Hopkins University Press, 1982.

Shepard, Alexandra. *Meanings of Manhood in Early Modern England*. New York: Oxford University Press, 2003.

Shepard, Leslie. Biographical Note to *Nennio, or A Treatise of Nobility*. Ed. Alice Shalvi. Jerusalem: Israel Universities Press and H. A. Humphrey, 1967.

Sherman, William H. *Used Books: Marking Readers in Renaissance England*. Philadelphia: University of Pennsylvania Press, 2008.

Silberman, Lauren. "*The Faerie Queene*, Book II and the Limitations of Temperance." *Modern Language Studies* 17.4 (1987): 9–22.

—. *Transforming Desire: Erotic Knowledge in Books III and IV of* The Faerie Queene. Berkeley: University of California Press, 1995.

Skinner, Quentin. *Foundations of Modern Political Thought: The Renaissance*. Cambridge: Cambridge University Press, 1978.

—. "Paradiastole: Redescribing the Vices as Virtues." *Renaissance Figures of Speech*. Ed. Sylvia Adamson, Gavin Alexander, and Katrin Ettenhuber. Cambridge: Cambridge University Press, 2007, 149–64.

Slater, Michael. "Desdemona's Divided Duty: Gender and Courtesy in *Othello*." *Travel and Travail: Early Modern Women, English Drama, and the Wider World*. Ed. Patricia Akhimie and Bernadette Andrea. Lincoln: University of Nebraska Press, 2019, 215–35.

Slights, William W. E. *Managing Readers: Printed Marginalia in English Renaissance Books*. Ann Arbor: University of Michigan Press, 2001.

Smith, Bruce R. *Shakespeare and Masculinity*. Oxford: Oxford University Press, 2000.

Smith, Helen. *'Grossly Material Things': Women and Book Production in Early Modern England*. Oxford: Oxford University Press, 2012.

—. "'A Man in Print?' Shakespeare and the Representation of the Press." *Shakespeare's Book: Essays in Reading, Writing and Reception*. Manchester: Manchester University Press, 2008, 59–78.

Smith, Ian. *Black Shakespeare: Reading and Misreading Race*. Cambridge: Cambridge University Press, 2022.

—. *Race and Rhetoric in the Renaissance: Barbarian Errors*. New York: Palgrave Macmillan, 2009.

Song, Eric. "Maybe She's Born with It: Spenser's Una, Milton's Eve, and the Question of Golden Hair." *Spenser Studies* 35 (2021): 213–44.

Staines, John D. "Pity and the Authority of the Feminine Passions." *Spenser Studies* 25 (2011): 129–61.

Stamatakis, Chris. "'With Diligent Studie, but Sportingly': How Gabriel Harvey Read his Castiglione." *Journal of the Northern Renaissance* 5 (2013).

Stern, Tiffany. *Making Shakespeare: From Stage to Page*. London: Routledge, 2004.

—. *Rehearsal from Shakespeare to Sheridan*. Oxford: Oxford University Press, 2000.

—. "Watching as Reading: The Audience and Written Text in Shakespeare's Playhouse." *How to Do Things with Shakespeare*. Ed. Laurie Maguire. Malden, MA: Blackwell, 2008, 136–59.

Stewart, Alan. *Close Readers: Humanism and Sodomy in Early Modern England*. Princeton, NJ: Princeton University Press, 1997.

Stewart, Stanley. "Sir Calidore and 'Closure.'" *Studies in English Literature 1500–1900* 24.1 (1984): 69–86.

—. "Spenser and the Judgment of Paris." *Spenser Studies* 9 (1988): 161–209.

Stone, Lawrence. *The Crisis of the Aristocracy, 1558–1641*. Oxford: Oxford University Press, 1979.

Sullivan, Paul. "Playing the Lord: Tudor 'Vulgaria' and the Rehearsal of Ambition." *ELH* 75.1 (2008): 179–96.

Suttie, Paul. *Self-Interpretation in* The Faerie Queene. Cambridge: D. S. Brewer, 2006.

Taylor, Gary. "Making Meaning Marketing Shakespeare 1623." *From Performance to Print in Shakespeare's England*. Ed. Peter Holland and Stephen Orgel. Basingstoke, UK: Palgrave Macmillan, 2006, 55–72.

Teskey, Gordon. "'And Therefore as a Stranger Give it Welcome': Courtesy and Thinking." *Spenser Studies* 18 (2003): 343–59.

Thaler, Alwin. "Spenser and *Much Ado about Nothing*." *Studies in Philology* 37.2 (1940): 225–35.

Thomas, Keith. *In Pursuit of Civility: Manners and Civilization in Early Modern England*. Waltham, MA: Brandeis University Press, 2018.

Tonkin, Humphrey. *Spenser's Courteous Pastoral: Book Six of the* Faerie Queene. Oxford: Clarendon, 1972.

Trafton, Dain A. "Structure and Meaning in *The Courtier*." *English Literary Renaissance* 2.3 (1972): 283–97.

Traub, Valerie. *Desire and Anxiety: Circulations of Sexuality in Shakespearean Drama*. London: Routledge, 1992.

Traugott, John. "Creating a Rational Rinaldo: A Study in the Mixture of the Genres of Comedy and Romance in *Much Ado about Nothing*." *Genre* 15 (1982): 157–81.

Tribble, Evelyn. *Early Modern Actors and Shakespeare's Theatre: Thinking with the Body*. London: Bloomsbury Arden, 2017.

Trolander, Paul, and Zeynep Tenger. *Sociable Criticism in England, 1625–1725*. Newark: University of Delaware Press, 2007.

Tylus, Jane. "'Par Accident': The Public Work of Early Modern Theater." *Reading the Early Modern Passions: Essays in the Cultural History of Emotion*. Ed. Gail Kern Paster, Katherine Rowe, and Mary Floyd-Wilson. Philadelphia: University of Pennsylvania Press, 2004, 253–72.

Van Elk, Martine. "'Our Praises are Our Wages': Courtly Exchange, Social Mobility, and Female Speech in *The Winter's Tale*." *Philological Quarterly* 79.4 (2000): 429–57.

Vasoli, Cesare. "Il cortigiano, il diplomatico, il principe: Intellettuali e potere nell'Italia del Cinquecento." *La Corte e il "Cortegiano"*, Vol. 2. Ed. Adriano Prosperi. Rome: Bulzoni, 1980, 173–94.

Vaught, Jennifer C. *Masculinity and Emotion in Early Modern English Literature*. Aldershot, UK: Ashgate, 2008.

Walker, Jonathan. *Site Unscene: The Offstage in English Renaissance Drama*. Evanston, IL: Northwestern University Press, 2017.

Walton, Charles E. "*To Maske in Myrthe*: Spenser's Theatrical Practices in *The Faerie Queene*." *Emporia State Research Studies* 9.1 (1960): 7–45.

Wareh, Patricia. "Humble Presents: Gift-Giving in Spenser's Dedicatory Sonnets." *Studies in the Literary Imagination* 38.2 (2005): 119–32.

Warley, Christopher. *Sonnet Sequences and Social Distinction in Renaissance England*. Cambridge: Cambridge University Press, 2005.

Weimann, Robert. *Authority and Representation in Early Modern Discourse*. Baltimore: Johns Hopkins University Press, 1996.

Weinberg, Bernard. *A History of Literary Criticism in the Italian Renaissance*, Vols. 1 and 2. Chicago: University of Chicago Press, 1961.

Wells, Robin Headlam. *Shakespeare on Masculinity*. Cambridge: Cambridge University Press, 2000.

West, William N. *Common Understandings, Poetic Confusion: Playhouses and Playgoers in Elizabethan England*. Chicago: University of Chicago Press, 2021.

Whigham, Frank. *Ambition and Privilege: The Social Tropes of Elizabethan Courtesy Theory*. Berkeley: University of California Press, 1984.

Whitney, Charles. *Early Responses to Renaissance Drama*. Cambridge: Cambridge University Press, 2006.

Williams Jr., Franklin B. "Commendatory Sonnets." *The Spenser Encyclopedia*. Ed. A. C. Hamilton et al. Toronto: University of Toronto Press, 1990.

Whittington, Leah. "Shakespeare's Vergil: Empathy and *The Tempest*." *Shakespeare and Renaissance Ethics*. Ed. John Cox and Patrick Gray. Cambridge: Cambridge University Press, 2014, 98–120.

Williams, Kathleen. *Spenser's World of Glass: A Reading of* The Faerie Queene. Berkeley: University of California Press, 1966.

Wiseman, Rebecca. "Courtesy, Cultivation, and the Ethics of Discernment in Book 6 of *The Faerie Queene*." *Sixteenth Century Journal* 47.3 (2016): 629–48.

Wofford, Susanne Lindgren. *The Choice of Achilles: The Ideology of Figure in the Epic*. Stanford, CA: Stanford University Press, 1992.

Worthen, W. B. *Shakespeare and the Authority of Performance*. Cambridge: Cambridge University Press, 1997.

Yamada, Akihiro. *Experiencing Drama in the English Renaissance: Readers and Audiences*. New York: Routledge, 2017.

Zunshine, Lisa. *Why We Read Fiction: Theory of Mind and the Novel*. Columbus: Ohio State University Press, 2006.

Index

Note: "n." after a page reference indicates the number of a note on that page. Literary works can be found under authors' names.